PROPHETIC

OF

Lady Eleanor Davies

CU00536199

WOMEN WRITERS IN ENGLISH
1350–1850

GENERAL EDITORS
Susanne Woods and Elizabeth H. Hageman

MANAGING EDITORS
Elizabeth Terzakis and Julia Flanders

EDITORS
Carol Barash
Patricia Caldwell
Stuart Curran
Margaret J. M. Ezell
Elizabeth H. Hageman
Sara Jayne Steen

WOMEN WRITERS PROJECT
Brown University

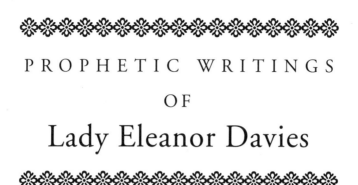

PROPHETIC WRITINGS
OF
Lady Eleanor Davies

EDITED BY

Esther S. Cope

New York   Oxford

OXFORD UNIVERSITY PRESS

1995

Oxford University Press

Oxford   New York
Athens   Auckland   Bangkok   Bombay
Calcutta   Cape Town   Dar es Salaam   Delhi
Florence   Hong Kong   Istanbul   Karachi
Kuala Lumpur   Madras   Madrid   Melbourne
Mexico City   Nairobi   Paris   Singapore
Taipei   Tokyo   Toronto

and associated companies in
Berlin Ibadan

Published by Oxford University Press, Inc.,
198 Madison Avenue, New York, New York 10016

Library of Congress Cataloging-in-Publication Data

Eleanor, Lady, d. 1652.
Prophetic writings of Lady Eleanor Davies/
edited by Esther S. Cope.
p.   cm. -- (Women writers in English 1350–1850)
1. Eleanor, Lady, d. 1652—Prophecies. 2. Prophecy—Christianity.
I. Cope, Esther S.   II. Title.   III. Series.
BF1815.E54P76   1995   248.2'9--dc20   95-1043
ISBN 0-19-507875-6 (cloth)
ISBN 0-19-508717-8 (paper)

This volume was supported in part by the National Endowment
for the Humanities, an independent federal agency.

Printing (last digit):
9   8   7   6   5   4   3   2   1

Printed in the United States of America
on acid-free paper

CONTENTS

v

FOREWORD

Women Writers in English 1350–1850 presents texts of cultural and literary interest in the English-speaking tradition, often for the first time since their original publication. Most of the writers represented in the series were well known and highly regarded until the professionalization of English studies in the later nineteenth century coincided with their excision from canonical status and from the majority of literary histories.

The purpose of this series is to make available a wide range of unfamiliar texts by women, thus challenging the common assumption that women wrote little of real value before the Victorian period. While no one can doubt the relative difficulty women experienced in writing for an audience before that time, or indeed have encountered since, this series shows that women nonetheless had been writing from early on and in a variety of genres, that they maintained a clear eye to readers, and that they experimented with an interesting array of literary strategies for claiming their authorial voices. Despite the tendency to treat the powerful fictions of Virginia Woolf's *A Room of One's Own* (1928) as if they were fact, we now know, against her suggestion to the contrary, that there were many "Judith Shakespeares," and that not all of them died lamentable deaths before fulfilling their literary ambitions.

This series is unique in at least two ways. It offers, for the first time, concrete evidence of a rich and lively heritage of women writing in English before the mid-nineteenth century, and it is based on one of the most sophisticated and forward-looking electronic resources in the world: the Brown University Women Writers Project textbase (full text database) of works by early women writers. The Brown University Women Writers Project (WWP) was established in 1988 with a grant from the National Endowment for the Humanities, which continues to assist in its development.

Women Writers in English 1350–1850 is a print publication project derived from the WWP. It offers lightly-annotated versions based on single good copies or, in some cases, collated versions of texts with more complex editorial histories, normally in their original spelling. The editions are aimed at a wide audience, from the informed undergraduate through professional students of literature, and they attempt to include the general reader who is interested in exploring a fuller tradition of early texts in English than has been available through the almost exclusively male canonical tradition.

SUSANNE WOODS

ELIZABETH H. HAGEMAN

General Editors

ACKNOWLEDGMENTS

The collaborative effort that is the Women Writers Project thrives on the contributions of all its members. Ongoing thanks are due to Brown University and its administrators, especially President Vartan Gregorian, Provost Frank Rothman, Dean of the Faculty Bryan Shepp, and Vice President Brian Hawkins. Members of the Brown English Department, particularly Elizabeth Kirk, Stephen Foley, and William Keach, have provided indispensable advice; many thanks to Marilyn Netter for her help in finding the WWP a new director. Gratitude is also owed to Don Wolfe, of Brown's Computing and Information Services. At Brown's Scholarly Technology Group, Geoffrey Bilder and Elli Mylonas are unfailingly resourceful and obliging in all matters, and Allen Renear is a rare source of energy and inspiration.

Working with Oxford University Press is always a pleasure; many thanks to Elizabeth Maguire for making the Series possible and to Claude Conyers for his unlimited patience, his unfailing sense of humor, and the laugh that goes with both.

A more committed set of colleagues than the WWP staff is hard to imagine. Project Coordinator Maria Fish facilitates all contacts with the outside world with her unerring knowledge of protocol and her considerable diplomatic skills. The computer textbase from which this volume was drawn approaches perfection largely through the efforts of Carole Mah and Syd Bauman. I thank Julia Flanders for defining the position of managing editor and easing me into the very big shoes she left behind. New Director Carol DeBoer-Langworthy deserves thanks for bringing a hearty serving of Midwestern pragmatism into the office. Others who have made this series possible include Elizabeth Adams, Anthony Arnove, Rebecca Bailey, Kim Bordner, Susie Castellanos, Paul Caton, Nick Daly, Cathleen Drake, Faye Halpern, Loren Noveck, Anastasia Porter, Kasturi Ray, Caleb Rounds, and Kristen Whissel.

ELIZABETH TERZAKIS
Managing Editor

ACKNOWLEDGMENTS

The debts I have incurred in the course of doing this project have a history that goes back before the project itself to my monograph on Lady Eleanor. Editing these tracts would have been exceedingly more difficult if I had not done that book first, and the many people who assisted me with it deserve acknowledgment here for their, often unknowing, contribution to this volume of Lady Eleanor's prophetic writings. For granting permission for copies of her tracts from their collections to be printed here I am grateful to the British Library; the Bodleian Library; the Beinecke Rare Book and Manuscript Library, Yale University; the Folger Shakespeare Library; the Houghton Library, Harvard University; the Henry E. Huntington Library, San Marino, California; the Provost and Fellows of Worcester College, Oxford; and the Public Record Office (London). In addition I want to thank the students and staff at the Women Writers Project for persisting in entering on computer and then seeing into print these idiosyncratic texts. Elizabeth Terzakis, who came to this project when it was in its final stages, has deftly dealt with its many idiosyncrasies, and Sara Jayne Steen has helped with the final rounds of proofreading. Julia Flanders has been a joy to work with. I have been repeatedly grateful for her efficient handling of details and her perceptive comments and suggestions. To my editor, Elizabeth Hageman, I owe very special appreciation for her patience with my many questions about editorial policies and with my resistance to clarifying prophecies that I believed were meant to be obscure.

ESTHER S. COPE

INTRODUCTION

Eleanor Davies' sixty-odd tracts are the principal record of her twenty-seven-year prophetic career. She became a prophet and began interpreting the will of God in history in 1625, just after Charles I had become king of Great Britain. On the morning of 28 July 1625 she was "Awakened by a voyce from HEAVEN" which told her, "There is Ninteene yeares and a halfe to the day of Judgement and you as the meek Virgin."[1] She identified the voice as that of the Old Testament prophet Daniel, and believed that he was giving her the information which he had been told should remain "closed up and sealed till the time of the end" (Dan. 12:9). Her responsibility was to announce to the world the date for the Day of Judgment.

Eleanor Davies was thirty-five years old in 1625. The fifth daughter of George Touchet, eleventh Baron Audeley and first earl of Castlehaven, and his wife, Lucy, daughter of James Mervin of Fonthill Gifford in Wiltshire, she had married Sir John Davies, the king's attorney in Ireland, in 1609. Prior to their marriage Sir John had attained some reputation as a poet and wit. He had published a number of poetic works, including *Orchestra* (1596) and *Nosce Teipsum* (1599). Like others in England's Irish administration, Davies regarded his place as a stepping-stone for professional advancement in England. In 1619, he left Ireland and the frustrations of his position there; six years later, in 1625, his ambitions had not been fulfilled. He was practicing law and hoping that the new king would make him a judge.

The scant and mostly retrospective information about Sir John and Lady Eleanor's domestic life makes its assessment difficult. Their two sons, one of whom was handicapped, died at a young age. Their only surviving child was a daughter, Lucy, to whom they gave the kind of classical education that they themselves had had, but that many of their contemporaries would have deemed appropriate only for boys. Thanks

---

1. *Her Appeal to the High Court* (1641), pages 80–81 in the present edition. Subsequent quotations in the Introduction from Lady Eleanor's works will be noted parenthetically. For a list of abbreviations for titles of tracts in the present edition, see below, page xxiv.

to the fortune Sir John had acquired through his investments in Irish land and his legal practice in England, the Davieses in 1623 secured a marriage for Lucy to Ferdinando Hastings, heir to the earl of Huntingdon. About the same time, they purchased Englefield, in Berkshire, to be their country seat. It was there that, two years later, just after Lucy had first gone to stay with her husband's family, Lady Eleanor heard Daniel's voice.

That experience at Englefield on 28 July 1625 became the keystone of Lady Eleanor's prophetic writings. She cited it repeatedly to demonstrate her credentials. Although she did not always use the same words in stating what Daniel had told her, she was consistent in her account of the circumstances in which she had heard him speak. Within days she set off for Oxford, where Parliament had fled from plague in London. There she delivered a tract interpreting Daniel's prophecies to George Abbot, the archbishop of Canterbury. Surviving evidence does not indicate the name of the tract or whether she had it printed prior to presenting it to the archbishop. *Warning to the Dragon*, her earliest extant tract and the only one dated 1625, declared on the first of its 100 pages that it was "the interpretation of the visions of the prophet Daniel" (6).

Warning to the Dragon and all but one of the rest of the many pamphlets or tracts that Lady Eleanor wrote and published between the summer of 1625 and her death in July 1652 appeared illicitly. (*Strange and Wonderfull Prophecies* was published legitimately in 1649.) Until 1641 illicit publications were those works printed by a press not certified by the Stationers' Company or those works not previously read and approved by the archbishop of Canterbury, the bishop of London, or some other designated official. In the 1640s when the Long Parliament dismantled the means by which the printing regulations had been enforced, it replaced them with a similar system under its own supervision. Most people in mid-seventeenth-century England, including Lady Eleanor herself, wanted freedom of the press only for those who agreed with them.

Apart from some comments in correspondence with her daughter and her denunciation of one printer named Paine in *Hells Destruction* (1651; 336), Lady Eleanor left little information about her printers and her dealings with them. Despite the risks involved in underground printing, especially prior to the abolition of the courts of Star Chamber and High Commission in 1641, many printers could be persuaded to undertake such work, although quality sometimes suffered as a consequence. Errors abound in Lady Eleanor's tracts; line spacing changes abruptly and whole signatures of several tracts are missing. She herself may have contributed to the imperfections of the printed texts. By quibbling with her printers about their charges and by letting their bills go unpaid, she may have negated the care she took in supervising them and in going over her work after it was printed in order to gloss and correct it.

In some instances Lady Eleanor claimed that she had sought but was denied permission for printing. In other cases, she probably did not even make a formal request. She certainly made no effort to conceal her authorship of the publications. She inserted her name in her prophecies, and, like the prophets of the Old Testament whom she regarded as models, she delivered her message to the very individuals whose use of authority would, she maintained, if they did not heed her, lead to divine judgment upon them and upon Britain. Her boldness in prophesying amazed and frightened her contemporaries.

Lady Eleanor lived at a time when England and Europe were fertile ground for prophecy. The religious ferment that had developed in the wake of the Reformation, and the political, social, and economic changes that were occurring, seemed to many observers to parallel the history of ancient Israel. Wars, assassinations, plagues, and other turmoil indicated that the events described in the Book of Revelation would soon follow. Using evidence from the Bible, prognosticators calculated the date for Judgment and the Second Coming. Both their conclusions and the form of their forecasts differed, however, some appealing to a wide and popular audience, others addressing an elite, or a scholarly, market.

In 1625, when Lady Eleanor published her first tract, there were few other women prophets in England. Although by the time she died in 1652 prophets of both sexes were more numerous, she stood apart from her fellows in a number of respects. Unlike Mary Cary and Anna Trapnel, who were Fifth Monarchists, or Mary Gadbury, a Ranter, Lady Eleanor cannot be linked with one of the many groups or sects that proliferated during the 1640s and 1650s. She never became a selfless, empty vessel for a divine message. Her aristocratic birth and attitudes remained an important part of her prophetic identity, and she published her prophecies herself rather than through the mediation of a clergyman or some other man, as did women such as Elinor Chanel or Sarah Wight. No one came to watch her have ecstatic experiences as they did Sarah Wight or Anna Trapnel. Unlike Catherine Chidley, who expressed views of the Independents in her published works, Lady Eleanor professed no direct links to any of the major religious factions. Unlike the Quaker women whose writings account for a major proportion of women's published writings during the years immediately following her death, Lady Eleanor did not attempt to preach. She saw herself as a prophet and a writer; the readers of her books were her audience.

Like other women who prophesied at the time, Lady Eleanor challenged the conflation of prophesying and preaching that characterized the missionary efforts of the century following the Reformation. Protestant preachers, who encountered persecution in their efforts to bring people the Word of God, saw themselves as prophets and in that guise justified speaking boldly to officials of both church and state. Because the post-Reformation Church of England, like its medieval predecessor, refused to recognize women as priests or preachers, the roles of prophet and preacher were for them necessarily distinct. Contemporaries recognized that God might choose women to be prophets and that women's nature made them receptive vessels for divine messages, but they also worried that the receptivity of women would make them easy prey for agents of the devil. If women had fallen for the devil's wiles, they were false prophets. Jesus had warned against "false prophets which come to you in sheep's clothing, but inwardly they are ravening wolves" (Matt. 7:15). Determining whether women were truly prophets fell to the men who in their capacity as clergy officiated in the Church. Lady Eleanor never won such recognition. Her claim to prophesy was her own, and she asserted it vigorously in her writings.

By prophesying without the permission of officials, Lady Eleanor challenged the hierarchical and patriarchal authority which was the basis of order in family and society and in church and state. As a prophet, she encountered more suspicion than support. The men who ruled the world in which she lived—husband, king, bishops, members of Parliament, and local officials—attempted in various ways to silence her. She saw her prophecies burned, experienced repeated arrest and imprisonment, and even endured confinement to Bethlehem Hospital (Bedlam) as a madperson. The attempts to discredit her had some effect. Lady Eleanor never attracted a significant group of followers, but apart from some rhetorical efforts at persuasion in her tracts, she did little to encourage adherents. Regarding her rejection by others as proof of the truth of her message, she considered writing, not conversion, her responsibility. She left Judgment to God and devoted herself to her profession.

Lady Eleanor's twenty-seven years as a prophet fall into three periods: 1625–33; 1633–40; and 1640–52. The conditions under which she worked changed, and her sense of identity as a prophet developed. Integral to her prophetic self was her aristocratic inheritance. This distinguishes her from other prophets both in her own age and in earlier ages. Whereas prophets more commonly repudiated their former selves in order to become vessels for a divine message, she incorporated her persona into her new being. Time and again she manipulated the letters and meanings of her name—her birth name (Touchet or Tichet), her married names (Davies and later Douglas), her father's titles (Audeley and Castlehaven)—to give them prophetic significance. In this volume, she is known as "Lady Eleanor," a slightly abbreviated form of "The Lady Eleanor," the signature she used on the title pages of many of her tracts.

Between July 1625 when she embarked upon her prophetic career and October 1633, Lady Eleanor focused her attention upon the royal court in an attempt to obtain recognition as a prophet. She hoped to persuade King Charles and his bishops to rid England of the threat of popery and to promote true religion, i.e., Protestantism. Her efforts failed. Charles held firm in his commitment to policies that she opposed. Although she attracted some attention by accurately predicting the death of her husband, Sir John Davies, who had tried to silence her by burning her writings, she made contemporaries, including the king himself, uneasy by her defiance of patriarchy. The apparent accuracy of other predictions about courtiers, including one that the royal favorite, the duke of Buckingham, would not live to see September 1628, augmented both her reputation and people's anxieties about her. Only months after Sir John's sudden demise in December 1626, she remarried. With her new husband, Sir Archibald Douglas, a Scottish captain, she engaged in a long and bitter series of lawsuits against her daughter's husband and his family to obtain possession of the estates that had belonged to Davies. Before long Douglas too came to oppose Lady Eleanor's prophesying. She suspected that his family (his grandfather had been tutor to King James and his uncle was dean of Winchester) was turning him against her in order to win royal favor, but she did not let this deter her. When Douglas, like Davies, burned some of her writings, she warned him that he would pay heavily for his conduct. His subsequent mental illness seemed to fulfill her prophecy. It also ended their marriage, in about 1633, for all practical purposes and destroyed her hopes that his claim to be Charles I's elder half-brother would allow her to achieve her prophetic purposes (*Her Jubilee,* 1650). Her own family had endured scandal two years earlier in 1631, when her brother, Mervin, Lord Audeley and second earl of Castlehaven, had been tried and executed for sodomy and for being accessory to a rape. By 1633, through a combination of personal factors and more general political and religious developments, Lady Eleanor was becoming increasingly unwelcome at court.

Between 1633 and 1640, the second period of her prophetic career, official opposition severely curtailed Lady Eleanor's prophesying. In the summer of 1633 she made clear her disaffection with the court and went to the Netherlands to have her writings printed. That autumn, shortly after her return to England, the Crown responded to her illicit publications and her petition against the appointment of William Laud as archbishop of Canterbury by summoning her before the Court of High Commission. Archbishop Laud burned her books, and the Commission ordered her to be imprisoned in the Gatehouse at Westminster. There she remained for two and a half years before she was released. In

1636, after she had vandalized the altar-hanging at Lichfield Cathedral, the Privy Council had her committed to Bedlam, and then in the spring of 1638 they transferred her to the Tower of London where she remained until September 1640.

Upheaval and civil war marked the final period of Lady Eleanor's prophetic career. Although she suffered imprisonment twice between 1640 and her death in 1652, she found reprieve from some of the trials she had endured in the 1630s. During the last twelve years of her life as a prophet, she enjoyed the loving support of her daughter Lucy as she closely watched the drama of public events and waited for the Judgment that Daniel had predicted. The execution of Archbishop Laud in January 1645, almost precisely nineteen and one-half years after her vision of July 1625, reinforced her faith in her mission and message even though the Second Coming of Christ did not immediately follow. Four years later in 1649 when King Charles was executed, Lady Eleanor once again believed the New Jerusalem was at hand. She published more prolifically than ever during the final period of her life.

Lady Eleanor's work survives in part because of her commitment to her prophetic task. Calling her tracts her "babes," she lavished maternal care upon them (*Everlasting Gospel*, 287; *Restitution of Prophecy*, 344). Her attention did not stop when she delivered a manuscript to the printer. She corrected and annotated printed copies, and in a number of instances she added handwritten dedications before taking them to designees. She continued to monitor the fate of her work by watching its reception and by including notes about subsequent events. She rejoiced in acknowledgment, such as the entry of her prophecies in the record of the Court of High Commission in 1633, and grieved about their "murder" when Laud burned them in the same year (*Everlasting Gospel*, 288; *Apocalyps, Chap. 11*, 1–2).

In a tract of 1644 Lady Eleanor described her daughter Lucy as "her alone and sole support under the Almighty" (*Her Blessing*, 129). Lucy contributed to her mother's recognition as a prophet by saving copies of the tracts. A volume containing forty-five of the titles, now in the Folger Shakespeare Library, probably belonged to her. Two additional tracts are now held by the Folger Library; eleven appear among the collections of the bookseller George Thomason (d. 1666), now in the British Library; ten among the Clarke Papers in the Library of Worcester College, Oxford; and a number in both the Bodleian Library, Oxford, and the Houghton Library at Harvard. Others are extant elsewhere. As far as I have been able to determine, only two of her tracts have been reprinted between Lady Eleanor's time and now: *Strange and Wonderfull Prophecies* (1649) has been reprinted three times, most recently in *Fugitive Political Tracts,* Second Series (1875); and *Restitution of Prophecy* (1651) by the Rota Press in 1978.

From Lady Eleanor's many tracts I have selected for inclusion here thirty-eight that illustrate the range and varied nature of her work during her prophetic career. Most of the extant tracts survive in print. Among the few exceptions are "Bathe Daughter of BabyLondon" (1636), from the Hastings Manuscripts at the Huntington Library, and "Spirituall Antheme" (1636), in the Domestic State Papers at the Public Record Office in London. Her longest piece, *Warning to the Dragon* (1625), was also her first. Its one hundred pages contrast with the brevity of her two broadsides, *Woe to the House* (1633) and *As not Unknowne* (1645), and her two-page *Benediction* (1651) to Cromwell. Although most of her work was in prose, she wrote *Given to the Elector* (1633) in ballad form. This was the poem that she addressed to King Charles's nephew, the Elector of the Palatine, Prince Charles of the Rhine, in 1633 and then revised and reprinted several times.

As she says in her prefatory general epistle to *Warning to the Dragon* (1625), Lady Eleanor regarded writing as an "office not a trade" (2), an activity that she approached with both professionalism and pleasure. Readers, on the other hand, have found the texts of Lady Eleanor's prophecies perplexing, weighted down with imagery and highly irregular syntax. Some sentences lack subjects or verbs, though others could pass the scrutiny of the most demanding grammatical critic. She explained why her meaning might seem obscure by pointing to the star that had guided the wise men to Bethlehem to see the baby Jesus. Using *Star to the Wise* as the title for a tract that she published in 1643, she asserted that her prophecy would be heard and understood by those who had ears to hear God's message. Although she stressed certain themes and cited some examples repeatedly, Lady Eleanor varied her approaches rather than belaboring them. Neither the carefully contrived pieces among her writings nor her corrected and annotated copies of her printed work indicate that she found composition burdensome. Her total output suggests that words came to her easily. In several instances she issued new editions of previously printed tracts which she had revised and adapted to apply to different circumstances. Although she took examples from everyday life and from familiar stories of the Bible, history, or legend, she also drew upon more specialized realms of scholarship and rhetorical techniques.

Lady Eleanor's aristocratic background, her keen intellect, and her extraordinary learning permeate her prophecies. While the details of her schooling are unknown, the texts of her tracts show that she knew Latin as well as English and was familiar with both the classics and the Bible. On several occasions she took up scholarly arguments about the translation of a particular biblical text. Like her husband Sir John Davies, Sir John Donne, and other writers of her day, she constructed elaborate imagery, puns, anagrams, and a host of other literary devices to make her points. She also made heavy use of biblical typology which paired individuals, ideas, and events from the Old Testament with those in the New.

Lady Eleanor's texts include many citations of verses from the Bible: a multitude of references to biblical persons, places, and events, as well as adaptation of passages to construct her own prophetic message for her contemporaries. Readers who check her citations will discover some discrepancies in wording because she used several different versions of the Bible and at times quoted loosely. Among her many phrases from the Books of Daniel and Revelation are "time and times and the dividing of time" (Dan. 7:25) and "Alpha and Omega" (Rev. 1:8); her imagery includes Belshazzar's feast (Dan. 5); Daniel's vision of the four beasts (Dan. 7); the two witnesses (Rev. 11); the Beast from the Bottomless Pit whose number was 666 (Rev. 13); and the Whore of Babylon (Rev. 17), whom she identified with the Papacy. She saw the Isle of Patmos where John wrote Revelation (Rev. 1:9) as Britain and herself as the "elect Lady" he addressed in his second epistle (2 John 1).

Editing Lady Eleanor's tracts has required me to violate her belief that explicating her words would be interfering with divine will. She believed that those who thought her message was in hieroglyphics were unworthy to understand its contents. I have been reluctant to defy the purpose of a woman who took her prophetic responsibilities so seriously. My awareness that I cannot be certain of the meaning or meanings she intended has also contributed to my hesitancy to embark upon this project. I ultimately overcame my reservations because examining her texts forces us to acknowledge Lady Eleanor as a woman of sensitivity, intelligence, and education. Through her writings we can gain an impression of her and a new look at the world of early seventeenth-century Britain.

Note on the Text

The thirty-eight tracts in this volume are transcribed from photographic copies of Lady Eleanor's writings, printed with permission of the libraries where they are now held: the Beinecke Rare Book and Manuscript Library, Yale University; the Folger Shakespeare Library; the Henry E. Huntington Library; the Houghton Library, Harvard University; the British Library; the Bodleian Library and Worcester College Library, Oxford; and the Public Record Office, London.

The headnote to each tract indicates, by library and shelf number, the copy of the tract on which the present edition is based. Tracts from the Folger Shakespeare Library are from the volume discussed on page xvii above, and catalogued under the Wing number of *Samsons fall:* D2010. All STC and Wing numbers are from the most recent editions of volume one of Pollard and Redgrave and Wing (1986 and 1994, respectively); for further bibliographical information, see the List of Abbreviations of Titles on page xxiv.

Although the present edition retains characteristic and idiosyncratic spelling, grammar, and hyphenation, it does not offer facsimiles of the base texts: the original layout, lineation, and woodcut illustrations have not been reproduced. Turned letters such as *u* and *n* have been silently emended, the letters *i, j, u, v, w* and long *s* have been regularized to follow modern usage, and some obvious printers' errors have been corrected (*rree* to *tree* on page 171, for example). Capital letters have been reduced to lower case when, for example, the second letter of a word at the opening of a tract is capitalized in the base text. Title pages have been regularized: multiple layers of emphasis have been reduced, and date and imprint information have been integrated into headnotes. Unless otherwise indicated, the place of publication may be assumed to be London. In some tracts (or portions of tracts) type faces have been reversed from italic to roman for easier reading; each of those places is recorded in a footnote. In the two tracts transcribed from manuscripts ("Bathe" and "Spirituall Antheme"), it has not been possible to show all of the nuances of Lady Eleanor's punctuation, variations in handwriting, or placement of her text on the page.

The following editorial conventions are used in the volume:

[as]   Roman print within square brackets indicates letters or words provided by the editor.

<as>   Roman print within angle brackets indicates handwritten letters or words that were added or that replaced deletions in the original text.

[*as*]   Italic print within square brackets indicates letters or words that were deleted or written over in the original text.

[ ]   Empty square brackets indicate letters or words that are illegible and places where the page is cut off.

Extensive annotations are printed in footnotes. To illustrate how Lady Eleanor annotated individual copies of the same tract differently, her notes from three copies of *Excommunication out of Paradice* (Wing D1987) are printed in this volume; in all other cases only the notes from the copy upon which the present edition is based are given. The annotations follow Lady Eleanor's punctuation even though she is not consistent (for example, she sometimes puts a period after "&c" and sometimes does not). Concluding punctuation is hers when it is within quotation marks; it is editorially imposed when it is outside them.

Notes identify only a fraction of the many references in the text. They assume that the reader will read the Books of Daniel and Revelation or Apocalypse upon which Lady Eleanor based her prophecies.

Notes reading "see [bib. cit.]" indicate places where the biblical passage provides an explanation of or background to the author's text; those reading "cf. [bib. cit.]" identify instances where she has created her own text from her biblical source. Where a tract depends heavily upon particular chapters of the Bible, e.g. *Warning to the Dragon* upon Daniel 7–12, the headnote states this rather than having individual notes make repeated references to those chapters.

Imagery, dates, and expressions that appear frequently in Lady Eleanor's texts, such as "Michaelmas" (the feast of St. Michael the Archangel, 29 September), or "Albion Army" (the British army, and those wearing white coats who are mentioned repeatedly in the Book of Revelation), are explained at intervals throughout the book rather than every time they occur. Although in Lady Eleanor's day the English still used the Julian calendar and thus began the year on 25 March rather than 1 January, this edition follows the modern system of numbering the year from 1 January, and clarifies Lady Eleanor's dates in notes; thus for her "10 January 1644," the note will read "1644, i.e., 1645."

Latin expressions such as *viz.* (namely), *ergo* (therefore), *finis* (end), *Anno Domini* (in the year of the Lord), or *cap* (chapter) that were common in Lady Eleanor's period are not translated in the notes, but longer Latin phrases and sentences are.

Selected Bibliography

Cope, Esther S. "Dame Eleanor Davies Never Soe Mad a Ladie"? *Huntington Library Quarterly* 50:2 (1987): 133–44.

———. *Handmaid of the Holy Spirit: Dame Eleanor Davies, Never Soe Mad a Ladie.* Ann Arbor, Michigan: Univ. of Michigan Press, 1992.

Davies, John. *The Complete Poems of Sir John Davies.* Edited by A. B. Grosart. 2 vols. London: Chatto and Windus, 1876.

———. *The Poems of Sir John Davies.* Edited by Robert Krueger. Oxford: Clarendon Press, 1975.

Greaves, Richard L. and Robert Michael Zaller, eds. *Biographical Dictionary of British Radicals in the Seventeenth Century.* Brighton: Harvester Press, 1984.

Hindle, C. J. *A Bibliography of the Printed Pamphlets and Broadsides of Lady Eleanor Douglas, the Seventeenth-Century Prophetess.* Rev. ed. Edinburgh: Edinburgh Bibliographical Society, 1936.

Historical Manuscripts Commission. *Report on the Manuscripts of the late Reginald Rawdon Hastings.* 4 vols. 1928-1947.

Hobby, Elaine. *Virtue of Necessity: English Women's Writing, 1649–88.* Ann Arbor, Michigan: Univ. of Michigan Press, 1989.

Mack, Phyllis. "The Prophet and Her Audience: Gender and Knowledge in the World Turned Upside Down." In *Reviving the Revolution,* edited by Geoffrey Eley and William Hunt. London: Verso Books, 1988.

———. "Women as Prophets during the English Civil War," *Feminist Studies* 8 (1982): 19–45.

———. *Visionary Women: Ecstatic Prophecy in Seventeenth-Century England.* Berkeley: Univ. of California Press, 1992.

Pawlisch, Hans. *Sir John Davies and the Conquest of Ireland: A Study in Legal Imperialism.* Cambridge and New York: Cambridge Univ. Press, 1986.

LIST OF ABBREVIATIONS OF TITLES

Following each abbreviation is the tract's STC or Wing number, its title as it appears in Pollard and Redgrave or Wing, and its date (new style). STC numbers are from A. W. Pollard and G. R. Redgrave, *A Short-Title Catalogue of Books Printed in England, Scotland, & Ireland and of English Books Printed Abroad, 1475–1640*, 2nd ed., rev. and enl. by W.A. Jackson, F.S. Ferguson, and Katherine F. Pantzer. London: Bibliographical Society, 1986. Wing numbers are from volume one of Donald Wing, *Short-Title Catalogue of Books Printed in England, Scotland, Ireland, Wales and British America and of English Books Printed in Other Countries, 1641–1700*, rev. and enl. by John J. Morrison, Carolyn W. Nelson, and Matthew Seccombe. New York: Modern Language Association of America, 1994. Lady Eleanor's tracts are listed under the name Eleanor Audeley in Pollard and Redgrave and under Eleanor Douglas in Wing.

Appeal from Court to Camp	Wing 1970A: *Her appeal from the court to the camp. Dan. 12.* (1649).
Appearance	Wing D1972A: *The appearance or presence of the son of man.* (1650).
As Not Unknowne	Wing D1973: *As not unknowne. This petition or prophesie.* (1645).
Bathe	[not in Pollard and Redgrave or Wing]: "Bathe Daughter of BabyLondon" (1636). Huntington Library, Hastings MSS, Religious, Box 1, folder 28.
Before the Lords Second Coming	Wing D1974: *Before the Lords second coming.* (1650).
Benediction	Wing D1975: *The benediction. From the A:lmighty O:mnipotent. I have an errand.* (1651).
Bethlehem	Wing D1978: *Bethlehem signifying the house of bread.* (1652).
Bill of Excommunication	Wing D1979: *The bill of excommunication, for abolishing henceforth the Sabbath.* (1649).
Blasphemous Charge	Wing D1981: *The Blasphemous charge against her.* (1649).
Crying Charge	Wing D1982A: *The crying charge. Ezekiel. 22.* (1649).

Reader   Wing D2005A: *Reader, the heavy hour
                                    at hand.* (1648).

Restitution of Prophecy   Wing D2007: *The restitution of
                                    prophecy.* (1651).

Samsons Legacie   Wing D2015: *Samsons legacie* (1643).
                                    [See *To the High Court.*]

Sign   Wing D2012AA: *A sign given them
                                    being entred into the day of judgment.*
                                    (1644; rpt. 1649).

Sions Lamentation   Wing D2012B: *Sions Lamentation,
                                    Lord Henry Hastings.* (1649).

Spirituall Antheme   [not in Pollard and Redgrave or
                                    Wing]: "Spirituall Antheme: Elea.
                                    Tuichet." (1636).

Star to the Wise   Wing D2013: *The star to the wise.*
                                    (1643).

To the High Court   Wing D2015: *To the most honorable
                                    the High Court of Parliament
                                    assembled, &c. My Lords; ther's a time.*
                                    (1643). [See *Samsons Legacie.*]

Warning to the Dragon   STC 904: *A warning to the dragon and
                                    all his angels.* (1625).

Woe to the House   STC 904.5: *Woe to the house.* (1633).

Writ of Resitution   Wing D2019: *The writ of restitution.*
                                    (1648).

As far as we know, *Warning to the Dragon* (STC 904) is Lady Eleanor's first printed tract. It appears to have been developed from an early version of a paraphrase and gloss of chapters seven through twelve of the Book of Daniel, *All the kings of the earth shall prayse thee* (printed in Amsterdam, 1633; STC 903.5), which Lady Eleanor intended to present to James I before his death in March 1625. Written after her vision of 28 July 1625 and apparently extant in only one edition, *Warning to the Dragon* contains the message Lady Eleanor took to Archbishop Abbot of Canterbury when he was in Oxford in August 1625. The present edition of this tract is based on a copy now in the British Library (shelf number 1016.e.22).

A WARNING TO THE DRAGON AND ALL HIS ANGELS.

LUKE, XXI.

Marke yee this wicked persons, & yee friends of the unrighteous MAMMON.

Take heed to your selves, lest at any time your hearts be over-charged with Surfetting and Drunkennesse, and the Cares of this life, and so that day come upon you unawares. For as a SNARE shall it come on all them, that dwell on the face of the whole Earth.

A SNARE O DEVIL.

Title. **THE DRAGON:** the Beast, Satan.

Epigraph. **Surfetting:** surfeiting; indulgence. **A SNARE O DEVIL:** an anagram for Eleanor Davies.

A GENERALL EPISTLE,
TO the fold and Flocke of CHRIST,
and to them that are gone astray, that say they are Apostles and Catholiques and are not, &c.

Grace be to you and Peace from God the Father, and from our Lord JESUS CHRIST, who gave himselfe for our Sinnes; and in the absence of his Body for a remembrance the Blessed Supper, till his second appearing. As often as we taste thereof, he takes it as a token we are not unmindfull of his tender mercy that tasted Death it selfe for us; so many
10 melting trials and torments, the innocent Lambe for a brood of Vipers, whose damme is Death whose sting is Sinne, he that washed us in his owne Blood unto whome there is no accesse but by Faith; Behold hee commeth, and every eye shall see him. To him be glory and dominion for ever and ever. Amen.

It seemed good unto me, having a perfect understanding given mee in these things, and the dispensation of them, an office not a trade; to roote out, to pull downe, to build, and to plant, by the grace and bounty of JESUS our Lord God. To present this Visitation to your view, joyning you together of the first Arke, and universall great House, ves-
20 sels of Honor and dishonor, some cleane and purified, others having need of purging.

Former things are come to passe, and new things I declare unto you; no age so weake, nor sex excusing; when the Lord shall send and will put his words in their Mouth. He powreth out his Spirit upon his hand-maidens; the rich are sent emptie away, even so Father for it seemed good in thy sight.

Pressed and constrained with obedience to him, and Duty towards you; saying no other things then the Prophets and Apostles did say

---

Line 4. **Catholiques:** Christians.

Lines 5–91. In the base text this section is in italics with roman emphasis; fonts are reversed here for ease of reading. Fonts follow the base text again beginning at line 92.

Line 11. **damme:** dame; mother. Line 19. **first...House:** see Gen. 7.

Line 25. **the rich...away:** cf. the Magnificat, Mary's hymn to God; see Luke 1:46–55.

should come to passe, that yee might know the certainty of those
things, wherein yee have beene instructed, whether you will heare or
whether you will forbeare.

It is a salve to annoint and open the eyes of the blinde, to bring them
that sit in darkenesse a light, to leade them out of the Prison-house; others by meanes of remembrance, (whose annoynting long since teacheth
them all thinges) to stirre them uppe; It is a true looking-glasse, a large
houre glasse, Phisicke for the sicke, wholsome for the whole, milke for
the young, and meate for the strong. It is upon Record due, an olde
debt One and Twenty hun-yeares since; Unto me is given this stone to
polish, unto me this grace is given.

It is as it were a new Song to be sung before the everlasting Throne, a
salutation for Strangers and the Brethren; if we love them that love us, if
we salute the Brethren only, what doe wee more then others; yea but
they come at the last houre, others having borne the heate and burthen
of the Day.

Shall not the lost Son be found againe, the Father of these that Blaspheme and are found lyers; But in the eye of our weakenesse their pros-
peritie will weave the webbe of envie; murmure not at the good-man of
the House; Is it not lawfull; is it not wrong (as he will) to dispose the
riches of his owne goodnesse; nay, rather may we not all say, we are
unprofitable, we have both gon out of the way, there is none that doth
good, no not one; nay, are not his Judgements according to truth; O
man grudge not his grace, dispute not his justice.

But they have bin, and will be to the worlds end, our persecutors and
slaunderers, need they not so much the more our Prayers; recompence
no man evill for evill; Therefore let the Congregations of the faithfull
Pray for them, poore, blind, distracted, naked, wretched people, and
give glory to God, who hath done away the vaile from these hidden
mysteries, that hindred our stedfast sight, Though to blinde mindes and
deafe harts, this vaile remaines still untaken away.

Line 45. **the lost Son:** the prodigal son of Luke 15:11–32.
Lines 47–48. **murmure…House:** see Luke 20:11.

60   Wherein for mine owne part, I challenge little, not so much as those that brought to the Tabernacle guifts of their owne spinning of Blew and other colours; But rather to be in the number of those servants, that drew out the wonderfull Wine for the Bridegroomes Feast, to beare it to the Governor and the Guests; though to cast in my myte with others I was never unwilling.

    Finally, to those that require a Signe, or thinke this Confidence; Boasting that high stiles are not steps for the declining age of this weake world to climbe, my defence is no shorter then free.

    Least any should thinke of me above or better then he seeth me to be,
70 as others to suspect a forged passe; To present you with Pearles of that sort or holy things, I forbeare at this time.

    If the debt be paid the secret of the multiplyed oyle is to my selfe; Though I shut the Doore or shadow my name, I feare no faces, smiles nor frownes, for the hope of *Israel,* to me no chaines are heavie, it is no bought nor stolne fire, my ability nor boldnesse extending so high; yet a Candle too high mounted for Sathan, and all his attempts to blowe it out, thrived the Gospell the lesse, rejected of the *Jewes.*

    But all alike hit not the marke, they presse forward, wranglers started aside like a broken Bowe, the match is wonne, one Foord is not knowne
80 to all Passengers; eleven strikes the clocke saith he, twelve saith she; doe these contradict those that are not against us or with us; Antichristians those that are not against us, are with us; Even so, glory be to him alone (the Set is ours) the houre and set time of whose Judgement is at hand; and O Lord remember thy servants *Abraham, Isaac, & Jacob, &* looke not to the stubbornnes, nor to the wickednes of this People, turne their harts, preserve thy Church, and his victorious Matie. to tread downe the power of his enemies, our Soveraigne gratious Lord and the Queene, annoint them with thy holy Spirit, Crowne them with Grace; and for-ren Princes, especially the Kings excellent Sister, with a happie life here,

---

Lines 62–63. **those servants...Wine:** see John 2:1–9.

Line 64. **myte:** small piece; cf. Luke 21:2–3. Line 67. **stiles:** steps over a fence.

Line 89. **the Kings...Sister:** Elizabeth, Queen of Bohemia, who represented the Protestant cause in Europe for many English people.

and eternall life hereafter. Be gratious to the remnant of JOSEPH, heare   90
I beseech thee the Prayer of thy servant.

The Servant of Jesus Christ:
O a Sure Daniel.
DANIEL, —I end al.

Postscript

To maske my name with boldnesse to unmaske Error I crave no Pardon, the
manner let none dispise; Dreames in times past have beene interpreted, our
Fathers in divers manners have beene spoken unto, the Winde bloweth
where it listeth.

Line 93. **O A SURE DANIEL:** a rough anagram for Eleanor Davies.

ELEANOR AUDELEY

REVEALE O DANIEL,

TO THE GREAT PRINCE, the Kinge of *Great*
BRITAINE, FRANCE, and IRELAND,
Defender of the Faith.

THE INTERPRETATION OF THE VISIONS OF THE
PROPHET DANIEL, *revealing the Man of Sinne; And the*
Morning Starre, before the comming of the Day.

In the Visions of this Prophet are revealed the same things contained in
the Revelatiō, which GOD gave to Jesus Christ, to shew unto his Servants things which must shortly come to passe; things that are not, to
bring to nought things that are: And as he signified to his beloved Servant JOHN, the Contents of the secret Booke by his Angell; Even so the
Lambe slaine by the eternall Decree purposed from the foundation of
the world; Declared the same things to the man greatly beloved, his servant DANIEL, unfolded in this present exposition; drawing the juice of
many sorts wanting roome and leasure, to lay things in order, wherein
the Scripture will repaire the want of methode. Being not willing for the
lighting of a Match to make a fire, when the stroke of a Flint is of more
facilitie; Speaking not to a People of a strange Speech and of a hard Language, but to the House of *Israell;* Avoyding mans enticing words;
things without life, give no life, that revealeth not the testimony of
Jesus; at whose Name, a name above every name, Let every knee bowe.
Heare all yee Children of my people, harken O Earth!

The first vision of this holy Prophet, was in the 1. yeare of the raigne
of BELSHAZZER, King of Babilon; from which spirituall Babilon takes
the denomination. One and Twentie hundred yeares since.

Wherein he saw the foure Windes of Heaven, or the losed Angels

---

Line 1. **ELEANOR AUDELEY:** printed backward in the basetext, to be read in a mirror.

Line 2. **REVEALE O DANIEL:** a rough anagram for Eleanor Audeley.

Lines 3–5 **GREAT PRINCE…Faith:** the title of King Charles I.

Line 13. **JOHN:** St. John the Evangelist, author of the Book of Revelation.

bound in the great River *Euphrates* the auntient bounds of the great
Roman Empire, that strove upon the great Sea, and the foure great
Beasts, that came up from the Sea divers one from another. These blowing Windes had no power to hurt, till the servants of God were Sealed
in the foreheads, at what time that Common-wealth became a Monarchy, persecuting the Church of God being then with Child, Travailing
in birth, crying and pained to be delivered of the man Childe, roaring
like a Lyon, the whole Forrest ringing, ruling all Nations with a Rod of
Iron; that breaketh in pieces and subdueth all things: He is *Alpha* and
Omega, so have the servants of God a Two-fold sence. Besides man
including some other of his Creatures, bearing the names of men, yet
being neither Man nor Beast; Praise yee him Sun and Moone, &c.

I heard the number of them: And here ended the Sealing of the first
Covenant, a yoake which our Fathers were not able to beare, to establish
the second, which is Spirituall, to put his Lawes in their mindes, with
the Pensell of his Grace to write them in their hard harts, a light Burthen, for the letter of the Law, graven in stone is the sentence of death;
But the Spirit giveth life to stony harts, that were dead in trespasses and
sinnes; yea, the whole valley of dead Bodies, turn'd into Stones and
Earth, from ABELL the first Borne, to the last man taken up in the Field,
they are all holy unto the Lord, their iniquitie is forgiven and forgotten,
as a Father, hee remembreth their sinne no more.

Of these were Sealed to bee of the seed of ABRAHAM, one hundred
forty and foure Thousand, twelve times twelve Thousand: Of which
faithfull Number JESUS CHRIST the Saviour of the world, the only
begotten Sonne of the living GOD, in the likenesse of sinfull Flesh
without Sinne, the Lyon of the Tribe of *Judah,* was sealed on the Eight
day of his Nativitie; The Lyonesse bringing but one, and but once in her
life.

That with the sprinckling and shedding of his Blood, both Covenants might be sealed; These were the first Fruits unto God, and to the

---

Line 32. **no power…Sealed:** see Rev. 7:3.

Lines 41–42. **the first Covenant:** that of the Old Testament, based upon law.

Line 43. **the second:** the covenant of the New Testament, based upon the gospel.

Line 48. **ABELL:** see Gen. 4.

60 Lambe, having the Token of the everlasting Covenant, of the great mysterie in those times, concerning CHRIST and his Church, put in the Flesh a Figure of the Heart.

Which first Covenant remaines to us a Patterne of tendernes, not made with hands, the Heart by a mutuall respect being now the Closet or secret part, whereby wee Gentiles are made the tender Spouse, the habitation of God, fellow heires of the unsearchable Riches, joyned to Christ the head, that in times past were the Children of disobedience and wrath, Aliens from the commonwealth of *Israell,* Strangers from the Covenants of promise, having no hope (without God) in the world, are 70 now, who were somtimes farre off; of all Nations, Kindreds and Tongues; uncircumcised Philistines, not of his Brethren; not of the House of his Father, By the blood of JESUS CHRIST made nigh members, of his Body, of his Flesh, and of his Bones; greater love and felicitie can none expresse.

Of which great mysterie, Hipocrites, next Harlots, whose counterfeit beautie deceives not him, whose praise is of men, and not of God; false Gods, are no partakers; the outward Token, being common to both. To assure us of which, receiving the earnest of his Spirit, that abideth, not crying Master; Carest thou not, that wee perish; but Abba, Father.

80 Thus our tackling lost without Anchor, to repayre the ruines and weaknesse of these decayed, sunke weather-tempest driven bottomes, such Treasures of Millions expended and bestowed, what burthen, what prizes, what things God hath prepared to bee the lading of these vessels of honour; Eye hath not seene, eare hath not heard, neither hath entred into the hart of man: To which, all the Transported affections felt or fained, injoyed without paines or feare, may seeme but light dotage, as Light and Darknesse compared, compared with the Crowne and weight of that Eternall blisse.

The Foure windes prepared for an houre, and a day, and a moneth, 90 and a yeare; are the powers of these four great Beasts; shewing their

---

Line 71. **Philistines:** enemies of the Israelites. Line 79. **Abba:** God; see Mark 14:36.

Line 80. **tackling:** ship's rigging. Line 81. **bottomes:** ships.

Line 83. **lading:** cargo. Line 86. **dotage:** foolish affection.

degrees of residence; also the finall Blast is included; The Sea are the Nations of the Earth.

The beginning and the ending, thus saith hee to the Sea: Waves drowning one another, swelling into Mountaines, for glory foaming out your owne shame. Saying, haile to the Wood awake, according to your owne understanding, you have made Idols and Images, not by my direction, but after the invention of the Craftsman, and have exalted your hearts and forgotten mee, giving my Praise to graven Images, and my glory to another for your God, (not setting me before your eyes) you have gotten a Divell, a false Prophet, whom I sent to prove you; that takes my lawes in his mouth, not of love, but for strife and envie: Thinkes he to say; Lord, Lord, in thy Name wee have cast out Divels, Preached, and Baptized; my answer is not unknowne to you both, though you thinke to plead ignorance, persecuting and dispising the number of my little ones.

You onely have I knowne, of all the Families of the Earth, whose transgressions doe hasten your Judgement; Therefore I will punish you for your iniquities, you shall bee like the Morning Cloud, and the early dew that passeth away as the Chaffe that is driven with a scattering whirle-winde out of the Flower, as smoake out of a Chimney vanishing away; And I will bee like a Lyon, as a Leopard by the way I will wayte and observe you, and as a Beare that is bereaved of her Whelpes, I will teare the Kall from your harts and devoure you, But to the faithfull I will bee a King, a Saviour; as an Eagle stirring up her Nest, fluttering over her young, bearing them upon the wing; So I will preserve mine inheritance, my Portion as the Apple of mine eye.

These are the words of the First, that was like a Lyon, his strength shall overcome the rest, and take their Dominion away, having no number of finite parts expressed; the time of whose undevided Kingdome is infinite and alwaies; As his yeares have no end, his Crownes are many; This is the Lyon of the Tribe of *Judah*, having of Flesh a tender hart; a mans hart was given unto it; The Prince of the Kings of the Earth, the

---

Line 109. **Chaffe:** husk or covering of grain.

Line 113. **Kall:** gall, bitterness; or caul, membrane.

first and the last; And because he is the roote, and made of the seed of DAVID; Hee is here accompted amongst these Beasts; This is hee that sate upon the white Horse, the Circle of the Earth, to judge and make War; beholding the Inhabitants like Grasshoppers; and a Bowe and a Crowne was given unto him; Hee is the Lord of Lords, the King of Kings, and of his Kingdome there is no end.

The second Beast like a Beare, the Seaventh head, that had Three ribbes in the Mouth betweene the Teeth of it, signifying, Three hun-dred yeares; this is the devouring Raigne of the Heathen Romaine Emperours, which lasted so long, licked by the Divell; In the Infancie of which Empire, the Sonne of God was Crucified, and the Citie of Jerus-alem destroyed, wherein the yearely Sacrifice or feast of the Passover was solemnized, that in her might be found the Blood of Prophets and Saints, and of all that were slaine upon the Earth, in which first seventie yeares, the Apostles and seventie finished their testimony what they had seene and heard, after which followed the over-spreading of abomina-tion spoken of by our Saviour, making the Sanctuary desolate, defiled with Carkasses which can neither see, heare, nor walke, abominable carrion, the house of Prayer, made the Gallery of the Divell, for his devices to stand in.

And this is hee that sate upon the Red Horse, Having a great Sword given unto him, to make Warre with the Church of God, devouring much Flesh, Burning, Scorching it with fire, Haile mingled with Blood, destroying Trees, and all greene grasse, smote every Herbe, and brake every Tree and here ended the first Woe with this second Beast, all fire and horrible Cruelty such as there was none like it in all the Land of spirituall Egypt since it became a Nation and shortly after began the next Woe, where the fire is not mentioned, because the smoake is so great, thicke darkenesse or heresie, false doctrine extinguishing the Light of truth, which shall continue untill the third Woe, Hell fire, and Brimstone or Blasphemy, issuing out of their Mouthes, a great crye

130

140

150

Lines 124–25. **hee…white Horse:** see Rev. 19:11. Line 141. **carrion:** dead, rotting flesh.
Line 143. **hee…Red Horse:** see Rev. 6:4. Lines 150–51. **the smoake…great:** see Rev. 6:12.
Lines 152–55. **the third Woe…Palenesse:** see Rev. 14–19.

from him that sits upon the Throne, when Rednesse shall be turn'd into Palenesse to the Maide behinde the Mill, the Captaine in the Dongeon, free and bond, because of the last Plague the second Death.

The third Beast that was like a Leopard, or halfe a Lyon, an Ape betweene Man and beast, whose feete or first footing, were as the feete of a Beare, that had upon the back of it foure Wings, like a Fowle or painted Bird: Two of the Eagle, and two of the Dragon; signifying his time, Foure hundred yeares before the comming in of Antichrist, then came the King of *Babylon* to Jerusalem, and besieged it, taking the advantage of the Night, what Linkes or Torches brought him thither I reade not, but Moonlight there was little, though hee were on his way or Wing, but letted Two hundred yeares before. 160

Bearing also foure heads, foure standing up for it, shewing the devision of the Empire into so many parts, being then too large and great for the government of one man. This is the Dragon of Egipt; that Monarchy that began with the Christian Emperours, whose deadly wound (Death to the Soule) was washed in the Blood, and healed by the Stripes of the heavenly Samaritan; There is now no healing of the Bruise, it is putrified, the Wound is grievous; the Leopard cannot change his spots; binde thy Tyre upon thy head, forbeare to cry: O Virgin daughter of Egipt, in vaine shalt thou goe up into Gillead and take Balme, or use Medicines, thou dost runne in vaine. And this is hee that sate upon the blacke Horse; the Ethiopian cannot change his skinne, lesse man then the *Minataure;* more Monster then a *Centaure,* ingendred of black Cloudes, carried about of every Winde, to whom is reserved the Blacknesse of Darknesse for ever: Blacke will take no other hew; having a 170

Line 163. **Linkes:** links; a kind of torch made of the shorter fibers of flax or hemp and pitch.

Line 165. **letted:** left. Line 169. **Christian Emperours:** the Holy Roman Emperors.

Line 171. **the heavenly Samaritan:** cf. Luke 10:29–36.

Line 172. **putrified:** putrid; infected.

Line 173. **Tyre:** biblical city which represented unrepentant evil.

Line 174. **Gillead:** biblical city which was supposed to have sources of healing.

Lines 175–76. **hee...blacke Horse:** see Rev. 6:5.

Line 177. **Minataure...Centaure:** In Greek myth, the Minotaur was half man, half bull; the Centaur was half man, half horse.

180 payre of Ballances given into his hand, without respect of persons, to measure to all men, rich and poore, free and bond, a measure of Wheate for a penny, and three measures of Barley for a penny; Hoe! every one that thirsteth, and hee that hath no money, Come buy and eate, give not your money for stones in stead of Bread, say not Ignorance is better then Knowledge, Neither hurt the Oyle and the Wine; Touch not the Lords annointed, and doe his Prophets no harme, that Nourish you with truth and understanding.

The last Beast the fourth, that is the Eight, and was Seven heads and is not, and is of the Seven, and goeth into perdition, that had great Iron 190 Teeth, that devoured and brake in peeces, and stamped the residue with the feete thereof, and was divers from all the Beasts that were before it; having a Miter of Tenne hornes, signifying also, though the Crownes be not here expressed, so many hundred yeares his Limitted time, the Tenne dayes of tribulation in the Apocalips, wherein the Divell shall have power to cast the faithfull into Prison; (After the Tribulation ime-diately of those dayes; Two shall be in the field, *&c.*) Nine of which number are expired, and some part of the last hundred, but how many are to come; by these hornes precisely cannot be aymed at without the Art or Science of Chronologie; This is *Judas* the Divell, the King of 200 *Babilon* and Egypt, the raigne of Antichrist Pope of *Rome,* count the Letters of his name for it is the number of his time, whose name is Death; hated mortally the King of *Rome* and *Italie:* This is hee that sate upon the Pale Horse, the sonne of Perdition, of all Complexions the darkest, neerest to corruption, threatning alone, a hart charged with so much wickednesse and malice as the Red Horse, all the sanguines in the Rayne-bow, and the Sword cannot set out more of Bruitish crueltie; had he winges to his will, and of time length to the height and bignesse of his insatiable minde; Nero, Titus, Domitianus, these beasts of the

---

Line 180. **payre...hand:** see Rev. 6:5; the balances, or scales, were a symbol of justice.

Lines 181–85. **Wheate...Wine:** Rev. 6:6.

Lines 192–94. **Miter:** mitre; a bishop's hat. **Tenne...tribulation:** see Rev. 2:10.

Line 196. **Two...field:** Matt. 24:40. Lines 202–3. **hee...Horse:** see Rev. 6:8.

Line 205. **sanguines:** reds.

Line 208. **NERO, TITUS, DOMITIANUS:** Roman Emperors, first century A.D., noted for persecution of the Christians.

Earth, their hearts and policies parraleld would seeme but a Curre cou-
pled or compared with this greedy Woolfe. A Bull as bloudy as the   210
Beare.

Whose land is covered with Locusts and Darknes; even darknes that
may bee felt rising out of the depth of the bottomlesse pit of Sathans
malice very grievous; yet had all the faithfull light in their dwellings that
they might not loose the way; for it was Commanded these Armies of
Scorpions besieging the holy City, having pernitious stings, both wayes
voluptuous and malitious, The power of the Enemy that they should
not hurt the grasse of the Earth, neither any greene thing, by any
meanes nothing should hurt them, but only drye Trees or boughs, bearing no fruite of repentance, those men that have not the Seale of God in   220
their gracelesse foreheads, that they should not kill these wretched
blinde miserable People, but that they should bee tormented five
Moneths, as in those dayes the most part, most Lamentable in the siege
of *Jerusalem* by Famine were tormented so long compassed with a
Trench, kept in on every side, Seeking death, and desiring to dye, &c.

This did the Lord because the Princes of Egipt, harkened not to
milde MOSES, but hardened their harts, and did evill in the sight of the
Lord, after the Abominations of the Heathen; Therefore saith the Lord,
I am against thee ô Dragon, which lyest in the Hart (the middest of the
Rivers) which said my Rivers ate mine owne, I have made it for my   230
selfe; I will put hookes in thy Clawes, and leave the Throne into the
Wildernesse, where there is no water; and all the Inhabitants shall know
that I am the Lord, because they have beene a staffe of Reede to the
house of *Israel,* when they tooke hold of thee by the hand, thou didst
breake and Rent all their shoulder, and when they leaned on thee, thou
brakest, and made all their loynes to be at a stand, with the Burthens of
Bricke and Rubbish thy Officers did lay upon them.

Thou hast given them Stubble for Straw, vapor of smoake for Vict-
uall; thou hast made their lives bitter unto them; Therefore the Lord is

---

Line 209. **Curre:** cur; snarling person or dog. Line 213. **the bottomlesse pit:** see Rev. 9:2.
Lines 215–16. **these Armies…City:** see Rev. 9:3–5.
Lines 226–27. **the Princes…MOSES:** see Exod. 7:13.
Line 235. **Rent:** rend; tear into pieces. Line 238. **Thou hast…Straw:** see Exod. 5:10–12.

240   against thee whose healed Wound is festred, turned wilde againe, become Antichristian and incureable, thou that haddest the Ballances in thine owne hand; Thou that art like a Leopard or a young Lyon of the Nations, as a Dragon; or a Whale in the Seas, with thy Diadem of Ten hornes, crowned with Ten Crowns, so many Antichristian hundred yeares, Nine of which accompt are cast, past, and expired.

Troubling the waters with thy feete, and fowlest their Rivers; the whole Sea of *Rome,* the third part of the maine Sea is become Blood; Behold the Lord is against thee and against thy Rivers, which are turned into Wormwood (woe due O *Rome*) and Hemlocke; Even the Third 250   part of the waters, the streames of Justice and Mercy are become poyson and Bitternesse; I hate and despise your Images, Feast dayes, Processions, Solemne assemblies, saith the Lord; who required those things: I commanded, Judgement should runne downe free as water, and Righteousnesse as a mighty streame; Woe the Bloody Citie.

You are impudent and disobedient Children, as the day of your Visitation, so are your sinnes hidden from you, when you shall say for shame to the Mountaines Cover us, and to the Rocks and Hills fall upon us; you will know your transgression, the long Wings of the morning, the Caves of Makadah shall not preserve you, Lightening, 260   Thundring Cannons, the whole Globe at a shot, shivering your Bodyes, sinking your Soules, and making your harts to hop: Eare never heard, neither hath entred into the hart of man such horror, forsaken of all, but the Divell and his Angells, burned and buried alive, of all the Creatures not a drop of water remaining, of Light not a sparke, Rebells these terrors as Shot or Hailestones from Heaven Pell-mell, shall drive you into a Bottomlesse gulfe headlong; the great day of his wrath is come, saying to the fiery Lake; Hide us from the face of him that sits upon the Throne.

Lines 242–43. **Thou…Seas:** see Ezek. 32:2. Line 246. **Troubling…feete:** see Ezek. 32:2.

Line 247. **Sea of Rome:** the See of Rome; the Papacy. **maine…Blood:** see Rev. 8:8.

Lines 248–49. **Rivers…Wormwood:** see Rev. 8:11.

Line 254. **Woe the Bloody Citie:** Nah. 3:1. Lines 256–57. **you shall…us:** see Rev. 6:15–16.

Line 259. **Caves of MAKADAH:** see Josh. 10:16.

When the faithfull scattered People shod with the everlasting Ghos-
pell of Peace, after all their labours and travaile in this Wildernesse, shall   270
enter into the Land of Rest: Here is the Body of the Beast destroyed;
PHAROAH and all his Multitude of unbeleeving Lowzie orders; even all
his Host of furious Horsemen as Locusts, eating every herbe, and all the
fruite of the Trees the haile had left, drowned in Hell Fyre the bottomlesse red Sea, that may boast rather of their Blaines and Boyles, then
Vermin, which their owne Magitians denie not to be the manifest finger
of God; vaunting they winne by their Cosening game term'd Chastitie,
the Joyes of heaven, and Secret bosome Almes in breeding Lice: Such
uncleane Ragges past mending, I did meane to cast away, but since you
will not heare MOSES and the Prophets, I will bestowe some labour to   280
ayre them for you, and your patch'd Coates waxen olde and bad to make
bags for heavenly Treasure, well may they stoppe Bottles when your
Reward is weeping and gnashing of Teeth; in those dayes, all the Water I
finde the Saints will supply you with, to coole your blistered Tongues.

Masters though to simple People you seeme to make straite steps, it is
no newes to say you incline too much on the left hand. Thinke yee the
Crownes like Gold can deceive us; or hayre as the hayre of Women; The
vayle of shamefastnesse, shewing sobriety and subjection: Thinke yee
those long locks like separited Nazarites, can cover your notted crownes
from the Raizer, or hide your pined Bodyes pinch'd of Provender like   290
neighing Horses prepared to the Battaile, It is not unknowne to us, the
golden Cup, and these gilden counterfeit Crownes like false Haire to
cover Baldnesse; Both came out of one Furnace: they are yet unpaid for.

Though ESAU should lend you Teares, yet shall yee come and worship before the feet of them, you now dispise and persecute; There is no
blessing reserved, the Mourning day is at hand, the Armour you beare
shines with the Brotherly affection you beare us, wee feare not your

---

Line 272. **Lowzie:** lousy; full of lice.   Line 273.   **Locusts…herbe:** see Exod. 10:15.

Line 275.   **may boast…Boyles:** see Exod. 9:9–11.

Line 277.   **their…Chastitie:** The Catholic Church required its clergy to take vows of chastity.

Line 278.   **breeding Lice:** see Exod. 8:17–19.

Line 289.   **Nazarites:** Jews who vowed not to cut their hair.   Line 294.   **ESAU:** see Gen. 23:38.

furie; Go yee Cursed, heere is your farewell, receive the Portion of Hipocrites, and eate the fruit of Lyes rejoycing and trusting in your owne
300 counterfeit Righteousnesse, painted flames, such false Coine will not
passe. Eternall life is free guift purchased by Grace; receive the wages of
Sinne; venemous Armies, the power of the Enemie led by the Starre
called *Wormewood,* To those that have not drunke or smoak'd out their
eyes, as visible as Lightning or a Lampe fallen from Heaven, threatning
Warre, Famine, with Pestilent Mortalitie; the fourth part, the whole
Christian world infected by that strumpet Hagge *Rome* and *Italie.*
Lastly, the name of his Palenesse was Death, because hee is the last, and
Hell followed with them with deadly malice, Raigning till the day of
Judgement, after which hee shall swimme with his fellowes, and bathe
310 in the Lake that burnes with Fire and Brimstone.

These three Beasts signified by the great Citie devided into Three
parts, so many severall persecutions of the Church under great *Babylon,*
With a bold stroake, the last is not drawne in cullours least to the life;
the fourth Beast (the false Prophet, their Popes falleth,) the bitter Starre
turning Judgement into Gaule of Aspes falne from Heaven, Signifying
the losing of his Keyes, (pride will have a fall) for which hee was cast out
of the presence of God: God and Mammon cannot be served together;
here hath hee the command of the bottomlesse Pit, smoaking with Heresie and ignorance; The Keys of the Kingdome of Hell, which trust so
320 much hee boasteth of, given him by the Dragon the Divell, to deceive
them that dwell upon the Earth; saying in the sight and opinion of
men; Let it be knowne this day, that I have done all these things at thy
word; that these are thy Keyes; I am thy Apostle; and if I be the man of
God, let fire come downe from Heaven and consume all those, that
obey not my orders, and Lawes; and at what time yee heare the sound of
my Instruments; fall downe and worship the Image, that I NABUCHAD-
NEZAR have set up, whose breath is in my hand, and whole are all my
wayes to glorifie mee; and who so falleth not down, &c,

Lines 302–3. the Enemie...Wormewood: see Rev. 8:11.

Line 307. the name...Death: see Rev. 6:8. Line 311. These three...Citie: see Rev. 16:19.

Line 315. Gaule: gall; bitter secretion, bile; see Job 20:14.

Line 316. the losing of his Keyes: see Matt. 16:19.

This *Baals* Prophet the last Beast, having devoured and broken in peeces the Roman Empire, exercising all the power of him whose Rome he usurpeth; the Lord saying, I that forme the Light, and create Darknesse; I that make Peace, and create evill, I will strengthen the Armies of the King of *Babilon,* and put my Sword into his hand. But I will breake PHAROAHS Arme, and he shall groane before him, with the groaning of a deadly wounded man; Moreover, thus saith the Lord of Hosts that keepes backe no mans pay.

The King of *Babilon* caused his Army to serve a great service against CHILDRIC King of *Tirus,* every head was made Bald of his Race, and every shoulder peel'd, yet had hee no wages for his Armie; Therefore the Land of Egypt shall bee his for his labour, because they wrought for mee saith the Lord; for there shall be no more a Prince in Egypt whose brightnesse was Excellent, and the forme thereof terrible to all the world; But rather a painted Image, a Vassoll, that the working of the poysoned Potion in the golden Cup, the mysterie of iniquitie bee not hindred, A base Kingdome the basest of all Kingdomes, neither shall it exalt it selfe any more above the Nations; for I will diminish them, it shall be no more the confidence of the house *Israell.*

Having now the spoyle of the Land for his Armie and the Sword and Ballances in his owne hand to make a prey of mercy and truth, with his Hornes and heeles as weapons to warre and weare out the Saints given into his hand untill a time and times; and the deviding of times, Three dayes and a halfe Two and fortie Moneths Three yeares and a halfe, halfe the mysticall weeke, untill the Day of Judgement; to make Merchandize of every thing, that no man may buy or sell without his Marke, marked with his fiends foote; which is his Seale, the signet of the Fisherman that beareth the name of the Beast.

The number of his name is then the number of a man, which is the number of his Age or Dayes, but this is the number of his Moneths; Naturall Beasts not living so long, the yeares being not so many as the dayes are to few. As one saith, the number of his Moneths are with the

330
340
350
360

Line 329. **Baals Prophet:** see 1 Kings 18:26–27. Lines 333–34. **I…Arme:** see Ezek. 30:21.
Lines 339–40. **the Land…his:** see Ezek. 30:25. Line 343. **Vassoll:** vessel; receptacle.
Line 354. **no man…sell:** see Rev. 13:17. Line 355. **signet:** seal used as a signature.

Lord; Also halfe the mysticall Weeke is delivered by the same measure. The latter Six Moneths added to the former Six hundred, making as compleat Fiftie, as Threescore make Five yeares; Here is Wisdome the counsell of times and seasons revealed, according to the eternall purpose, which the wisedome of the Father put in his owne power, God hath numbred thy Kingdome and finished it, thou art weighed in the ballances, thou tyrant, that boastest of thy wit, and art found wanting graines innumerable, thy Kingdome is divided, and given to the people of the Saints of the most Highest, whose Kingdome is an everlasting
370   kingdome &c. Therfore let him that readeth count this number well, and well marke, the marke of the Beast, is the Signet of the Fisherman, which men take in their right hand, wherewith his Band are branded in the foreheads, and this is the Caractor and colours that distinguisheth his Traine-Souldiers from the followers of the Truth.

    Therefore thus saith the Lord to the King of *Babilon,* Antichrist thy dayes be few, The great day of my wrath is at hand, even for the Elects sake, and the Soules that rest under the Altar, crying for Execution and Vengeance upon thee, whose Bodyes thou hast beheaded, burned and buryed alive, slaine for the Testimony they held, the time is shortned,
380   thy Bishoppricke shall bee voyde, and become a habitation for Divells; and because thou remembrest not to shew mercy, by swift destruction thy memorie shall be cut off from the Earth, thy Damnation slumbreth not, as a theefe in the night, and as a snare it shall come shortly upon thee; Thou hast loved cursing, in blessing thou hast not delighted, but as a cloake for Covetousnesse, selling to thy Marchants for money, those foule oyntments to fill thy Bagge, calling and crying from thy Exchange and darke shoppe; if any man Thirst to commit Whoredom, spirituall or carnall, Treason, or Murther, let him come to mee and drinke of my Golden Cuppe, Incest or Parricide; *Hoc misterium firmiter profitemur;*

Lines 362–63. **Six Moneths...yeares:** 666, the number of the Beast.

Lines 365–66. **God...it:** Dan. 5:26.

Line 374. **his Traine-Souldiers:** see Rev. 13:17; the trained bands or soldiers were those parts of the militia in Stuart England who trained regularly for fighting.

Line 387. **if...Whoredom:** cf. John 7:37.

Line 389. **Hoc...profitemur:** This divine mystery is being steadfastly revealed (Latin).

what doe yee lacke; wee can sell you for Gold, Silver, and pretious   390
stones, thin Wood, Brasse, Iron, and Marble, all manner of Vessells, in
Nunneries or Stewes, what will yee give; These execrable odors, and thy
Brazen browed Bulls, casting flakes of Fire and fulminations in the sight
of men from their noysome Nostrills and Thundring throates, as with a
Garment thou hast cloathed thy selfe, thou hast robbed mee even of
this whole Nation, therefore prepare thy selfe thou cursed for everlasting fire, prepared for the Divell and his Angells, which shall enter into
thy Bowells like water, and soake with thine oyntments, as oyle into thy
Bones, and mingle with thy marrow; thus let the Enemies of the Lord
bee rewarded, yea, in the meane time let them be their own execution-   400
ers; let one JUDAS with Poyson burst out the Bowells of another; let their
hope be as the giving up of the Ghost, and their righteousnesse wherein
they trust, in thy remembrance as water that passeth away; Let them
curse, but Blesse thou ô Lord to whom vengeance belongeth, shew thy
selfe, lift up thy selfe thou Judge of the Earth, and to this proude man of
Sinne render a reward; let him not have the upper hand, sitting upon
the Throne of Iniquitie in thy Temple, shewing himselfe that hee is
God, Consume him ô Lord with the Breath of thy mouth, and destroy
him quickly with the Brightnesse of thy comming.

Lastly, this Beast his habitation is compared to a woman for Sorcer-   410
ies, shamelesnesse and gorgious trimming, arrayed in Purple and Scarlet, the Virgin daughter of the King of *Egipt*, is become the Whore of
the King of *Babilon*, the faithfull Citie is become a Harlot, having in her
hand a Cuppe full of abominations, Witchcraft and Blasphemy, viz.
worshipping Idols of Gold and Silver, Brasse, Wood, and Stone, mixing
holy things with filthy excrements, remission, the forgivenesse of sinnes,
and calling the foule Sinagogue of Sathan, the Church of God, and
these are the spices and spirits wherewith her Cup is brewed; and this is
the Golden Cuppe wherewith the Kings of the Earth have been made so
drunken with, a Cup of *Sodome*, Wine mixed with the Blood of Drag-   420
ons, and stirred with the stings of Aspes; Is this meate indeed, and

---

Line 420. **Cup of Sodome:** see Rev. 17:4; the city of Sodom was known for its corruption
(Gen. 19:20).

drinke indeed, the sawce commeth after; Is this the true Mother; is this
the Woman shee is taken for, with Eagles wings; her childe caught up
unto God and to his Throne, and having a crowne of Twelve Starres; in
no wise in her there is no Bowells of a Mother, though they strive to the
end of the world.

   Her Judgement followeth; And a name was written upon her forehead *BABILON,* The Mother of Harlots, and Abominations of the
Earth, the Print is not small, yet not so large as the mysterie is deepe; It
430 was written, and therefore to bee read: Thus, the hidden mystery of this
Enigmaticall writing is here, the secret of numbers to teach us to number her dayes; The numbers are these, and I heard the number of them,
Two hundred thousand thousand horsemen, having breast-plates of fire
and Gunpowder or hiacinth, force and furie in stead of faith and love,
alluding to the double number of NINUS Horsemen, wherewith he subdued so many Nations in Seventeene years: The double confirmation of
this mysterie seventeene hundred yeares also, being the limited time
fixed to finish her warre, which began with the Lambe, and ended in
subduing his Saints and Servants; And as the fiery Army needing no
440 fuell, were to the Army of NINUS, consisting of Twenty hundred Thousand, amounting a hundred to one, so is the accompt of the time, when
the spreading Vine of the Earth, the clusters of her Grapes being ripe,
she shall be cast into the great wine presse of the wrath of God. These
Tyrants, (here is wisdome to looke into these accompts) shall make her
desolate and naked, and eate her flesh, and burne her with fire, for God
hath put it in their hearts to fulfill his will, when *Babylon* the glory of
Kingdomes, shall be as *Sodome* and *Gomorah,* the time is neere, the
dayes shall not bee prolonged.

   The Father of this goodly Baby, (yet auncient, no novice in her
450 whoredome) for so hee nameth himselfe, there is no need to name him

---

Lines 423–24. **Woman…Starres:** see Rev. 12:1–14.

Lines 428–29. **BABILON…Earth:** Rev. 17:5.

Line 433. **Two hundred…horsemen:** cf. Rev. 9:16.

Line 435. **NINUS:** Assyrian king who built Nineveh.

Lines 446–47. **when Babylon…Gomorah:** see Jude 7.

(at whose entrance the Fourth Angell or Winde was loosed) as hee is sufficiently notorious, so is he mistaken Sathan that old Serpent, begetting the Impe of Fornication, before ever the Beast and his false spouse came together, deceivers as seldome wanting cloakes of craft to hide their shame, as their of-spring faile in Lyneaments and likenesse to their Parents, seven heads no lesse markes then Mountaines, seeing as incredible as superfluous and monstrous, were it not the Evidence and demonstration of that Sinagogue to prove her title and visibilitie, drunken with the Blood of Saints and Martyrs, In steed of her Mothers milke and breast shee sucks her hart-Blood, whose Father was a Lyer and a   460 Murtherer from the beginning.

To Administer the rites of their unrighteous mistery; This City Bab, hath Citie Gossips, NINEVY is not invited; she repented at the Preaching of the poore Prophet, shee is none of them; But *Babylon* for her Pride and impudency at this Antichristian solemnity or shew of Christianitie; The Mother of Harlots; for her stiffe neck is preferred before her, whose name this shamelesse place, never to be outworne or blotten out, beares in her fatall brazen forehead.

Besides, this Lady sitting upon her Beast, seventeene Kings to beare up her Traine, decked with Gold and pretious Stones, and Pearle, whose   470 name is also *Semiramis* or *Jesabell,* for magnificence millions of men, viz. a hundred times Twenty hundred Thousand; Her Altars, Images, Sorceries, and Blood of Prophets and Saints, Saying in her hart, I sit a Queene and am no Widow; a Lady for ever, I am, and none else besides mee; there are Seven Kingdomes.

Five are fallen downe dead drunke, upon whom the Lord hath poured out the spirit of deepe sleepe, and closed their eyes, they shall revert nor rise no more; After slumbering the other Two, (though they have falne from the truth,) shall stagger and come to themselves againe;

Line 451. **Fourth...Winde:** see Rev. 7:1.   Line 456. **seven...Mountaines:** see Rev. 17:3, 9.

Line 462. **This City Bab:** Babylon; babble or infantile talk.

Line 463. **NINEVY...repented:** Nineveh; see Jon. 3:5.

Line 471. **Semiramis:** the queen of King Ninus of Assyria. **Jesabell:** Jezebel; queen of King Ahab of Samaria.

Lines 473–74. **I...Widow:** Rev. 18:7.   Line 476. **Five...downe:** Rev. 17:10.

480 and that Must now growne sower and stale, their lust shall be little to taste thereof againe; The first Kingdome or ONE IS, are the Brittish Islands, the right Inheritance of King JAMES the first of that Name of Great *Britaine* and *Ireland;* for the Iles feared the Judgement of the Lord and saw it; Even the ends of the Earth were afraid and drew neere. The other is not yet come, and when it commeth, it can continue no long space, the end of the world is so neere.

O sencelesse poore Beasts who hath bewitched you; why lye yee still, who hath bitten you; arise, choose not Death rather then life; how are yee swolne, why should your Carcasses be dung, and meate for the 490 fowles of Heaven? Why will yee dye, stand up; why goe yee backward; what astonishment is this that hath taken you; be recovered, understand, halt not, yet heare the word of the Lord; curst cattell, backsliding Heifers hee delighteth in Mercy; provoke not him with your strange vanities and Bruitish abominations; The day of the Lord is at hand.

Therefore awake yee Drunkards, weepe and howle all yee drinkers of Wine, because of the new Wine the Deepe Cup, the day of the wrath of the Lord is at hand; yee Kings of the Earth and Rulers of *Sodome,* who have committed fornication, and lived delitiously with this indulgent Witch, the mother of Harlots; when yee see her brought to the stake 500 and utterly burnt with fire; how will yee stand, for strong is the Lord who Judgeth her; what will yee say; yee shall stand a farre off, or wish in vaine the Mountaines to cover you, howling and gnashing your Teethes for feare of her Torment, whose sinnes as the smoake of her Burning have reached up unto Heaven; saying alasse, alasse, *Sodome,* alasse, *Babylon, Rome* the great Citie, the head of the Monarchy; for in the twinckling of an eye, an houre unlookt for, thy Judgement is come, is that a time to cast dust on your heads?

Never more shall we heare in thee the voyce of Harpers and Pipers, awaking and calling for rewards to Saints and our Lady; and Trumpeters

---

Line 481. **The first…IS:** see Rev. 17:10. Lines 484–85. **The other…come:** Rev. 17:10.
Line 495. **weepe and howle:** Joel 1:5.
Lines 499–500. **brought…burnt:** the usual punishment for heretics.
Line 508. **Never…Pipers:** see Rev. 18:22.

when wee doe our Almes; Never more shall wee see in thee Idolls or
Images so auntient, the curious device of the Crafts-man, nor the sound
of the grinding Milstone; our Altars decked as a shop, shining with the
light of so many Tapers and Candles. Nor the voyce of the Bride-
groome, called the head, and [t]he Bride by Prelates and so many Kings
our holy Mother; The Net is spread, shee is taken in the Snare, in grinding the face of the Poore, shee that so much glorified her selfe, in a day
and an houre her Plague is come.

The Thrones of these Earthly Kingdomes cast downe the auncient of
dayes shall appeare; his long Traine, and the great white Throne
whereon he sate, from whose Face the Earth and the Heavens uncleane
in his sight fled away, in whose presence ministred Thousand thousands, and Ten thousand times Tenne Thousands; also the Two Witnesses are brought forth, the Books of the Law and the Prophets, to
Judge every man by his workes, or according to his faith, for if they
beleeve not the writings of MOSES; how can they beleeve his words of
whom MOSES wrote, These Bookes shall accuse them, the witnesses
which God the Father beareth of his Sonne; The other Booke is the
Booke of Life, written with the names of Saints that shall live for ever;
To whom the just Judge shall deliver the possession of that Kingdome
that shall never passe away to be destroyed, but remaineth for ever, even
for ever and ever.

The foule Beast, some of his purtenances will be wanting if his
hornes be not farther Considered; foure came up out of the North part
of his head, the French Emperours; of the Southside six Spanish;
before whom, there were Three of the first, their Race pluckt up by the
Rootes; amongst these came up an other little Horne about the midst of
the time: in this Horne were eyes, like the eyes of a man, in workmanship striving to set Nature a patterne; curious in all Arts, and doing
honour to vertue, but wanting the gift of grace, opened a fearefull
Mouth; the King of the East, whose looke is more stout then the highest
of his fellow Hornes.

Hitherto is the end of the matter of these earthly Monarchies, and

---

Lines 522–23. **the Two…forth:** Rev. 11:3.

the day of Judgement hath beene also declared the matter of the end: The Story is yet but chalked out, Therefore in these following Visions is contained more at large, the occurrence of those dayes before mentioned, even to the end of the world; Wherein my desire is, not as hee that rowleth a stone to returne upon himselfe, but to make it a twisted Threefold Cord, to draw up the weight that presseth so hard of infidelitie.

550   The Prophet beheld till the auncient of dayes did sit to Judge the quicke and the dead, and the Beast cast alive into the Lake Fire, his Body destroyed and given to the Burning flame, to be tormented day and night, for ever and ever.

DANIEL. Chap. VIII.

In the third yeare of Belshazzer a Vision appeared unto Daniel alone, even to himselfe, and hee heard a mans voyce that called, saying; Gabriel, make the man understand the Vision; so he came neere unto him, and said; O Sonne of man, the time of this Vision extends to the end of all things; behold therefore I will make thee know what shall come to
560   passe, even to the last day, the great day of Wrath and Indignation, for at the time appointed the end shall be.

MEDES AND PERSIANS	SEND MEE SPANIARDS
THE ROUGHE GOAT.	THE GOTHE ROAGUE.

The first matter given him to understand, is the breaking in peeces of the Roman Empire, which spiritually is called *Sodome* and *Egipt;* where also the members of our Lords Body are Crucified, signified by the Ram, the Hee Goate is the *Turke;* The *Roman* Emperours the Two hornes in the East and West, are also signified by the Kings of *Media* and *Persia.* The foure Kingdomes standing up out of that Nation, are
570   the Isles of Great *Britaine, France, Spaine,* and *Turky.*

Lines 546–47. **hee…himselfe:** in Greek myth, the punishment of Sisyphus, who was condemned to roll a stone endlessly uphill.

Lines 562–63. **MEDES…ROAGUE:** two anagrams.

Line 565. **spiritually…Sodome:** see Rev. 11:8.

Lastly, the Goate himselfe shall be hunted by a King of a fierce Countenance, not regarding the person of the old, nor shewing favour to the young, casting downe some of the hoast of PHAROAH, and of the Starres to the ground: For the transgression against the daily Sacrifice was the Hoast given over: A King understanding darke sentences which are some part of the holy Scriptures, through policie and supposed wisdome, he shall cause the craft of the Divell to prosper, for by Peace and affected pittie, and satisfying the ambitious mindes of some Christians, he shall not only draw them to denie the faith, but many others following their example: Not by his owne power, but by the Divells policie he 580 shall be mighty, whose looke is more stout then his fellowes, But by the great day of the Lord, he shall be broken without hand.

Now in those dayes, when the Goate was come close unto the Ramme, and had cast him downe and stamped upon him; The Prophet that beheld as by a perspective these remote things, heard also one Saint speaking, and an other Saint said unto that certaine Saint that spoke, how long is the time from this Vision to the end of the world, that the holy Citie of God, and his chosen People be no longer trodden under foote; And hee said unto mee unto Two Thousand Three hundred dayes; Then shall the Sanctuarie bee cleansed, and the holy People Jus- 590 tified.

The dayes bee so many yeares to the end of the world, beginning at the Vision, which was about the yeare of the world, 3425.

Of the certaine Saints speaking, or the number of wonderfull secrets, I omit to speake, that to the most part might appeare (being in this Land, and these late dayes) but some tale of a Phenix, though to bee testified of more then five hundred men and women besides my selfe.

DANIEL. Chap. IX.

After these Visions in the first yeare of DARIUS the Son of AHASHUERUS, the Prophet understood by Bookes and Computations, the number of 600 yeares whereof the word of the Lord came to JEREMIAH the Prophet,

---

Line 575. **Hoast:** host; bread in the Holy Communion.

Line 596. **Phenix:** phoenix; bird which rose from the ashes, a symbol of resurrection.

concerning the desolation of *Jerusalem,* that seventie yeares should be
accomplished; And whilst hee was speaking in Prayer, and presenting
his supplication before the Lord for the holy Mountaine the People of
God, even for the holy Citie the Church, that to the end of the world
must be trodden under foote, whereof that ruinous place the Citie of
Jerusalem, is a figure trodden downe at this day. Yet was this *Hebron*
built seaven yeares before *Zoan* in *Egipt.*

  The man GABRIEL which was caused to flie swiftly, touched him and
610 said (alluding to the former matter of his studie and meditations, as of
troublous, appetites, and Cogitations somtimes Dreames are derived) O
DANIEL I am come unto thee againe to give thee more skill and understanding; Seventie weekes are determined upon the holy Citie, signifying the time, not onely when the Sonne of God by his suffering should
make reconciliation for sinne, but a time and times and part of time,
three dayes and a halfe, halfe the mysticall Weeke, to make an end of
Sinnes to finish transgression, and to make a new Heaven and a new
Earth, wherein dwelleth everlasting righteousnesse to seale up the
Visions and Prophecies with the Seale of assurance, that all these things
620 are past and true, and to annoint the most holy King and Kings, and
Lord and Lords, the first and the last.

  And here againe the Angell GABRIEL willeth him to know and understand the things of which he shall informe him; The first is this, that
from the going forth of the Commandement, which is the beginning of
the Creation to the building of the new Jerusalem, the second comming
of *Messiah* the Prince the Sonne of God, it shall be Seaven Weekes or
Seaven Moneths, as it is spoken by EZEKIEL the Prophet; Then the desolate Citie the Sanctuary shall be walled in, in a troublous time, to
make a seperation betweene the Sanctuary and the Prophane place.

630 And in the middest of this Propheticall weeke, after Threescore and
Two weekes, *Messiah* shalbe cut off, the Son of God shalbe Crucified
and be delivered unto the *Gentiles,* & they shal scourge him & put him
to death, the People of the Prince (for it was not lawfull for the *Jewes* to
put any man to Death) these People the *Roman* Nation shall destroy the

---

Line 607. **Hebron:** city in Canaan to which the Israelites came (Num. 13:22).

Citie of *Jerusalem* and the Sanctuary; at the end of which Warre there shall begin a floud of Fyre (kindled in our Saviours dayes) during the Raigne of those Ethnick Beares, and the abomination of desolation standing where it ought not; then let him that is in *Judea* flye to the wilde Mountaines for safety; for in those times Judgement did begin at the house of God; and if first Justice did begin at his Children and Ser-   640
vants in this life, what shall the end bee of his Enemies, whom hee hates in the world to come, that have not obeyed the Gospell of God.

These Flouds the Serpent will cast out of his Mouth, a time and times & halfe a Time, to trie them of the holy Covenant, their bold-nesse, what confidence they have concerning the Lords oath, and whether they will persever in this holinesse and righteousnesse all their dayes to their lives end, and not rather feare his power, who is Sathan the Prince of this world, or at least the furious cruell hands of his tortur-ing Instruments.

Whose lives cannot satisfie their malice; for had not the senselesse   650
earth shewed more pitty then they, opening her Mouth to helpe these poore outcasts, their torments had beene endlesse; Sooner they may swim, and sinke in their Blood, then daunt or foyle their courage, not abashed for their Boasts, threats, nor fiery Brands they feare them not at all; their Triumphs are graven upon the Palmes of the Lords hands, hee forgets them no more, then a Mother forgets her new-borne Sonne, her sucking childe, when the Tongue cleaves to the roofe of the Mouth for Thirst, to have compassion on him; be of good cheere, you have peace in Christ, though tribulation in this world; persecutions are but like the Travell of a Woman, who hath sorrow because her houre is come, but as   660
soone as shee is delivered of the Childe, shee remembreth no more the anguish, for joy a man-childe is borne into the world.

The Lambe, the Bread of life shall feede them, they shall hunger nor thirst no more; hee shall wipe all Teares from the eyes of his Children; these vilde Bodyes, subject to all infirmities, shall then be made like his

---

Line 643. **Flouds...Mouth:** see Rev. 12:15. Lines 650–51. **had not...they:** see Rev. 12:16.
Line 660. **Travell:** travail; labor in childbirth.
Line 663. **The Lambe...feede them:** Rev. 7:17. Line 665. **vilde:** vile.

owne glorified Body, of more perfection then our first Parents, a living
Soule that shall not dye to Sinne; neither shall the heate of the Sunne
smite them; for hee shall have mercy upon them, and leade them to living Fountaines of truth, cleere as Christall; these that come to him, or
670　overcome the world, hunger no more, they have rest and peace for
paine, and by their white Robes and Palmes in their hands, the Ensignes
of peace and victorie; they shall be knowne, neither to be Heretiques or
Schismatiques, but his servants that have fought for his Kingdome that
it should not be delivered up unto Antichrist.

　　The followers of him, who shall shortly tread these Traitors in the
great Wine-presse of the wrath of God, who have turned away their
Eares from the wholsome Scriptures, the Leaves of which are for the
healing of the Nations, that they might be rubbed with the Prophane
fables of Drunken doting old wives.

680　　But with all the faithfull the Lord shall confirme his truth and Covenant for a Weeke from the beginning of the world untill the last end
therof; This week is Seven thousand yeares, consisting of yeares,
Moneths and weekes; finished when the Kingdomes of this world, are
become the Kingdomes of our Lord, and of his Christ, and hee shall
Raigne for ever and ever: When the Tenth part of the Citie fell, the
Tenne dayes of Tribulation are ended; Seven thousand names of men
slaine in the great Earthquake, *Dies Solis, Dies Lunæ, Dies Martis, Dies
Mercurii, Dies Jovis, Dies Veneris, Dies Saturni;* the remnant were
affrighted, and gave glory unto the God of Heaven.

690　　For wee must not be ignorant of this one thing, that one day with the
Lord is as a Thousand yeare, and a Thousand yeare as one day; In the
middest of which Weeke, the Lord shall cause the oblation and Sacrifice
to cease, saying, Sacrifice and Offering thou wouldest not, but a Body
hast thou prepared mee without spot, for the redemption of the trans-

---

Lines 671–72. **white…peace:** see Rev. 7:9.

Lines 675–76. **who…Wine-presse:** see Rev. 14:19–20.

Line 685. **the Tenth…fell:** Rev. 11:13.

Lines 687–88. **Dies Solis…Dies Saturni:** Sunday, Monday, Tuesday, Wednesday, Thursday,
Friday, Saturday (Latin).

Lines 690–91. **one day…yeare:** 2 Pet. 3:8.　Line 692. **oblation:** solemn offering.

gressions that were under the first Testament. The Blood of which first Testament of Beasts, God enjoyned to purifie the patternes of heavenly things, the Vessels of the Ministrie, but the heavenly things themselves with better Sacrifices (which are the Consciences to purge them from dead workes, that they may be cleane vessels to serve the living God.)

Thus hee once suffered, the uncreated in likenesse of a Creature like feeble sinfull flesh, sowne in weaknesse and dishonour in the Dust, but raised in Power & the Brightnesse of his Fathers Glory, the expresse Image of his person, over whose excellent Nature, voyd of violence and deceit, the Grave could get no victory, no more then the wombe can keepe backe a sonne at the time of perfection, redeemed from the Bowels of the Earth, and ransomed by the riches of his owne unsearchable Treasure and quickning Spirit.

This seeming ugly Serpent, rather some shadow or his skin, at whose approach men turne pale and quake more terrified then hurt; But rocking Babes the faithfull a sleepe, others run raving with staring frenzie for feare, as if this once appointed so were fits to be chased away, not calling to minde the Resurrection of JESUS CHRIST, hath opened his Jawes, his Sting cut out and nayled to the Crosse, that bold Champion scorning to be his executioner, setting his victorious foot upon the Traytors head, by spirituall alliance kinne to the Divell, proud of advantage, bites the Heele of our Saviour with his rotten Teeth, for want of his Poysoned sting.

But heare ô Death unstop thine Adders eares from whose Molesighted eyes, the light of Repentance is hid, behold thy time and Plague is at hand; thy pined crying Prisoners, thou shall restraine their libertie no longer, that say our Bones are dryed and our hope is lost, when shall we dwell in the Land of the living; behold, thy Caves and Castles shall be destroyed & broken downe, and the Earth that opened her Mouth and swallowed up the Flood shall cast it up againe in the twinkling of an Eye, thou shalt give up thy accompts, for of the Sonnes and Daughters of the Lord, thou shalt not keepe backe so much as the least, whose names are written in the Booke of life.

700

710

720

Line 718. **Death…eares:** see Ps. 58:4.

And lastly, Viper, seed of the olde Serpent, thy sentence is for that bold attempt; Fuller of malice then hurt, thy house shall be burned with unquenchable Fire, the Place sowne with unsavory poysoned Salt, and thy Carrion-carkasse swallowed up of thine owne Brood the second Death.

All which mysticall Weeke or Seaven Moneths formerly mentioned, as it is spoken by the Prophet EZECHIEL; The Land of *Israell* shalbe burying of *Gog* that Sathan, that the Land may be cleansed.

Hitherto are the matters talked of between the man GABRIEL and the Prophet.

DANIEL. Chap. X.

In the third yeare of CYRUS King of *Persia*, a thing was revealed to Daniel (whose name was called BELTESHAZZER) and the thing was true but the time appointed was long. These are the things not only come to passe, in this latter age of the world, but at this time and in this day; signified by the Son of God to the Prophet.

PRINCE OF PERSIA. —I CAN POPE FRIERS.

Divell. *I can Pope Friars. Man hold up my Traine?*
Pope. *Kings I Depose, and all their Race, to Raigne.*
Divell. *And Popes to Friers I can turne againe.*

The Prince of the Kingdome of *Persia*, (that Lord by whom the Lord of Lords was withstood,) is Sathan the Divell, MICHAEL one of the first Princes that came then to helpe him; This is JAMES King of Great *Britaine*, and the man who is raised on high: The one and Twenty dayes; the Lord making no forfeiture, are so many Hundred yeares, beginning at the Vision, and ending this present, 1600. And so long the words of this Vision have been closed & sealed up; Even till now the time of the end.

This most Blessed person the Saviour of the world, remained with the Kings of *Persia*, the *Roman* Emperors (signified so unto DANIEL

Line 735. **Gog:** see Ezek. 38, 39.

Line 744. **FRIERS:** friars; brothers (members) of religious orders such as the Franciscans, the Carmelites, and the White Friars.

Line 750. **JAMES:** King James I (reigned 1603–1625).

being the present Monarchy) till there arose up a new King in *Egipt* which knew not JOSEPH, and said unto his People; Behold, the People of the Children of *Israell* are more, and mightier then wee; Therfore set over them Taskmasters to afflict them with Burthens, but the more they 760 did afflict them, the more they multiplied and grew. These Kings placed in the highest Thrones, to walke in his Statutes to execute his Judgements, but because they gave more Eare, and harkened rather to false Prophets then to ELIAS and MOSES, for severitie and meeknesse; Representing the Law and the Gospell, suffering their Bodies to lye dead in the streets in an unknowne Tongue, even hee the Lord departed from them; and with the sword of his Mouth will fight with their Prince Sathan, renewing alwayes his old quarrell against the Church of God.

And here these Kings forsaken of JESUS CHRIST, for one secret friend which is the Divell, they have two open Enemies, the *Turke* and the 770 *Pope,* making their Crownes his footstoole, this did not CÆSAR, by these Three the Empire being devided; what can remaine but the bare Image; or the Image of the Picture of him, whose deadly wound was healed: Bearing at this day, as Thunder goes before Lightning, for their fatall device, the sad Fowle blazoned with the ominous Colours of the blacke Horse; for feare, but halfe displaying her wings, in stead of her beake shee casts her heads, the Eagle hath Mued her Feathers; Though thou exalt thy selfe as the Eagle, and though thou set thy neast amongst the Starres, thence will I bring thee downe saith the Lord.

These things hitherto mentioned concerning the last Vision is the 780 preamble for this that followeth, for here the Sonne of God whose eyes were like a flame of fire, and his feet like fine brasse, saith he will shew unto the man greatly beloved, that which is noted in the Scripture of truth, which is the *Revelation*, the sayings of which are faithfull and true, that there is none, or but one, that holdeth with him in these

---

Lines 757–58. **there…JOSEPH:** Exod. 1:8. Lines 765–66. **suffering…streets:** Rev. 11:8.
Lines 771–72. **by these…devided:** Rev. 16:19.
Line 775. **blazoned:** displayed, as in coats of arms.
Lines 777–78. **Mued:** mewed; shed or moulted. **Though…Eagle:** see Jer. 49:16.
Lines 781–82. **the Sonne…brasse:** Rev. 2:18.

things, which is the true Interpretation of the Scripture, but MICHAEL our Prince of Great *Britaine* and *Ireland,* that fights and contends with the Enemies of the Lord, about his Body, disputing with them, have transubstantiated & changed the truth of God into a lye, worshipping
790 and serving the Creature more then the Creator, for which cause God gave them up, &c.

Now followeth that that is noted in the Scripture of that Prince. After the Temple of God was opened in Heaven, wherein was seene the Arke of his Testament, overlaid round about with gold, wherein was the golden Pot that had Manna, and ARONS Rodde that budded, and the Tables of the Covenant, And over it the Cherubins of glory, covering the Mercy-Seate, and Lightnings and voyces, and Thunders, &c. This is the Millitant Church that brought foorth the Man-childe, the word of God, caught up unto God, and to his Throne, after which the Woman
800 fled into the Wildernesse, where shee was fed A thousand two hundred and threescore dayes, which are so many yeares.

The first accompt beginneth from the destruction of *Jerusalem,* when the abomination of desolation, did stand in the Holy place, the yeares being the same spoken in the last Vision of the Prophet DANIEL, though thirty yeares be taken away, because the Court without the Temple was left out, given unto the Gentiles, for the Raigne of the first Christian Emperour.

These yeares doe reach to the dayes of those blessed Men, when the light of the Gospell did first begin to shine, after the great Mist, lasting
810 a Thousand two hundred and ninetie yeares, dayes of darknesse and gloominesse of Cloudes, and thicke Mists, when the third part of the Sunne was smitten, and the third part of the Moone, and the third part of the Starres, which are innumerable; After these dayes were past, there was warre in Heaven, MICHAEL and his Angells, fought against the

---

Line 789. **transubstantiated:** Transubstantiation is the Catholic doctrine of the mass, which holds that the wine and bread are changed into the blood and body of Christ.

Line 795. **ARONS Rodde:** see Exod. 7:10–12.

Lines 799–800. **the Woman…Wildernesse:** see Rev. 12:14.

Lines 811–12. **when…smitten:** Rev. 8:12.

Dragon, and the Dragon fought, and his Angells the Jesuites, and prevailed not, neither was their place found any more in Heaven.

Heaven is here taken in this place for the Church of God, the fray is fought by seconds, by MICHAEL is meant King JAMES; The Dragon needs little exposition, It is the Pope, for MICHAEL overcame by the blood of the Lambe, and by the testimony of so many Bishops, and other faithfull, crowned with the Glory of Martyrdome; Therefore rejoyce yee Church of God, yee Congregations of the faithfull, and ye Professors that dwell amongst them, and woe to the Earth and to the Sea, the Congregation of that Sinagogue the Sea of *Rome,* Sathans seate, where Sathan dwelleth, for the Pope, the Dragon, the Divell is amongst you, having great wrath, because he knoweth he hath but a short time, two woes are past, and behold the third woe commeth shortly.

Blessed are the Dead that dye in the Lord, for they rest from their labours, and their works follow them, and this is the truth noted in the Scripture of Truth, of MICHAEL, And God make the name and Throne, of the King of his Sonne, better, and greater then his.

Though I owe no defence for the name of an Angell given to a Mortall man (in this Prophesie) yet to satisfie as well the Envious as the Ignorant, they shall finde the Sonne of God sometimes called by the name of the first ADAM, DAVID who shall feede his Flocke like a Shepheard, and gather his Lambes with his arme, and carry them in his bosome, stiled a man after Gods owne Hart; and in another place from his owne Mouth, holding it no derogation to his Divine Nature, to apply to himselfe by Parables the properties of an austere Master, a Cruell usurer, or the unjust Judge, May by the same Authoritie give the name of MICHAEL, or like unto God in some respects unto this Prince who fought the battell of the Lord, more like an Angell then a Mortall Man; as to the other the name of Dragon, because he spake as a Dragon.

820

830

840

Line 815. **Jesuites:** Jesuits; a Catholic religious order, which worked hard to reconvert Protestants to Catholicism.

Line 817. **fray:** fight. Lines 823–24. **woe…Sea:** Rev. 12:12.

Lines 832–33. **no defence…man:** a justification of the apparent blasphemy in identifying King James with Michael.

As this young Dragon hath acted his part, his Syer or Damme the old Dragon, his markes may not be forgotten, whose Hornes have been formerly mentioned in a Miter and Diadem, his seaven Heads are so many Rulers, as it were Husbands or severall sorts of Magistracy, governing that Commonwealth, and the seaven Crownes are seaven Hundreth 850 yeares, beeing the time from *Romes* foundation to the first Emperour. *Equæua polo, Eterna, Antiqua, Caput Mundi, Celsa. Deum locus. Cœlestis.* Names of Blasphemie.

DANIEL. Chap. XI.

DARIUS the med. — i dreamed thus.

Besides this Prince of victorious and blessed memory, who came to helpe the King of Kings, that sate upon the white Horse, whose name is the word of God, to fight the Battell in Heaven against the Prince of the Kingdome of *Persia,* here is an other of like happy memory, that hath the Honour to have his name Recorded in this holy antient Prophecie, 860 Constantine the Great, named, Darius the *Mede,* raigning thirtie yeares. In the first times of which renowned Monarchy the Lord stood to confirme and strengthen him. After whose time three Kings stood up together in *Persia,* dividing the Empire, which breach, made way for the fourth, the fourth Beast, corrupted with Riches and libertie; Farre richer then they all, By whose strength through his riches, Christian Princes were stirred up against Marhomet, growing not a little great by their ruines.

And a mighty King shall stand up, the great King of *Tyre,* the absolute Monarch thereof, and all the dependences Northward, that shall 870 rule with great dominion, and doe according to his owne will, and when hee shall stand up the fundamentall Lawes of his Kingdome shall bee broken and infringed; And the Kingdome shall be divided towards the foure windes of Heaven, and not to his posterity, nor according to

---

Line 851. **Equæua...Cœlestis:** Of the same age as the earth, eternal, ancient, head of the universe, lofty, the place of God, divine (Latin).

Line 854. **DARIUS...THUS:** an anagram. Line 856. **the King...Horse:** Rev. 19:11.

Line 860. **CONSTANTINE the Great:** Roman Emperor, fourth century A.D., who granted toleration to the Christians.

Line 868. **the great King of Tyre:** see Isa. 23.

his Dominion which hee ruled, for this Kingdome shall be pluckt up, even for others, besides those that were planted therein; his naturall subjects by a dispensation being freed from their oath of obedience.

Caroli Magni Christianissimi Romanorum Imperatoris
Corpus hoc conditum est sepulchro.

After this the King of the South was strong, and he was strong above the King of the North, and he had dominion, and his Dominion is a great dominion.   880

These two Kings, the King of the North, and the King of the South parting the ten Hornes, the Princes of *Tyre* and *Ethiopia;* In the end of yeares they shall joyne themselves together, for the Kings Daughter of the South shall come to the King of the North to make an agreement, but shee shall not retaine the power of the Arme, neither shall he stand nor his Arme, or they shall be Childlesse, and she shall be given up, And they that brought her sent away destitute of a Father, and for saken of her Brother.

But out of a branch of her rootes, which are her Father and her Mother, signifying their Incestuous Mariages, One shall stand up in his Estate very hardy, and shall come with an Armie, and shall enter into the fortresse of the King of the North; or the King of *Tyre,* and deale against them and prevaile; And shall carry Captives into *Egipt,* their Gods and their Princes, and with their Pretious Vessells of Silver and Gold, and hee shall continue more yeares then the King of the North in the Monarchy; So the King of the South, or the King of *Ethiopia* shall returne into his owne Land, the Land of Dust and Ashes, where his worst Enemies doe not envie his quiet possession: But his Sonnes who succeeded each other in the Monarchy, shall be stirred up against the King of the North, and shall assemble a great multitude of Forces, and one of them shall certainly come and overflow with a floud of Fury, and   890 / 900

Lines 875–76. **his naturall...obedience:** The pope freed Queen Elizabeth's subjects from obedience when he excommunicated her.

Lines 877–78. **Caroli...sepulchro:** Most Christian Charlemagne, Emperor of the Romans. This body is founded on the grave (Latin).

Lines 882–83. **These two...Hornes:** Rev. 13:1.

Line 891. **their Incestuous Mariages:** according to Lev. 20:20-21, childlessness is the consequence of incestuous marriages.

shall passe through, and prevaile against them of the Holy Covenant; But after that hee shall returne and be stirred up, even to his Fortresse or best Fenced place by them.

And the King of the South, or one of these Brothers shall be provoked with Choller, and shall come forth and fight with the King of the North, who shall set forth a great multitude, but the multitude shall bee given into the hands of his Enemies, and himselfe shall be his Prisoner carried a Captive into *Ethiopia*.

And when the King of the South, or this *Persian* King hath taken away the multitude, his heart shall be lifted up against God; and he shall cast downe many of his servants Tenne Thousands; but neither hee nor those that come after shall bee strengthened thereby.

(For at the end of Yeares, which are now expired, there shall certainely come a King of the North, and hee shall set forth a multitude greater then the former, a great Army and with much riches, and hee shall doe according to his owne will, &c.)

And in those former dayes there shall many stand up against the King of the South; also the Robbers of the Christians, these Extortioners shall exalt themselves, to establish the Vision of the Prophets, and the Figures of the Law, which Prophecied untill JOHN; for the first things that are but shadowes, are now vanished away, to establish the second, but they shall fall, So the King of the North shall come and cast up a Mount, and take the most fenced Cities; and the Armes of the South shall not withstand, neither his chosen People, neither shall there bee any strength to withstand, But hee that commeth against him, shall doe according to his owne will, and none shall stand before him; and hee shall stand in the glorious Land which by him shall be consumed; Hee shall also set his face to enter with the strength of his whole Kingdome, and upright ones with him; thus shall hee doe.

And hee shall give him the Daughter of Women, or a Queene by decent, whose Royall blood was corrupted, and stayned by the usurping authority of a Tyranous Husband, but she shall not stand on his side, neither before him, for hee dying shee was brought home, and shortly after Married to another,

After which agreement dissolved, and the League broken, his Successor shall turne his face unto the *Brittish* Iles, and shall take many Prisoners, but a Prince for his owne behalfe, rather then the honour of God of a happy daring shall cause the reproach offered to cease without his owne reproach, hee caused the shame to turne upon him that opposeth and exalteth himselfe above all that is called God. The Lord sometimes providing the remedy before the sore, as carefull Physitians have Drugs in store for all diseases, preparing the disobedience of VASTHI, and the unlawfull divorce, for the preservation of the *Jewes*, to hang proud HAMMON and all his wicked Sonnes, so this Prince throwing under foote his Cappe of Maintenance (whose visage was unmask'd, by a Munke not long before) those *Babel* Monasteries, unmeete Cages for such Craignes, Ostriges, and chanting Owles, digesting not only all the thorney-Choaking Heresie of false Prophets, but the rusty Purgatory fictions of Heathen Poets, The doings of these uncleane and hatefull birds, Though as the eating of doung I loathe them in my Mouth, yet since our Saviour and Lord himselfe vouchsafed to cast his Eye towards those secret privie places, bidding us take heed of their Deserts, I may not stop my Nose or Mouth for nicenesse, but rather thinke it my part to empty such houses of office, if weakenesse did not prevent and hinder my willingnesse.

Yet with mine owne hand according to my might (God willing) I will throw one stone at this *Thracian* Witch, the wicked Prophet; If I cannot breake his head, I will breake his Harpe if I can, before hee passe headlong downe to Hell the streame: Neither will omit her Holinesse (though her native Soile and Sex may challenge some favour) how they shall walke then, Inseparably hand in hand togither; And as certaine of their owne Poets mention, her untimely Death, stung by the false Scorpion, that lurk'd so close in the grasse, of his gamesome villany.

1020

1030

1040

Lines 1024–25. **disobedience…divorce:** see Esther 1:12 and 2:4.

Line 1026. **HAMMON:** see Esther 7.

Line 1027. **Cappe of Maintenance:** a cap borne before the monarch at the coronation.

Line 1029. **Craignes…Owles:** cranes, ostriches, and owls; see Isa. 38:14, Lam. 4:3, Job 30:29.

Lines 1030–31. **Purgatory…Poets:** Protestants rejected the Catholic belief in purgatory.

Line 1039. **this Thracian witch:** Hecate or Persephone.

Line 1040. **his head…his Harpe:** those of Orpheus; in Greek myth, Orpheus was a musician whose wife, Eurydice, was killed by a snake. While mourning her, Orpheus was attacked and killed by Thracian women, and his severed head continued to sing as it floated down the river.

This Beast (or rather Divell) for so hee seemes by his description, by the stamping of his Oxe feete. Long teeth of Iron, nayles of Brasse, and ten Hornes, or at least some horrible Monster in his likenesse, takes upon him to give, by his Marke to all the world most cursed Dispensa-
1050 tions: To please HEROD it shall be lawfull to Marry his Daughter to her Husbands owne Brother, the Uncle to his Neece: Thus unnaturall he is not satisfied in most prodigious manner to abuse himselfe, but others must doe Incestuously by his Example. These vomited things, are now savory meate, neither can Sathan, cast out Sathan: Then it is granted they can Erre, which Cunning lesson had he not learned of his lying Father, his Kingdome long since, had beene divided and broken in pieces. Bee it never so unlawfull, like the Law of the *Medes* and *Persians,* the Decree may not be changed.

Thus out of the sentences of the holy Scripture, this Spider sucks
1060 somtimes his poyson, saying in his Hart, "All the Kingdoms of the Earth are mine, My Father the Divell hath given them unto me, and rather of my Estate then abate a button; I will teach men as many lyes to damne them, as wee can both invent, that with the breath of my Mouth I blow in and out the fire of Purgatory, where People beleeve some Soules are blood-raw, others rosted to death, that I make the Creator, sacrifice and sell their Saviour, which puts me in minde of *Judas* my Brother, whose hanging I could heartily lament, had hee not like a pas-sionate foole, so ill playd his last part.

"Admit of his weaknesse he did repent, is a wise man the Trumpet of
1070 his owne shame? to say he had Err'd to be his owne accuser, what did he gaine by this; some say forsooth, This Confession of friends and foes, might be, to leave the subtill Elders, and their generation the *Jewes,* without excuse, though wee eate both of one Sop, I like not the Exam-ple, I meane the manner; It is olde and weake, and lame Arguments will follow fast enough; Idle Confessions, are no secrets to me, I like not his tragicall speech, it was timorous, had it beene by boasting, scoffing, or

---

Line 1050. **HEROD:** ruler of Galilee, first century B.C.; see Matt. 14:4–10.

Lines 1055–56. **his lying Father:** the elder Herod; see Matt. 2.

Lines 1060–61. **All…Earth:** Ps. 128:4; the tract by Lady Eleanor (STC 903.5), on which this tract is probably based; see headnote, page 1.

to advance his service, as it proved earnest, more might bee said in his defence. I doe the same my selfe: but let it passe, my plot was no pen to blot his name, and had it prevailed, the fire is witnesse, his frailtie had never flowne so farre. 1080

"When I call to minde my predecessors, no small puffe can blow my pride downe, shall I degenerate, or not follow their steps, JUDAS the Apostle, and JULIANUS the Emperour, no Ring-leaders of that Nazaren poore Sect, that leave the certaine Blisse of this world, to beleeve Scripture promises made to the Fathers had I beene in their dayes, though they were couragious, both faithlesse, and false enough, I can lift my heele as high as theirs, I had gone before them in their owne craft.

"Yet since it was not remorce of Conscience, but the ungratefull answer of the chiefe Priests, and all his hopes frustrate, this cast the Man away, my Pardon as beneficiall to him as to others, shall cost him noth- 1090 ing, this accident upon that ill advised answer: WHAT IS THAT TO US LOOKE THOU TO THAT, was the first motive that made me coine Absolution, which passeth now for currant Silver, being all the Fees the desperate Traitors get of mee towards their hanging, this ditch-water I give the poore soules for Aqua vitæ, when they goe to the Gallowes."

If some will say this stone is cast too far, I say but a Dreame of like, or lesse horror, would have started, or as throughly awakened themselves to behold so great a Tyrant, a Prince so gratious & good, his Kingdome with so much pride, and spitefully invaded; All his naturall Subjects become disobedient Rebells, except a Remnant of some few, forsaking 1100 their lives, that lov'd not their lives to the Second Death, suffering for their loyalty & love unexpressable, fiery exquisite bloody torments, his Cittizens amongst whom hee Inhabited, with one voyce Crying out all at once. Away with this Man, saying, we will not have this Man to raigne over us, himselfe (ô gentle Dove) dumbe as a Sheepe before the sheerer, hanged by the hands as an off-scouring, set up like a Marke for an Arrow, reviled, made a derision, as their Musicke, to his People,

---

Lines 1083–84. **JULIANUS:** Julian the Apostate, Roman Emperor, fourth century A.D., who turned away from Christianity and persecuted the Christians. **Nazaren poore Sect:** Nazarites who were committed to asceticism. Paul was accused of being a leader of their sect (Acts 24:5).

Line 1095. **Aqua vitæ:** the water of life (Latin). Lines 1104–5. **we will…us:** Luke 19:14.

Line 1106. **off-scouring:** defilement.

sweating drops of blood downe to the ground, the barres of sorrow preventing the passage of Teares, (all in vaine) in so strong an Agony, more for griefe and anguish of them and their Children? then his owne feare, of those unspeakable paines and torments, Crying with a lowde voice, unable to conceale that passion, MY GOD, MY GOD, WHY HAST THOU FORSAKEN MEE, my tongue cleaveth to my jawes, thou hast brought me into the dust of death through his tender Mercy, shedding from his pierced side, blood from the wound, for a sensible Testimony of a true Sacrifice, and water to Baptise and wash them, whose hard hearts could not weepe for themselves. He wiste the Spirit of the Lord, was departed from him.

Stones rent, the Earth quaking, not Ghosts walking, but Graves opening, and dead Bodyes amazed, and awaking, The whole Globe Mourning in Sable blacknesse, except Man, at the dreadfull Funerall of this most mighty Prince; The Sonne as Chiefe, covering and hiding his astonished face, with hideous Cloudes, as blacke as Sackcloth of haire, to utter the height and depth of silent speaking sorrow, by whose darke vaile and traine the shadow of Death, turning the Day to Night, wherein all Creatures are a Corps, and the world but a Tombe, detesting and abhorring his Beames of light should beare witnesse, the true light of Men, by mankinde was so ungratefully and unkindely extinguished, the expresse Pure Image of the Maker, the Prince of life, The Person of God, (not made) turn'd to a lumpe of Clay, by a shamelesse accusation, an unjust sentence, and a cursed Executoner. To Slay these Lords that have dominion over us, hee pulled the house downe upon his owne head, the mightie deliverer of *Israel*.

His God head and death being Incompatible, choosing rather to forgoe, and forsake the one, then forget his promise, leave the will of his Father undone, or his worke unfinished; His sufferings being by a

---

Lines 1112–13. **MY...MEE:** Matt. 27:46.

Line 1117. **wiste:** wist; knew.

Lines 1120–23. **The whole Globe...Sackcloth:** see Matt. 27:51–52; sackcloth was coarse fabric used for mourning or penitence.

Lines 1132–33. **hee pulled...head:** cf. Judg. 16:30.

vacancy of Power, as sometimes cold, may abate and abolish the sense of feeling, yet retayned by the vitall parts, the losse is not irrecoverable. Whose Hart would not melt, Haire stare, and Hands become faint, to write or heare such a story. 1140

Yet here is not an end, what shall he doe, now chased as a Bird betweene Heaven and Earth since his resurrection, pull'd by Bitts to peeces, throwne to hungry Hell-hounds, the Divells Dogs, Caniballs; did not his power to deliver his Darling, surmount the greedy arrogant policie of these *Barbarians;* spoken without aggravation both one Spaune, acting (in their Copes, I might say, party coloured fooles Coates) like painted Peacocks, the part of HECUBA, the franticke Troyan Wives and POLLIXINA; Such pompe and gaudinesse of Masking garments, being fitter for the Theator then the Temple, the state thereof requiring rather Mourners with all their BACCUS Savage Ceremonies, 1150 apish and affected Fashions, No Vice on a Stage, with senselesse jests to move the vulgars laughter, good folkes ashamed; So rediculous, without understanding babling like Parrots or Children, a Tongue they know not; yet no Babes or Children in Mallice, Pyping without distinction; Pricketh not this the hearts of the hearers, twanging upon a Harpe, Instead of an Egge, asking a Scorpion; and saying *Amen* to any *Pater-Noster.*

Is there any sorrow like this, whose Mirth is so great; whose heart so hard; as not to be greeved for this affliction; can wee forbeare to bow our selves, and not to Travell for these paines; To heare the Arke not 1160 only is taken, but helpe Lord alas, to see the Heire apparant of the living God so dishonoured and mangled amongst his Enemies! O the wonder

---

Line 1146. **Spaune:** spawn; offspring or product. **Copes:** cloaks worn by bishops.

Line 1147. **HECUBA:** Trojan queen.

Lines 1148–49. **POLLIXINA:** Polyxena; Hecuba's daughter whom the Greeks killed on Achilles' grave. **Masking garments:** costumes worn for court masques, entertainments thought by some to be sinful.

Line 1150. **BACCUS:** Bacchus; Roman name for the god of wine.

Lines 1156–57. **Instead…Scorpion:** Luke 11:12. **Pater-Noster:** Our Father (Latin); the Lord's Prayer.

Lines 1160–61. **the Arke…taken:** see 1 Sam. 4:11.

of wonders, a lying Wonder, to see creatures endued with sense and reason, beleeve a senslesse Miracle; here is the Doctrine or spirits of Divells, three uncleane spirits, Three Frogs forg'd one like another, or a false lye spit up by the Divell, the Beast, and the false Prophet from their uncleane slimy Mouthes, Into the Ovens and kneading Troughs of the Kings of the Earth, and of the whole world, to gather them to the Battell of the great Day of God Almighty; Also to decide the question

1170 (with full consent) when this doctrine working miracles was conjured up. When Transgressors are come to the full; the water dried up, that the way of the Kings of the East might bee prepared; The *Tartars* whose looke is more stout then his fellowes. Righteous art thou ô Lord, which art, which wast, and shall be, because thou hast judged thus; for they have shed the Blood of Saints and Prophets; and thou hast given them up to blaspheme the God of Heaven, to beleeve a lye, false teachers that teach, thou hast given them Blood to drinke, the Blood of the living God, as it were the Blood of a Dead man; here is a sore lye, a grievous Soare, well may such mad Dogs gnaw their Blistered Tongues.

1180 Then shall stand up in his estate, a raiser of Taxes in the glory of the Kingdome; but in few dayes hee shall bee destroyed in the strength of his Age, neither in anger, nor in Battaile, but in a sport of Tilting by a splinter in his Eye.

And in his estate shall stand up a vilde person, or a Luxurious, to whom they shall not give the honour of the Kingdome, but he shall come in peaceably and obtayne the Kingdome by Flatterie; and with the Armes of a Flood, or as the sodaine inundation of *Nilus;* so shall the Faithfull people be overflowne from before him, they shall bee broken by a cruell Massacre, yea, also the Prince of the Covenant, and after the

1190 league made with him, even the Great King of the North, hee shall worke deceitfully with the holy people; for hee shall come up and shall become strong with a small people, he shall enter peaceably even upon

---

Line 1163. **endued:** endowed. Line 1165. **three uncleane spirits:** see Rev. 16:13.

Lines 1171–72. **water…prepared:** Rev. 16:12. **Tartars:** Asian followers of Genghis Khan.

Lines 1182–83. **in a sport…Eye:** the way in which King Henry II of France died in 1559.

Line 1187. **Nilus:** the River Nile.

the fattest places of the Province, for he shall doe that which his Fathers
have not done, nor his Fathers Fathers, he shall scatter among them the
prey, spoyle and riches of the wicked; yea, and he shall fore-cast his
devices against the strong Holds of Sathan for a time, not to the End;
And he shall stir up his Power and his great Courage against the King of
the South with a great Army, & the King of the South shall be stirred up
to Battell with a very great and mightie Army, but hee shall not stand
for they shall fore-cast devices against him; yea, his owne Dogs (stiled   1200
Gods) that feed of the Portion of his meate shall destroy him.

After whose decease his Army shall overflow, and many of the righteous shall fall downe slaine, and both these Kings hearts shalbe to doe
mischiefe, and they shall speake lies against the knowne truth, both at
one Table, but it shall not prosper; for yet the end of all things shall be
at the time appointed, Then shall hee returne into his owne Land with
great riches, and little profit; and his hart shall be against the holy Covenant; therefore the next blow was at the hart. And he shall doe exploits,
and returne to his own Land.

At the time appointed, hee shall returne even the King of the North   1210
spoken of before, that should certainly come after certaine yeares with a
great Army, and a multitude greater then the former with much riches,
and shall come towards the South, but it shal not be as the former, or as
the latter; for hee shall wound as it were his owne sides. The Ships of
Shittim shall come against him; therefore he shall be grieved and
returne against his owne strength, and have indignation against the holy
Covenants; So he shall doe; he shall returne, and have intelligence with
them that forsake the holy Covenant; these Ships built with pretious
Wood, whose Anchor is the Lord, tossed too and fro with flouds of
ungodly men in the Sea of *Babilon,* and compassed with the Waves of   1220
Death; but when they cry unto the Lord, and are at their wits end. Hee
who walketh upon the Sea, draweth nigh unto them, and bringeth
them out of their distresse; he maketh the storme a calme, as a Childe,
even so suddenly he stilleth the roaring Waves of this Tempestious Sea,
lifted up with the stormy windes of Sathans malice.

Lines 1221–22. **Hee…Sea:** Jesus (Matt. 14:25).

Therefore thus saith the Lord unto *Tyrus,* O thou that art Scituate at the entry of the Sea; which art a Merchant for the People for many Isles. Thus saith the Lord God; O *Tyrus* thou hast said, I am a perfect beautie. Thy Borders are in the midst of the Seas, thy buildings have perfected

1230 thy beautie; they have made all thy Ship Boords all of Firre Trees of Senir; they have taken Cedars from *Libanan,* to make Masts for thee; of the Okes of *Bashan* have they made thine Oares; the Company of the *Ashurites* have made thy Benches of Ivorie, brought out of the Isles of *Chittim;* Fyne Linnen with broydered worke from *Egipt,* was that which thou spreadest forth to bee thy Sayle, Blew and Purple from the Isles of ELISHAH, was that which covered thee, &c.

And Armies of the ungodly shall stand on his part; they shall pollute the Sanctuary of strength, and shall take away the daily Sacrifice, and shall place therein the abomination, that maketh the house of God des-

1240 olate, turning it into a Den of Theeves (the daily Sacrifice, or the Lords Supper shall be taken away to place the Divells Idoll, the Supper of the Lord, instituted in remembrance of our Redemption; as the Passeover was a Commemoration that the Lord passed over the houses of the Children of *Israel* in *Egipt,* when hee smote the *Egiptians* and delivered them. DAVID a man after Gods own heart, poured out unto the Lord, the Water of *Bethelem,* that he so sore longed to drinke, the blood of Mortall men, that went in jeopardy of their lives, yet damned people are told they drinke of God our Lord JESUS CHRIST his heart-blood. Shew-ing themselves more thirsty after it, then the greedy *Jewes,* these blood-

1250 suckers will have it before his side be pierced.

And such as doe wickedly against the Covenant, to breake the Com-mandements of God, the vow, vowed in their Baptisme, by which they forsake the Divell; with all the Covetous and Carnall desires of the flesh; these uncleane vilde persons shall be corrupted by flatteries, and easily drawne from the truth, to beleeve a lye, that they may bee damned, that hath pleasure in unrighteousnesse, but the People that know God and

---

Line 1226. **thus…Tyrus:** see Ezek. 27:3. **Scituate:** situated.

Line 1231. **Senir:** cf. Ezek. 27:5–7. Line 1234. **broydered:** embroidered.

Lines 1245–46. **DAVID…Bethelem:** see 2 Sam. 23:15–16. Line 1248. **they:** the Catholics.

feare him, shall be strong, he shall cover their heads in the day of Battaile, and they shall doe exploits, yet they that understand among the People, and their Teachers that instruct them; these shall fall by the sword, and by flame and imprisonment, and by spoyle of their goods 1260 many dayes; yet feare none of these things, for hee that neither slumbers nor sleepes, will arise and take his owne quarrell into his hand, and you shall be holpen with a little helpe; Therfore trust not in multitude of Forces, neither them that will cleave to you with flatteries, for they will worke deceitfully, as they have done in former times, nor expect a finall end of these persecutions, Sathan will sift, the tayle corne is his owne. If they call the Master of the house BELZEBUB, what respect can yee looke for that are of the houshold. And the King shall do according to his will, and hee shall exalt himselfe and magnifie himselfe above every God, and shall speake marvelous things against the God of Gods, great words 1270 against the most High, and shall weare out the Saints of the Most high, and thinke to change times and Lawes, and shall prosper till the indignation bee accomplished, for that, that is determined shall bee done, Neither shall he regard the God of his Fathers, nor desire of Women, neither shall she retaine the power of the Arme, being a branch of ungrafted Roots; nor regard any God, but shall magnifie himselfe above all; In his estate hee shall honour the God of Forces and Battell, being terrible to the servants of God and his Enemies; a God that his forefathers knew not; or an Altar shall he honour with Gold and Silver, and with Pretious stones, and pleasant things; thus shall hee doe in the most 1280 strong holds with this God, a stranger for many yeares to the Apostles and their followers, whom he shall acknowledge and increase with glory; and hee shall cause in stead of Shepheards, Dogs and Wolves, in sheep-skins, to rule over many, as Lords over Gods heritage, and they shall not onely devide the Land for filthy lucre, but make Merchandizes of mens Consciences. But if GOD spared not the Angels, what shall become of these cursed Children, that have not onely lost the Flocke,

---

Line 1263. **holpen:** helped. Line 1266. **the tayle corne:** taxable corn.

Line 1267. **BELZEBUB:** Beelzebub; the Devil.

Lines 1283–84. **Dogs…sheep-skins:** cf. Matt. 7:15.

but gone astray and runne away themselves, following the way of
BALAM the Son of BOZER, who loved the wages of unrighteousnesse,
1290 having eyes full of Adultery; even when they speake their great swelling
words of Vanitie and Absolution; at that time they allure to the Lusts of
the Flesh, and much Wantonnesse, leading simple women into Captivi-
itie, promising libertie, that are themselves the servants of Corruption,
wallowing in the Myre like filthy Swine to cleanse themselves by wresting the Scriptures to their owne destruction, licking up againe the unsavorie meate themselves could ill disgest not long agoe, and running
downe headlong into the deepe Lake of Fyre and Brimstone, whose latter end is worse then their beginning; it had beene better for these men
to have continued Heathens as they were at first in the pollutions of the
1300 world, then after they have knowne the way of righteousnesse, to turne
from it, crucifying the Sonne of God afresh, and putting him to open
shame.

And at the time of the End shall the King of the South push at him,
with all his Spanish Pikes, and the King of the North shall come against
him like a whirlewinde, with Chariots and with Horsemen, and with
many Ships, The Lord of Hosts send them Victorie; and he shall enter
into the Countries, and shall overflow and passe over; hee shall enter
also into the glorious Land *Domina gentium,* and many Countries shall
be overthrowne; but these shall escape out of his hand, even *Edom* and
1310 *Moab,* and the chiefe of the Children of AMMON his Confederates, he
shall stretch forth his hand also upon the Countries, and the Land of
Egipt shall not escape; But hee shall have powers over the Treasures of
Gold and of Silver, and over all the Precious things of *Egipt,* and the
Libians and the *Ethiopians* shall bee at his steps. But tidings out of the
East and out of the North shall trouble him, therfore he shall goe forth
with a great furie to destroy and utterly to make away many; And hee

---

Line 1289. **BALAM:** see Num. 31:8. Line 1294. **Myre:** mire; mud.

Lines 1296–97. **running downe...Brimstone:** see Rev. 20:10.

Line 1304. **Spanish Pikes:** weapons made of wooden shafts with points of iron or steel; the Spanish were particularly well-known for their infantry's use of pikes.

Line 1308. **Domina gentium:** Lord of the nations (Latin).

shall plant the Tabernacles of his Cedars Pallace betweene the Seas in the glorious holy Mountaine; yet he shall come to his end, and none shall helpe him.

Therefore take up a lamentation for the King of *Tyrus,* whose Cedars are for the building of both Houses; and say thou hast beene in EDEN the Garden of GOD; every pretious Stone to garnish the foundation was thy Covering, the Ruby, the Topaz, and the Diamond, the Berill, the Onix, the Jasper and the Saphire, these things were prepared for thee. Thou art annointed the Cherube that Covereth, thou wast upon the holy Mountaine of GOD, and thou hast walked up and downe in the middest of the Stones of Fyre: but because thou hast lifted up thy heart, and said; I am GOD, I have subdued three Kings. I sit in the middest of the Seas, and hast defiled thy sacred Houses, I will bring thee to Ashes, and none shall help thee. As I live, saith the Lord, I will even doe according to thine anger, and according to thine Envie, which thou hast used out of thy hatred against them, and I will make my selfe knowne amongst them, when I have judged thee, and thou shalt know that I am the Lord, and that I have heard all thy Blasphemy, which thou hast spoken against the Mountaine of *Israell,* Saying, they are layd desolate by Massacre, they are given us to consume by the sword; thus with thy mouth thou hast Boasted against Mee, therefore shortly when the whole Land of *Israell* rejoyceth, I will make thee desolate, then thou shalt know that I the Lord doe Sanctifie *Israell,* when my Sanctuary shall bee in the middest of them for ever.

Therefore, ô King of the North, arise from thy Throne, lay thy Royall Robe aside, and cause a Decree through *Tyrus* to be published; saying, Let them turne every one from his evill way, and from the violence or unnaturall shedding of Blood, that is in their hands, &c. Who can tell if GOD will turne and repent, and turne away from his fierce anger, that wee goe not into Perdition.

Line 1320. **lamentation:** cf. Ezek. 28:12–25.

DANIEL. CHAP. XII.

James, Charles,—are Michaelss.

And at that time shall Michael stand up, the great Prince that defends
1350   the Faith, Charles King of Great *Britaine, France,* and *Ireland,* which
standeth for the faithfull Children of our Nation, the Saints of the most
Highest. As the Angell of God, so is my Lord the King, to discerne good
and bad; therefore the Lord thy God will be with thee for ever.

And there shall be a time of trouble, such as never was since there was
a Nation, even to that same time, blessings and great felicities, being for
the most part accompanied with Corrections, and extraordinary
Calamities; Devotion and Religion of happinesse, in this life the Highest, not exempt from superstition and heresie; And at that time thy People shall bee delivered; Every one whose name is found written in the
1360   Booke, &c.

AL TRUTHS CESAR.

Behold the Lord is at the Dore, as a man come from a farre journey; All
that sleepe in the Dust of the Earth, shall heare his voyce and awake,
and come forth, those that have done good to the Resurrection of life;
These have their part in the first Resurrection, and those that have done
evill unto the Resurrection of Damnation. Then the Angell came
downe from Heaven, having taken from the false Prophet the Key of
the Bottomlesse pit, having in his hand a great Chaine, hee shall next
lay hold on the Dragon the Devill; and hee shall bee bound a Thousand
1370   yeares, or one day, which is all one with the Lord; he shall shut him up,
and set a Seale upon him, for the wrath of the Lord that day, shall bee a
sufficient marke that the Nations be deceived no more.

This Thousand yeares is the great day of the Lord, to poure out his
wrath and just indignation upon his Enemies; But the wise Virgins with
Palmes in their hands, that have not beene deceived by the subtilty or
force of flatterers, shall shine in their Robes, as the brightnesse of the

---

Line 1361. **AL…CESAR:** an anagram for Charles Stuart; a picture of a crown is printed above.
Line 1362. **the Lord…Dore:** cf. Rev. 3:20. Line 1366–68. **Angell…pit:** Rev. 20:1.
Lines 1374–75. **wise…hands:** see Matt. 25:1–12.

Firmament; Kings Daughters attended by honourable Matrons, as Starres for ever and ever, prepared for the Bridegroomes Marriage, whose Wife the Bride and Queene, hath made her selfe ready clothed in fine Linnen cleane and white, arrayed in a Garment of Needleworke wrought with Gold of Ophier, the Daughter of *Tyre* shall bee there with a Gift; she shall be brought to the King, with gladnesse and rejoycing, they shall enter into his Pallace, saying, O King, thy Throne is for ever and ever, thou lovest righteousnesse and hatest wickednesse; therefore God thy God annoynt thee with gladnesse above thy fellowes. 1380

After this Thousand yeares the great Day of the solemnitie finished, the Bride being safe in her closset and Marriage chamber, Sathan the olde Serpent shall be loosed a little season, as Prisoners are set at libertie when they goe to the place of Execution to receive his finall sentence of everlasting Damnation; yet hoping in his vaine imagination and hart that cannot repent to deceive the Nations that are at rest, to take a prey, to goe up to the Citie that is in safetie that needs no Wall, neither the light of the Sunne or the Moone, &c. 1390

Unto whom the just Judge frō his Throne of Glory with a terrible looke, for furie, jealousie shall come up into his face, shall say unto him; Art thou he whom I have spoken of in olde time by my servants the Prophets to give the Nations warning of thee, how thou diddest not onely like a foole deceive thy selfe, when thou saidst, I will ascend up and be like the most highest, but like a cursed creature didst deceive their innocent Parents, be prepared therefore, and prepare thy selfe and all thy Company, and see whether thou canst be a guard unto them; or what defence they can make for themselves who could not be ignorant, and ought not to be carelesse, because by mine owne Mouth I gave them warning, that after many dayes thou shouldst be visited and brought a Prisoner into the Land which is now brought backe from the Sword and cleansed, though it lay waste a time, and the Villages thereof unwalled. For these I commanded them straightly to watch both 1400

Lines 1377–81. **Kings...Ophier:** see Rev. 19:7 and Ps. 45:9.

Line 1383. **O King...for ever:** Ps. 45:6. Lines 1387–88. **Sathan...season:** Rev. 20:3.

Lines 1392–93. **the Citie...Moone:** see Rev. 21:12–20 , 23.

concerning the things I fore-told them should come to passe; as also of this houre, lest like a Theefe, or as the Flood came upon their fore-fathers the Ungodly, they should be surprised unawares, because I told you of these things before depart, I know yee not, nor that Captaine your false Prophet, are yee those that eate my flesh and drinke my blood, whence are yee, I never knew you more, then you knew mine, or Me; cursed and deformed crew, with stiffe neckes, double crooked hearts, deafe Adders, and blinde People with eyes, goe yee cursed into everlasting fire.

Wee have eaten and Drunke in thy presence, all the world was taxed by the Prince of our Nation; and thou hast taught in our streets; Their iniquitie is the greater, thrust them out. Lord, Lord, come out Dogs and Swine, Apes and Satiers, hence here all Lyers, Scoffers at the truth, uncleane persons, for here shall enter in no wise any thing that defileth, neither whatsoever worketh Abomination, or maketh a Lye, but they which are written in the Lambes Booke of Life.

But thou ô DANIEL, shut up the words, and seale up this Booke to the time of the end; Now that the whole world might take notice, and discerne when this Sealed Prophesie shall be opened, the time is more then once repeated, even at the time of the end, when the King of the South shall push at the King of the North, and the King of the North shall come against him like a Whirlewinde, for till then, though many shall run too and fro by the Art of Navigation, discovering an other Hemisphere, Sayling by the Compasse and the Needle, found out by expert men, and knowledge increased, furnishing Magnificent Libraries with printed Bookes, By which two Arts, chiefly the Gospell shall bee published to all Nations; yet the Character of this Booke shall not bee read, till the time of the end; which time is easie to be knowne, even without the Notice of the yeares closed up in this Booke; where Eagles are gathered together, you suppose some Carcasse to be there: The Fig tree, when her Branch is yet, tender, and putteth forth her leaves, ye

---

Line 1409. **lest...Theefe:** cf. Matt. 24:42–43. Lines 1417–18. **all...Nation:** cf. Luke 2:1.

Line 1420. **Satiers:** satyrs; in Greek myth, creatures part goat and part human, associated with drinking and revelry.

Lines 1436–39. **where Eagles...neere:** cf. Matt. 24:28, 32.

know that Summer is neere; *Jerusalem* when it was compassed with Armies, the Desolation was nigh. In like manner, when yee see these things come to passe fore-told you, know the end is nie, even at the dore; But of the day and houre knoweth no man, no not the Angells that are in Heaven; neither the Sonne but the Father; the accompt in this Booke of note, being by Centuries of yeares.

Then I Daniel looked, and behold there stood other Two; the two Olive Trees, the Tree of Life, either of them bearing Twelve manner of Fruites, the Two Witnesses into whom, after Three dayes and a halfe, the Spirit of Life from God entred; and they stood upon their feet. The one on this side of the banke of the River; and the other on that side of the bank of the River; The foundations of the wall of the City, Jesus Christ himself being the chiefe corner stone.

And one said to the man clothed in Linnen, that was upon the waters of the Rivers, that cryed with a loude voyce, as when a Lyon Roareth; Lord wilt thou at this time restore againe the Kingdome of *Israell,* how long shall it be to the end of these wonders, or tell us when these things shall bee, and what shall bee the signe of thy comming, and of the end of the world.

And he held up his right hand and his left hand to Heaven, shewing his Resurrection and Ascension, and sware by him that Liveth for ever and ever, Heaven and Earth shall passe away, but my Word shall not passe, neither this froward generation; this Nation till all these things bee done spoken of by my Mouth and the Prophets; there be some standing here, which shall not taste of Death, till they see the Sonne of Man comming in his Kingdome, his servants will fight for him. So shall even all my words be fulfilled.

It is not for you to know the times and seasons which the Father hath put in his owne power; But goe thou thy way and rest, and stand in the Lot. Seale up those things which the Seven thunders uttered, and write them not, it shall be for a time and times and halfe, then all these things shall be finished, as a Henne gathereth her Chickens, or as a scattered Army in that day the Holy People shall be gathered together, in the meane time many shall bee purified and made white by the fiery Tryall;

Lines 1462–63. **some standing…Death:** Matt. 16:28.

The wicked shall doe wickedly, and shall not understand, but the wise, it is given unto them to understand the misteries of the Kingdome of Heaven.

And from the time that the daily Sacrifice shall bee taken away, or the yearely Passeover by the destruction of *Jerusalem,* to place the Abomination that maketh desolate; there shall be a Thousand Two hundred and Ninetie dayes; Heere is the Measure of the Temple, and the Altar, and 1480 them that worship therein; And here is also the breach of the first Commandements, spoken of by our Lord; the abomination that maketh desolate not only the Sanctuary but the Citie; the first ripe Apples that hang so high against the Sunne; The Divell thought if hee could reach these, the rest were his owne; therefore to plucke them downe in the primitive times, he began to reare his Ladder in the holy Places to set up his plurality, adding the Images of living Mortall men to be worshipped with Divine honour, and vaine supplications, as if themselves were present, making no doubt, having no egresse and regresse in time to bring his owne amongst them into the nomber, in which expectation 1490 hee sayled not much; for who is this here, that sits in the Temple of God, as if there were Two Gods, besides his PIGMALION-like Image; the parts of which are seldome colde, if there bee heate in the Kisses of such holy People.

The swiftnesse of time is such, I cannot gather all the Spices and dropping Myrrhe of this Tree, I can fixe no longer speaking what manner God will sit alone in his holy Temple, abhorring not only the people but the place where a Coleague is joyned with him in office; therefore of the next branch.

Suppose a man after his Marriage to a young Virgin, should say, my 1500 experience is more then yours, I cannot alwayes walke hand in hand with you, neither may I keepe you in a Cloister that will not be for your health or my profit, neither must you forget your Covenant to bee subject to my desires not tending to the harme of either of us; I love you as mine owne Body, if I should not love you, I should not love my selfe,

---

Line 1479. **the Measure…Altar:** see Rev. 11:1–3.

Line 1491. **PIGMALION-like Image:** In Greek myth, Pygmalion was a sculptor who made a beautiful statue, which he married when Aphrodite gave it life.

you are tender and faire without blemish or blot, so I would have your minde also without spot or wrinckle like your face, many strangers will strive to bee your Servants; not all for your beautie but some for malice and envie to me: Though your intent be good in all things, yet because I am very jealous of mine honor, entertaine none in that manner; though they be silent for a time, and conceale themselves, in the end 1510 they will draw your affection from me; Besides, much resort though shee be never so chaste, is dalliance the marke of a knowne Harlot, which sort of women I would have you differ from, and no marke I know more fit to put `a difference betweene you then this; For much entertainment will not only waste our substance, better imployed upon more necessary occasions, but consume time in unprofitable idlenesse.

Is there no consequent, yes doubtlesse, I am the Lord thy God, thou shalt have no other Gods but me; thou shalt not make Images of any likenesse to bowe or humble thy selfe before them; for of my honor I am a jealous God, you are mine, I bought you to enjoy the libertie of 1520 my service; I brought yee out of the house of bondage, which no other God could doe; thou shalt love the Lord thy God, and keepe his charge and his Statutes.

When yee goe forth to shew the way of truth to other Nations, this spirituall dalliance, which in the end turnes to whoredome, beware of it for it shall bee a marke betweene them that hate mee and you that keepe my Comandements; and though I will not at any time bee farre from you, yet you shall fall by Captivitie and persecution to spread my name, or for the Triall of your Faith, when you see their Idolatrie pull downe their high Places, Preach against them; say, Little Children, ignorant 1530 people that understand not the slights of Sathan; Beware of Idols, tender natures encounter strongest motions; Top-sayles are first assaulted; No man so well knowes his owne frailtie, as the Lord your God knowes how prone Devotion is to Superstition.

Also when yee goe in and out amongst the Heathen folke, or if the Lord give them into your hands, as the *Amalikites* were given into the hand of the Children of *Israell,* when the Prophet said; what meaneth

---

Line 1517. **I am…God:** cf. Exod. 20:2–6.
Lines 1536–37. **Amalikites…Israell:** see 1 Sam. 15:20.

this bleating in mine eares; SAULS excuse shall not availe you; to say, we set them up for Saints before the Lord, the Images of JUPITER for Jesus Christ; the Statue of HERCULES for CHRISTOPHER; VENUS and the little Lad, for the blessed Virgin, as holy as Scarcrowes in a Garden of Cowcumbers.

You that cannot make one haire white or blacke, will yee goe a Whoring after your owne inventions, to humble your selves before Pageants, Pictures, Images with eyes that see not, Eares without hearing, &c. More senslesse then a Beast; yet these rare Mamets, the light of the Sunne is too darke for them without Candles; when the Members of Christ goe naked, these must bee cloathed, not for warmnesse but for wantonnesse; and these are the Babyes made and dressed by the Divell, and decked to please his Children, abhorred, and abominable in the sight of the Lord.

Lastly, with these lines the Temple of God is Measured, and them that worship therein. Measuring is for Numbering; place is put for time, and sometimes space a thousand six hundred furlongs; Signifying the persecution of the Church so many yeares, reward her even as she rewarded you. To rise therefore and Measure the time, begin from the taking away of the daily Sacrifice or the Destruction of *Jerusalem,* and count a thousand two hundred and threescore yeares, wherein for the absence of the Church in the Wildernesse, the two Witnesses did Prophesie clothed in Sackcloth, so many yeares of Mists and darknesse, to these must be added some dayes of faire weather, a hundred forty and foure thousand, amounting to foure hundred yeares and odde, having their fathers name written in their foreheads, these sing as it were a new song; These are Virgins not (defiled with women) Chaste conversation,

Line 1538. **SAULS excuse:** see 1 Sam. 15:15.

Line 1539. **JUPITER:** in Roman myth, the ruler of the gods.

Line 1540. **HERCULES:** in Roman mythology, hero who performed twelve great labors. **CHRISTOPHER:** saint who protects children.

Lines 1540–41. **little Lad:** in Roman myth, Cupid, the son of Venus.

Line 1542. **Cowcumbers:** cucumbers. Line 1545. **eyes...hearing:** cf. Mark 8:18.

Line 1546. **Mamets:** maumets; idols. Line 1554. **a thousand...furlongs:** see Rev. 14:20.

Lines 1561–62. **a hundred...thousand:** see Rev. 7:4.

not commanding laciviousnesse, by forbidding Marriage, waxing worse
and worse.

The Temple was not built in a day, it is three Stories; the foure hundred yeares are to be devided into three severall parts, Seventy yeares
and odde, untill the destruction of *Jerusalem,* when the Apostles finished their testimony, thirty yeares are restored for the raigne of 1570
CONSTANTINE the great, the remaines remaine for these last times, being
the same eighteene thousand Measures spoken by EZEKIEL the Prophet,
the Measure of the Temple within are not summed up, I presume not to
looke into the account, the Measure of it round about without, I heard
the number of them cast up, Eighteen thousand Measures, every Measure sixe Cubits, according to the Measure of a man. That is, of the
Angell, three hundred yeares & odde; and the name of the City from
that day shal bee God is there, that said Son of Man, the place of my
Throne, and the place of the soles of my feet, where I will dwell in the
middest of the Children of *Israell* for ever, and my holy Name shall the 1580
house of *Israell* no more defile, &c.

Blessed is he that waiteth and commeth to the thousand three hun-
dred and five and thirty yeares, these are the blessed times of JOHN
WICKLIFFE & JOHN HUS, both famous Martyrs, and burning Lights, set
up to shew forth the state and beauty of the truth, one burnt alive, the
other after hee was dead, being hard to judge in which of these, the
Devill the Father of lyes, Antichrist his crucifying Sonne, and the
Dragon, expressed most malice; from which cursed triplicitie, three
Monsters of the bottomlesse Pit, God deliver us, who will give us a
Crowne of life; Come Lord JESUS, the grace of our Lord JESUS CHRIST 1590
bee with you all.

Amen.

Last of all, the whole world is numbred and those that worke abomination therein, and the delights thereof, weighed in the balances, are
found lighter then vanitie it selfe. There is nineteene yeares and a halfe

---

Line 1572. **eighteene...EZEKIEL:** see Ezek. 48:35.

Lines 1583–84. **JOHN WICKLIFFE:** Wyclif; fourteenth-century English religious
reformer. **JOHN HUS:** fifteenth-century Bohemian religious reformer burned as a heretic.

to the day of Judgement, July the 28. M.DC.XXV. Sixe hundred and threescore Moneths are excluded, from this last Age of seventeene hundred yeares. And I thinke that I have also the Spirit of God.

DANIEL.

1600   *Hee that is unjust and filthy let him bee so still, and hee that is righteous and holy, let him bee so still; for behold hee will come quickly, and his reward is with him. Blessed are they that doe his Commandements.*

FINIS.

Line 1600. **Hee…him:** Rev. 22:11–12.

In this broadsheet (STC 904.5) printed in Amsterdam in 1633, Lady Eleanor prophesies Judgment upon the house of Derby, whose members she claimed had inflicted great wrong upon her own family. The present edition of this tract is based on a copy in the State Papers, Domestic, at the Public Record Office (shelf number SP 16/255/19), where it is bound with *All the kings of the earth shall prayse thee* (STC 903.5), also printed in 1633.

WOE TO THE HOUSE.

Interpretation.

Anagr. { ELIZABETH STANLEY. THAT JEZEBEL SLAIN.   *Anagr.* { ANA STANLEY. A LYE SATANN.

So she wrote letters in Ahabs name, and sealed them with his seale, and sent the letters unto the El-ders, and to the Nobles that were in the city. She wrote in the letters &c. Set two men sonns of Beliall before him, to beare witnesse against, saying, &c. And the men of the city, the Elders, and the Nobles who were the inhabitants of the city, did as Jezebel had sent unto them. And there came two men, children of Belial, and the men of Belial witnessed.

Decembris 1626.   Aprilis 1631.

Title. **THE HOUSE:** the house of Derby, whose coat of arms is displayed on the broadside. Elizabeth and Anne Stanley were daughters of Ferdinando, earl of Derby, and his wife Alice.

Anagram. **ELIZABETH STANLEY THAT JEZEBEL SLAIN:** The Countess of Huntington, mother-in-law to Lady Eleanor's daughter, was, by this anagram, Jezebel, the wicked wife of biblical king Ahab (2 Kings 9:7–10). **ANA STANLEY A LYE SATAN:** Anne Stanley, countess of Castlehaven, wife of Lady Eleanor's brother, Mervin, was, by this anagram a lie of Satan.

Line 1. **she...name:** cf. 1 Kings 21:8.

Line 8. **Decembris 1626:** date of the death of Lady Eleanor's husband, Sir John Davies, and beginning of the dispute between Lady Eleanor and her daughter's in-laws over his property. **Aprilis 1631:** date of the trial of Lady Eleanor's brother Mervin for sodomy and accessory to rape.

Appeared personely S^r. George Hastings of Middlesex K. Knight, and Thom ass Gardner of the middle Temple Esqu-lyer, and by vertu of their Corrp. oath made, faith &c.

And behold the word of the Lord came to Elijah, saying, Arise meet Ahab &c. Hast thou killed, and allso taken possession, in the place, &c. and the doggs shall eat Jezebel by the walls of Izeerel.

And when hee came, behold the Captaines of the hoast were sitting, and hee said, I have an errand to thee, O Captaine. And Jehu said, To which of us all? And hee said, to thee, O Captaine. And when Jehu was come to Izeerel, Jezebel heard of it, and she painted her face, and tyr'ed her head, and looked out of a window, &c. And hee troade her under foote.

Anagr. { MERVIN AUDELEY.
M'EVEL VINEYARD.

No, No, my vineyard FOWNTH-IL doe account,
A fruitfull h-il, from Tower hil did mount,
My soule from Lyons, thence on Angels wings
In Abrahams bosome Haleluiah sing.

ISAIAH 5.
Now will I sing, to my beloved, a songe of my beloved to his
vineyard, my beloved &c.

Lines 9–14. A printed sidenote reads "Before Sr. Henry Martin, Judge of the prerog:" **the prerog:** the Prerogative Court of Canterbury, which handled the proving of wills and administration of estates.

Lines 9–10. **George Hastings...Thom ass Gardner:** attorneys who served the Countess of Huntingdon and her family.; the spelling "Thom ass" seems an intentional insult. **Esqu-lyer:** Instead of Esquire, the title Gardner claimed, Lady Eleanor contends that he was a liar.

Line 11. **Corrp. oath:** corporal oath; oath taken, as in court testimony, when the taker touched a sacred object while swearing.

Line 12. **Elijah:** see 1 Kings 21:17–23.

Line 16. **Jehu:** king who had Jezebel killed (2 Kings 9).

Line 21. **MERVIN AUDELEY:** second earl of Castlehaven and brother to Lady Eleanor.

Line 24. **FOWNTH-IL:** Fonthill; Mervin, Lord Audeley's estate in Wiltshire.

Line 25. **Tower:** Mervin, Lord Audeley, was executed at the Tower of London in May 1631.

First printed in Amsterdam in 1633, this tract—as Lady Eleanor says continually in her later writings—contributed to her being called before the Court of High Commission and being imprisoned in the Gate House at Westminster. Although, as far as we know, no copies of the edition of 1633 survive, *Given to the Elector* represents such a critical point in Lady Eleanor's prophetic career that the 1648 edition (Wing D1992) is inserted here. The setting for this tract is the history of Babylon told in the Book of Daniel and, especially, Belshazzar's feast (Dan. 5). In various extant copies of this (1648) edition and also of an edition published in 1651 (Wing D1993), annotations by Lady Eleanor point out parallels between events in Babylon and in England. *Amend, amend; Gods kingdome is at hand* (1643; Wing D1967) is another version of this tract. Yet another version, printed in 1649 with the title *Strange and wonderfull prophecies* (Wing D2014), is apparently the only one of Lady Eleanor's tracts to have been printed with government authorization. The present edition of *Given to the Elector* is based on a copy now in the Library of Worcester College, Oxford (shelf number AA.1.12.[1]).

GIVEN TO THE ELECTOR
PRINCE CHARLES OF THE RHYNE
From the Lady *Eleanor, Anno* 1633. at
her being in *Holland* or *Belgia*.

Title page. The title pages of the Worcester College copy shows a hand holding a pen that is writing "Mene peres" (Dan. 5:25–28). A handwritten annotation beneath it reads "For His Excellence the Lo[rd] gener[al] the worde of the Lorde of Hosts accomplish[t]".

Title. **the ELECTOR:** Prince Charles, nephew of King Charles of England, was the ruler of the Rhine Palatinate and thus one of the German princes entitled to elect the Holy Roman Emperor. **her being…Belgia:** Lady Eleanor travelled to the Low Countries to publish tracts which she had not been allowed to publish in England, and to appeal for help to the Elector's mother, King Charles's sister, Elizabeth, Queen of Bohemia.

1648. Reprinted.
To the happy READER.

Whoso readeth, let him understand, &c.
Matth. 24.

Like as in days of Noah, *foreshews*
when comes the Son of Man,
What posture in, the Church found then
concludes as it began:
Bids thee number by the Floods age,   5
number the dreadful Day;
Baptisms voyce accords thereto,
no Babe, as much to say.

Ætatis 1600 compleat.

A Table,
Shewing what Affinity between Great Babylon *and* Great
Britain, *with significant Names.*

Daniel, Judgement of God.

Nebuchadnezzar, bewailing of the Kindred.

Belshazzar, without treasure, or a searcher for treasure; he last of the
Caldean Kings.

Mene, number, &c. *Mene-Laus,* power of the people.

Also *London, Babylon,* confusion signifying; and *Scotland* otherwise
10   called *Caledonia: Baby-Charles* bids him beware (whose Anrgr.)
Charles be: Belchaser.

And so from *Nimrods* days unto *Nebuchadnezzars* about 1700 years, the
Roman Empires date out, puts into the number.

Line 8. **Mene-Laus:** Spartan king who went to war against the Trojans to recover his wife,
Helen; also "number Laud," Lady Eleanor's warning to Charles I.

Line 10. **Caledonia:** Roman name for north Britain or Scotland. **Baby-Charles:** James I's
name for his son, who became King Charles I in 1625.

To the Palsgrave of the *RHYNE*,
Charles Prince Elector:
The Palm of the Hand, *Dan. Cap.* 5.
The Tune to, *Who list a Soldiers life,* &c.
Psal. *I will utter my grave matter on the Harp.*
By the Lady *Eleanor, Anno* 1633.

1. To *Sion* most belov'd I sing
   of *Babylon* a Song,
   Concerns you more full well I wot
   then ye do think upon.
   Belshazzar, lo, be hold the King   5
   feasting his thousand Lords;
   Phebus and *Mars* prais'd on each string,
   every day records.

2. The Temple Vessels of Gods House
   boldly in drank about:
   His own ('tis like) were made away,
   bids holy things bring out;
   Praising of Gold and Brass the gods,
   of Iron, Wood and Stone,
   See, hear, nor know not, out alas,   15
   praised in Court alone.

   As when Prague lost, he feasting with Ambassadors was betrayed, &c

3. A hand appears lo in his sight,
   as he did drink the wine,
   Upon the wall against the light
   it wrote about a line   20

Title. **Palsgrave:** title of Prince Charles, the Elector. **The Palm of the Hand:** Dan. 5:5 (Geneva Bible). **Who…life.:** popular ballad to whose tune this song can be sung. A picture of one staff of the song is printed above the first line. **I will…Harp:** Ps. 49 (Geneva Bible).

Line 3. **wot:** know.

Line 7. **Phebus:** Phœbus; in Roman myth, the god of fine arts. **Mars:** the god of war.

Line 10. Sidenote. **Prague lost:** At the Battle of White Mountain, 8 November 1620, Roman Catholic imperial forces gained control of Prague, and the Protestant Elector was forced to flee.

In presence of his numerous Peers,
    not set an hour full,
In loyns nor knees had he no might,
    chang'd as a gastly skull.

4. Who might it read, alas, the thing,   25
    Belshazzar loud doth shout;
Calls for Magicians all with speed,
    came in, as wise went out.
Caldeans and Southsayers sage
    the meaning whoso can   30
Of *Mene Mene* third Realms Peer
    in Scarlet Robe the man.

*Which nume-
ral letter of
Mene Tekel U-
pharsin.
MUIL.
Entred then
(shews) into
the day even
of Judgement,
&c.*

5. His Majesty forgets to Sup,
    Nobles astonish'd all;
Musicans may their pipes put up,   35
    stood gazing on the wall.
The pleasant wine at length as sharp,
    too late, till thought upon
Division of another strain
    unfolds the fingers long.   40

6. When to the Banqueting house so wide,
    where host of Lords did ring,
So wisely came the graceful Queen,
    said, *Ever live, O King.*

Line 26. Sidenote. **numeral letter:** letters which were Roman numerals.

Line 31. **Peer:** an English noble.

Line 33. **His...Sup:** Charles did not eat the night before his execution.

Line 36. **wall:** This word is underlined and followed by an asterisk; an underlined, handwritten annotation in the margin reads "on scaffold".

Lines 37–40. A handwritten annotation in the margin reads "His Head Severd from His Bodie:"

Line 41. **Banqueting house:** These words are underlined; a handwritten annotation in the margin, followed by an asterisk, reads "A cave".

Needs trouble, O King, thy thoughts no more, 45
    forthwith shall it be read;
Daniel *there is, who heretofore*
    like doubts did overspread.

7. Could all interpretating shew
    which profound man soon brought, 50
On whom confer the King needs would
    his orders hight unsought.
Needless preferments yours reserve,
    Sir, keep your gifts in store;
High Offices let others gain, 55
    there's given too much afore.

8. Yet unto thee shall here make known,
    resolve this Oracle true,
Sure as in thy Banquetting house,
    where all that comes may view: 60
The Vessels of my God are brought,
    the palm salutes thee know
Herewith; for these profan'd by thee
    threatneth the fatal blow.

9. O King, even thou, the most high God 65
    unto thy Grandsire bold,
Caldean Land, a Nation fell
    gave them to have and hold.
The Royal Scepter and the Crown
    advanc'd whom he would have, 70
And whom he would he pulled down,
    could put to death and save:

Caledonians or Caldeans signifying union mingling or as Devils.

Line 59. **house:** This word is under- and overlined, and marked with an asterisk; a handwritten annotation in the margin reads "Euen Whi/[te] Hall as somti[ ] Cardinall Woollseys House so[ ] /[and the] churche must retu[rn]". The edge of the page is cut off.

10. Till walking at the twelve moneths end
       subject full Tides to fall;
    Excellent Majesty how gone,   75
       Court exchang'd for the Stall.

Nebuchadnez-
zar, a Father
and Grandfa-
ther both sig-
nifying, or a
Godfather.

    Thy Grandsire on as came to pass,
       at all yet minded not,
    As if a feigned Story but
       his miserable lot.   80

11. Expelled was for words escap'd,
       memory can speak well,
    Hardened in pride, unheard of such,
       the wilde Ass with did dwell:

As multitudes
grazing at S.
James of late

    Sent to the Ox it owner knows,   85
       undreamt of this his doom:
    Fowls their appointed time observe,
       wots not the Night from Noon.

12. Whose Heart made equal with the Beast,
       driven out with those that Bray;   90
    The Diadem as well fits thee,
       Ass, go as much to say.
    Until return'd came to himself,
       knew him that rules on high,
    Over the sons of men appoints   95
       what Office they supply.

13. During which space, this Assyrian,
       what watch kept night and day,
    Thus metamorphos'd, over him,
       lest makes himself away.   100

Lines 74–80. A handwritten annotation in the margin reads "[J]anuary Last/[W]itness/ Horss/
[ ]aning/[ ]here/&c." The page is cut off.

Line 86. Sidenote. **S. James:** St. James, the area where Charles I was executed.

Line 97. **Assyrian:** someone from Assyria, a kingdom hostile to the Israelites; a term of
derision applied to Nebuchadnezzar.

Fields, woods as well ring out, as men
    for woe; and Ecchoes call
Mercy this savage King upon,
    in holy Temples all.

14. Bewaild dejected soul, thus faln,   105
    fed now grazing full low,
Whilst they bedew the ground with tears,
    discerns not friend from foe.
Earth that of late made seem to dawn
    with songs of Triumph high,   110
Fleeth each wight abas'd as much
    among the Herd doth lye.

15. By Star-light for device who gave,
    as graven on his Shield,   The King of
An Eagle mounted on the Crest,   Scots Hart
    a Hart in silver field.   given by
Extold again his God as high,   *Douglas,* &c.
    blessed him all his days:
Others reputes them as nothing,
    alone proclaims his praise.   120

16. Whose seven times till served forth,   King & queen
    in vain for rest to crave;   of Scots both
Whom Devils Legions do possess,   put to death of
    a Monarch turn'd a Slave.   late.
Deposed thus, thou knewest well,   125
    Belshazzar, O his Son,
And renown'd so deliverance his
    voyced by every one.

Lines 113–19. A handwritten annotation in the margin reads "[ ]entry[ ]owels traytors [ ]ad &c".

Line 115. **Crest:** shield or insignia as in a coat of arms.

Line 116. **in silver field:** silver background in a coat of arms.

Line 121. Sidenote. **King & queen:** Charles I's grandparents, Henry Stewart, Lord Darnley (never actually crowned king), and Mary, Queen of Scots.

1605. No-
vember the
fifth.

17. A day a Trumpet made to sound
     for Generations all;   130
And with a Feast solemnized,
     that no time might recal:
The memory of such an act,
     yet as it had not been,
Thy Favorites who are more this day,   135
     or matched to thy Kin.

18. Then they adoring Wood and Stone,
     Statutes forsake Divine;
Meditate carved Statutes on

How matched
with *Arundel*
and *Weston,*
&c.
his Allies.

     in Faction do combine   140
With Enemies of God most high,
     to thrust him from his Throne,
And thus hast lifted up thy self
     so facile and so prone.

19. Against the Lord of Heaven thy King,   145
     not humbling of thy heart,
But stiffned hast with pride thy neck
     unto thy future smart.
Behold polluting holy things

Altars again
adored.

     with Sabbath so Divine,   150
Idolatry and Revels in
     that day and night made thine.

20. But he in whose hand rests thy life,
     even breathe thy ways all,
Thou hast not glorified him   155

Line 130. Sidenote. **1605. November the fifth:** the date England celebrates the discovery and prevention of the Gunpowder Plot, an alleged Catholic conspiracy to blow up the king and Parliament.

Line 141. Sidenote. **Arundel and Weston:** Thomas Howard, second earl of Arundel, and Richard Weston, later earl of Portland, together sponsored an amendment to the Petition of Right (1628) to save the royal prerogative.

Line 147. **pride thy neck:** This phrase is boxed and marked with an asterisk.

sent this wrote on the wall.
God numbered thy Kingdom hath
ended; the Hand points here,
In Ballance his weighed thee too,
the set hour drawing neer.　　　　160

21. How light soever by thee set,
　　thou as thy weightless Gold,
　　His Image wanting found much more
　　lighter then can be told.
Parted, divided thine Estate,
　　given to the *Medes* is;
At Hand, the Hand bids it adieu,
　　finish'd thy Majesties.

FINIS. 1633.

1648. September

So filled to the brim the Cup
　　thy Nephew tasted first,
Miserably that was in France
　　imprisoned by Lewis the Just.
Before it came about to thee
　　forty-five in, to him
When filled up the measure had,
　　twenty five did begin.

Sidenotes:

Crowned
and married
1625. was de-
feated 1645.
(Trinity feast)
the Lyons
chased.
Serves also for
the Eagle put
to flight. The
Swedes inva-
ding the Em-
pire about
1625. and last-
ly the Turk.

O Mene Tekel
Upharsin,
{Anagr.}
Parlement
House Kin:
in number
about 666.

Line 160. A handwritten annotation across the top of the page reads "Highe of [　]Last". The top of the page is cut off.

Lines 161–68. Sidenote. **Crowned…1645:** Charles I. **Trinity feast:** the eighth Sunday after Easter, 1 June in 1645; parliamentary forces defeated those of Charles I at the Battle of Naseby on 14 June 1645. **The Swedes…Empire:** in the Thirty Years War (1618–48).

Heading. **1648. September:** when Lady Eleanor reprinted the tract.

Line 2. **thy Nephew:** Charles I's nephew, to whom the tract was dedicated.

Line 4. **Lewis the Just:** Louis XIII, king of France.

Line 6. **forty-five:** 1645, when Charles I's forces were defeated at the Battle of Naseby.

Line 8. **twenty five did begin:** Charles I's reign began in 1625.

As eyes a flame of fire reveals
    like measure for thy pains,   10
In whose right hand the Pen or Shaft
    missing not Heart and Reins.
From Mene Mene, *doubled twice*
    established even
Parliaments Writs stoln too on thee;   15
    and so take leave, Amen,

$$\left\{ \begin{array}{l} \text{Reveale} \\ \text{O Daniel} \end{array} \right\} \text{Anagr.} \left\{ \begin{array}{l} \text{Eleanor} \\ \text{Audeley.} \end{array} \right\}$$

FINIS.

Line 11. **Shaft:** This word is underlined and marked with an asterisk.

Line 15. **Parliaments Writs:** official summons to assemble a Parliament.

To the Kings most Excellent Majesty: The humble Petition of the Lady *ELEANOR*, 1633.

Shews to Your Majesty,

That the Word of God spoken in the first year of your happy Reign to the Petitioner, upon Friday *last early in the morning did suffer: The B. Beast ascended out of the Bottomless Pit, the Bishop of* Lambeth, *hearted like a Wolf, having seven Heads;* viz. *making War seven years, hath overcome and killed them: Certain Books condemned to be burnt, their Bodies shrouded in loose sheets of paper (by the Prophets being authorized:) This is the third day; if your Highness please to speak the word, the Spirit of life will enter into them, and stand on their feet, &c.*

So craving no other pardon, shall pray, &c.

And going on the Word of God to the King (Rev. 17. cap.) The Beast that was, and is not, even he is Eight, and is of the Seven, and goes into Perdition.

At the Court of Whitehal, Octob. 8. 1633.

His Majesty doth expresly Command the Lord Archbishop of *Canterburies* Grace, and his Highness Commissioners for Causes Ecclesiastical, That the Petitioner be forthwith called before them, to answer for presuming to Imprint the said Books, and for preferring this detestable Petition.

Sidney Mountague.

Concordat cum &c. Tho: Maydwell.

Lines 4–9. A long sidenote printed beside this passage reads "July 28. 1625. these words saying, *There is Nineteen years and an half to the Judgement day, be you as the meek Virgin.* (Fulfilling *Rev.* 11. ver. 5.) 1644. he on a Friday morning Janu. 10. Beheaded or killed, who burnt that testimony with his own hand, in the presence of so many."

Lines 13–18. A handwritten annotation in the margin reads "As Hee 48 aged 1648". A long sidenote printed in the margin reads "And accordingly accomplished on both, as the King at his coming forth 47. so the other seven years compleat and eight current Archbishop before his going into prison, translated that was 1633. Septem. 19. to his Metropolitanship, including also the very seventh and eight moneth And *H:7* and *H:8*. their Character. So again the aforesaid 19 of Septem. whose Coach and Horse with the Ferry-Boat, going (as it were) into the Abyss, which sunk down ascended again."

Lady Eleanor endorsed the autograph manuscript from which the following transcript is taken with two phrases: "By the waters of Babylon wee sat downe & wept" and "Misterye of god in the revelation xv & xvi chapter". She takes her text from Revelation 15–16 and identifies biblical places and events with those of Britain in her own day. In the word "BabyLondon" Lady Eleanor conflates Babylon and London, and the spa at Bath becomes the site for the Whore of Babylon of Revelation 17. The manuscript transcribed here (Henry E. Huntington Library, Hastings MSS, Religious Papers, Box 1, folder 28) is apparently the unique extant copy of this tract.

Bathe Daughter of BabyLondon
woeman sitting on seven Mountains
Beholde—revela xvii-9

XV chap:	A signe in heaven great & marveilous Seven Angells &c:	Bathe of Britains seven wonders not the Lest.
	as it were a glassie sea mingled with fire	scalding hote sea colored.
	Them that had gotne the victorie stand (at or) on the glassie sea.	by guides supported
	Seven Angell came out of the Temple clothed in pure white Linnin. girded	cleansed daylye. neare the church.
XVI chap:	And I heard the Angell of the waters saye Lord &c	some noteable judgement observed &c then.
	And the fourthe angell powred his vial out on the sunn &c	a drye summer &c
	And Men Boyled in great heate blasphemed for theire paines and soares &c (repented not)	such maladies cured by the waters

10

71

Sixt Angell powred out his vial. sixt daye waters drawne
and the waters were dryed up. daye of preparation for
Kinge of Kings

20 And I sawe three uncleane spirits fowle ennoughe. Spirits
like froggs come out of the come out of the devils.
Mouthe of the Dragon Beast false & out of the mouthe
prophet. of the POPE

For they are the spirits of devils.
goe unto the Kings of the
Earth. and of the whole world. Theire embassadors

Blessed is hee that keepeth
his garments & without
Lest hee walke naked &c. shame cursed.

30 Gathered into a place called
in Hebrew Armagedon signifieth
Hill of good tideings. hill of Apples
or fruite &c

And great Babylon came in By her Beware before
remembrance&c too Late. repent.
It is Don: .Elea Tichet.

Landsdowne
Mountains Clarknesdowne &c
Warlesdowne

Line 18. **the waters:** at Bath.

Line 36. **Elea Tichet:** Eleanor Touchet, Lady Eleanor's birthname.

Lines 37–39. **Landsdowne...Warlesdowne:** hills near Bath (written on the verso of the manuscript).

Lady Eleanor endorsed these manuscript verses (Public Record Office, SP 16/345/104) "Spirituall Antheme" and subscribed them from "Litchfeild January. 1636," i.e., 1637. In the preceding December, as she explains in *Bethlehem* (Wing D1978—page 369 in the present edition), she had vandalized the new altar-hanging at the cathedral in Lichfield, sat on the bishop's throne, and declared herself "primate and metropolitan" (archbishop and bishop). She remained in the city until mid-February. Even though the Privy Council acted immediately to order that she be confined to Bethlehem Hospital (Bedlam), bad weather prevented the messengers who bore that order from reaching Lichfield. The tract inserts the beast (Rev. 13) into stories of men possessed with devils (Matt. 8:28–33; Mark 5:1–20; and Luke 8:27–39). The manuscript transcribed here is apparently the unique extant copy of this tract.

ELEA. TUICHET

When hee was come to the other side of the contrye, of the Gergesenes, there mett him two: possessed with Devils Coming Out of the Tombes.

8 Math: Mark.

Travelors poore Tombes thes. avoide & flee.
Wide Mouthes untam'd. No chaine that Beare can Tye.
Insasiable worme, Tongue Brideled Bee.
Spirits uncleane which restles rage & Crye.
Devils administer. adjure. yee see.   5
Epicure swine feeding. Chok'd Thousands Twaine.
Named Legion. in his righte. Minde againe.

Soe howese of god poluted smell & veiw.
A fayre of Fatherless; weepe Thames & Trent
Theifes theire correction howese fitter for you.   10
Heere Marrage. Lawe. Bonds. all assunder rent.
A Mercement for. Empted uncleanness Strive

Title. **ELEA. TUICHET:** Eleanor Touchet, Lady Eleanor's birthname.

Line 6. **Epicure swine feeding:** Followers of the ancient Greek philosopher Epicurus were popularly regarded as dissolute lovers of pleasure.

Line 9. **Thames and Trent:** English rivers; cf. James 5:1. Line 12. **Mercement:** fine.

Men Mercieless. Lett this Whipp. smale suffice.
Fetters beware. A Touche. to you bee wise
Braune to digest in Choler. not refuse   15
Friendly Musterd. a little. to peruse.

You Ducking Lowe. rooteing. yee that Beraye
Your rayement white, Fryers, [ ]
    awaye no staye.

Litchfeild January. 1636

Line 17. **Beraye:** defile; but possibly bewray, reveal.
Line 18. **Fryers:** friars; members of a Catholic religious order. [ ]: The deleted word is illegible.

This tract (Wing D1971) is the first of Lady Eleanor's tracts surviving from the 1640s and thus from the period after her confinement to Bedlam and the Tower of London. Beginning by comparing herself to Joseph (Gen. 37), she proceeds to interpret Nebuchadnezzar's dream (Dan. 2) and other prophecies of the Book of Daniel, comparing for example King Charles's agreeing to the Long Parliament's attainder for the execution of the earl of Strafford with Nebuchadnezzar's ordering the death of his wise men. In 1646 Lady Eleanor published a different and longer tract under a similar title (Wing D1972—page 181 in the present edition). The present edition of *Her Appeal to the High Court* is based on a copy now in the Thomason Tracts in the British Library (shelf number E. 172[33]).

THE LADY ELEANOR, HER APPEALE TO THE HIGH COURT OF *PARLIAMENT.*

PSAL. 123

Behold, even as the eyes of Servants looke to the hand of their Masters, &c.

Mat. 8.4

See thou tell no man, but goe thy way, shew, &c.

TO THE HONORABLE ASSEMBLY OF THE High
Court of *Parliament.*

Most Honorable *Lords,* Noble *Knights,* and *Gentle-men*: This *JOSEPH,* and about to take his flight, hated hetherto, for the *Evill-report* brought of his *Brethren:* Also a Striplin grown up of 17. yeares; many collours or peeces whose Coat too, craves Your patience, to heare him a few words here.

The Preface.

The roade way not to baulke, a preface omitted neither to the *reader:* complement, although layd aside, soft lineing of that sort, these therwith prefaced not; rather preferred for all weather serviceable, a peece of
10   plaine Leather. In Paradice our livery made up without hands, that of Skinnes: And for that precious Stone without hands cut out; this peece or appollogie serving, set here without coullours or flowers, as for enammeling such, having none Artificiall.

And heretofore a shew, having bin of these handled: Though the substance unmanifested or maine summe; Times mistery unknown that treasure, till the Evening and fullnesse of time, as those Trenches filled even with Water before the fire fell, and purifying-pots, those first with Water filled: likewise the mistery of times and seasons so late revealed, made knowne for the fayling of the future. This good Wine kept till
20   now.

And this thing now, who knowes not too well; tedious to touch and fowle: but Blaines and Running-Soares nothing else all over, from the Elbow unto the feete: so this annoynting commended to all, for the blessed *Readers* and *Hearers* both:

Farwell. From *Kensington,*
the *Angell signe.*
Whitsontyde, 1641.

Line 3. **Striplin:** stripling; youth. **17. yeares:** the time elapsed since 1625, when Lady Eleanor had become a prophet. Line 4. **Coat:** see Gen. 37:3.

Lines 6–25. In the base text this section is in italics with roman emphasis; the fonts have been reversed here for ease of reading. Fonts follow the base text again beginning at line 26.

Line 7. **baulke:** balk. Lines 16–17. **Trenches…Water:** see 1 Kings 18:35.

Lines 25–26. **Kensington…signe:** an inn in Kensington (a suburb of London), identified by a sign over its door. **Angell:** perhaps presented as a sign of God's presence.

The LADY *ELEANOR,* her appeale to the
high Court of *PARLIAMENT.*

DAN. 2. 34.   30

Thou sawest till that a Stone was cut out without hands, which smote the
Image upon the feete: That of Iron, and Clay, and brake them in peeces, &c.

Heere these touching the *Iron-age,* remaines of time, a tast thereof; the
Sonnes of the Prophets for their use, needlesse; as into the water to cast
a Logg, wherein a sticke cut downe, but thrown sufficeth, or to give a
touch, &c. As farre either from building upon others foundation, theirs
&c. The lanthorne unusefull, when the Moone giving light at full, not
trespassing in that way here, nor borrowing either &c. And so farther of
the latter dayes, these even being become drosse changed, even commanded these by him.   40

The Judge all-sufficient, God able to change all, and them reforme:
As doubtlesse the end, the finall day before of doome refined reformed
to bee: to this end commended by us, and being high time to make
some preparation; the tydings of a troublesome time cut of, unfruitfull,
&c.

In short shewed, those sharp dayes shortned, the brittle feete parted
those, a warning peece, as followeth.

In peeces broken, destroyed at the last, though nothing than mettle
lasting more: That stone then unmoveable, invincible, the everlasting
Law, as the workemanship of the Creators finger, moreover his heavie   50
hand therewith: None other that great Image but sprituall aspiring
BABYLON the fall of both, the other *Babell* likewise that taken, going
before the end of the World; like this dreame the World gone in a
moment. And before the worlds departing, not without a Cutting blow
threatned forthwith, as when that hasty Decree sent forth his Proclamation for his own Nation; those wise men to be destroyed. That first
borne Monarchy, *Babylons* great revolution, visible even in our Horizon
that end or time, closing with the time of the end, and from the hand
also a faire signe after to appeare.

Line 33. **tast:** taste. Lines 34–35. **Prophets…Logg:** see 2 Kings 6:6.

Line 37. **lanthorne:** lantern. Line 39. **drosse:** impurities.

Line 44. **cut of:** cut off. Line 48. **mettle:** metal.

60   And here so much for paralizing of this expensive time, with that time of wantonnesse, in his reigne not found currant. In which want none found: of weakenesse willfulnesse begetting, lifted up like the empty Scale, when the full descend: The Sunne like at lowest, making then the longest shaddow. Thus represented in this Mirror of former times, the present age the visage thereof, &c. Also, no spare body unwildy growne and great, every way dangerous division therby unable to stand upon the feete: Not spared by Her, whose song the Worlds far-well these. Disburthened in this ensuing briefe. And plaine to bee in undoing this knot too, the *Iron-age* done, finished, although this peece

70   difficult to digest, somewhat, &c.

Thou sawest, till that a Stone was cut out without hands, &c.

The summe of these words signifie, the *Burthen of Gods word in the last dayes*, of a truth disclosing the time of the end. And of premisses the conclusion following: So unexpected Judgements foretold from them: Also made evident the end of time. Here *Stone* sharpening *Iron*, and striking fire, High favours (for the most part) not without a heavie hand imparted: like *Jacob and his Brother*, the unlike twinnes begotten, or the Blessing in one hand, a Rod of correction in the other, and of which fire already kindled, loving Kindnesse and Judgement, going hand in hand

80   together, the evill times but touched onely.

Thou sawest, till that a Stone was cut out without hands, which smote the Image.

The Signe in the feete; So in these last dayes: see here, and behold fulfilled, how that very saying:

Thou sawest till that, &c.

By Thee beheld, as much to say, to read a certain Manuscript, the weighty Stone become a Booke, not waiting long for Priviledge, Imprinted, howsoever sooneafter.

Certainly, in what yeare testifying the Worlds disolution, Manifested

90   with a heavie one: In the yeare One thousand six hundred twentie five.

That great Plague yeare, out of Darknesse, when the Visions trans-

---

Line 68. **this ensuing briefe:** the prophecy that will follow.

Line 77. **Jacob and his Brother:** see Gen. 25:23.

lated *of the Man, greatly beloved DANIELL.* For the great dayes breaking forth, cleared those clowdy Characters: As delivered not without a token, since made good, the Brittle standing of his owne Kingdomes, dedicated to the KING of Great BRITTAINE, Defendor of the Faith.

And of whose making to justifie here, by whom Published; though hitherto by authority with-stood.

ELEANOR AUDELEY, handmayden of the most high GOD of Heaven, this Booke brought forth by Her, fifth Daughter of GEORGE, Lord of CAS-TLEHAVEN, Lord AUDLEY, *and Tuitchet. NO inferior* PEERE *of this Land, in* Ireland *the fifth* EARLE.   100

Which name blotted a House or Castle, of late fallen by the ancient of dayes: His Kingdomes misteries displaying, nor chosen any obscure Motto: *God hath devided thy Kingdome, and numbred &c.*

And farther, *of this Stone; of the Builders cast aside:* the Summe of this Booke or Subject, besides the day of Judgement revealed, *even that Some standing here, shall not tast of Death, till they see that day.* Herewith fell upon the *ROMAN-EMPIRES* disolation. The World, the great *MAN:* the disolution ushered with *GERMANIES* overthrw unexpecting: As moreover one last serving these Feete, great Brittaines foote too, and   110 *Germanie* divided both betweene two opinions, Religions, and Buisnesses, where never since a Nation such distractions. For Plagues and greivances, such inward and outward ones, striving to outstrip one another.

Heere-withall foreshewed, the Furious Progresse of the *French* and *Spannish Forces*, with those Leagues not in force now. Notwithstanding corsse Marriages, &c. never before so.

The Kings of the North, by those *France* signified: Likewise the Kings of the South, the *AUSTRIAN Family*, these like whirlwinds tossing the World up and downe from this side to that, &c. AND for the   120 shutting up of this Treatise, lastly; with a Salutation concluded for the Son of *Peace*, if he had been there saluted, &c.

And at that time shall MICHAEL stand up, the great Prince, &c.

Line 95. **KING…Faith:** part of the title of Charles I.

Line 97. **by authority:** phrase indicating that a book's publication was permitted.

Line 104. **God…numbred:** Dan. 5:26–28. Lines 106–7. **even…day:** see Matt. 16:28.

Angel land, or ENGLANDS-ILAND, therefore the *Arch-angels Name;* here the halfe name and abbreviated words, the age or time shortned betokning, &c. And for future things derided their Musique. *Daniels* Prophesie shut up prohibited, this time of trouble, their's come to passe notwithstanding. So passing or poasting to the time, at last of deliverance, the blessed resurrection. Heere unfolded that treble or threefold
130   Coard, not easily broken nor altred: Sworne with a high hand, that meeting a *Trienniall* &c.

For a time and times, and halfe, (or part) from the halfe of Seaven, *the hand pointing at the seaventeenth-hundred yeare:* That very time, about the halfe but fulfilled of the last Centerie, as five hundred yeares filling up a Period. Lastly, given under the hand lifted up, *even five thousand yeares compleate* for the age of the World. The Worlds Ages too, parted into three parts, allotted two thousand yeares a peece, or thereabouts. The shortest lot drawne last, for a time and times, and halfe; shortned in the behalfe of *His Elect.*
140   From *Adam* unto *Abraham, (offering of his sonne)* the first Stage or time; so unto *Jerusalems* destruction the second. And the last or third, to the end of the World, the glorious *Resurrection,* &c. And yet farther, for the fortunate figure of five, *(Blessed is he that waites and comes)* &c. Here two hundred and ninety, and three hundred and five and thirty, amounting to six hundred twentie-five, signifying thereby, the yeare wherein unsealed the Booke of the Prophet *Daniell,* 1625. and 17. yeares current, sithence a time and times and halfe Likewise, this Bookes Resurrection-time also appointed, waiting for the appeasing neere of these stormes and troubles, a Peaceable time: *God was not in the*
150   *Wind, not in the Earthquake, not in the Fire: after the fire, at last, the small still voyce.* AND so finished this Booke. (Beyond expectation,) but so came to Passe in the yeare aforesaid, 1625. Shee awakened *by a voyce*

Line 128. **poasting:** posting; travelling. Lines 129–30. **threefold Coard:** Eccles. 4:12.

Line 131. **a Trienniall:** A triennial act, ensuring that Parliament must meet every three years, had been passed earlier in 1641.

Line 139. **His Elect:** those chosen by God for salvation.

Line 140. **Abraham…sonne:** see Gen. 22. Lines 147–49. **God…voyce:** 1 Kings 19:11–12.

from HEAEVN, in the Fifth moneth, the 28. of *July,* early in the Morning, the Heavenly voice uttering these words.

"There is Ninteene yeares and a halfe to the day of *Judgement,* and you as the meek Virgin. These sealed with Virgins state in the Resurrection, when they not giving in Marriage."

And to take heede of *Pride,* or to that effect spoken or added: But as for the Golden number that heeded well or heard: the cleare voice of a Trumpet inclining thereto; and like the chaffe of the Summer-threshing-flowre scattered. When the Cittie flying or Fled from the Pestilence, that Sommers great Visitation, the fifth monethes Farwell, *July* 28. the Heavie hand, in that very weeke, as weekely the number certified, five thousand deseased of the Plague: Moreover; the ensuing Weeke, giving up the reckoning more full, the number of the dead, amounting to five thousand five hundred and odd, &c. there stoppt or stay'd immediately, as much to say; but a spanne the Worlds age, graven with that deadly Dart, and never to be forgotten, within few dayes how scarce a token? So suddenly ceasing then.

Vers. 36. *This is the dreame, and wee will tell the interpretation thereof before the King: thou art this head of gold.*

The Iron touched with the Load-stone, turnes towards the North, Great *Brittaines* foure Crownes or Kingdomes: This gyant-Image armed at all points, *England,* Angel-gold fought the first fight, incountred *Romes Dragon,* put to flight his Anges.

The Reformations Leader, the other inferiour Kingdome, *France* the Breast and Armes of *Silver,* sometimes subiect to this *Ilands-Crowne,* beares onely the *Lillyargent* for Armes, &c.

Another third Kingdome bearing, rule over all: of brasse, *Scotland;* Bell Mettle, *the Belly and Thighes,* the Breeches to wit, or blessing wrestled for, having shrunck a sinnew, halting too.

160

170

180

Line 153. **FIFTH moneth:** July, under the old calendar when the year began in March.

Line 159. **Golden number:** number used in calculating the date of Easter.

Line 170. **VERS. 36:** Dan. 2. Line 172. **The Iron…North:** as in a compass.

Line 173. **foure Crownes:** England, France, Scotland, and Ireland.

Line 178. **the Lillyargent:** The French royal arms were silver *fleurs-de-lis.*

The *fourth kingdome of Iron, the feete Ireland broken in peeces by an army,* their old customes turn'd into new Lawes, & divided between two *Religions,* our *Ladies & our Lords* at strife together: *but Woman, what have we to doe with thee, but Potters earth and myrie clay, but water with wine compaird.*

And drawing here to the end, or foote of this *Image:* The *fourh Monarchies heavie estate,* & that fourth Kingdome weighed both here together, where *Princes* and *Nobles* going a begging: The basse set on
190   Horse-backe commanding, without doubt the *Gentiles* their returne, to wallow in the mire, or *Heathenisme-covetousnes and Idolatry:* this massy peece importing and expressing no lesse. And further, the *Iron feete* as inferring besides *Irelands denominations,* the names of *Ferdinand,* by whom the devision of these dayes, left for a Legacie to his heires. Also, of that *Arch-engin* great peeces, Volues of shot where distance of so many miles, not securing without hands or mercie in a moment. Towers trodden under foot, and Ships as townes broken in peeces: doubtlesse which cruell Invention among *Christians,* sounding the *Alarum* of the day of *Judgement* at hand, by those thunderbolts discharged. And in
200   dayes of old, had the mighty Volumes bin, those of late Imprinted, out of doubt repented they had, But this *Joseph they knew not the holy Scripture.* So old dayes presedents made for the future, the Fathers as it were laying up for the Children, & more tolerable in the day of *Judgement* for them, then for these times, and these of that rare Art also of the Presse, as wel as peeces, in an instant performed, drawn within the compasse *of this stone, cut out without hands, become a mountain: the Kingdome of heaven at hand,* pointing therat to be revealed *too.*

Lastly, this name of *Charles,* no small Favourites of the *Fisher-man* taken in his nets, stooping to his unsavorie toe; so come to the *French*
210   *and Spanish* Emperours. And *Charles the great,* since whose daies, a

---

Lines 184–85. **Woman...thee:** John 2:4.

Lines 191–92. **massy peece:** associated with the mass, thus with Catholicism.

Line 193. **Ferdinand:** archduke and Holy Roman Emperor, 1619–1637, and thus a key figure in the Thirty Years' War. Lady Eleanor associates Ferdinand's name with *ferrum,* Latin for iron.

Line 195. **Volues:** volleys. Line 204. **that...Presse:** printing.

Line 210. **Charles the great:** Charlemagne, crowned Holy Roman Emperor in A.D. 800.

thousand yeares expired neere: Feete of the longest size, of the Tenns. Fowre of his Race succeeding in the *Westerne* Empire, setting in *Europes-Ocean* that eye of the World. No little one, either the other great toe, *Charles the fifth, & of his successors some six of them.*

Thus of two thousand and two hundred yeares standing, this great *Image;* foure stories in height, or a nayle driven to the head: layd upon the Anvill by those, in all Arts so able, that further amplification unnecessary, but commended *these.*

DAN. verse 44. *And in the daies of these Kings, shall the God of heaven set up a Kingdome, which shall never be destroyed: and the Kingdome shall not be left to other people, it shall break in peeces.* 220

Finally, for a watch word also these, let fall; *at the end of twelue monethes, &c.* verse, 29 And the end of all these at aimed, either Heavens departing: for without some farther mistery, doubtlesse not. Even the not knowne day and houre, shewed about New-yeares-day, when that good time falling, or twelfe-tyde, there then to watch, as those night-watchers, the happie Shepheard, our example.

And *Nebuchadnezer* for examples sake too, for the future chastised, by whom an Act published the earth throughout, for those that walke in Pride to beware. And signes and wonders for to observe from above; which some carelesse observing not, othersome not discerning not, as blockish. So this sonne of the Morning, walking in his majestie, the heavie sentence falling, as foretold by the Prophet *Daniel,* for to avoyd the Tree, whereof the leaves faire, and fruit much; as much to say, a faire Pedigree, Kings and Princes growning thereon. And the axe laid to the trees roote, wherefore to shew mercy at length to the poore: Counselled for lengthning of his well-faire and tranquillity; lest of the lash tasting as well as others. 230

And upon greatnesse, none to presume, this *Daniel,* penning feigned *Tragedies,* none sets forth plain this great *Assiryan* how; taking his 240

Line 214. **Charles the fifth:** sixteenth-century king of Spain and Holy Roman Emperor.
Line 219. **DAN. verse 44:** Dan. 2:44. Line 224. **twelfe-tyde:** twelve days after Christmas.
Line 237. **lash tasting:** being punished.
Line 240. **Assiryan:** enemy to the Israelites.

Sabbaticall progresse. In all hast driven from his privy Chamber, how doing in the fielde open Pennance, also grazing before his Palace, feeds with his fellow Asse: And like *Eagles-plumes*, those stareing locks of his overgrown; a heavie crowne or capp, to keepe his head from cold. Also Oxens pushing hornes-like, thereto crooked nayles as *birds of prey*, the inseparable crown and septor so going together: Pride and cruelty here, which *Brutish condition* before served out, that *apprentiship* before added excellent Majesty, &c. and Lords seeking to him, constrained to cast those high lookes lower, little dreamed of that estate: sometime who from the *Bed to mind calling the grave no doubt, and thoughts in their owne likenes begetting Dreames.* By this great *Monarch dreamed, thought he saw an* Image & *a stone of that greatnes, certainly lay thinking, when he gone the way of all flesh, gathered to his fathers, upon some peece in his own likenes some everlasting Monument.* From whose sudden awakning and up rising also, the *Prophet revealing earthly dominions and Monarches, the heaven therewith passing away in a moment of time, even mortallities change for no other passage this, or place of* Scripture. But like these mettels foure, the Elements melting, so live for ever, &c.

FINIS.

DANIEL,
I end all.

In the first two editions of Wing's *Short-Title Catalogue,* Lady Eleanor's petition *To the High Court* and *Samsons Legacie* were numbered as two separate publications (Wing D2015 and D2011, respectively); in the 1994 enlarged edition of volume one of Wing, *Samsons Legacie* is listed as part of Wing D2015. In *Samsons Legacie* Lady Eleanor expands and develops a theme she had used in *Samsons Fall* (1642; Wing D2010): King Charles and Queen Henrietta Maria, she argues, were reenacting the biblical story of Samson and Delilah (Judg. 14–16). The present edition of *To the High Court* and *Samsons Legacie* is from the Thomason Tracts now in the British Library (shelf number E. 96[19]); the petition is dated by Thomason 14 April 1643. Although on page 14 of *Samsons Legacie,* Lady Eleanor refers to the present year as 1642, she may have written that just before 25 March when the year 1643 began; similarly, the date 1642 at the end of the petition refers to January 1643 according to the new calendar.

TO THE MOST HONORABLE THE HIGH COURT OF *PARLIAMENT* ASSEMBLED, &c.

My *LORDS;*

Ther's a *Time for every thing under the Sunne,* and if any; for to bee abrupt and breife in ever, tis *NOW* when *Time* so precious is with your Lordships: under the Sunne there is nothing but a supernaturall Course to be taken, Touching the *Cure* of such unnaturall condition'd *Times:* The Almightie his Word the only *Balme* then, and *Soveraigne* remedy when ye have tryd all: If any therefore doe amisse and miscarry of you: Blame your selves none but the *Parliament:* For I shall of no little *Burthen* discharge my selfe here who can but say, and tell you. I have a receipt of such rare opperation and vertue given me; That within few days it shall bring Him againe to Himself, I meane the *KING;* after absent so long from his *Parliament:* whose Character if ye please to observe; This is his: 10

Line 1. **My LORDS:** addressed to members of the House of Lords.

Line 10. **receipt:** formula or prescription.

Lines 11–12. **KING...long:** Charles left Westminster in January 1642, i.e., 1643.

He that no Chaines could binde him, (Marke Evangelist the 5th.) *That had been often bound with fetters and with Chaines pluck'd assunder by him. And the fetters broken in pieces, neither could by any man be tamed;* as much to say, *neither* Oath, *nor* word, *or* promise *availing, or any reason of force to parswade with Him, as the* Holy Ghost speaking plaine: *by that adjuring in* Gods Name; *and by asking his* Name *too, saying,*
20 LEGION, *for they were many, who spake not with the Lest:* Nevethelesse, not more feirce then fearefull of the *Lords* comming, *this man wounding himself thus.*

And thus have made tender unto your Lordships; Of my service, whether or no yee accept thereof: for to bring His Majestie to you, Setting as afore time cloath'd, &c. And doing withall what Ye shall aske or desire. As for the Caveliers what They shall doe all of them, even crave a Passe here, to take Shipping for the *Low-Countries*, and *Germanie* to be gone away; the *Boors* will entertaine them willingly, S^t. *Matt*: the 8. *gives Notice of two, so exceeding feirce that none might passe by that way,* to wit,
30 that Dutch Duke, or Prince possessed with an uncleane Spirit, out of his WITS; he to returne also without delay Home againe, beyond Sea.

1642.   Waiting on your
The 3^d. of   *Lordships Commands*
January.   ELEANOR

The Holy Ghosts
New-yeares-gift.

Line 23. **tender:** offer. Line 26. **Caveliers:** Cavaliers; King Charles's supporters, royalists.

Line 27. **Passe…Shipping:** official permission to sail. Line 28. **Boors:** Dutch peasants.

Line 30. **Dutch…Prince:** probably Prince Rupert, King Charles's nephew, who was in the royalist army.

Line 32. **1642:** i.e., 1643.

Line 35. **New-yeares-gift:** In the seventeenth century, new year's gifts were presented at the beginning of January.

SAMSONS LEGACIE.

JUDGES, the 16. Chap. &c.

And as instanc'd or brought to *his* Tryall, here found light; *SAMSON* guiltie that way: which *Vow* of his, had he unhappily not violated, a businesse that: Of no mean weight, what *Fetters of Brasse bound him had;* none of what kinde soever. *Samsons fall, lost himself hereby, dispossessed of the* Spirit *of the* LORD.

By him discovered *the Almighties counsell unto the* Lords *Enemy, could not with-hold or refraine, told her all his heart;* she acquainted is therewith bee it whatsoever: Such a blind thing is *Love;* They into such Thraldom brought which harbour it: suspected nothing because he *lov'd* her, or *doted rather.* That whosoever they were, was able with a looke of his *Browe,* to put them for ever to silence, wherein his soul so farre ingag'd, any to attempt but the motion, &c.

And farther shewed, how in his *allegiance having toward his Master and Lord fayled: Both stript of that great strength of his, Lost both his* Eies, *not only boord or put out,* faine to be lead afterwards by a Ladd: But *put in prison, beside grinding in a Mill:* To tast of restlesse HELL, that wearisome being. *Even* takes *Essaye* of our *Saviours Cup;* indeede these in some things to *Samson* belong onely: able but for to turne his weary sides without other help, or by a wals side *to* go, which before had *The Lord his support; The* Philistims *his Lords now:* a heavie change, of no other estate worthy, had taken his pleasure and so came of it.

One Trusted with that high place of Government: Twenty yeares therabout, as it appeares. Crownd with so many favours; That had the *Eternall words direction his light:* set so light by alhough chastised never so severly the bage of his Masters heavy displeasure, none commiserate his Complaint bee it whatsoever, *whether marked, shorne or noted.* He *which wist not the* Spirit *of the Lord was departed from him, when He had*

10

20

Line 9. **Thraldom:** servitude. Line 17. **Essaye:** taste. Line 20. **Philistims:** Philistines.

foolishly departed from the Lord: And if GOD spared not *Samson,* others
much lesse that have him for their lesson.

30 Who could have supposed, warn'd before hand too, what trust to be
reposed in them. That upon a Womans assault her charms such a Forte
rendered up: without any reason rendred *But to please* Her, *was not that
Riddle disclosd enough:* who would not have layd another wager, as great
as *Samsons?* That this man could never have been over taken so, that had
been mistaken so much in Her before, *named his Heifer;* and *this*
woman she of the *Philistims* breed too, both of them one in effect: or
two witnesses appearing as it were: Herewithall bidden to take heed all,
of Close-underhand-dealers: For *the holy Ghost* is not without a double,
or two-fold meaning in *these* thirty *Shirts* wrap'd *up,* & thirty *Shirtes*
40 *those;* not only *Judas* His livery-Coates *or Coate-armes expressing, but our
bleeding dayes* wherein such Plundering and *intolerable* Theifts:

  For which betraying of the trust, as one beside himself; beside being a
Prisoner, made a by-word, or one for a meane Occupation fitter, or
trusted when *His eyes bee out rather then other-wise: In steed of a* Saviour
or Deliverer, *hee delivered into the hands of such, &c.* Which kindnesse
for; To none other *Bound, but to Her:* beside *his* willfulnesse, *whose Parents* some-time could not prevaile with *Him,* or any other: Is during the
remnant *of his wretched dayes,* ordain'd for to beare *those shakels and fetters,* Brassen ones for suretiship, and better securitie: *Thus armed by Her*
50 *from Head to Foote &c.*

  But *her* Ladyship *urged him, She prest him* Daily, vext his Soule, his
Conscience to the *Death.* Moreover, by *Lulling of him as much againe,*
was kept in a *Dreame, untill* layd *himself flat at her* Feet: By such maine
Strength was *Samson* over-mastred by his *Mistres,* who *so often* gives the
Allarum; The *Philistins* SAMSON, &c.

  But to bring these home a little *farther,* to these last dayes, without

---

Line 40. **Judas…armes:** the marks of a traitor.
Line 41. **bleeding dayes:** a reference to the civil wars during Lady Eleanor's lifetime.
Line 43. **by-word:** an object of scorn or contempt. Line 48. **shakels:** shackles; bonds.
Line 49. **suretiship:** assurance, security.

Over-laying Your patience *I hope,* shewed great *Brittains low ebbe,* like *Samson what passe brought to.*

The worlds wounder *for blessing and bounty from above beyond all theirs not unknowne;* a dreadfull Name, *farre* and *neere:* Now by His Majesties *warfare* being *fettered* and in *Armes;* become the game and musicke of the World. 60

Those (as it were) away *hidding* and *running before time,* crowding as fast, and covering *house-tops,* fearelesse *now* of *Samson.* In which difference difficult to judge; whether *for Might and Majestie* more reverenced, then dejected at last and dispised: Certainly manifested as *great Imbecillitie in subjecting himselfe to a Womans waywardnesse, therewith carryed away so and transported.*

But these not for disputation sake; but made for dispatch, not so wide and full of stuffe as others are acknowledged: If it fit close, tis as becoming *Joseph* in makeing himself known to his Brethren, in hast told them, I am *Joseph:* So now it was not you that sent mee hether, but GOD 70

So was it of the Lord; no thanke to *Samson, Samsons saying, she pleaseth me well: When neverthelesse it displeased his Father and Mother. They saying; is there never a Woman among thy Brethren or people, &c.*

The almightie for bringing his owne Counsell and purpose to passe; suffers much, and forbeares long: the Holy Ghost thus saying, hee sought an occasion against the *Philistins,* GOD on his side, he needs not feare any. The Time was come of their fall: at last which stricks home, though hardly like the Thunder at first heard. 80

And to be som-what lowder, or plain herein: was not an occasion sought also against that House of Lords and Commons, by that unexpected progresse without *President* or Example of Progenitors, when he separated Himself from his Head-Kingdoms Parliament Assembled

---

Line 58. **passe:** juncture; critical position. Lines 61–62. **game and musicke:** entertainment.
Line 70. **stuffe:** contents; text. Line 71. **Joseph…known:** see Gen. 45:1–4.
Line 80. **stricks:** strikes. Line 84. **progresse:** journey or tour. **President:** precedent.
Lines 84–85. **he separated…Parliament:** Charles I left Westminster in January 1642.

then, for rooting that Slip out, blind *Herisie Her* Majesties *darling,* grown unto such a height. Without doubt with as ill, or worse successe taken in hand, then hee which but lost his life, good *Samson:* When the House of Peeres and Commons those two Pillars, charged with a heavie

90   taxe of *Treason,* purposing to lay violent hands next: first rob'd of their good Name; and then of their Life lastly, brought about by Lyers in waite for that purpose. And thus his causlesse falling out, the occasion of these such unspeakable miseries; he carried away from His Parliament thus, by the Church of the LIBERTINES and ROMES CHURCH, proceeding from a loosnesse or carelesnesse of goodnesse: the good affection not set by of those, to have been Equaliz'd, if not preferr'd before Forreine states; a greater honour then proginey (common to all) to discharge such a Stewardship well. The office of a Crowne *(a good name, Proverbs.* 22) as our Eies open'd, and Wofull evidences

100   thereby given to understand: That not old *Samuel,* godly *Queene Elizabeth* was rejected, tender hearted unto every one. But herewith wee which were not content: But nay, we will have a King to reigne over us, whatsoever coming to passe.

How soone verified, the old true proverbe, seldome comes a better: for unto *Samson* as at his end; so befallen us. More slaine in one yeare, then since the Conquest in the Reigne of so many Kings and Queenes of them cald to sacrifice their Lives for the Truths testimony: commanded to rest a little season. Blessed innocents were who changed have their scarlet for white robes, *calling a loud, how long O Lord* Revela. 6.

110   &c.

Line 86. **blind…darling:** Charles's queen, Henrietta Maria, was a Roman Catholic and thus a heretic in the eyes of the Protestant English.

Lines 89–90. **House…Pillars:** cf. Judg. 16:29–30. **charged…Treason:** In January 1642 Charles charged several members of Parliament with treason.

Line 94. **LIBERTINES:** Lady Eleanor's meaning is unclear. "Libertines" could refer to licentious people or to extreme religious sectarians.

Line 97. **progi018y:** progeny; heirs. Lines 98–99. **a good name:** see Prov. 22:1.

Line 100. **Samuel:** see 1 Sam. 8:5-9.

Line 106. **the Conquest:** William the Conqueror's defeat of England in 1066.

Lines 108–9. **Blessed…robes:** see Rev. 6:9–11.

And every haire of Times head grown precious, never recald; and if ever perrilous to loose it, as tis now reveal'd here; and unloos'd the mistery of time, how *Samsons seven-fold ropes pluck'd asunder, even drawn from them; like* Pharaohs *double Dreame,* where the thing was one, likewise these broken *Withes and ropes* reach to this sevententh hundered yeare present not alone; But to that sevententh yeare of the Kings reigne, a time of greater famine then *Pharaohs,* when the plentie was not known, by reason of the scarcity following so grievous.

And now great *Brittaine* newly so stiled, accompanied with no few Honours that started up, have in this sevententh hundred yeare; Even as those knots undone all and broken, with *Irelands* green plantation by the rootes pluck'd up: This *knot or union so fast made, how is it come to nothing, but all up making ready in Armes;* that beside a *Coate-armes* borne, no other appearance at all remains, suddenly like *his armes* become *when be awaked; great Brittains peace even so brittle stands as those ropes, &c.* Compard unto towe, or a piece of thred, choaked with *Match and Powder now:* for the sweet sents of *peace* and *plenty* injoyed Long: And handled *Thus:* Notwithstanding, not unfore-told. None *Considers of that handwriting,* though *in* the Yeare, 1633. shewing, His Kingdome is devided and numbred &c. *Belshazzar, it shall be easier for him in the day of Judgement.*

120

130

Line 114. **Pharaohs...Dreame:** see Gen. 41.

Line 115. **Withes:** bonds or shackles of twigs.

Lines 116–17. **But to that sevententh...reigne:** 1641.

Line 119. **great Brittaine...stiled:** When James VI of Scotland succeeded to the English throne in 1603, the royal title or style changed so that he was King James I of Great Britain, rather than king of Scotland, England, and Ireland.

Lines 119–20. **no few Honours:** James I granted many honors and titles, including the new one of baronet.

Lines 121–22. **Irelands...up:** Ireland erupted into war against the English rulers in 1641. **knot or union:** the joining together of England and Ireland with Scotland.

Lines 123–24. **beside...remains:** The new royal coat of arms is the only tangible remainder of the British union of Scotland and England.

Lines 126–27. **towe:** a piece of wool or flax; also a rope used for towing. **choaked...now:** smothered or filled with the paraphernalia of war. **sents:** scents.

Line 129. **that handwriting...1633:** Lady Eleanor's prophecy, *Given to the Elector.*

By the Prophet *Jeremiah:* PASHUR *which smote him, was rebaptiz'd:*
Who gave him that Name Compounded as unluckie as it was Long;
MA:GORMISSabib namely restles or feare round about being no lesse then
great Brittains very *Motto:* Wherefore to make it good unto His Majestie two Names be attributed a Godfathers and Godmothers here:
toward his regeneration Baptized in their teares, for *Salt that is wanting.*
Now from *Samson: JAMES* SON derived, and also Mother *Rachels*
Name; hers added: drawne from *CHARLES,* to weare it for a Favour, as
long as he lives here; *weeping because they were Not,* or were lost, *would
not be comforted &c.*

    The Lyon become a Noted sheep; signifies: *for Rachell is a sheep,* but
herewith to give nevethelesse some comfort: *Thy Kingdome come &c.*
Then the only remedie when all is done; *Come Lord Jesus.* For what Thy
Kingdomes are come unto, none need to shew it: They speake for themselves, round about plainly: and thus *Samsons* story their state sets *forth,*
no newes either Your hangings and Tapstery makes it not a stranger, but
Common blind *Ale-houses* not without it, His lying in her Lapp a sleep,
whilst she pooles him &c.

    And without streining this *Legacie of his* too, besids those ropes puld
in pieces, which became as singed with fire. With His *Brazon Chains,* as
the one Stands for *Match,* the other toward your pieces of *Ordnance.*
Fastend this also on our *Effeminate* time, *his seven Locks,* Left to this last

140 (margin, line marker)

150 (margin, line marker)

Lines 132–34. **PASHUR…MA:GORMISSabib:** see Jer. 20:2–4.

Line 136. **Godfathers and Godmothers:** Although in Lady Eleanor's day both godmothers and godfathers attended a child's baptism, only the godfather named the child.

Line 137. **Baptized…wanting:** see Matt. 5:13.

Line 138. **Now…derived:** a rough anagram linking Samson to James's son, Charles. **Rachels:** an anagram of Charles; Rachel was the mother of Joseph and Benjamin (Gen. 35:24).

Line 140. **weeping…Not:** Rachel wept for her children (Matt. 2:18).

Line 142. **The Lyon…sheep:** The lion is the symbol of the British monarchy; "Rachel" is the Hebrew word for sheep.

Line 144. **Come Lord Jesus:** Rev. 22:20.

Lines 147–48. **Your hangings…Ale-houses:** The story of Samson and Delilah was frequently portrayed not only on tapestries and other wall hangings, but also on the walls of alehouses.

Line 149. **pooles:** pulls. Line 152. **Ordnance:** military supplies.

hundred yeare: shewing what weaving and curlling we have of FALSE-
HAIRE, by that going away of His, with the *Webbe* fastend to the
Beame; whose locks therein woven by her: who said; Thou sayest false,
(*or*) hast mocked mee, &c. Expressing *how men forbidden expresly long
Haire, yet the sonnes of God will weare it:* some of them looking thereby
more like the sonns of Divels.

And so farther, *for the green Withs and new ropes provided of old, long*   160
since for such Hellhounds, whose smoaking tongues as Links set on fire
already, notwithstanding RACHA, *he who cals his Brother so, he shall bee
in danger of a Counsell, &c.* and so much for those *Withs and ropes;*
unusefull neither for great *Brittains Navie and Taklings,* together with
Irelands Plow-Taklings and other uses, as aforesaid.

And neverthelesse like the *Plague-tokens* of their inevitable end: The
hastie Messengers, likewise so many *Judgements* sent forth suddenly
forerunners of the dreadfull daies approach: *All prepared alike to meete
the Son of God, as those Hoggish Gergesens, when all the Citie came out to
meete Him, and besought him to depart: And now truely fulfilled. The wed-*   170
ding is prepared, but they which were bidden, were not worthy, &c.
(Matth. 22.) *For nothing but in eating and drinking, and giving in Marriage, is this your hastening To his Comming? Cleansing your selves of all
filthinesse.* But returning to Times cutting off, which no more returns.
That great Man sealed in the forehead, or front with 1642. *Noahs dayes
even shall declare the meaning of that scentence from our* Saviours mouth;
that no flesh saved except those dayes be shortned, as much to say: *shall*

Lines 154–55. **FALSE-HAIRE:** the wigs often worn by the royalists; also false heirs, those
who claimed authority or property illegitimately.

Lines 157–58. **men...Haire:** 1 Cor. 11:14.

Line 161. **such Hellhounds...fire:** fiends like Cerberus, the three-headed dog who guarded
the underworld in Greek myth.

Lines 162–63. **RACHA...Counsell:** Matt. 5:22.

Line 164. **Taklings:** ships' rigging or horses' harnesses.

Line 169. **Hoggish Gergesens:** see Matt. 8:28–31.

Lines 173–74. **Cleansing...filthinesse:** 2 Cor. 7:1.

Line 175. **That great...1642:** see Rev. 7:3. Line 177. **no flesh...shortned:** Matt. 24:22.

come short of his dayes, at the time of the Deluge alluding to it, when all flesh perished, *except eight persons.*

In like manner from the *Incarnation*, (when *God became man, thought not scorne to take our Nature upon Himselfe,*) From which time to his second comming, Parrallels it Thus. But as the dayes *of Noah* were, so shall the comming *of the sonne of Man bee:* For as in the dayes *before the flood, untill the day Noah entered into the Arke. And knew not untill the flood came, and tooke them all away: So shall also the Comming of the Sonne of Man bee.* And so all before the comming of the last day also *forewarnd* to be, appeares plainly (*Matt.* 24.) Dated with the present yeare, 1642. *Two shalbe in the feild, two* Armes, to wit, *Two women shall be grinding at the* Mill, *&c.* and of our miserable devission, so much for a watch-word shall serve.

The seventh Angels Trumpet (*Revela.* 10.) give his voice on *Noahs side*, beside that Angell that set his *Right foot upon the sea, &c.* Whose feete as Pillars of fire: with that little Booke open in his hand: Even great *Brittains* revealed forewarning, That Ilands vissitation: *That there be some standing here not only, but throughout the World: that shall not tast death, till the day of Judgement.* And so take eate this little Booke, the sacrament of his comming at hand:

As herein is no small mistery Conteind too, twofold double Witnesse appearing like all the rest: *Judges the* 15.20. *verse, And he Judged Israell twenty yares, in the dayes of the Philistins, &c. verse* 31. and 16 Chap. *And he Judged Israell twenty yeares.*

Also, when the sonns of GOD became Tyrants, and carnall (*Gen* 6.) My spirit shall not strive alway with man: for that he also is flesh. *Namely, how great soever:* Yet his dayes shall bee an hundred and twenty yeares: It includes *Times reigne;* This twenty yeares to be put upon his last score. The Prophet *David* foresaw this weeke (*Psalm.* 90) *A thousand yares in his sight, are but as yesterday.* The Apostle *Peter: One day with the Lord, is as a Thousand yeares, and a Thousand yeares, as one day.* Daniel the Prophet, that Master of *Arrethmatitians:* confirms that weeke thus;

Line 181. **thought not scorne:** did not despise. Lines 182–86. **as...bee:** Matt. 24:37.
Lines 195–96. **some standing...Judgement:** Matt. 16:28. **eate...Booke:** Rev. 10:9.

He shall confirme his Covenant with many for a weeke, and in the middest 210
of the weeke oblation shall cease, &c. The Messiah slaine, and the Cities
Desolation, to wit; in the fourth Thousand yeare: Wherein not only
shewed *Messiah* his dayes cut off: but *Time,* the sonne of Eternitie, his
dayes too shortned: Even one Thousand yeares fulfilled, or compleat.
For the Gospels Progresse:

The 20. of the *Revela:* Thus speakes; *That they lived, and reigned with*
Christ, a Thousand yeares: before these Idolatryous times of late[. And]
therefore in respect of Time past, (our Saviours late comming Then)
The Apostle *Paul,* after this fashion admonisheth. *The Time is short,* as
much to say; *And to be shortned. For which cause, as if we possessed or* 220
enjoyed nothing Corinth.7.

And here adding but in a word or two, of the LORDS day; that also
cut off: how this *Samson* hath been shaffed: This *Samson-day,* how it
hath been observed and kept, after what spirituall fashion; Even the
LORDS house haunted by *Spirits of Divels,* no few amongst those
Tombes, &c. Holding their Spirituall-Courts there, whose daily Office,
and Occupation was, before their being cast out of *Pauls,* Either to
make many forsweare themselves; Or to fill Prisons, with those call'd by
them, *Puritans:* and now, *Rownd-Heads.* For which senslesse, rediculous
Name, not amisse with the Prophet, to bestowe these for a *Girdle:* 230
always to bee girded with feare, round about *MAGORMISSABIB:*
those Characters compounded of GOG, & MAGOG: Compassing the
Camp of the beloved Citie of the Saints: Whose number &c. *Revela.* 20.
consisting of *Papists,* the Queenes Armie, and prophaine *Protestants,*

Lines 210–11. **He…cease:** Dan. 9:27.

Lines 222–23. **the LORDS…off:** Lady Eleanor contends that Charles I encouraged violation
of the sabbath by reissuing the *Book of Sports* in 1633.

Lines 225–27. **Spirits…Pauls:** the bishops and other ecclesiastical officials who held church
courts at St. Paul's cathedral prior to 1641.

Line 228. **forsweare themselves:** The ecclesiastical courts required defendants to take the
oath ex officio and swear that they would answer all articles against them, and thus in effect
testify against themselves.

Line 229. **Rownd-Heads:** a derisive term applied to parliamentarians, many of whom were
critics of the church courts.

Line 232. **GOG, & MAGOG:** the nations which were to be deceived by Satan (Rev. 20:8).

before the day of *Judgement,* being let loose: These like *Herod* and *Pilate,* that were made friends, at variance before.

And wherewith observ'd, as it deserves no other, as others have serv'd God, professing themselves his servants, and going contrary: as it were your servant &c.: likewise by them as supposed. Their *Name* but used
240   for the abusing or betraying of their person; having first craftily gone about to cut the throats of so many: by giving them another *Name:* But to return; Thus this Sabboth too discarded: not onely Excommunicating the Lord *prophets and servants, &c.* but turned into a Day of Carding, and Diceing, with sweating *Pastimes: Goe for thy labour, sit downe and* spinne, *and* weave; plough, *and* ditch, *from henceforth in the sweat of thy face Eate thy bread: Come no more into the garden of God;* so much for harkening to the *Serpents* voice: The flaming Sword beware: *Neither be grieved with him,* crying; *O my sonne Absolom my sonne, my sonne Absolom.* (also) *O my sonne Absolom, O Absolom my sonne, my sonne:* The *Sab-*
250   *oths* double *Eclips:* as much to say, or twice Chang'd and alter'd: That harkend not to that voice rather, saying *verily my Saboths shall ye keepe, even he shall be cut off, that worketh thereon.* That day which was given *for* a perpetuall signe: *Exodus* 31. &c. No marvell or wonder therefore; our Houses though vissited by the Spoyler and Plunderer with our day-labour, turned into Daies and Nights-warding and watching.

Neverthelesse, not cut off without declaring in the place (of this *Judas-day,* more like then the *Resurrections*) a lawfull Successor herewith shewed, &c. upon *Mathias-day,* how the Lot fell in the yeare 1633. that Mundaies first day of the weeke. In which aforesaid yeare, the *Beast hee*
260   *also asscended then out of the bottomlesse Pit; The son of* perdition: The

---

Lines 235–36. **Herod and Pilate:** see Luke 23.

Lines 243–44. **Carding...Pastimes:** games that Charles I and his bishops permitted on the sabbath.

Line 246. **Come...God:** cf. Gen. 3:17–23. Line 248. **O...Absolom:** 2 Sam. 18:33.

Lines 253–55. **our Houses...watching:** cf. Matt. 24:42.

Lines 257–58. **Judas-day...Mathias-day:** Lady Eleanor's terms for the violated sabbath and its replacement; see Acts 1:15–26.

Line 259. **Beast:** reference to Laud, who was appointed archbishop of Canterbury in 1633; see Rev. 13.

last Arch *B.* gone to his owne place Now; by whom the word of God, in the Moneth *October* 23. was burnd, suffered Martyrdome by a Candle, *from his owne hand,* at the High-Commission board Sacrifiz'd. And at this time, two Armies striving in the fielde for Possession, and in *Barke-shire* and *Oxfordshire,* where the *Heavenly* voice was *heard first* at *Engle-field-house:* The *prime Shire* imediately *carried thereupon* to *Oxfords* Parliament *to bee published, &c.* In the *first yeare* of the Kings Raigne, it being a *Roule* a *manuscript, revealing* the day of Judgement, &c.

For which *Cause now* againe, a great *meeting of the Prophets;* as sometime in the daies *of John,* that *Conjunction then: Isaiah, 6. An ancient* Saint complaining thus, *Woe is mee, I am cut off,* (or undon) *because I am a man of uncleane lips, &c.* When as those Heralds of Armes present, *Each of them with six wings, twaine they covered their faces with, with twaine covered their feete, with twaine did fly: holy, holy, holy Lord of hostes; cryed one to another, &c. The whole earth is full of thy glory:* And here to bring these home to the dayes of *John,* in the *Revelation, &c.* prophecying to his *Time,* even to the end of the world; being *Times Voices expresly:* for no other then a third Sabath to be through the earth, as exprest by the foure *Beasts,* and foure *Evangelists,* &c. give all their voices also, saying; *holy, holy, holy, Lord God almightie, which was, which is, and which is to come:* And for more light in this matter; (*Revela.* 4.) *The seven Lamps of fire before the Throne, &c.* which are called the seven *Spirits:* signifie no other then *Munday,* to be a Spirituall day. (*Chap.*5.) Signified thus, *There stood a Lambe in the middest of the Elders, having seven eies, and seven horns, which are the seven* Spirits *of God, sent forth into all the earth:* To wit, *Sunday* the middle Sabbath; the *Eie,* as it were, to the *Gentels,* that great light for seventeene hundred yeares space.

270

280

Lines 261–63. **last Arch B.:** Archbishop Abbot, who died in 1633. **the word...Sacrifiz'd:** Laud's burning of Lady Eleanor's writing in 1633.

Line 268. **Roule...manuscript:** Manuscripts were sometimes in the form of rolls; cf. Ezek. 3:1.

Line 269. **great meeting...Prophets:** Lady Eleanor's description of Parliament; cf. Rev. 22:9.

Line 271. **Woe is mee:** Isa. 6:5–7. Lines 272–75. **those Heralds...glory:** Rev. 4:8.

Line 283. **Munday...day:** Lady Eleanor maintained, without an explicit scriptural basis, that the new sabbath of the Second Coming would be Monday.

Line 287. **Gentels:** Gentiles.

Likewise the Horns, the new Sabbath, *Munday*, as afore shewed: As the
one proclaiming the first *Resurrection* or comming; So the other the
290 Last, in the seventeth hundred yeares to be recal'd. And thus our eternall
Sabbath, & these Sabathdayes, both in one, sealed up in the little
Booke.

Farthermore, for an addition these; shewing beside how the Worlds
ages being cast into three parts. That had not those daies before the
Flood, been cut off or shortned; the Deluge had not been till *Noahs*
Death, which lived 300. Yeares after, &c. *Enoch* his walking with God,
confirms it: *Walked with God* 300 yeares after his begetting Children: as
much to say, weary *Time* three hundred yeares, Comes before his *Time*.
High time of such daies to be disburthened.

300 And to touch this New-day with a coale from the Altar, shewed also
the one even Munday purified, and the other remooved: As appeares in
that Massage sent *Herod,* who had shut up the Lords Messenger: Sonne
of *Herod* the great so Sir Nam'd, That be-headed Him: setting abroach
his *Blood* for his Birth-day: better he never had been borne: *John* of *too*
high a *spirit* to feed him with *flattery, tooke* our Saviour for *John* risen
againe, or some walking Spirit. The Lord sends him word of the *Resur-*
rection, saying; *go tell that FOX, behold I cast out Divels, and will heale to*
day, and to morrow, and the third day I shalbe perfected: Neverthelesse I
must walke to day, and to morrow, and the day following, &c. bids him
310 doe his worst; as much to say: which Ambassage,whether delivered it
were, or no, wee read not.

But doubtlesse for admonition spoken unto all spirituall *Herods,* neither being curious whether these came to her eare, indeavouring rather
to unlocke or open the meaning of that. How coming to passe, *Herod* or
Hayreod, to be Sur-named *Reynold the Fox.* Not onely because *John*
called our Lord, *Innocent Lambe,* made their prey, but his eare dedicated

---

Lines 295–96. **Noahs...Yeares:** Gen. 9:28. **Enoch:** see Gen. 5:22.

Line 300. **a coale from the Altar:** a coal left from a burnt offering on an altar; title of Peter
Heylyn's controversial tract (1636) defending Laudian policy concerning altars.

Lines 303–4. **Herod...Birth-day:** see Matt. 14. Lines 305–6. **tooke...againe:** Luke 9:7–9.

Line 307. **go tell that FOX:** Luke 13:32. Line 310. **Ambassage:** message.

Line 315. **Hayreod:** a rough anagram for Reynold, the crafty fox of satirical fables.

to her so, his *Dalilah*. Very likely he did weare some odde Locke, Fox-
tayle-like, a scourge, as it were, of hayre, portending how, together with
his Souldiers, our Saviour should be stript, scourged, despised, and
mocked by him.   320
Wherefore before that *Easter*, this word or mocke sent him, that
before had given his consent: Onely for a rash words sake (as made an
eye-winesse of his valour) to be-head such a one, for such a woman,
partly because of his alliance, &c. Then lessen himselfe. His greatnesse
makes himselfe a fire-brand of Hell rather: And although this Fox, the
first of that Name, is said to be exceeding glad to see *Jesus,* of whose
coming then questionlesse he was foretold, in that word sent unto him;
notwithstanding, to those questions of his, vouchsafed no answer at all.
As much to say, he had and would make good his word in the end, &c.
Thus shee in such obedience to her Mothers instruction; He standing in   330
as much awe of them both, those *Philippian* Dames. And so much for
an *Old Case* new reported.
And as in the Gospell the five Yoke of *Oxen*, these serves for
OXFORDS Meridian, which belong to His Majesties invitation: *Hath*
MARIED a wife, and cannot Come, &c. Yoak'd in the yeare, 1625.
unequally. Also that Term of *FOX,* or *OXFORD,* to wit: Ominous to
long Gownes; *Samson* Companion too crafty for him; afords them that
subject likewise to worke upon. So againe Lastly: What Lacke yee? Doe
you lacke Match, and Powder, or Cable-Ropes, or any Brasse &c.: Fetters toward Field-pieces, or long Haire any to weare? Or *Irish Withs?* Of   340
these as much as yee please: *SAMSON* is provided for you, Bound to
serve is, as long as he Lives. Even hee with those grinding Gun-powder.
That Mother and Daughter in the *GOSPELL: Two women shall be*
grinding &c. The last dayes watch-word, so much shall hereof suffice.
Onely these, (*Matt* 24.) Then *shall two bee in the Field, &c.* As it serves
for this yeare 1642. with the sevententh hundred yeare: So *Samsons*

Lines 330–31. **He…Dames:** see Matt. 14.   Line 333. **five Yoke of Oxen:** Luke 14:19.

Line 335. **Yoak'd…1625:** King Charles married Henrietta Maria in 1625; cf. Luke 14:19–20.

Line 337. **long Gownes:** worn by the scholars at Oxford.

Line 338. **What Lacke yee:** Luke 22:35.   Lines 343–44. **Two…grinding:** Matt. 24:41.

sacrificing here his Life. Hee bearing as it were, the gates of Hell and Death: Also, these beares date about this present *EASTER,* set forth in Honour of the glorious Resurrection, his Life, and End.

350   And hetherto from Thence &c. Your Silence on all sides, which concludes Consent: Wherefore I Conjure and Charge the aforesaid *Evill Spirits, or Legions, no more here to enter into this Kingdome from henceforth:* Goe downe into Hell, out into the farthest part of the Earth: *get thee hence, &c.* Glory, Honour, and Blessing.

From the Blessed *LADIE,*
her *Day* in *Lent, &c.*
1643.

None offer without *Priviledge,* to Re-print *These.*

Lines 351–53. **Evill…henceforth:** cf. Luke 8:29–30.

Lines 355–56. **LADIE…Day:** Lady Day; 25 March, Feast of the Annunciation of the Virgin Mary.

Lady Eleanor's title for this tract (Wing D2013) evokes the star that guided the wise men to Bethlehem to see the newly born Christ child. She regarded the Christmas story as a precedent for her own, seeing herself as the virgin whose books would announce the Second Coming. She also described Daniel's voice speaking to her in July 1625 as a "morning star." The wise are those who understand her message, in contrast to those who, in their self-asserted wisdom, claim she is mad. She presents the tract as a petition or address to Parliament and thus follows a course employed by many individuals and groups to obtain relief from grievances. The present edition of *Star to the Wise* is based on a copy in the Thomason Tracts in the British Library (shelf number E.76[28]), dated by Thomason 25 November.

THE STAR TO THE WISE.

To the high Court of Parliament,
THE HONORABLE *HOUSE* of *COMMONS:*
THE Lady *ELEANOR* her Petition; Shewing
cause to have her Book Licensed,
BEING
The Revelations *Interpretation.*

Malachy 4.2.
*For unto you who fear my Name, shall the Sun of
Righteousnesse arise with healing in his wings.*

The Star to the wise.

To the High Court of Parliament,
The Honorable House of Commons;

The Lady Eleanor *her Petition, &c.*

Happy Reader and Hearer; for so he who reads, and keeps the words of
this last Prophecy, revealed to be at last: The Revelations shewing
Things which shall shortly come to passe: And as the golden leaves of
that fruitfull Tree, shewed to be for the healing of the Nations, *Their
Blessed Peace-maker,* saying, *And there shall be no more curse:* So the
whole Prophecy directed unto our Nation, provided for these dayes of
ours; That Soveraign Plaister, when such unnaturall Division, sowed by
the old Serpent; The very foul Disease of the *Kings-Evil,* &c. saying
therefore, *I Jesus have sent my Angel.* And so, touching Malignant
humors, for the most part resorting about the Ears, in which parts, not
a little dangerous; wherefore, *He that hath Ears to hear, let him hear;*
being the burthen of every charge, to the Churches, concluded therewith; proclaiming his coming to be shewed aforehand to his servants,
saying, *I am Alpha and Omega, the first and the last;* The Lord of Sabbath; as evident, by holding the *seven* stars in his right hand; and That
Book sealed with *seven* Seals, like *Pharaohs* Dream doubled, even the
established time; and so many dayes as from the *first Adam* to the flood
of waters, so from the *second Adam* to the fiery Lake, That flood of Fire
and Brimstone; And therefore the second Death so called.

And as that Token set in the clouds: The streightned Bow that bound
himself thereby, so here crowned with the Bow, bindes it with an Oath,
By him that lives for ever, That Time shall be no longer. But as the seventeenth hundred yeer revealed to *Noah,* shews Times mystery contained

10

20

Lines 3–4. **golden…Nations:** Rev. 22:2.

Line 7. **Soveraign:** effective, curative. **Plaister:** plaster; medicinal bandage.

Line 8. **the old Serpent:** Satan. **the Kings-Evil:** scrofula, a disease which was believed to be
curable by a monarch's touch; also the wrongs brought on by the king, Charles I.

Line 11. **He that hath Ears:** see Rev. 2–3. Lines 15–16. **That Book…Seals:** see Rev. 5.

Line 16. **Pharaohs…doubled:** see Gen. 41.

Line 18. **the second Adam:** Christ. **the fiery Lake:** Hell.

Line 20. **The streightned Bow:** the rainbow; see Gen. 9:13.

in that little open Book; (The shortnesse of Time) also revealed to be
before the end: Even the days of Baptisme, likewise how long preached,
to such disobedient spirits; as farther by *his right foot on the waters,* and
his left on the earth: The times measured, the first *Noahs* dayes, by the
second *Noahs* dayes: to wit, in the seventeenth Century, his coming in
the clouds, who rewards every one according to his service; For the
name of a Christian serves not; But his end worse then his beginning.   30
That after the House swept and garnished, with *seven* foul spirits that
goeth and berayeth it. And afar off, as in the one bewrayed, how long
the preaching to the last of Baptisme, as here in alluding to those dayes;
By *sevens* when every clean, &c. entred into the *Ark,* By the unclean
seven spirits entred into him, whose end worse then his beginning. So
he expresly speaks in another place of the worlds begining and end, to
know one by another: *As the dayes of Noah were, so shall the son of mans
dayes be also;* As the dayes before the Flood, One thousand seven hundred yeers; as much to say, To both alotted alike. And so in *Luke* the
Eleventh, a touch given going afore, for better discerning the time;   40
when they said, *He by the Devil cast out Devils.* Much like now, as to
beleeve that an army of another Religion should come to defend the
true Religion. Where the end of Antichrists Kingdom, shewed also further, By such a King, as it were against himself divided; or a man possest, that goes about to make away himself.

And had the old world warning; and are the last dayes cast out of
remembrance; and is his Promise come utterly to an end? Though saying, *Ye shall not see me, till ye say, Blessed is he that comes in the Name of
the Lord.* And behold, *I will send you Elias before the great and dreadfull
day;* as *Eli* signifying the Name of God, &c.   50

And so much for those dayes, when the sons of God took them wives
of the Daughters of men, taken with their Sorceries.

And this yet held a sencelesse thing, or a fancie to expect it: Though

---

Line 26. **his…waters:** see Rev. 10:2.   Lines 27–28. **the second Noah:** Christ.

Line 31. **That…spirits:** Matt. 12:44–45.

Line 32. **berayeth:** disfigures.   **bewrayed:** revealed.

Line 42. **army…Religion:** The Scots, with whom the English Parliament had just made a
treaty, practiced a different form of Protestantism than did the English.

Line 49. **Elias:** Elijah (Mal. 4:5).

shewed, even thus it shall be when the son of man shall be revealed, (*Luke* 17) like giving in marriage, and revelling: And with such Buildings and Plantations &c. a fair warning to prepare for it.

And cursed *Jericho* that burnt with fire *seven* dayes, or a weeks warning that had, where *Rahab* saved her Fathers house there, by a Line for token, &c. And was the hand-writing at that Feast, sent to him, He of
60   that first Monarchy, the last of them, who was weighed in the Ballance, &c. and found a lost Body, &c. And by reading the Prophet *Jeremiahs* Books: He that understood then the number of those yeers, that *seventy* yeers should be accomplished in *Jerusalems* desolation: Wherefore not by reading now of that Book, where bidden, *Let him that hath understanding, count the number of the Beast,* 666. &c. To understand also, how long the Churches captivity under spirituall *Babylon:* The Antichristian Monarchy, and aged now 43. and 1600. Even as signified in his *seven* heads, and Ten horns, those crowned: his age, So in her whores forehead, written too that Name of hers: Not of the blessed Virgins giv-
70   ing, of a certain; and so much for that. He ridden, and ruled so long by her, no longer to be indured: and which great Harlots City, not unknown. Beginning here, with the everlasting Gospel, shewing, as coming to passe in *Augustus* his Taxin dayes, there sending forth his Decrees to have all the world Taxt. That second *Cæsar,* when he the second person in Trinity, came to pay the Ransome of all; Also in his Raign, those Taxing dayes of his, Not over the world unknown: These Burthens never so imposed, before He the second of *Great Britains Monarchy:* Likewise revealed the second coming of our Lord, when that time comes to passe: *And good will towards Men, Peace on Earth.*
80   So farther with That past, comparing This troublesome time: When

---

Lines 58–59. **Rahab…token:** see Josh. 2, 6:17. **the hand-writing at that Feast:** see Dan. 5.

Lines 62–63. **seventy yeers:** see Jer. 25:11.

Line 67. **aged…1600:** Lady Eleanor was writing in 1643 when Charles I was forty-three.

Lines 68–69. **So…hers:** see Rev. 17:5.

Line 73. **Augustus:** Augustus Caesar, Roman emperor (Luke 2:1).

Lines 74–75. **second Cæsar:** Augustus. **second…all:** Christ (1 Tim. 2:6).

Lines 77–78. **second…Monarchy:** Charles I.

all the city so troubled, and He who mockd with God, faining He would worship him, was himself mockd; after they made of his Counsell, having sent them to *Bethlehem,* &c. in revenge fell upon poor Innocents, under such an age spared none; who to that Fox returnd not any more, but went another way, supposing before their God they should have obeyed him: Whose Treasure then they laid it at his feet; given as it were to the Churches use; made their Omage there.

And in city and country, early and late, such keeping watch by day and night both, to keep out wolves inwardly, those late Bishops; as when the watchfull Shepherds visited, and were told where they should finde *The Lamb of God:* And the Churches watchmen likewise assembled. Wherefore as Thou *Bethlehem,* not the least, so inferior to none of *Great Britains* Villages, Thou KNIGHTS-BRIDGE by Name; for such service of thine, found worthy to afford such a Plaister, *To the Honorable* KNIGHTS and BURGESSES in the Commons House, which was delivered by their worthy Speaker; Being made of the root of *Jesse* and pure Oyl-olive, & from the Hospitall of the diseased and dismembred, not distant far, doubtlesse remembred all those maimed in Gods service and slain, in preferring This place, made the receptacle of His Sacred Oracle, that oyntment.

Where the *Spittle* and the *Bridge,* in those Letters signified, *the Spirit and the Bride;* & as *Bethlehem, The House of Bread,* signifying, &c. so, *Let him that is athirst, come:* for here, *The wedding of the Lamb, The offspring of David;* Even as the inseparable Witnesses in the Sacrament: Those places where the Word of God resides, like the Bread & Cup.

90

100

Lines 81–84. **He...Fox:** Herod (Matt. 2 and Luke 13:32).

Lines 90–91. **watchfull...God:** Luke 2:8–11.

Line 92. **Bethlehem:** Hospital of St. Mary of Bethlehem, the London mental hospital known as Bedlam.

Line 93. **KNIGHTS-BRIDGE:** London suburb where Lady Eleanor was living in 1643.

Line 96. **root of Jesse:** Jesus claimed to be descended from Jesse, David's father.

Lines 97–98. **Hospitall...far:** King Edward III had made a grant for such a hospital in Knightsbridge.

Lines 101–2. **the Spittle:** a house for the reception of the poor and diseased. **the Spirit and the Bride:** see Rev. 22:17.

And thou *Hide-Park,* none of the greatest, yet makes up the Harmony, before the wedding all rejoicing; The trees of the Wood also utter their ayrie voice, where the Court of Guards service weil worth the marking and observation; those Bulwarks there so watcht round about; and here to proceed with the everlasting Word of God; there the flaming sword also; the Tree of Life guarded thereby, which turns every way on the East of it; and as it were the Cherubims returnd, displaying in the air their golden wings, those Colours of theirs; like as the Man, when droven out to till the ground from whence he was taken; and so the *Thorn,* and the *Thistle,* and *Herb* of the Field, his portion with his Wife, sent away in their Buff-coats and skins, to take their progresse.

In vain neither those Pales pluckt up, laid open that Inclosure; for every one to make their Fuell of it: But the fore-runner of the little Books disclosing, the day of Judgements time discovered, Times race or finishd, &c. and so of those inlarged Horns of the *seven*-headed Beast, ranging without meane or measure, crownd with so many Crowns, *The mystery of Time there but sets forth.*

And *Britain* derived from *Brute,* having the *Beasts Name* as it were, and left the good angels, nothing ever since *Prospering* or *Thriving;* shewing also how He to *Oxford* now droven to go, a Prototype or figure of Time, sealed in his very brows or forehead, being aged 43. And thus as he participates of Times age like it. So tyrant Time to be no longer; but in the seventeenth hundred yeer cut off; a copartner with him, of his Estate also and Condition, which in the seventeenth yeer was expelled of his Raigne forborn so long.

And thus, as the way shewed where kept now the Tree of Life; so farthermore of what nature it is; a Tree hard and stony, the Fruit not to be medled with, or toucht at first; though none more mellow and soft then

---

Line 106. **Hide-Park:** Hyde Park; a public park in London.

Line 108. **ayrie:** airy; lofty. **weil:** well. Lines 110–11. **the flaming sword:** see Gen. 3:24.

Lines 113–14. **Man...out:** Adam, driven out of the garden of Eden.

Line 116. **Buff-coats:** naked, without clothing; also the attire of soldiers.

Line 117. **Pales pluckt up:** stakes or fence pulled up.

Line 123. **Brute:** Brutus, legendary founder of Britain, supposedly a great-grandson of Aeneas, the Trojan who had founded Rome.

Line 125. **He:** Charles I.

it afterward; and because of a restraining vertue, its good Name taken away, like the Medlars crowned fruit miscalled.

And so another place belonging to the city, in these dayes of such distraction, worthy to be thought upon, *Bethlehems* Hospitall, *Their House of Bread;* for the witlesse sent to This, as the Wisemen to the other, those Sages, &c. in some respects to That not inferior, where some Barn or the like, made the Bed-chamber of the blessed Lady; and He there 140 born, our Bread from heaven, and for a signe given the Shepherds, of his racking on the crosse, that was put into the Rack or Manger; and by a Woman aforehand anointed; and other like signes and tokens.

Whether these betoken nothing too, appeal to the wisdom of our age; or to be such an unlikely thing; that he who wrote that brotherly Epistle (going before the *Apocalypse*) to a Lady, saying, *He had many things to write unto her.* Whatsoever it was which appears not there, but referred to another time or meeting; That from another Lady, *The Revelations Interpretation* of her writing, should be sent to Divines for their assent to the same, written by that Divine, &c. where such a meeting of 150 theirs, in a time of so much distraction of the Church.

Where touching or importing an inspiration; what phrase of speech more meet and proper, then that of, *Mouth to Mouth; That our joy may be full?* for a full expression of our Lords coming to be revealed to a woman; That secret disclosed.

And *the wind blowing where it lists;* wherefore not serving to bring these about from the Isle of *Patmos,* to *Great Britains* Islands, when testified he cometh, he cometh. The Islands may be glad therof, &c. *Psal.* especially at such a time of perplexity and woe; and for the redemption of wounded prisoners too, so miserably relieved, and others for their 160 hurts and maims, disabled ever to help themselves.

Wherefore then not to be revealed to us, before others in such case:

Line 135. **Medlars:** the brown, apple-like fruit of the medlar tree, eaten only when decayed.

Lines 140–41. **He...heaven:** John 6:35.

Line 142. **racking on the crosse:** stretching apart, torturing. **Rack:** a holder for fodder; a place where prisoners are held; a means of torture.

Line 144. **betoken:** mean. Lines 145–46. **he...Epistle:** St. John the Evangelist (2 John).

Line 148. **another Lady:** Lady Eleanor.

Lines 153–54. **Mouth...full:** see 2 John 12, Geneva Bible.

and as soon to his handmaids as his menservants; the spirit of God to be poured on them: and so now, as well as then, when she had the first happy sight of him, after his rising, which was sent to tell and inform them where they should meet him *first:* and what odds between *seven* Churches visited, or sent unto: and *Henry* the sevenths Chappell, in such a Church: and in the seventeenth hundred yeer of Grace; where the *Assembly of Ministers,* &c. sitting in that place, dedicated or conse-
170 crated to his memory; whose sons Royall Issue so soon reedified or reformed the Church so much gone to decay; renewed in such a short space of Time, The Scriptures buried in another Language, Life not only infused into them; but sent forth as far West, as even East in former dayes.

And now in the West, to us since this thing to be revealled, (the Mis-terie of the Lord of Sabbaths Coming) wherefore to *Westminster,* Not directed too: where the Kingdoms Great Counsell meeting shewed there where they shall meet *Him* coming in the Clouds.

And of late the Red Rose and the White also, By the scriptures that
180 were delivered out of thraldom, how soon reconciled, being disunited before: The *Bread and Cup in the Lords Supper* reunited, having been judgled away By the old Serpents policie, because bidden to divide it,

---

Line 163. **as soon...handmaids:** see Joel 2:29.

Line 164. **she:** Mary and Mary Magdalene (Matt. 28).

Lines 166–67. **seven...sent unto:** Rev. 2–3. **Henry...Chappell:** at Westminster Abbey.

Line 169. **Assembly of Ministers:** At Westminster in 1643 some English clergy, a few laymen, and some Scottish observers met to reform the church. They prepared a new order of worship, the *Directory for the Public Worship of God,* to replace the *Book of Common Prayer.*

Lines 170–71. **whose sons...Church:** Henry VII's son, Henry VIII, and his children, especially Edward VI and Elizabeth.

Line 172. **The Scriptures...Language:** Henry VIII authorized the translation of the Bible from Latin into English.

Line 177. **the Kingdoms Great Counsell:** Parliament.

Line 179. **Red...White:** used to symbolize respectively the royal houses of Lancaster and York which, in the fifteenth century, fought against one another for the English throne.

Line 181. **The Bread...reunited:** Prior to the Reformation only clergy took both wine and bread at the sacrament; afterwards the laity did also.

Line 182. **judgled:** juggled; made to disappear by magic.

The Cup amongst them, as other allowance have none for it. So begins with the one first, intending not to forbear the other long: *Eves* Daughters moved for their sake, layes hold of the fruitfull Vine, whose Embleme, those Branches to keep within their own walls: or because the Spirit *first* moved upon the waters, And he in hold now himself the very Antichristian Serpent, by whose crooked unluckey, hands kindled this Kingdoms cruell Combustion again: shewed how Gods word *first,* even that burnt by him, together with the revealed last coming: the Handwriting applied to this Nation, being Sealed therewith, that Seal Manual. To *Belshazzar* that was sent heretofore. And now whether his Kingdoms: He which was so much incensed hereat, be Divided and Numbred, or he absent and found wanting, or this be proved a false alarme sent to him, who tatken With *Belshazers* loosenesse, the occasion of this befalne him: as for more proof of it, Moreover, &c.

Moreover of the Holy Oracle, that Handwrighting *reinterpreted by her for an express signe, Which in the yeer 1633 was to the* Elector Palsegrave *Dedicated upon the letters of his name* The palme of the Hand, &c. Charles Be: *for* Belshazer: *bidden beware the Hands of the* Medesis: *and he being after so imprisoned in* France. *With the premises referred to the worlds judgement: What mould* Pharaohs *heart made of, whether the Handwriting hath not been fullfilled and double, Brittains Blowe.*

And as of late came to passe these: So let his repentance come to late, when praying it were to do again, give him for his doings, of that Sop his belly full, till his Bowels gush out with that arch Traytor, his fellow *Judas,* let the Executioner be without his fees no longer: his Gown and Girdle, Win it and wear it, who hath drawn this Curse upon us: and for

190

200

Lines 189–90. **Gods…him:** Laud's burning of Lady Eleanor's writing in 1633.

Lines 191–92. **Seal Manual:** the sign manual, a small seal with which the king authorized documents; cf. Rev. 5:1.

Line 198. **the Elector Palsegrave:** Charles I's nephew, Charles Louis, elector of the Palatinate, to whom Lady Eleanor had dedicated *Given to the Elector* (1633—page 59 in this edition).

Line 200. **Medesis:** Medicis, the family of the Queen Mother of France, Charles I's mother-in-law, known for their Catholicism and involvement in European politics.

Line 202. **What… made of:** cf. Exod. 7:3.

Lines 206–7. **that…Judas:** Laud, whom Charles I had appointed archbishop.

whose cause (with those companions of his) these fleeing the very place
210   where they sat: here repair to the Second House for this Licence for the
Lambe and the Bride, She having made her self ready, like *Joseph* and
Mary, but betroathed as yet, this pair: So the other House of Parliament:
Our Saviours second Coming assigned to them, to give Order for this
his Licence, In due consideration of a Sihne, or the twelve Signes given
rather for a token, as not unknown to both houses, &c. Which was
delivered to their Speaker (taken out of the Revelation, Chap. 12.) *And*
there appeared a great signe in Heaven: a woman Clothed with the Sun and
the Moon under her feet: And upon her head a Crown of twelve Stars.
Interpreted this way: The *Celestiall Woman* clothed with the Sun, to wit,
220   the Suns entring in *Virgo,* the bowels and belly: Shewing the time of the
Churches great deliverance, about Michaelmas to give her enemies for
ever the overthrowe: as signified by *Michaels* victory and the Dragons
fall, and which piece of Scripture thus expounded, be presented to them
in the moneth of August. Not unlike that of *Jonas* in the *Whales* belly,
that signe of the *Resurrection* then as this now of the *generall time* at
hand.

And thus his Eexcellencie here, the Generall for the House of Parliamets defence, as that Archangel signifying Ezcellent to omong the
Angels, and by War in heaven. The Division of tha high Cout set forth
230   where *Saint John* ascends a degre higher then the Prophet *Daniel* speaking likewise of the troubled time of the end: Thus, *And they that turn*
many to Righteousnesse *shall shine as the Stars in the Firmament,* the *Par-*

Lines 210–11. **repair...Bride:** The House of Lords would be responsible for trying
Archbishop Laud, whom the House of Commons had impeached, and thus for preparing the
way for the Second Coming (Rev. 21).

Line 212. **other House of Parliament:** the House of Commons.

Line 220. **Virgo:** the Virgin, an astrological sign.

Line 221. **Michaelmas:** 29 September, Feast of St. Michael the Archangel, who was
responsible for saving the believers from Satan.

Line 224. **Jonas...belly:** Jon. 1:17.

Lines 227–30. **the Generall:** the earl of Essex; also Michael the Archangel. The words
"Eexcellencie", "Parliamets", "Ezcellent", "omong", "tha", "Cout", and "degre" are printed here
as spelled in the base text.

Lines 231–32. **And...Stars:** Dan. 12:3.

liaments signification, *The Firmament* firm for ever: as much to say, To sit there fixt, &c. as they, *Daniel* and *John,* joyned in Commission for these dayes.

And so the day of Judgements Epitomy, This Battell here in heaven amongst us here before his coming, that testifies he rewards every one according to his work; as they have done by others, even served with the same themselves; Their *toes pared too,* taken lower.

And shall our loins be girt, and lights burning to prevent bodily dan- 240
ger, so much preparation: And shall all be in such security, when that dreadfull time, and no signe at all then on the posts of our doors: But the destroyer coming into houses of his servants also: When a[t] the Devils storming, because he knows he hath but a short time, shews expresly the time is to be foreknown.

And the Nations angry for that time of wrath come; The time of the dead to be judged (*Rev.* 11) shews the Churches Intelligence aforehand of that time; far be it from us to be like the deaf Adder; That because once accursed for harkning when forbidden. Therefore to forbear, charm the Word of God never so strongly and sweet; like the blinde 250
Jews under colour of shunning Idolatry, and the like, that fell to be such Blasphemers of God.

Preaching ye have alway, and may hear them when ye please, and their large Dedicatories and Volums may License them daily: But the little Book,The Spirit of Prophesie, Not alway that.

And lastly, here for testifying the burthen of the Word of the Lord revealed to her, by so many voices with one consent, shewed as follows, touching this Firstling the Word of God, where and when the same came to her: In the *first* yeer of his Raign, when His first Parliament called at *Oxford.* Whether he now returnd; a great voice from Heaven 260
then, speaking to her, revealing in what yeer the day of Judgement; and

---

Line 234. **Daniel...Commission:** The Book of Daniel and John's Book of Revelation describe what will happen at the time of Judgment.

Line 236. **Epitomy:** epitome; representation or summary.

Line 239. **Their toes pared too:** Judg. 1:6–7. Line 246. **the Nations...come:** Rev. 11:18.

Line 248. **like the deaf Adder:** Ps. 58:4. Lines 254–55. **the little Book:** Rev. 5:1.

Line 257. **her:** Lady Eleanor. Line 259. **first Parliament:** in July 1625.

so at what time of the yeer, or how long that time; she the Daughter of the *first* Peer or Baron, her *first* Husband the Kings *first* Sergeant, &c.

And in *Berkshire,* the first of Shires at her house at *Englefield,* about the end of July; which moneth, nam'd after the *first* Emperour, heard the voice of God there.

And for publishing the same, from thence went immediatly to *Oxford,* that *first* University; To the Parliament then delivering the tydings of the end revealed, &c. in a Writing given to the prime Bishop
270 *Abots;* which being printed, was afterward burnt by his Successour in his *first* yeer, 1633. whose Passe given him before, &c. and with this Signe annext to it, That the great Plague presently should cease, which came but to its height the next Week after.

And so came to passe, after that Weeks great Bill, which amounted to Five thousand six hundred or neer, being the *first* Week of *August,* 1625. as it were the Worlds age, The mysticall Weeks reckoning.

And then so suddenly vanished, that before a Moneths end, or there-about, scarse any token or appearance thereof, the City so long shut up, open again in a manner cleer.

280 Thus from that presaging place or Name of *Englands* bloody Field: *Englefield* neer *Reading*-Town, where the Term kept, that remarkable yeer, for so many Examples of Extraordinaries produced.

And now where the day of Judgement, the great Day of Battels approach (as hath bin declared) was proclaimed, &c. There in those two very Shires, of Berkshire or Birchshire) and in Oxfordshire. What we have not so much as heard the half of, others have by wofull experience felt the waight of it. Where two such Bodies of Armies so large, Whose

---

Lines 262–63. **she…Baron:** Lady Eleanor's father claimed that he was first among the barons at the coronation of King James. **her…Sergeant:** Sir John Davies.

Line 265. **first Emperour:** Julius Caesar.

Lines 269–70. **prime Bishop Abots:** Archbishop Abbot of Canterbury.

Line 274. **great Bill:** Bill of Mortality, a weekly report of deaths in London and the surrounding area.

Line 278. **City…up:** People fled from London or took refuge in their homes during the outbreak of plague.

last Blow, after that cruell Fight, was within a bowe-shot of the afore said House of *Englefield:* at Theill village; and these belonging to this place of Scripture, wherefore worthy of notice, Luke the 17. *Where Lord shall thy Coming be revealed:*) when replyed, *Where the bodie is the Eagles will resort.* As Gods Word without a high and heavy hand never digested, or obtaining passage, but like the Passeover, ever eaten with bitter Herbes, That Fast of the Lambe.

The Raven is sent forth before the Dove, likewise before him: That same that had his raiment of Camels hair, girt with a Letherne girdle coming before him, in whose Coat, not so much as a seam. And Here the still, or soft voice sent with everlasting peace, the last, before the good time bring the true Olive Leaf.

POSTSCRIPT. Revela.

And here The Cup none debard of it: He that is athirst Let him Come, &c.

Knights-Bridge, November. 1643.

Lines 288–89. **within...village:** at the Battle of Newbury.

Lines 295–97. **The Raven...Dove:** see Gen. 8:7–8. **That same...seam:** John the Baptist and Jesus.

Line 298. **the still...sent:** 1 Kings 19:12. Line 299. **true Olive leaf:** see Gen. 8:11.

This maternal blessing to a daughter (Wing D1991) stands out against the numerous examples of fathers' benedictions to their sons that survive among papers from aristocratic families of Lady Eleanor's day. Here, as elsewhere in her tracts, Lady Eleanor combines the personal and the prophetic. Motherhood was important to her, and although she described her books as her babes, letters attest that the attention she gave to her prophetic writings did not interfere with her affectionate relationship with Lucy, her only surviving child. In 1649, in *The new proclamation* (Wing D1998), she explicitly acknowledged Lucy's contribution to prophecy by printing Lucy's answer to her own letter inquiring about the translation of Philippians 2:6. She dedicated another tract, *Sions Lamentation* (Wing D2012B—page 271 in this edition), to her daughter in that same year, on the occasion of the death of Lucy's eldest son. In *Her Blessing* Lady Eleanor conflates the biblical story of Jacob and his sons (Gen. 29–45) with that of Britain's James I, and the beasts of Daniel's vision (Dan. 7) with the beasts that heralds used in coats of arms to indicate genealogy. The present edition of *Her Blessing* is based on a copy in the Thomason Tracts in the British Library (shelf number F. 10[1]). Thomason dated it 23 September 1644.

FROM THE LADY ELEANOR, HER BLESSING

TO HER BELOVED *DAUGHTER*, The Right HONORABLE *LUCY*, COUNTESSE OF Huntingdon

The Prophet DANIELS *Vission*: Chap. 7. *In the first yeare of* Belchazer *REX, &c.*

FROM THE LADY ELEANOR, HER *BLESSING*
to Her beloved Daughter, &c.

Whose new Interpretation, not with *Froath* filled up, or Interlarded
with differing Opinions of others, such old peices having No affinity
and agreement *with* this BRITISH *garments* or displayed COATE *by*
blessed Prophets pend: So what the *Veritie* of those *fouer great Beasts,*
divers one *from* another, *which should arise &c. Who so would understand*
& know their mistery for this very time reserved, hitherto with the *King-*
dome of Heavens great seale shut up.

Distinguishing not only *Nations* but *Times:* The very truth of it:
N'other then the severall Coate, Armes, *given or borne by him,* the first
of great *Brittains Kingdoms or Monarchie.*

Not unlike *Jacobs united Familie his Wives Children, and Children of*
the Hand-maids. The aforesaid Crowns foure, *concerning whose peice of*
super-artificiall Heraldry unknown to those Heralds of the King of great
Babylon (Dan. 3.) even at hand proclame the ancient of dayes, *the*
aproach of that great day of his. So goe thy way Daniel, *for the words are*
closed up and sealed till the time of the end, which: *Not only the Time,* but
unfolds unto what *Nation* or *Language,* revealed those glad Tydings, as
by the Word (Sealed) given to understand thereby. *Even where the great*
Seale the Impression thereof, those fouer Coates or Beasts, *styled Kings*
which shall arise, &c. And the *Coine* stampt therwith and the like, &c.

And so the first *in the likenesse of a Lyon with Eagels wings, &c.* first
displays the armes of *England* and *France,* and then *standing upon the*
feet like a man, a Lyon rampant (to wit) *Scotlands coate,* where the other

---

Line 1. **Interlarded:** interspersed or interlayered.

Line 3. **COATE:** outer garment; coat of arms; clothing indicating one's profession.

Lines 9–10. **first…Monarchie:** James I (1603–1625).

Line 12. **Crowns foure:** James I and Charles I claimed to rule over England, Scotland, France, and Ireland.

Lines 18–19. **great Seale:** the wax emblem or mark used in England to signify royal authorization of documents. **styled:** called or given the name of.

Line 20. **Coine stampt:** Coins bore the royal coat of arms.

Line 22. **armes…France:** The English lion and the French *fleur-de-lis* appeared in the first and fourth quarters of the British royal coat of arms in Lady Eleanor's day. The Scottish arms appeared in the second quarter, and the Irish in the third.

Line 23. **rampant:** standing on one hind leg, as the lion appeared on the arms of England.

the *Irish* Instrument, or Harpe evident also out of Tune, &c. That no need to say, *I am Joseph,* or over-verball to be in this case.

No more requisit then their asking either whether or no thy sonns coate this of so many colours or peices, as in the field, now those inumerable colours, &c. That were HE living, our Father *JACOB* would say, *some evill beast had devoured us,* to behold such blood shed amongst brethren and cruelty, as Since the Creation such a flood, the old *Serpent* never casting out of his mouth, and so like *Joseph sold to the Midianits,* our wofull estate, sale and rapine made, *by Malignant* brethren *&c.* But such miserable Shipwracke with us being no news, shall returne to those misteries of *Heraldry.*

The frequent Oraments of your House wherefore to explain them farther, but needlesse; nor endlesse Figures *here borrowed out of old Orators Bookes,* suffices for figurative Demonstrations such, *to render their meaning truly, running the way of the plaine rather for the ancient of dayes his comming to prepare the way.* So *for my Commission thus.*

And farther as to you not unknown especially at what time your Mother became a Writer or Secretary, concerning the unsealing or interpreting this obscure peice to open *the Vission of Daniel, though no obscure persons of the seed of the KINGS and of PRINCES.* Even in the yeere 1625. undertaken this burthen, following his steps, who declares when *HE* wrote first in *BELCHAZARS* first yeere, the last of those *Caldeans* of great Babylon.

Also shewed in that great plague yeere, when the City shut up: This Vission then opened, *whereof even* Then a Signe *or* Token, *not without a touch* given *in those* words. But *thou O Daniel shut up &c. (Dan.*12) And thus where every word a *mistery,* cannot passe over *them,* as none of the least His being so often saluted or stiled so highly of the *Angel: O Daniel greatly beloved man,* as much to say too, *O KING of great Britaine!* as Kings and Prophets; Brethren, *Let him that reads* Daniel *understand.*

And as it extends to this time also, beares Date forty foure; directly

---

Line 25. **Joseph:** Jacob's son.

Lines 29–30. **such...brethren:** in the English civil wars.

Line 35. **Oraments:** possibly a pun that invokes oratory (public speaking or place of prayer); possibly a misprint for "ornaments," including coats of arms.

the present *Yeare* as these beareing Record of time and place, &c. of whose storming daies thus. *And Daniel spake and said, I saw and behold upon the great* Sea, *the foure Winds strove,* and foure great Beasts *came up, divers one from another* (to say) *from beyond sea,* the occasion of such divission, ready to be swallow'd up in these swelling Seas.

60   *The first like a* LYON, *and Eagels wings,* (Daniel 7.) *I beheld till the* Wings *were pluckt thereof: And lifted up from the Earth, and made stand upon the* Feete *like a MAN:* And *a MANS* HEART *was given unto it,* viz. The LYONS Passant (*regardant*) turn'd into the Rampant, &c. After her decease, a *Virgin* Princesse of renown'd *MEMORY, ENGLAND* stil'd great Britaine, and then these foure severall *Coates* given, &c.

    (And this Sayling on; or pursuing *the* Subject:) *And behold another* Beast, a *second like to a* BEARE, *and it raised it selfe upon one side: And had three* Ribbs *in the mouth of it, between the teeth of it.* N'other then as it were displayed *The three* LYLLIES: The *Armes of FRANCE,* to the full 70 given by this KINGDOME, where Nothing but a meere Shadow, or the bare Coate of it Left, *Leaves in stead of Fruite:* Besides, how by a She-Beare, as this N'other: Three devided KINGDOMS rent in peices. The *Ribbe* or *Side,* beares Witnesse thereof, The second *SEXE* its Character.

    And so farther from *This saying, too well prooved; (Arise and devoure much* FLESH:) even what *Date* it bears needlesse to say: *Her MOTTO the Mother not of the* Living *Child,* but of *Divissions and* Massacres, *where* inclusive the ador'd *Sacrament* called the *MASSE:* Thus uttered Her Voice, *Let it bee neither Thine,* nor *Mine, but devide it: destroy it utterly, &c.* No such *Coate* then, like to have any Affinitie with *Solomons* 80 Ivory Rament or Robe: as the *Ensigne of Peace, the* LILLY *of the field,* but

---

Line 55. **present Yeare:** 1644.

Line 63. **LYONS Passant (regardant):** In heraldry a beast passant had the right foreleg raised as if walking; a beast regardant was looking back over its shoulder.

Line 64. **Virgin Princesse:** Queen Elizabeth I.

Line 69. **LYLLIES…FRANCE:** the *fleur-de-lis,* which are irises, not lilies.

Lines 71–72. **She-Beare:** Lady Eleanor believed that Charles I's queen, Henrietta Maria, a French princess, was responsible for Britain's troubles.

Line 76. **Mother…Child:** see 1 Kings 3:16–28.

Line 77. **the ador'd…MASSE:** Lady Eleanor's view of Catholic beliefs.

Line 80. **Rament:** raiment; clothing. **LILLY of the field:** see Matt. 6:28–29.

rather a Slippe come out of the *Bear-garden*, unworthy to behold the *Sunne:* became *degenerate and so wild:* Sometime to none of the *Flowers* of Parradise inferiour.

And another like *LEOPARD*, Lyon-like *SCOTLANDS Coate* the truth of it displaied Thus: *Which had foure* Heads, *and foure* Wings *on the backe of it,* as it were a Heralds Coate, or KING AT ARMS, &c. So great *BRITAINS* foure KINGDOMS or *Crownes* proclaimes by them: And this the Summe of it; shewing Then revealed the time of *END,* when united *These foure aforesaid, &c. As hereby farther appeares.* (*And Dominion was given unto it:*) No small addition, after Her dayes raigning forty foure Yeares, for *Scotland* to give such a Large *Coate* by a Prince as *unfortunate* in His *Progenie* and *Successor;* As in *his Predisessors* or *Parents:* Wherefore liken'd to the LEOPARDS Spoted skinn those sable spots or *drops.*

And behold a fourth BEAST like a *HARPYE,* or some such *Monster,* having great *Iron Teeth,* and *Nayls of brasse,* to be short, *the Irish Harpe demonstrated,* likewise the very wrest as it were a little Horne, of which *Instrument not a little out of tune,* as insues, stamping all underfoote *Gods Law, Humaine Law.*

And so farre for the *Harpe, Like the very forequarter or ribbs informe or likenesse,* as strung in that manner ribbwayes, *whose short Horne the expresse Character of tirrants of no long continuance,* raising up and setting lower, like the wrest according to their will made a law, *changing and altering* when they please.

90

100

Line 81. **Slippe:** a twig or plant cutting; also a young person. **Bear-garden:** one of several London sites of bear and bull baiting, regarded by Lady Eleanor as a den of iniquity; an allusion to France, whence Henrietta Maria came.

Line 84. **SCOTLANDS Coate:** coat of arms; Scotland's coat of arms included a lion rampant and a red *fleur-de-lis.*

Line 86. **KING AT ARMS:** the chief herald.

Lines 90–93. **raigning...Yeares:** Queen Elizabeth I. **Prince...Parents:** James I's progeny were: Henry, his eldest son, who died in 1612; Elizabeth, who was forced with her husband, Frederick, to flee from their kingdom on the continent; and James's successor, Charles I, king at the time of Britain's civil war. James I's father was Henry Stuart, Lord Darnley, who was murdered in 1567; his mother was Mary Queen of Scots, who was executed in 1587.

Line 94. **sable...drops:** dark spots. Line 95. **HARPYE:** in Greek myth, a winged monster.

Line 96. **Irish Harpe:** The harp appears in the Irish coat of arms.

Line 97. **wrest:** tuning key for a stringed instrument. Line 102. **tirrants:** tyrants.

Informing moreover *concerning the blaspheming blasts of the little Horne, that had eies like a man, and such a mouth,* as much to say, *that mouth speaking such great things, a Womans and no Mans.*

Her Proclamations at her command, *the great Seale, the Elders and the Nobles,* so with the Story goeing on of that Idolatrious time, *Come see* now *that cursed Womans spirit, she cast downe, &c. cunjured up,* as it were, *walks up and down,* that like her selfe of her unnaturall Dogs, *Acteon* like eaten (*of her none left to bury) Jezebel* by name, *Woe to the House,* whose signification, so no other then a stolne peice by the Poet, very like to be, as that for another: *Borrowed from Elias, Elevation, also the fable of Phaeton,* That *Prophets* being sought for as though some where had falne or miscarried.

Whose *misteries* or *morralls* in so high esteeme among the *Heathen* against many may rise in *Judgement,* of *whom reverenced no more Divine Oracles* further more, to weigh or unite those times, *with our heavie* days, *Likewise Peace,* though voiced, *Jacobs voice like and the hands of Esau,* yet such divisions and slaying of all hands, *nothing but peace,* put the question *as though he sought nothing else,* is it peace, *and thus saith the King, is it peace.*

And ever and againe, *Thus saith the KING, &c. Is it peace, JEHU.* New Propositions as it were. And Sir as long as her *Sorcerors* inforce doeing what she pleaseth, *what hast thou to doe with peace,* also at her last cast (when this Motto, *who is on my side* who) *who troode* HER *underfoote,* her inchanting voice, *Had he* Peace *that slew his* Master? (As it were *to looke to his* Head) This blood-thirsty Mistres of *Charmes* and *Spells* like Satans falling those aspiring Spirits.

Line 112. **Jezebel:** a wicked queen who, like Actaeon in Greek myth, was devoured by dogs (2 Kings 9:36). **Woe to the House:** the title of Lady Eleanor's 1633 tract against the house of Derby; see page 57 in the present edition.

Line 114. **Elias:** "Elias" and "Elijah" were two forms of the prophet's name.

Line 115. **Phateon:** Phæton; in Greek myth, he drove a chariot of the sun for one day with disastrous results.

Line 116. **falne:** fallen. Lines 120–21. **Jacobs...Esau:** see Gen. 27.

Lines 122–23. **is it peace...peace:** 2 Kings 9:17–22.

Line 127. **who is on my side:** 2 Kings 9:32.

So alike the time possest, now see what a double portion powr'd out of the curse what one leavs, another taks, *He that escapes the Sworde of Hazael Jehu slayes, and hee escaping Jehus Sword Elisha slayes,* because the Land devided as those waters by him parted with the mantell of *Elias,* wherewith *Sayled over Jordan River,* and such virtue in it, bein worne out by them, much more vigere then and Spirit in their Books being perused and studyed upon.

And Mother and Daughter alike too. Now she cast into a languishing bed, consumed to nothing an *Anatomy,* &c. scarce any thing to bury.

The occasion of this LANDS *deep* CONSUMPTION *SHE,* And wast made *thereof: Woe to the House of God,* and the House of PARLIA- MENT both, the nursing mother of *DRAGONS,* those *Sonns* of *BELIALL* in armes, for as her name is, so is she MARRAH: *The GALL of bitternesse.* 140

But because the *Daughter of a King* as *JEHU* speake, *Here forborne the Remainder, buryed in silence,* for so births PREROGATIVE *surmounts* or *goes* before *that gain'd* by Marrage *as desent* and *blood,* a Character not to be blotted out, where with follows the state of VIRGINITY, the pres- idence theirs, *Not in subjection as others.*

And for *ELIAS* progresse in the SPIRIT: The returne of those long expected dayes, Let the READER be pleased for his satisfaction to turne but (to the *Apocalyps* the 11) And see in his COMMISSION to the *Gentills. What date it beares there, concerning the revealed time of the Res- urrection, &c. even behold the Sevententh Centurye it measured out by moneths and dayes, amounting* unto three years and halfe, the halfe of seaven like the time nothing, but divission, including the great misticall weeke, exprest severall & divers wayes. A touch *of* which time *folded* up 150

Lines 132–33. **taks:** takes. **He that escapes...slayes:** 1 Kings 19:17.

Line 134. **waters...Elias:** see 2 Kings 2:8.

Line 138. **Mother and Daughter:** Henrietta Maria's mother, Marie de'Medici, had wielded considerable power in France after the death of her husband, Henry IV.

Lines 142–43. **Sonns of BELIALL:** devils. **MARRAH:** echoes Henrietta Maria, the name of Charles's queen; see Exod. 15:23.

Lines 145–46. **Daughter...silence:** see 2 Kings 9:34.

Line 149. **Not...others:** Married women were subject to their husbands' authority.

with that *sevenfold* marriage, put the *question* in the *resurection whose wise*, &c.

160   Wherefore of the last (turned) Houre-Glasse of time, Thus *(Revel. &c.) And in the same Houre a great Earth Quake and the tenth part of the CITY fell, and slaine Seven Thousand, Decima Pars, &c. and* thus pend with the *Character* of the present when *Elias* his *dayes shall appeare againe,* their Resurrection or *Revolution,* as it were by a beseiged City its modell, and yeelded or rendered up by the affrighted remnant, when such publike Thanksgiving, saying, *Wee give thee thanks O LORD GOD Almighty, which art and wast, and art to come.* Utter'd (times) treble voices, to weigh the time, &c.

     And as a Reformation time, to the greatest part hatefull & unsuffer-
170 able: *so the day of Judgements tydings as wellcome,* like the writs of Parlia-
ment *that news* to many also dreadfull, and detestable to the world, these makes it sufficiently plaine, *and the Nations were angry the time of the dead was come that they should be judged, &c.* (ergo or viz.) *to be man-ifested* to the *Gentills,* and so like the last Supper aforehand, shewing his death, likewise *commands the little booke open'd to be received and eaten,* as much to say, *The last day revealed to be or afore shewed the Lords second comming, &c.* Also by two witnesses, to witt, the Bookes of *Daniel* and St. *John, although reproved for his firy Spirit:* That he was forward and sudden *in calling for the day of Judgment as it were:* Then who knew not
180 of what *Spirit he was.*

     And here like *Elias* and *Elijah* not to be parted (*those twain goeing along further with the last time,* those aforesaid mourning moneths 42. And a Thousand two Hundred and Sixty dayes, and three dayes and a halfe, &c. (*Revela.* 11.) all *but sounding the great dayes Alarme in the sev-enteenth Century:* Then to watch *as the time for the Elects cause promised to be cut off and shortned,* to witt its comming short of 2000. yeares, and so much for times sentence, to be no longer (*Revela.* 10.) *And the Sacra-mentall tree of life,* or Bookes of the old and new Testament, afore men-

---

Line 162. **Decima Pars:** tenth part (Latin).

Lines 163–64. **Elias...againe:** Mal. 4:5; Matt. 17:10–13.   Line 167.   **treble:** triple; soprano.

Lines 170–71.   **writs of Parliament:** summons calling for the assembly of Parliament.

Line 181.   **twain:** two.   Line 185.   **the Elects cause:** that of those chosen for salvation.

tioned, *And he therefore that shall add or deminish* from the set time
written by those witnesses *let Him expect the plagues also proceeding out of*   190
their mouths, Pestilence and Warre, &c. otherwise that might have *escaped*
death no few with *Elias* have been taken alive up, debarred *from* entering the rest, &c. as that figure of the Resurrection, double witnessed by
Elijah a touch of whose Corps therby one raised up againe, but let
downe into this Sepulchare.

So againe looking backe to *Daniel* touching the *little Horne* declaring
or sounding the brevitye of great *Brittaines* Monarchie, (*Whose looke
more stoute then his fellows)* more over thus I considered the *Hornes, And
there came up another little Horne, before whom three of the first Hornes
were pluckt up by the roots,* the truth of it as much as to say, *That he the*   200
first Heire of the red rose and the white. Whose ISUE three of them
Crown'd Princes childlesse, *deceasing without Heires of their body,* the
Crown of *England* fell to *Scotland, and great Brittaine so stiled,* then
wherefore blazoned by those great *Beasts foure being from name of Bruite
derived, whose Unicorns* Horne become as short as his fellowes. Looke-
ing of late as though al by conquest had been his, so according to his
will wresting and altering whatsoever, and possest with no little willfull-
nesse as well as pride, proceeding *from Ephnesse* and *Shallownesse.*

And so from *HENRY* the fourths taking possession of the *Kingdome,*
regained by *EDWARD* the fourth of those royall Rose ten in number   210
(giving the dunn Cow) so many even from the House *of Lancasters*
usurpation untill the *diadem* fell to be *Scotlands* lott, all which displayed
by those *Horns, ten and another little Horne, &c.* as *Corone* being derived
from *Cornua,* and *Carolos* a Diminative, &c.

Line 192. **Elias...alive:** see 2 Kings 2. Line 194. **Elijah...againe:** see 1 Kings 17:17–24.

Line 201. **first Heire...white:** Henry VIII, whose parents, according to popular tradition, joined together the red rose of the House of Lancaster with the white rose of the House of York.

Lines 201–2. **ISUE...childlesse:** Edward VI, Mary, and Elizabeth.

Line 204. **Bruite:** Brute or Brutus, legendary founder of Britain; also a beast.

Line 205. **Unicorn:** beast added to the British royal arms with James I's accession.

Lines 209–10. **from Henry...EDWARD:** from 1399 until 1461. **royall Rose ten:** Ten monarchs ruled between Henry IV and James I.

Line 211. **dunn Cow:** rough-skinned shark.

Lines 213–14. **Corone...Cornua...Carolos:** crown, horn, Charles (Latin).

For sayling on, the Wind serving faire still, or *for proceeding with the* Map *of great Brittains last Parliament, so manifest,* that whose Image this, who needs to doubt, as a little *farther,* I shall hold on, &c. (*I beheld, then because of the* great voice *of the* word which the Horne spake, *I beheld even till the Beast was slaine and his body given to the* burning flame:)

220   Some may say hath God care *of Oxen?* Yes doubtlesse beholds even such a Den or Draught *of restlesse beastlinesse* day and night, St. *James*-Fayre *so called,* not without Cause their Priviledge of late abolished: As hereby appeares the Modell every of those Courts put downe: Where so long such Lawlesse *doings* there, &c.

(As for the rest of the *Beasts,* They had their *Dominion taken away:* BUT their *Lives were prolonged*) as Hee no little or inferiour Beast for one, *whose voice set a Note lower,* brought to the barre, though so long deferred, *yet whose Judgement sleeps Not.*

And then the Ancient of dayes, sitting in his Judges Robe, and Locks

230   like Snow, Even *the day of Judgement clothed in the Parliaments likenesse:* And the Parliament clouded under, or shadow'd out by the day of Judgement. *His comming in the Clouds, so all in their pure wooll, set forth & wooll Seats;* and thus much for that: *The judgements shall sit, and the Bookes were opened,* the Bookes of the Old and New Testament also: *Nothing covered that shall not be disclosed too, and proclaimed.*

Likewise by those *Legions of Angells,* beside the Parliaments everlasting sitting, the warre raised *by them* set forth, *like Dooms day as it were,* when the Elements melting and the *Heavens* shaking, & *Stars falling,*

Line 220. **Oxen:** the beast; "Oxon." is the Latin abbreviation for Oxford, the center of the Royalists.

Line 221. **St. James-Fayre:** a fair held in London by a grant from King Edward I, on the eve and day of St. James and for five days afterwards.

Line 223. **those Courts put downe:** the courts of Star Chamber and High Commission, abolished by statute in 1641.

Lines 225–26. **Dominion...prolonged:** The bishops lost their seats in the House of Lords in 1642; although Laud was impeached in the winter of 1640–1641 and twelve others were accused of treason a year later, none had been executed by September 1644.

Line 227. **brought to the barre:** brought to court for judgment.

Line 233. **wooll Seats:** Lords in parliament sat on wooden benches covered with woollen cushions.

like those Valies of Thunder-Bolts with lightnings *such a firy Streame now making way:* the generall dayes *Epitome* & the conclusion of all these, *Dan. 7.*   240

(*And the Kingdome and Dominion, and the greatnesse of the Kingdome* under the whole Heaven, *Shall be given to the Saints of the most high (OR RULERS) whose Kingdome is an everlasting Kingdome.*)

As to no other, given such a high stile, except unto this Kingdome, &c. Hitherto is the end of the matter concerning the end, *and as for Daniel his countenance changed,* and his cogitations troubled. The troublesometime before the change, *fore saw* even *our* evill times, *His heart bleeding too, &c.* And as *Daniel* signifying the *judgement of God,* so that *Monsterous fourth Beast,* as much to say; *a Viperous generation:*   250

Herewith is signyfied like *Josephs* & *Pharoahs* dreams doubled, even the seventeenth hundred yeare: By this very measure doubled to bee likewise: a *Time and times, & the deviding of time,* or three and a halfe, (viz.7.) *Surge & metire templum, (Revel.* 11.) follows *tempus & tempora, & dimidium temporis.* The Resurrctions time hereby measured even in the present *Century* cut *in the midst too* (as it were) *Paradventure fifty there, &c.* And paradventure there shall lacke five of fifty, exprest in the day of judgements very language, as *shall not the Judge of all the earth doe right,* and *Abram* he but Dust and Ashes then.

With whom saying, *Now I have taken upon me to speake,* cannot here   260 rest shewing farther, as *Noah outlived* the Flood, three hundred years and dyed, two thousand years after the Creation, likewise *now* the time abated or comes short 300. years, wherefore the disolution in the seventeenth hundred yeare, and thus cut off so many yeares, like the shortned dayes of *Enoch whom God tooke,* who lived three hundred yeares and *Eternitys* forerunner *begat Metheuseliah,* thus five *hundred* years amounts to a PERIOD, *as deeply sworne the Time should be longer, (Revela.* 10.)

Line 239. **Valies:** volleys[?]. Line 240. **Epitome:** summary of the chief points.

Line 245. **stile:** style; title or form of address.

Line 251. **Josephs...dreams:** see Gen. 37 and 41.

Lines 254–55. **Surge...temporis:** Rise and measure the temple (Latin); Rev. 11:1; time and times, and half a time (Latin); Rev. 12:14.

Line 259. **Abram:** Abraham; see Gen. 17:5–7.

measured by the CREATORS his right hand lifted up, *Tempus non erit amplius, sed in diebus vocis septimi Angeli: Times mistery revealed, &c.* as
270   promised to be witnessed by the Prophets, *his servants concerning* times TRUMPET then put to silence time no more, &c.

And lastly for MICHAELMUS (1644) *That happie halfe yeare herein included,* a time and times and halfe also, *to disperse the Forces, &c. Revela. the* 12. *and Dan. the* 12. concerning *Michaels alarme,* there signified and so like a Thiefe in the night as this fearful night vission, appeares even the end stolne upon the whole world, or comming as the travel of a Woman misreckoning sometimes taken before *SHE* looks.

Also farther for this last of Parliaments, & *whereas Gods word able to speake for it selfe of full age,* other argument whatsoever, needlesse, it
280   being of a quicker returne, *shall presse another place of Scripture,* as briefly explaind as others afore, *Reve.* 10.9. *Concerning that Albion Army, and Aleluja voices where even the revealed time of the Lords comming.* And the writs of this happie Parliament sealed up in one: *Scribe Beata, &c. They that are called to this meeting,* &c. All sealed with the Unicorne in pure Paper, as it were mounted on white Horses, or like the great shew. both going together: as noted &c.

Nomen scriptum quod nemo novit, the Parliaments name in another language, viz. *et vocabant nomen ejus verbum dei. The Word, &c. et cum Justitia judicat, et pugnat. And upon his head many Crowns with a gar-*
290   *ment dipt in blood, deep Scarlet clothed,* and on his vesture, and upon his legg written, &c.

Namely the Colour and Garter of the order the Knights of St. *Gorge* (*Ecce equus Albus*) likewise from *Chival* and *Equus.* And thus the

---

Lines 268–69. **Tempus…Angeli:** Time will not be filled, but in the days of the voices of seven Angels (Latin).

Line 277. **travel:** travail; labor; childbirth.

Lines 281–82. **Albion Army:** those in white robes (Rev. 7:13–14) and Britain's army; "albion" means white; it is also a poetic term for England.

Lines 283–89. **Scribe…pugnat:** Lady Eleanor mingles Latin and English in giving the text of Rev. 19:9–11.

Line 292. **Color…St. Gorge:** The Order of the Garter was England's most prestigious order of knighthood. St. George was its patron saint.

Line 293. **Ecce equus Albus:** Behold a white horse (Latin); Rev. 19:11. **Chival and Equus:** "horse" in French and Latin, respectively.

Knights and Esquires of both Houses displayed, of what house, and so from the name of *Oxford,* thus, *et vidi Beastiam et Regis terræ et exercitus,* &c. Revela. 10.9.

And for the aforesaid warre so farr as for the motive, *Meritrice magna qui corrupit terram in prostitutione sua, &c.* Hath bin shew'd afore where she painted like her Images that downfall of Hers before theirs.

Also added these to the premises because injoyned not to part, or put asunder what is joyn'd, shewed *Farthermore, The great Image, (Dan.* 2.) even *armed at all points,* the verity of those foure Metals, *ore* Argent, &c. the very same likewise divers one from another. Apertains to *the foure great Beasts the one rising out of the Earth, the other out of the Sea.*

So contains Cæsars Superscription even *the Roman Empires age,* written in in those Characters of the 3. Ribs, 4. Wings and the 10. Horns and then *those Eagles wings so lifted up pluckt too,* notwithstanding *Germanies* manly looks, that Saxon state: like this great *Statue* unable *longer* to stand upon its feet, not unlike *Irelands estate,* the modell of that *Empire* in such a flourishing condition, *and as the blow then in the* 17. *yeare of the present reigne,* so the other in the 1700. &c. broken so soon in peices: *Wherefore the world but like a Dreame vanished:* Like his suddain awaking in a moment forgotten all, &c.

But now returning to great *Brittains brittle condition* againe: *That union dissolved and broken in peices since his dayes:* He the head of GOLD, as by those peices called *JACOBUS,* after his name, &c. And he the ROMAN SPANISH Emperour by his tribute of late, since the *Indies discovery, who makes up the head of Gold too:* And all this but to

300

310

Line 295. **et…exercitus:** and I see the Beast and the land of the King and the army (Latin).

Lines 297–98. **Meritrice…sua:** The great prostitute corrupts the land in her prostitution (Latin).

Line 302. **ore Argent, &c:** gold, silver, etc. (French).

Line 305. **Caesars Superscription:** his heading or address (Matt. 22:20–21).

Lines 307–8. **Eagles…Statue:** Lady Eleanor compares the eagle, used as the ensign or insignia of the army of ancient Rome (Caesar's army) and the symbol of the Holy Roman Empire, to the statue or image in Dan. 2:32–34.

Lines 310–11. **17…reigne:** 1641, the date of the Irish "Rebellion."

Line 316. **JACOBUS:** gold coin named after King James.

Line 317. **the ROMAN SPANISH Emperour:** Charles V, king of Spain (1516–1556) and Holy Roman Emperor (1519–1555).

manifest and shew. *That God is a Revealer of Secrets in these dayes also:*
320 Reveales the deep and secret things, *And maketh known what shall be in*
the Latter dayes; by divers & severall demonstrations, as this for another. Of
the *Axe laid to the roote: That tree or pedigree whose fruit much of such a*
hight, reached up to Heaven, *this Jacobs Ladder, &c:* And now but the
Stump end remains as yee see.

The very Woods every where proclaims it, where the Axe never put
so to the Root, *such selling, &c. And so the Axe that fell into the water, by*
a sticke cast into it, caused to swime: The Morrall thereof no other then
the *Resurrection time revealed to be by the Spirit of prophesie.* As much to
say, As the late hand writing for a seale or signe of it, *a sufficient prophet-*
330 *icall proclamation though not on the Walls, &c.* in the Banquetting-
House, yet not unknown to Lord to few how these applied. *Thy King-*
dome numbred, and thou found wanting, &c. and come to passe *too,* as
published and printed, 1633. *sufficiently* known, *in meeter to his Majes-*
tie from great Babylon *transferred to great Brittain.*

And so this but the truth of it (*shewed in the* 12. *of the Revelation*)
How Satan because he knows his reigne or time to be short: is ready to
devoure the Woman even for the truth of the Resurrection time
revealed, *as most proper to be performed by that sex a Woman by whom*
death came to be the Messenger of Life. And so, *WOE TO THE INHAB-*
340 *ITERS of the EARTH, and of the SEA, &c.*

And since a pleasing Theme (as tis said) makes a good Orator, and
sure I am a worse time then this never known or ever heard of, so then
the time the end discovered, although *pend* somewhat hastily or unper-
fectly, &c. being like the hony: and like the hony gathered out of so
many parts, I shall the lesse need to excuse it unto such as have a ful
knowledge of the Scriptures, That should it be written at large a Chronicle or a booke as ample as those tables, of the Mapps of the World
could I suppose not contain it.

Line 322. **the Axe laid to the roote:** Matt. 3:10. Line 323. **Jacobs Ladder:** see Gen. 28:12.
Line 326–27. **the Axe…swime:** 2 Kings 6:5–6.
Lines 329–31. **late hand writing…Banquetting-House:** cf. Dan. 5.
Lines 339–40. **WOE…SEA:** Rev. 8:13.

Not sutable to the little book, being but an *Epittomie* as it were, and
so much for being not voluminous, especially when the time so short
too: as by *Tyrant time his reigne expired,* shew'd to be and these the
apointed Scutchins for his Hersse apeared, those winged *Beasts devour-*
ing times likenesse, &c.

As by this one wittnesse more produced or set forth: *asigned to the*
present, even in the dayes of these Kings, or united Kingdoms: *Shall the*
God of Heaven set up a Kingdome which never be distroyed. And the Kingdome shal not be left to other, &c. And shall breake in peices, even to
the same effect, with that (*Dan.* the 7.) *The greatnesse of the Kingdome*
under the whole Heaven, for ever given to the Saints (or Rulers, &c.) which
shall breake in peices, &c. viz. By those ordinance or orders of Parliaments, and feild peices, &c.

And yet not so strange as true; notwithstanding such a troublesome
time *O let Ismale live as it were,* prefer'd before *Isaac to be his Heire,* And
Absolons life before *Solomon the wise (O Absolon my sonne Absolon)* Like
Egypts Leekes & Garlike before *Canaans* Grapes, &c. And so preferred
this worlds vanity & folly before everlasting Righteousnesse, *endlesse Joy,*
life eternall, and now ended thus this point of Honour, displaying the
Ancient of dayes his Kingdome your portion to you dedicated: that so
punctually have discharged that duty of the first commandement with
promise, in so much and such dishonour endured, have bene your
mothers Copartner, even You, her alone and sole support under the
Almighty. *So Veni Domine Jesu, gracia Domine, &c.*

350

Line 352. **Scutchins:** escutcheons; badges showing coats of arms.
Line 356. **Kingdome...distroyed:** Dan. 2:44. Line 361. **feild peices:** artillery.
Line 363. **Ismale:** Ishmael; see Gen. 16:15.
Line 364. **Absolon:** Absalom, David's son; see 2 Sam. 18:33.
Line 365. **Egypts Leekes...Canaans Grapes:** Num. 11:5.
Line 372. **Veni...Domine:** Come Lord Jesus, gracious Lord (Latin).

Cheshunt, Herts. EN8 9SL
www.tesco.com

VAT NO: 22043021

THANK YOU FOR SHOPPING
WITH US

TESCO

Every little helps

If you change your mind about
your purchase, please retain
your receipt and return it to the
store with the product as sold
within 28 days.

Conditions apply to some products,
please see instore for details.
Your statutory rights are not
affected.

Tesco Stores Ltd
Registered Office
Tesco House, Delamare Road
Cheshunt, Herts. EN8 9SL
www.tesco.com

VAT NO: 22043021

THANK YOU FOR SHOPPING
WITH US

TESCO

Every little helps

H-M went to France? → France enemy again? → Ⓕ defeated repeatedly. low morale

1644

2 years into the war Sides well & truly chosen.

KJV 32 yrs old!

Ⓟ war Marsten moor. inclue Summer high morale

According to the title page, Lady Eleanor published *A Prayer or Petition for PEACE. November 22.1644* (Wing D2001) when King Charles I was moving triumphantly toward Oxford. Shortly before, the royalists had defeated the parliamentary army at the second battle of Newbury, not far from Englefield, where Lady Eleanor had heard Daniel's voice almost two decades earlier. The promised Second Coming of Christ offered some hope in seemingly discouraging circumstances.

No copies of the 1644 tract seem to be extant. The copy in the Folger Library volume on which the present edition is based begins with what appear to be the first seven pages of the 1644 tract and then proceeds, on page 8, with "A Prayer or Letter for the Peoples Conversion and Deliverance from their Distraction, June 1649." Another copy, also listed by Wing as D2001, in the Library of Worcester College, Oxford, has different pagination and contains a number of minor textual variations. It too begins with what appears to be the original tract and then on page 9 proceeds to "A Letter or Petition from their tedious Distraction for a speedy deliverance," dated at the end November 1649. A third version of that letter is appended to *A Discovery,* the version of *Sign* (1649; Wing 2012AA—page 277 in the present edition) which lacks the full title page. Two slightly different versions of *Prayer,* both dated 1645 (Wing D2002 and D2003), are extant in the British Library.

A PRAYER OR PETITION
FOR PEACE.
November 22. 1644

Behold, your house is left unto you desolate; And verily ye shall not see me, till ye say, Blessed is he that cometh in the Name of the Lord.

Epigraph. **Behold...the Lord:** Luke 13:35.   A handwritten annotation in the margin reads "without whom yee can doe Nothing:"

A PRAYER & PETITION FOR *PEACE.*
By the Lady *Eleanor.*

O Lord, the\<n\> great and dreadful God, as we have sinned deeply and
offended, guilty of no less then open Rebellion, by excluding thee, fleeing from thy presence with one voyce (as it were) *We will not have this*
man to reign over us (or) *He defers his coming,* as others; Even departed
from thy Precepts and Judgements set before us: so here prostrate before
the foot-stool of thy Throne, implore nevertheless pardon and forgiveness.

For this no stoln or secret transgression committed, but with a high
hand; and so much the rather presuming on this access, because hith-

10   erto the vulgar (the burthen and heat of the day though theirs) those
sheep yet not guilty or accessary to this trespass or capital Crime, or of
thy return opposed, as manifest in hearkning not to the loud voyces of
the Propets accomplished thy Messengers: But to our Kings, Princes,
Heads and Rulers, which appertains, so straitly commanded, saying,
What I say unto you, I say unto all, Watch; the *Gentiles* watchword also
charged in readiness to be; and signs of the time they not them discerning, such and such express evident Signs and Tokens, haste, watch'd over
them, as since this a Nation, or under the whole Heaven. the like
unknown, witness, The Irish Massacres Winter flight, and Sabbath

20   journey, those bloody pestilent Vials, so violently poured out (without
doubt) not since the Flood as in this present Century.

Line 1. **O Lord…deeply:** words likely to be used in confession.

Lines 3–4. **We will…over us:** Luke 19:14.

Lines 5–6. **prostrate…Throne:** a position of humility appropriate for a petitioner.

Line 8. **stoln:** stolen; accomplished by stealth.

Line 10. **the vulgar:** the innocents; the common people as opposed to the rulers.

Line 11. **capital Crime:** a crime punishable by death.

Line 14. **straitly:** strictly. Line 15. **What I say…Watch:** Mark 13:37.

Line 19. **Irish Massacres:** Reports of massacres of Protestants by Catholic rebels in Ireland reached England in October 1641.

Line 20. **pestilent Vials:** see Rev. 16–17.

Thus neither (awakened or) taking warning (by Forraign Nations) as Beacons lighted our neighbors houses set on fire first, like *Jacob's* setting in the front the handmaids and their children: which alarms so lightly weighed, til suddenly at last, like *Sampsons* sevenfold new Cords and green withs, all pluckt asunder when linked so fast and knit, *France* with *Great Britain, Spain* with *France, Germany* with *Spain;* together with these late married Isles or united Kingdoms, now in widows forlorn woful Estate, or worse, as divorced; sometime that as had it been a new world, with such *Creations* flourishing, & Titles all new *Names,* even   30
walking like days of old, also become as those, when God repented he made *Man,* brought to a like Ebbe or fall, as those insasciable Gyants, Great *Britains Babel* Towering thoughts confounded.

And now behold, O Lord, through a high and heavy hand abased and so low brought, humbled to ashes and sackcloth, from the highest to the lowest; then tread not on a worm, break not the bruised reed, the wounded smite them not; but hear us out of the deep, O thou our Anchor, hope and present help, ready to be consumed and swallowed up, if thou calm not and asswage those working tempestuous Seas, through unruly raging winds let loose, wrought and contrived; And so   40
with him praying in his posture, *Elijah,* when as without *Rain* so long, forty two Moneths (that prophetical Number prest so much, of Three years and a half) he bowing himself double, or kneeling on his head; also behold such our Estate turned upside down, since the year 1642, *since the War began*
defer us not these miserable Isles and Kingdoms of ours, whose

---

Lines 23–24. **Jacob's...children:** Gen. 33:2.

Lines 25–26. **Sampsons...withs:** see Judg. 16:11–12; a "with" or "withe" is a shackle made of twigs or branches. *of Willow*

Line 27. **France...Spain:** Marriage alliances had linked these kingdoms: Charles I of Britain with Henrietta Maria of France; Philip II of Spain with the princess Elizabeth of Valois; Philip of the house of Hapsburg with Joanna of Spain.

Line 28. **late married Isles:** The accession of James VI of Scotland to the English throne in effect married the kingdoms of England and Ireland with Scotland. James took the title King of Great Britain.

Line 32. **insasciable:** insatiable. Line 33. **Babel:** see Gen. 11.

Line 41. **Elijah:** see 1 Kings 18.

Storehouses exhausted, like those Rivers dryed up, and like the dead Trees, burnt up our Nation and Habitation, torn between two She-bears, like those Forty two ungratious Infants.

To conclude (O forsake us not! thou of unspeakable Mercy) cause
50 thy face to shine upon us, for the Lords sake, our alone Savior Jesus Christ, made of the womans seed according to the flesh: A woman making her first witness of the resurrection [*and ascensions* [ ] *Joyful*] tidings to the<m>. [*Church*]: Let thy mighty voyce be heard, that speakest sometime to the Fish, the Fig-tree, the Deaf, the Dead, and very Devils subjects; And at whose motion the Sun and Moon moved not, stood still, heard him; and turnest the hard Rock into standing waters, &c. also the waters of this city, heal them; say the word and it is DONE, that henceforth let there be no more DEATH, no more Killing and Slaying, stay thy Hand She beseeches thee.

60   A Prayer or Letter for the Peoples Conversion and
          Deliverance from their Distraction, *June* 1649.

And O Lord of Sabbaths, our King, the God of Hosts sitting between the winged Cherubims, enclosing thy glorious Throne; That without delay vouchsafest to hear the humble address of thy Handmaid, and the waters according held of our Brittish *Jericho,* witness the very next moneth, *Decemb.* the 5th *Anno* 1644. a conjuring Letter from the other side, as would answer at the day of Judgement the contrary, &c. to lay aside Arms, whereas about three moneths after, the Enemy waxt at thy consuming presence like melting wax, calling to Rocks and Hills, or
70 fleeing to hide them were put to flight: He vanished in that fashion disguised, amazing those that knew him, signed with the years of thy right arm, 1645. owing since the horrible design *Anno* 1605. *November* the

---

Lines 47–48. **She-bears…Infants:** see 2 Kings 2:24.

Lines 51–52. **woman…resurrection:** see Luke 24. [ ]: The deleted word between "ascension" and "Joyful" is illegible.

Line 55. **Sun…moved not:** Josh. 10:12–14. Line 64. **vouchsafest:** condescend.

Lines 65–66. **waters…Brittish Jericho:** see Josh. 5. **next moneth:** after she had written her prayer of November 1644. **conjuring:** conspiratory; deceitful, bewitching.

Line 72. **horrible design…1605:** the Gunpowder Plot; see note to line 130 on page 66.

5th which faction (he the four and twentieth of those Alban Elders, prostrating his Crown so low) combined with.

And the Sword of War sheath'd thus, as when *Elias* the *Prophet* his Supplication presented, just three years & six months after their departing the City, he in that maner led in a string, from 1641. *January,* until 1645. *June,* that blow[ ] before his downfal. Notwithstanding, Justice her Sword drawn since Kings, Princes, Head-Rulers, going to wrack, great Trees felled down, as well as those of lower growth amended; like that restless mans Estate, *taking unto him seven spirits more unsufferable,* after the House swept and adorned, the Epilogue or End worse then the beginning, pointing to the Spiritual Function; especially, *seeking high places, earthly preferment, whereat all aym.*

Then here croaching at thy blessed feet, for a blessing on the Jubiles insuing year: O heavenly bounty, royal mercy, greater then *Solomons* exceeding fames report, suffices we have bin and are of thy Justice, not wanting an open example, *a hissing to all Nations,* guilty of no petty Treason, thine own Servants and Citizens, *Shuting thee out, conspiring against thee;* outed by disloyal Tenants: with those Husbandman also saying, *the Inheritance shall be ours, to us and our heirs;* accomplished signs and tokens when, the Creation groaning to be delivered, accompanied with the peoples voices or distempers restored to their old liberty: *Kingdom against Kingdom,* witness, *brethren Nations strugling like*

80

90

Lines 73–74. **he…twentieth:** Charles I was the twenty-fourth English ruler since the Norman Conquest in 1066; see Rev. 19:4.

Lines 75–76. **Elias…Supplication:** see 1 Kings 19; "Elias" and "Elijah" were two forms of the prophet's name.

Line 77. **1641. January:** i.e., 1642, when Charles I left London and Westminster.

Line 78. **1645. June:** date of the victory of the parliamentary army at Naseby and capture of the king's cabinet, containing his correspondence. [ ]: There is a blot on the page.

Line 79. **going to wrack:** being destroyed or ruined.

Line 83. **Spiritual Function:** the responsibility of clergy, particularly bishops, for the care of souls, in contrast to any temporal authority they might exercise.

Line 85. **croaching:** crouching. **Jubiles:** The Jubilee year, every fiftieth year, was to be a year of restoration and liberation (Lev. 25:10).

Line 88. **hissing:** see Jer. 19:8.

Line 90. **outed:** put or driven out.

Esau *and* Jacob, *one house storming the other,* the Devil the old Serpent, for his part storming too, his time because knows of no longer continuance; a day of publique Thanksgiving, deserving rather then sitting up their own horn, or to be admired of the world.

How is it then that they do not understand, blaspheme thy name so nigh: 100 rave on the world; notwithstanding, *What have we to do with thee, O Jesus,* conjured before the time, *to torment them not,* both sex discovering, *like the dog returnd to his excrement, and Sow to the mire,* how cleansed from filth, or in grace growing up, how long the graceless world in these budding times, also besotted, look back with *Lots* wife, to a sink of sin and corruption, [*with whose incesstious Daughters the Kings of the Earth matched, for the Mothers sake disinherited, they and their heirs referred to their salique slavish*] Law, [*wresting that, That the Lillies spin not, &c. as the pillar displays of salt.*]

[*With*] his Play-house [*for another*] whether not recorded in *Ahabs* 110 reign by our Scotish Bethmite, also (as it were) execrable, *Jerichos* edifice Erected: *The foundation laid in his eldest Son, and the gates in his yongest son, executed at the gate;* that after demolished those cages, or Monestaries of theirs, for an acknowledgment of the powder plots escape; dedicated that Monster everlasting like Theator, to the Devil for his Sabbath-service, and other such like.

New *Jerusalems* precious foundations and gates, ought rather much to have looked after, or to have considered the Arks building, which

---

Line 95. **Esau and Jacob:** see Gen. 27.

Line 97. **day of publique Thanksgiving:** observed periodically in seventeenth-century Britain after victories or after relief from plague or famine.

Lines 100–1. **What...O Jesus:** Mark 1:24. Line 104. **Lots wife:** see Gen. 19:26.

Line 105. **incesstious Daughters:** Lot's daughters bore him children (Gen. 19:36).

Line 107. **salique:** salic; the French law which excluded women from inheriting the throne or passing the right of inheritance to their children.

Line 109. **Ahab:** ruler reproved by Elijah for allowing idolatry in Israel (1 Kings 19:17).

Line 110. **Bethmite:** perhaps Bethlehemite or Bethlemite, someone in Bethlehem Hospital, i.e., a mad person.

Lines 111–13. **eldest Son...yongest son:** see Josh. 6:26. **cages...theirs:** centers of Catholicism. **powder plot:** Gunpowder Plot of 1605; see note to line 130 on page 66.

Lines 114–15. **Theator...Sabbath-service:** to some of Lady Eleanor's Puritan contemporaries the theater appeared to be an institution of the devil.

century the seventeenth, we then were entred; the Ark as in length Three hundred cubits measured out by the days of the year, so in breadth fifty, answerable to the weeks thereof; the hight of it thirty cubits, according to the days of the moneth, &c. [*So*] <Whether> teach us to number ours, the sum of it.

That merciful Lord, except infused special grace: Since so it is, as derive their Name, from *BRUTE, So are they,* may as well speak to the Ass and Adar to hear, *What the Spirit saith unto the Churches,* or to cause [*by means of a stick or rod, cast in*] an Ax to swim, grown (thou seest) so brutish and blockish, well shadowed out in seeing men like Trees walking: without which from above avails as much, as before the Scriptures speaking in the vulgar language: *That blessing although not equivolent to the former; how hear we every man in his own language, we born,* &c. yet a door, not remote therefrom. <Thoughe prophising all to thes days.>

From whence emboldned do beg, give them leave like as when bitten by fiery Serpents, those vipers; by another beheld in the same likeness were healed; so by these leaves taken from a womans hand, by them [*eaten*] (as it were) live may for ever: They by reason of their knowledge puft up hitherto, even of times and seasons mistery to take their fill, not in season till the [*evening of time this last* <of>] age <s>.

And since to have knowledge of the disease, though the first step to recovery suffices not: The Medicine if not attained, give them the Spirit of discerning, since come to maturity the Tree of Life, a qualification for of our first parents expedition, the tree reserved, that casting an eye upon the Map of the world that then was, the Ark Baptisms figure, whereby to measure or parallel the Gospels pilgrimage and the Floods age together, lifting up the same voice, the swelling Seas sounding their

120

130

140

Line 119. **cubit:** measure of land derived from the length of the forearm; see Ezek. 40.
Line 124. **BRUTE:** Brutus, legendary founder of Britain; also a beast.
Line 125. **Adar:** adder; snake. Line 126. **Ax to swim:** see 2 Kings 6:6–7.
Line 127–28. **brutish and blockish:** savage and stubborn. **men…walking:** Mark 8:24.
Line 129. **the vulgar language:** that of the common people.
Line 130. **how…language:** see Acts 2:6. Line 134. **these…hand:** the pages of the tract.
Line 135–36. **by reason…puft up:** cf. 1 Cor. 4:18–19.
Line 142. **the Ark Baptisms figure:** Noah's ark as a parallel for baptism.

alarm, climbing over Rocks and Mountains, besides an universal flood a
year or two ago, over the face of the earth, told then before, *There shal be
signs in the Heavens, in the Sun and Moon, and in the Stars,* the Sea roaring, people at their wits end distracted, &c. witness this sign, A new
Star, as seen in the East, the one 74·years before *Jerusalems* destruction
150   or judgment, so the other in *Cassiopei* its aspect or influence to the great
Year 1644. extented *Rev.* 7,14, 21. refer'd to it; Which Messenger Star
likewise appeared seventyfour years before our being entred into the
very day of judgment, with no ordinary apparitions in the Heavens, *The
powers of Heaven and Earth shaken both.*

So look upon us amended Lord, [*like the backward Spring,*] with
those ungrateful graceless Lepers (asked) *Where the nine,* &c. cursing
hitherto, where thou blessest, such returns. O send down upon the time
to come, (though have sinned a great sin) a blessed shower of commiseration for which so much. And for this stollen touch, as vertue when
160   gone from thee, 1649.

FINIS.

Line 150. **Cassiopei:** Cassiopeia, a northern constellation in which a new star had appeared
and then disappeared in 1572.

Line 154. A handwritten note in the margin reads "As August last &c."

Line 156. **ungrateful graceless Lepers:** see Luke 17:12–19.

Lady Eleanor publicized her own 1633 condemnation of Archbishop Laud by printing her petition against him in this broadsheet (Wing D1973). To emphasize her point, she placed the warrant for her appearance before the High Commission immediately following the petition. The present edition of *As Not Unknowne* is based on a copy in the Thomason Tracts in the British Library (shelf number 669.f.10[22]), where it is dated 21 March 1644, i.e., 1645, thus not too long after Laud's execution on 10 January 1645. By publishing the broadsheet at that time, Lady Eleanor could remind readers that she had been right to condemn him. Because this broadsheet has no title, it is ordinarily cited by its first words.

As not unknowne, though hath long beene deferd: Neverthelesse this Petition or Prophesie (on Record) not uncomplished: witnesse the present yeare, 1644. When as he on a *Friday* morning was killed or sufferd then: Who little supposed such a *SOP* prepared for his Lordship. (*Mat.* 24.) Saying, *The Lord of that servant shall come in a day and an houre hee lookes not for:* Even unprepared, as much to say, fore-warn'd. Although, that because the day and houre none knowes. Therefore thinks to put off the *Time made knowne of* HIS *comming,* with that Shift: *Who shall cut assunder that false Prophet,* or as the Word renders it, *Cut off* (to wit) his Head, with that Arch Hypocrite gracelesse *Judas,* bursting *Assunder* His very sentence, both served with one *Writ.*

Doubtlesse *an houre and a day,* Not dreamed of in his *Diarie,* where sets down the 19. of *September,* 1633. Was translated to be Arch *BB* But not by whose high authority the *Lords day cut off, the Sabboth translated into a day of such prophanation.*

Line 2. **Prophesie (on Record):** Because Lady Eleanor's petition of 1633 had led to the High Commission's proceedings against her, it was in the records of that court. **uncomplished:** unaccomplished.

Line 3. **he:** Laud. Line 4. **SOP:** a piece of bread soaked in water or wine.

Line 9. **Shift:** contrivance or stratagem.

Line 10. **Arch...Judas:** a comparison of Laud and Judas.

Line 12. **his Diarie:** Laud's diary was published in the course of the proceedings against him.

Line 13. **19. of September...Arch BB:** the date Laud became archbishop of Canterbury or, in Lady Eleanor's opinion, Arch Blaspheming Beast.

And thus having shewd: *The Beast like his Sabbaticall reigne finishd,* seven yeares compleat and eight current that was Arch *BB.* of *Lambeth* (or *Bethlam*) before his going into Prison rewarded as he had shut up and silenced others.

20   Also for his *Majesties* reference thus, how presumptious so ever the imprinting seemd then of those Books, where prayed to beware *the hand writing,* yet how true: Not behind hand with Him, in applying great *Babylons* judgement at hand. *Dan. 5. dedicated unto the present REIGNE;* needs no other *but referrd to such raging division* the Occurrents of the *Present. And* with that *for another* of the great Prince *Michaels* standing up, *when such an* unparalleld troublesome Time (Cap.the last) *also shewd to be directed to our distracted Nation of Great Brittain, in the* Arch *Angels name, given to this Island.* So notwithstanding these stiled presumptious and detestable: Have made bold presumd 30   to publish the fore-shewing of them in the yeare 1633. When little expected such a blow so nigh, His Majestie then crownd in *Scotland,* With the Arch *B* hornd here, whose absence and Acts he, weighed with his the last of those *Assyrians,* found as full of *Levity,* or *No lesse wanting.*

Lines 17–18. **Lambeth (or Bethlam):** the London palace of the archbishop of Canterbury or Bethlehem (Bedlam); an anagram.

Line 21. **those Books:** Lady Eleanor's works printed in 1633, especially *Given to the Elector.*

Line 24. **raging division:** the war between royalist and parliamentary forces.

Line 27. **Cap:** Chapter.   Line 28. **Arch Angel:** St. Michael.

Line 31. **crownd in Scotland:** Charles in 1633.

Line 32. **Arch B:** archbishop.   **hornd:** horned; applied to bishops because of the shape of their mitres or caps.

Line 33. **Assyrians:** enemies of Israel.

TO THE *KINGS* MOST EXCELLENT MAJESTIE.

The humble Petition of the Lady Eleanor. 1633.

Most humbly sheweth to Your Matie.

That the word of God spoken in the first yeare of Your happie reign unto
the Petitioner, upon *Friday* last did suffer early in the morning: the
B:BEAST ascended out of the Bottomlesse pitt: having seven Heads,   40
&c. seaven Yeares, *viz.* making Warre hath overcome, and killed them:
Bookes sealed by the Prophets. By the Bishop of *Lambeth* horned like
the Lambe, harted like a Wolfe, are condemned to be burned at *Pauls-
Crosse*, where our Lord crucified, &c. This is the third Day, that their
dead Bodies shrowded in loose sheets of paper. Lye in the streets of the
Great Citie, &c. more cruell and hard harted, then other tongues and
Nations, who will not suffer them so to be buried. If your Highnesse
please to speake the word the spirit of life will enter into them they will
stand upon their feete, &c.

Craving no other pardon, humbly as in   50
duty bound shall pray for your Matie.

The word of God to the King, Revela: 17. *October,* 1644. *The BEAST that
was, and is not: Even Hee is the eight, and is of the seven, and goeth into
perdition.*

Lines 43–44. **Pauls-Crosse:** outdoor pulpit in London where banned books were burned and
punishments administered.

Line 45. **dead Bodies:** see Rev. 11:8.

Lines 50–51. **Craving no…Matie:** traditional ending to a petition.

Line 52. 17. **October, 1644:** the first day of Laud's trial.

At the Court at *White-Hall, October* the 8. 1633.

His Majestie doth expresly command the Lord Arch-Bishop of *Canter-buryes Grace,* and his highnes Commissioners, for causes Ecclesiasticall. That the Petitioner be forthwith called before them, to answer for presuming to Imprint the said bookes, and for preferring this detestable petition.

Sydney Mountague:
Concordat cum originale factâ colatîone
per me Thomam Maydwell, no librum publium

Line 61. **Sydney Mountague:** the official who signed the warrant.

Lines 62–63. **Concordat...publium:** Agreeing with the original made and collated by me Thomas Maydwell, not freely published (Latin); note verifying that this is a valid transcript.

The title of this tract, *Great Brittains Visitation* (Wing D1994), addresses directly the conditions in Britain which corresponded to those prophesied as prelude to the Second Coming. As she does on a number of other occasions, Lady Eleanor discusses her subject by commenting upon chapters 1 and 4–10 of the Book of Revelation. She also draws comparisons between the year 1644 and the time of the birth of Christ (Luke 2). Although the title page says the tract was printed in 1645, *Great Brittains Visitation* was probably written in 1644. The present edition of this tract is based on a copy in the British Library (shelf number Tab.603.a.38[9]).

GREAT BRITTAINS VISITATION.

By the Lady *ELEANOR*.

Title. **VISITATION:** an act of God, especially an affliction; also an ecclesiastical dignitary's inspection of his jurisdiction.

THE APOCALYPS PROLOGUE

Wherein a revolution or returne, Exprest, as in those dayes it came to passe, when as City and Countrey opprest so: By such an universall imposd taxx: Inns so full that for our only Saviour to be borne in. No place but an open Stable afforded: And thus like the truth which no Corners or Curtaines requires. The joyfull tydings they in the wide field, First saluted with them: Shepheards that kept watch the glory from the Lord by night which shone round about them.

So lastly at his second comming, or returne also reveald to be afore hand, the watchfull Pastors saluted: over Spirituall Flocks from him,
10   saying: *I am Alpha and Omega, the morning Starre and evening both: the first and the last.* As this the Lord of Sabbaths Angel whose countinance as the Sun, and lighted at the evening of time with the seven Starrs, &c. And Golden Candlesticks all watch Lights round about him, even so farther for the little Booke of Life, who had its Swadle-Bands (as it were unloosd: with Seven fold Seales bound so fast up, when wonderfull acclamation such in heaven & Earth (Revel. 5) as came to passe with the Angel; a multitude of the Heavenly Host suddainly praising God: Luke 2 such Corispondencie ever between the Son of God, and Gods Word which for ever and ever indures. Maugre the Old Serpents malice.
20   And his Angels, let loose againe, as in the dayes of the Gospels first pro-gresse. <revela 9>

And therefore to say the truth, Though the Bottomlesse pit freely opend, no wonder: affording beside evill Spirits their Fellowship, Muni-tion also of all Kinds, And the winds let loose out of their Prisons, And Wrathfull Vialls the last powrd out, Who shall commisserate their Con-dition? when open house or Court (as it were) kept in Heaven, inviting all, Darkenesle not withstanding preferd at last shall be before Light. Like those frivolous and light excuses made of marriage: its mutability

---

Lines 1–36. In the base text this section is printed in italics with roman font for emphasis; the fonts have been reversed in this edition for ease of reading. Fonts follow the base text again beginning at line 37.

Line 14. **Swadle-Bands:** swaddling clothes in which babies were wrapped.

Line 19. **Maugre:** malgré; in spite of (French).

Line 27. **preferd:** preferred; favored by the monarch and offered a place.

preferd above the estate of Angels: And before eternall life: Farmes their
Leases or the like, as sold their life in blessed Paradise for such a toy.   30

Thus no marvel, although the infernall pit opend, where those
Legions of Wormes or Locusts swarming out. Our Pruining Hookes
have turnd into Swords, our union into division; And so much for these
present vigilent dayes of ours from which nothing conseald is, or hidden, even the things in the little golden booke as with no little expedition are presented here.

THE REVELATION OF JESUS CHRIST Interpreted.

Shews how ONE Isle calls unto another, *The Ile of Pathmos,* unto the
Iles of *Great Brittaine.* The great day of the Lords comming revealing it:
Whereof let the Isles be glad, Now or Never.   40

Of whose Visitation *from him which is, and which was, and which is to
come:* what date the time beares, the first witnesse these, *And from the
seven Spirits in sight of the Throne or nearest there unto,* vers. 4. Which as
it signifies or figures the present Century, *or the last seven hundred years*
Also points at the present reigne, when it began, about *Easter,* witnesse
these: *And from Jesus Christ the first begotten of the dead,* And the Prince
of the Kings of the Earth, *Unto him that loved us, and washed us from our
sins in his owne Blood, verse 5.*

Even as two for failing can witnesse, *Sonne and Father both:* crown'd
or *created Kings,* about the aforesaid *Resurrection feast kept,* concluded   50
thus: *And hath made us Kings and Priests unto God and his father, to him
be glory and dominion* for ever and ever Amen, verse 6. *Behold he commeth, &c.* as much to say, the last father and sonne of that kind from the
Conquest: since when hath been 24. of them, making up the blessed
Prophets and Apostles number.

And so farewell *the blessed yeares of Grace,* and time to be longer as in

---

Line 29. **Farmes:** purchases by contract; cultivates.

Lines 32–33. **Pruining...Swords:** cf. Mic. 4:3.

Line 45. **reigne...Easter:** Charles I acceded to the throne on 27 March 1625, about two
weeks before Easter Sunday.

Line 50. **Resurrection:** Charles I's father, James I, had acceded to the throne on 24 March
1604, also about two weeks before Easter Sunday.

Lines 53–54. **from...24:** twenty-four rulers since the Norman Conquest of England in 1066.

the yeare 1625. was revealed *to his Hand-maid,* the *first* yeare of his reigne, *to whom the day of Judgement being at hand declared:* was dedicated in a booke by her: And the generall Resurrection to bee in his
60 dayes as from the Prophet *Daniels* mouth given to understand: concerning the aforesaid time: *And at that time shall the great Prince Michael stand up, which standeth for the children of the people or defender of the Faith,* even Great Brittaines troublesom *time,* pointing thereat with the plagues pursuing one another for mortality as never since a Nation the like: Of whose *Inauguration or standing up at the aforesaid* Resurrection feast thus signified: *Many of them that sleepe in the dust of the Earth shall wake,* some to everlasting life, *&c. Dan.* 12.

And for a faithfull witnesse *So goe thy way Daniel,* as no few in their Mother Earths Bosome dayly take up their lodging of free cost, *till*
70 *Michael his alarme awakens them,* where also the yeare 1625. (*untill which dayes Daniels visions to waite*) Thus cast up two Hundred & ninety daies and three hundred and five and thirty, 625. (*Dan.* 12.)

But going on with *John whose name to no Nation better known then unto Ours,* who stiles himselfe your Brother and companion in tribulation, in the Isle that is called *Patmos,* where confined *was on the Lords day visited by the Holy Ghosts Angel, the* First voice saying, *I am Alpha and Omega, and what thou seest write in a Booke and send it, &c.* Wherupon being turned, saw that dreadfull appearance, *ONE all looking from head to foot like fire,* that stood in the midst of those candle
80 stickes of Gold, and therupon falling dead at his feet by a touch of his Septer, the seven Starrs in his right hand, being againe revived come to himselfe: was againe charged to write the things to come, the mistery of the seven starres which he saw in his hand, the Lord of Sabbath *Even to display times Coate by* CHARLES *Waggon or Wayne,* to wit the seventh present Century, about the midst of it, even to looke for the generall Resurrection time, as present, past, *and future here with times voice testified from him which is, and which was, and is to come.*

Wherefore in the day of Judgements likenesse was presented unto him the Booke of the Old and new Testament, that Alpha and Omega: Whose

---

Line 84. **times Coate:** coat of arms or symbols. **Wayne:** wain; an older English word for wagon; perhaps also a pun on wane (decline).

Body as it were clothed and girt. The Bible in gilt paper bound with 90
brasse Clasps which in such a yeare beares date, 1700. *When interpreted*
the booke of the Revelation as whatsoever spoken in darkenesse or in the
Eare assur'd to be made cleare as the light. And he that hath an eare let him
heare what the Spirit of prophesie saith, and in time repent and amend,
or expect a blow for *his paines, when he stands at the doore and knocks so*
long, the Comforter sent saying, behold I come quickly. And he shall Sup,
and sit with mee that hears my voice opens the doore.

CAP. 4.

Though hastning with winged time: yet some more Evidence requisit in
this a matter of such weight the day of judgement: And so shewes a 100
doore opened here, as much to say, *Nothing conseald or hidden, as heav-*
ens cathederall shewed here, the voice saying come up heither, I will shew
thee things to come. The Resurrection propheticall alarme verily, like that
afore, *I am he that was dead and am alive, &c. and have the Keyes, &c.*
First saw where the ancient of dayes sate, Inthroned under a Canopey,
raine bowe like: Where all in Priestly Vestments round about *those*
Elders with restlesse Thundering voices extolling his name who lives for
ever and ever. *And Holy, Holy, Holy, crying out as it were glory be to the*
Father, &c. Amen. For whose pleasure all things created. As for the
lamps before the Throne, *to wit* the year of God call'd the seven Spirits 110
of God, of the same influence with the seven Stars, requires no farther
repetition being both one: Neither these in the likenes here of Saints
and Angels, in Heaven *whose wings so full of eyes before and behind signi-*
fying those eye witnesses their watchfullnesse and as personating the blessed
Prophets and Evangelists: So lastly farther for the *mysterie or morall* of
these crown'd Elders expresly shews, How many intered Princes in this isle
since the conquest which in the space of seven hundred yeares last past
in Alablaster Shrowds clothed, That have cast their Crownes before the
Throne or before the great day.

Lines 90–91. **Bible…Clasps:** Bibles were often bound in this way in the seventeenth century.

Line 99. **winged time:** In Greek myth, Hermes, the messenger of the gods, was portrayed with winged feet.

Line 116. **intered:** interred; buried.

Line 118. **Alablaster:** alabaster; translucent gypsum or calcite.

120   CAP. 5.

And without boasting or amplifying, these the truth in few words: *This blessed Booke first cryed, He that hath an eare let him heare. And here by a strong Angel proclam'd: Who is worthy to open the booke in the right hand of him sitting upon the Throne:* No other then the misterie of times and seasons, in the yeare of the worlds Redemption, 1625. to be reveald or unseald. And because this so difficult (no man found *worthy, &c.*) John *that therfore much wept,* by that Elder willed to weep no more. *Informed ECCE LEO radix David, vicet, to open the booke and loose the sevenfold seales:* being not improper to explain this likewise, as he said, *I am*
130   *Joseph, so am I David,* This name of mine enterd here: by that Elder even *Daniel,* as much to say, *Goe thy way John, let those words satisfie thee* spoken to *Daniel:* The words are sealed up untill the time of the end, *Thou shalt stand in thy lott,* &c. (*Dan.* 12.) Reservd till a time and times and halfe: Pointing to the present Century so signified in behalfe of it, three periods and a part, &c.

  So dignus est agnus, viz. Anno Domini, in such a yeare of our Redemption, the first yeare of such a reigne. These Sabbaticall Seales unloosed witnesse, *For thou hast redeemed us and made us Kings and Prophets and we shall reigne.*
140   Even so let every Creature in the sea, namely the Isles Blesse those right hand yeares, with that Grand Jury, the 24. Elders before the Throne falling down. Who give up their Verduit, *Davids* Keye hath prevaild honour, glory, and blessing, &c.

                              CAP. 6.

And the Sonne of Thunder this fourth Evangelist that heard the day of Judgements Sommons, *The noise of thunder as it were, one of the seven*

Line 128. **ECCE LEO…vicet:** Behold the Lion of the tribe of David (Latin); Rev. 5:5.

Lines 129–30. **I am Joseph:** Gen. 45:3.

Line 136. **So dignus…Domini:** So worthy is the lamb, that is, in the year of our Lord (Latin); Rev. 5:12.

Line 141. **Grand Jury, the 24:** between twelve and twenty-three people served on a grand jury; see Rev. 5:14.

Line 142. **Verduit:** verdict.   Line 145. **fourth Evangelist:** John.

Seales being unloosed: One of the foure Beasts saying come and see: As much to say, *display'd* times and seasons mistery: *In the seventh Century,* And unto what Nation, this new Song of the Lords comming dedicated: as no unnecessary *circumstance time,* a thing observed of old, when the word of the Lord came unto them.

For evidence here of the Conquerer & *Rufus,* here behold *their ancient* Seales: *Where first saw a White Horse,* and *He that sate on him a Bowe, and a Crowne given unto him.* The English bowe renown'd farr and neere: (verse 2.) Whereby cleere as day given to understand *the Sonne of God reveald out of the Scripture to these very Isles. Wherefore listen O Isles.*

And this misterie of time sealed with the yeares four seasons, their discriptions, *The Sun like a Conquerour: and Gods word like the Sunne which overcomes whatsoever* Dispells all darkenesse, saying: *He that hath an eye come and see:* The worlds eye, like an expert Horseman upon his Carreer: running his restlesse course about, who first enters the victorious crowned yuory Ramme, the *Wholesome Spring more then Gold to be embraced, the Odorifferous Spring giving to every creature Life.*

The second Rider so furious, he on the Red Horse, giving all one word, Come and see: Not difficult to be discern'd, the *Crabb at all points* armed, *Summers scorching rayes: when red as fire all:* Slaying in Armes as it were with Sythes and such like no short weapon.

The third a Blacke Horse, he *that sate on him, a paire of Ballance in his hand, in his proper colours and complexion signified not inferior to his fellowes, as Automes voice* cleeres it, who these Celestiall Horsemen, *or Riders* were, a voice heard in the midst of them, saying, *A measure of Wheat for a peny, and three measures of Barley.* And hurt not *the wine and oyle,* even the Sun in his circuit passing by the *Equinoctiall,* weighing

150

160

170

Line 148. **times and seasons mistery:** see Acts 1:7. Line 149. **new Song:** see Rev. 5:9.

Line 152. **Rufus:** king of England 1087–1100, son of William the Conquerer.

Line 154. **English bowe:** English archers, using the longbow, were famous for their contribution to victories over the French during the Hundred Years' War.

Lines 159–60. **He…an eye:** cf. Rev. 2:29. Line 161. **Carreer:** career; fast-moving course.

Line 162. **Ramme:** Aries, astrological sign of spring.

Line 165. **Crabb:** Cancer, astrological sign of summer.

Line 173. **Sun…Equinoctiall:** the autumn equinox.

equall houres to day and night: *Thus all the world come and behold also the fourth seasons misterie,* explained in this new Calender or Prognostication.

The fourth a pale Horse, he that sate one him called Death. Or like the last day so gastly and *paile* the grizled Goate with his Beard. *Hoary Winter its wann visage that starvs with hunger young and old,* shaking every Limbe.

And these Characters pointing at those foure Beasts, *Aries, Taurus, Leo, Capricorne, Like as the foure Evangelist.* By winged Beasts foure, full of eyes. Which Motto, *come and see,* may serve them to *which rests not Day nor Night.*

And after foure of the Seales opened the mistery shewd of the foure seasons, the Suns restlesse course (to say) finish'd. *The next offer'd to considerations veiw, in this Story or Treatise, is the blessed case of those poore Soules intreated a little Season to rest: till their* Fellow Souldiers and Brethren *killed* as they, Whose Blood for the Testimony they held crying so loud, *How long Lord,* &c. to wit, to the day of vengeance, as behold defferd no longer the day of Judgement immediatly which followes in its dreadfull likenesse, when as fullfild, white robes given likewise to *the rest of their brethren arrayed,* (to wit) *in cleane Shrouds.*

Then Time *to his untimely end comes, whose thride of life suddainly cutt off, of whose sable Hearse thus, & what mourners accompanying the corps of time, about 44. aged in the midest of his dayes:* First the quaking Earth Mother of all in such a consumption. The Sunn next as black as Sackcloth of haire, coverd all over. And the Moone overwatched with her red face looking *like blood,* the condoleling *Heavens* shedding their stars in stead of teares as fast, impatient windes as loud: their shrill Throat setting forth, ready to rent all assunder with Sighes hollow Grones.

So all departing as they came: the Heavens as it were quartering those

---

Line 178. **grizled Goate:** Capricorn, astrological sign of winter.

Lines 181–82. **Aries…Capricorne:** astrological signs: the Ram, the Bull, the Lion, and the Goat. **foure Evangelist:** Matthew, Mark, Luke, and John, symbolized respectively by a man, a lion, an ox, and an eagle.

Line 193. **Shrouds:** shrouds; burial garments. Line 194. **thride:** thread.

Line 196. **44. aged:** The century and Charles I were both forty-four years old.

Line 202. **quartering:** the division of a shield or coat of arms into four parts.

Ancient Coates the foure Seasons, which were like Scutchens roled up together like a Scrole: The Islands carried away with the violence of the Seas uproare: Each acting a part, the Kings and Great men ringing out such a Peale, *all* flying away and hyding themselves for the great day of his wrath to come as who able to stand, routed *all,* surprised in such a moment *darkenesse.*

CAP. 7.

And these like *Jacobs* Ladder reaching at last to Heaven Gate: (*Ascen-*   210
dentem abortu solis:) *Behold saw foure Angels standing on the foure Corners of the Earth holding the foure Winds that they should not blow, &c.* Even gives to understand in what year the Finall blow, saying: *hurt not, &c.* till we have sealed so many, *And there were sealed a hundred forty and foure, &c.* of the servants of God in the fore heads, as much to say, the yeare of God, 1644. when compleat, then the disolution comes quickly or is at hand. *And thus like the Covenant of late sealed, where so many names also the months of the yeare, setting their hands as it were twelve times twelve.* verse 4.

And as including the yeare compleat or accomplished, 44. till when   220
those pernitious winds restrayned not to hurt the Earth nor any Tree: *So Aludes to that fruitlesse tree after the fourth yeare to be for borne,* no longer interceded, for in the Gospel. Wherefore *Sir,* these are to let you know it is spoken to your *Majestie,* the last of those crowned foure and twenty Elders, *being full forty foure aged, and reigning since aged* 24. *saying* Sir *thou knowest who they are, verse* 14.

That Albion Regiment, these Folke in white Robes fleeced and fam-ished as yee see, the very condition of Prisoners taken by you: The Prophet *Isaiah* gives notice of it, They are his words too, *Listen O Isles,*

Line 203. **Scutchens:** escutcheons; heraldic shields.

Lines 205–6. **ringing out…Peale:** ringing the church bells, which occurred on occasions of mourning and of celebration.

Line 210–11. **Jacobs Ladder:** Gen. 28:12. **Ascendentem…solis:** Ascending prematurely to heaven's gate (Latin).

Line 217. **Covenant:** the Solemn League and Covenant, an alliance made between Parliament and the Scots in 1643; also the Covenant or pact between God and the Israelites; see Gen. 17.

Line 222. **fruitlesse tree:** see Luke 13:7–9. Line 227. **Albion:** British; white.

230   *&c.* 49. Cap. That thou mayest say *to the Prisoners goe forth, to them that are in darkenesse they shall hunger and thirst no more, neither shall heat nor Sun any more smite them,* for the Lambe in the midest of the Throne having the seven eyes, *which are the seven spirits of God, shall wipe away all teares from their eyes.*

And more over for these words *aforesaid, as* serving for the midest of the Century, about the yeare, 44. So points at the very halfe yeare, *about Michael the Arch Angells Feast, the aforesaid Blow,* or last Blow, *there about till when those hurtfull winds restrained,* Michaelmas riggs so called.

240   As aforeshewed forbidden to hurt the Wine and the Oyle: all speaking as it were with *Automns* boysterous *voice,* a greater Blow then great Babylons, when that hand writing appeared, writen by that Angels hand, that Prince affrighting and his numerous Peers, not a little.

CAP. 8.

And *like as about halfe an houre after the clocke had stricken,* shews about the space of halfe an houre there was silence in Heaven, after the seales were opened which imports not only when a vacancie in the Church. *These Angels their standing before God then, preparing themselves to sound, but shews withall a space of time allotted to repent of their contempts stood*
250   *in, and cruelties before his men of warre sent forth.* But the marriage of the Lambe being ready they unworthy that were bidden: The censure fil'd with Alter Coales is cast downe the curse defer'd no longer, the aforesaid seven Angels so highly preferd, sound fire and sword, woe to Land and Sea.

And so the great Ship its being lanchd forth, shewed at large, ver.12. *likened to* Etnas *burning mountaine with like Sulpharous smoaks smiting of Sunne Moone, and Starrs, the third parte: and with such a spacious Lampe like a Starre even well named Wormewood: verily the Arch Bishops Charecter,* His lanching out or advancing both goes together: Bishops

---

Line 238. **riggs:** storm or strong wind.

Line 252. **Alter Coales:** coals left from a burnt offering on an altar.

Line 256. **Etnas burning mountaine:** volcano on Sicily.

Line 258. **Wormewood:** the name of a bitter plant.

and Ships able both to choake all with their smoakes and the like. The very root of bitternesse made of it, and this the meaning of this unluckey Starrs falling burning as a lamp. The contriver of this third kingdoms cumbustion this aforesaid high Officer in the Church, also with the yeare of God 1633. *September accompanied, when he translated as in truth this Prognostication serves from the yeare 1625. untill 44. compleat. The third Angells proclaimes it: Witnesse Woe, woe, woe, treble woes to the Earths Inhabitants* to wit, *England, Scotland* and *Ireland.* And so much for these Angels alarme imparted concerning the third part of creatures in the Sea distroied: and the third part of Ships. And the third part of the lights of Heaven smitten, and to slay the third part of men, Saying come and see or behold great *Brittains Mapp, as visible as the Heavens foure Seasons shewd in the Calender.*

Even *Lucifers* being cast downe lik lightning in our dayes First the Arch Bishop in whose custodie the Keys of the AByss power given him to imprison, Levie Taxes, wage warre at his pleasure, the loose Reines laid on his Necke that breake his owne the portion *of that aspiring Hypocrite full of the misterie of Iniquitie: And so much for the misterie of that malevolent Starre.*

CAP. 9.

Proceeding one with these calculated for this Kingdom shewing, as *Heaven* open'd and those horsemens comming proclaim'd come and see. *Also open'd the bottomles pit, ecclipsing the Sun and Ayre, set open by him the Sonne and Heire of perdition, father of that generation of Vipers: So Dragons and Deeps, like the evill spirits confesse and praise God when men faile.* For discovering whose comming at hand the day of judgements standing at the doore, the very current coine demonstrated of this Kingdome all horsemen, money made their Gold that odored Masse occasion of evills all, *Begetting such uunaturall doings, Warrs, and Imprisonments, desired death where it flees away, of late like Hell throng'd*

260

270

280

Lines 262–63. **third kingdom:** England (Scotland had erupted into war in 1638, Ireland in 1641, and England in 1642).

Line 264. **translated:** moved or transferred. Line 273. **Lucifer:** the devil.

Line 274. **AByss:** Abyss; also AB's (archbishop's).

Line 284. **Deeps:** abysses. Line 287. **odored:** smelly; perhaps punning on "adored."

290 *as full every where. Of which flying current halfe crowne peices Currentium
in Bellum, with Crownes on their heads, what peices of Plate they are no
need to aske or goe farre to inquire,* whose Image with deformed haire,
Hermophradite Locks, none of that mayden Queens doubtlesse with
Breast plates all, &c. such tormenting doings and Dolers unknowne in
her dayes.

And so much for those signes with that star of the bottomlesse pitt in
the likenesse of *Scorpio and Sagitarious, with faces like men, but as the
nose in the face or the like so difficult whose to discerne, whose superscription or discription, & with our* old Gold plainly called the Angel of the
300 aforesaid AByss (that Distroyer) not without a double signification like
those names, *Abbadon and Apollyon,* giving to understand withall as
under the Angels feet the Scorpion or Dra*Anglia* giving the Angells
name fatall to the Old Serpent *to receive there his fall.*

And here one woe is past (The sower of debate and division Anata-
miz'd) *And two woes more comming after, passing over how farre Civill
warre exceeds other. the Navyes preparation comes next, those winged Horses
of the Sea with Lyons heads and Serpents tayles.*

The winds withall prepared for an houre, a day, a moneth, and a
yeare, which Angels foure commanded to be loosed bound in the East
310 as it were: or Babylons great river *Euphrates,* not only points at that suddain hand writing sent but to the yeare of 1644. past as much to say,
then the third woe the day of judgement comes after or quickly, like a
Theife. Of which *Horse men even* bound *in the narrow Seas saying. He
heard the number of them or list of their names, with fire and smoake and
Brimstone issuing out of* their tayles the very firie Lake, to behold with
stinging great Gunns or peices chargd as here peices of all kinds num-

---

Lines 290–91. **halfe crowne peices:** coins. **Currentium...Bellum:** occurring in War (Latin).

Lines 292–93. **deformed...Locks:** In contrast to the short hair of the Roundheads (the parliamentarians), the royalists were known for their long hair and thus might be called hermaphrodites for combining long hair with their soldierly profession. **mayden Queen:** Elizabeth I.

Line 294. **Dolers:** grievings.

Line 297. **Scorpio and Sagitarious:** astrological signs, the Scorpion and the Archer.

Line 301. **Abbadon...Apollyon:** Hebrew and Greek names of the angel of the bottomless pit.

Line 302. **DraAnglia:** a word evoking and linking dragon, angel, and England.

berd, of late since discovered the *Indies,* And so farre for a discoverie of the time also, and these serving to explaine the rest: And the rest of the men that were not killed, &c: (verse 20.) repented not that they should not serve Divels of Gold and Silver, &c. (*Dæmonia*) neither repented they of their murthers, Fornications, and Theifts. As much to say, which had quarter for their lives, being Prisoners, yet so beastly as it Were come of the breed of bruit beast rather then man kind, like these monsters between a Horse and a Foule, some GRIFFINS winged or the like, with such renting teeth Ruffins of the pit of Hell halfe Divels: So to them, calling themselves Bishops out are none theirs the Keye of the kingdome of darkenesse.

CAP. 10.

The Misterie of God open in the Angels Hand (whose Face like the Sun) to give a touch againe of it not amisse, as crownd with the dayes of the Flood being 1700. yeares after the creation. So the very yeare 1625. under his hand beares date before this Odoriferous little Booke to be reveal'd, The Burthen of God Word received from Angelicall hands, The blessed Sacrament or Seale eaten of the Lords comming at hand, & therfore commanded to be publishd even proclaimd beyond Sea also, wherefore to his Lyons voice adds his speaking posture the one of his firie feet setting upon the sea the other on the Earth pointing to Heaven with a high hand, sweares in his wrath the apointed time is come.

By him above who lives for ever and ever, calling withall Heaven and Earth and Sea to witnesse with the things that are therein that time shall be no longer.

As displaied afore by things Celstiall and Terrestriall from the celestiall signes peices of coine and ships & great peic[ ] And as having shewd this booke his commission no lesse sweet thed Manna to his

---

Line 320. **Dæmonia:** demons or devils.

Line 322. **quarter for their lives:** exemption from being put to death.

Line 324. **GRIFFINS:** mythical animal with the head and wings of an eagle and the body of a lion.

Line 325. **Ruffins:** ruffians; brutal and villainous people.

Lines 326–27. **Keye…darkenesse:** cf. Matt. 16:19.

Line 343. [ ]: There is a blot on the page.

mouth, how distastfull so ever to others (persecuted by Antichrist,) Most willingly is taken though not unforetold how bitter a pille it would prove: So might be insisted on his writing to a LADIE (willing her) not to salute with Godspeed then of the factlon of Antichrist. But unwilling to be voluminus to intrude too farr on the bounds of patience 350   in distracted times.

FINIS.

_____

Line 347. **LADIE:** 2 John 1.

In the Church of England, Whitsuntide (Pentecost), the seventh week after Easter, commemorates the Holy Spirit's descent upon the Apostles. In this tract (Wing D1990) Lady Eleanor, who expected the Day of Judgment and the Second Coming before another year passed, offers her creed for what she believed would be the last Whitsuntide. She expresses here her belief in the possibility of "Redemption for all the DAMNED" (page 160, line 89). This belief distinguished her from the orthodox Calvinists, who were strict predestinarians. The copy on which the present edition is based is in the Library of Worcester College, Oxford (AA.1.12[32]). The other extant copy of *For Whitson,* which lacks pages 7–10 and which has part of page 5, all of page 6, and all of page 11 crossed out, survives in the volume of Lady Eleanor's tracts in the Folger Shakespeare Library.

FOR WHITSON TYDS LAST *FEAST:*
THE PRESENT, 1645.

ACTS the first:
The same JESUS *shall come, in like manner as yee have seene him goe, &c.*

Title. **THE PRESENT, 1645:** A handwritten annotation beneath these words reads "Lecesters Loss: revela. xi /The second woe is past: &c."

THE LA:ELEA: HER CREED OR Confession.

Verily as We all Beleeve *in* GOD, *the sole* Creator *of all* Things *that were made in the* beginning: *So* according *to His* promise *made also; Concerning the* Womans *SEED, of which the* Serpent, on forfiture or *pain of his* head, forewarn'd to beware: *do beleeve in our Lord* JESUS hee the *very* GOD: *alone* Redeemer of the *World,* born *of the VIRGIN, which Conceived by the Holy Ghost,* our only Sanctifier.

Who after he had finished on *the sixt day the* worke of *Our Redemption, and* rested the *seventh, rose* againe; And was by the *space* of *six*
10 *weekes* seen, *whose last Commandement* was to wait *for his* Fathers promise, of *the Holy Ghosts* comming *in whom We also beleeve.*

Wherfore of beleife not slow: in those Things written by the *Prophets* and *Apostles,* doe for mine own part *Confesse,* how *incredible soever* it seems to *Others,* I farther beleeve the second *Comming* of the *holy Ghost,* imediately before the *day of Judgement* acording to that spoken by the *Prophet Joel,* saying: GOD *saith,* afterward it shall come to passe, I will powre out my Spirit upon all flesh, before the great and terrible Day of the LORD: *Namely, on the Gentiles, their* Sonnes *and* Daughters *likewise:* And I will shew Wonders in the Heavens (*beside a New Star, not*
20 *long* since never) more frequent signes, & in the Earth *Blood, and Fire, and pillars of Smoake, &c. Witnesse such* warr, throughout *the* Christian world.

Of which last dayes, give *ME* leave to say, in *Grace* and *Giftes of LEARNING;* how *Rich* soever They *esteem* themselves: The *Gentiles* neverthelesse of a *Comforter,* more need had *Never,* how *much* soever *presume upon their Holinesse:* Supposing like the *Jewes* a *Saviour* for them *unnecessary,* which held themselves *so just:* And so *because* Christians already *cleansed;* likewise no more *need to be beholding:* Thus all *con-*

Line 1. **CREED OR Confession:** part of the church's liturgy; cf. the *Book of Common Prayer* (1604) and the *Directory for the Public Worship of God* (1644).

Lines 4–5. **Womans...beware:** cf. 2 Cor. 11:3–4; in Lady Eleanor's time, beheading was the punishment for members of the nobility who committed treason.

Lines 10–11. **his Fathers...comming:** Acts 2:33.

Lines 16–22. **Prophet Joel...world:** cf. Joel 2:28–30.

cluded under unbeleif, & *fearfull* blindnes, *unmindfull of that Charge, to feare by others wofull fall,* and not to bee highminded, Rom. 11. *And so for farther* justifying *this point touching* Prophecie *for ever not extinguished. But as the* Latter raine *no lesse requisit then the former,* though for a time ceas'd: Shall proceed *on with the everlasting* Gospel, *concerning the case of the* Gentiles *cut off,* in case of unbeleife.

As even the two witnesses *comming against them with* firie mouths, *that thinke to* quench *or silence the* Spirit of Prophecie, *well called Spirituall* Sodome *and* Egypt *that Citie. And he the* Beast as Bruitish, *ascended out of the Bottomlesse pit (as it were)* Judas *spirit conjured up, or* Herod *that* Fox, *together with the* Nations *or* Gentiles *as outragious as the* Jewes, *because these two* Prophets *tormented them, whose testimony publish'd,* the Old and New Testament those, *Luke* 21. *There shall be signs, &c. who* Maugre *their enemies stood upon their feet again: the* Spirit of life *entering into them.*

Intruth *as much to say, the* Prophet Daniel *stiled greatly beloved: and this favourite* Disciple, *their sealed* Bookes (*reserved for the end*) open'd *or to be* interpreted, *like themselves* lying dead and revived: *by the* Angels, *touch or hand. And as those sent two and two: before the* Lords face, even so the Messengers of the Resurrection, the two *witnesses* sent to prepare the Judge of quicke and dead his *comming* Revel. 11. Whose foes incensed so against them for the same. As the little Booke open in the Angels hand (Revel. 10) declares. Commanded to be eaten, *verily no* other then the Sacrament of the *Lords* returne sworne in his wrath as it were even times finished reigne, or dayes to be shortned.

And for this so distastfull to the world; *therfore* heavie judgements and Plagues and Warre appointed the day of Judgements forerunner as worthy of no other, when come to passe on earth such distraction, and the World six thousand years aged too, as in the sixt Century of *Noahs* age the Flood came upon the Earth, but so many dayes of the weeke (as it were,) in the *Lords account.*

And thus *he* one of the *witnesses John* bidden to arise, and measure

30

40

50

60

Lines 38–39. **Judas:** the apostle who betrayed Christ. **Herod that Fox:** see Luke 13:31–32.
Line 42. **Maugre:** in spite of (French).

the *Gospels Progresse* as it were, the Temple, how long until the rising
from the Dead, from his dayes bearing date 1700. yeares as the halfe of
seven gives it plainly, sealed up in those *Propheticall Characters,* the 42.
Moneths given them to prophecie, or a thousand two hundred & sixty
dayes, and so a time & times and halfe agreeable to the present division.
& *thus* both agreeing in one, stiled by the Prophet *Daniel,* a time and
times and the deviding of time, *whose Commission to* continu *so long:*
And then *he* whosoever *shall* oppose it *Though* never so great: as here he
stiled the *God* of the earth *no* lesse, these two as freely to proclaime open
70   warre so often as they please, to smite the *Earth* or *Land* with *Pestilence
and such Judgments, as those* Vials *of wrath* directed to the present *Century shew,* so much suffices: and how they were rewarded, their Sackcloth changed into a glorious cloud, and their Foes so much tormented
with their testimony, *how at the same time such an Earthquak the City
falling upon them,* except a Remnant which upon Repentance or peace
made, escaped.

And all these but speaking one thing in severall *Languages* (to wit) *the
Resurrections loud voice,* and that of the Ascension: as *ascendite huc*
added to those Propheticall firie tongues of theirs or fire proceeding out
80   of their mouths, if any will harme them suffices for the insuing feast
also, when fully come or finished wherefore with the 24 Elders that
great Councell or States sitting upon their seats forever with one consent and voice Let great *Brittain likewise* say; *Wee give thee thrice humble
thanks O eternal Trenity, which art, and wast, and art to come,* because
thou hast taken to thee thy great power and hast reigned.

And I beleeve *lastly,* though a *Mistery* none of *the lest,* like the *grace* of
God *bestowed upon the* Gentiles, *held as impossible* a point with the *Apostles: That after the last* Period *expir'd, ther is a* Release *out of* HELL,
Redemption for all the DAMNED, *Although granted that* sentence *Irevo-
90   cable,* Goe yee Cursed, &c.

And the unpardonable sinne, not in this world *nor that to come so given:
And the fire* unextinguished, *yet proves their* sufferings *not of like* nature

---

Line 78. **ascendite huc:** Come up hither (Latin); the direction given to the Remnant (Rev.
11:13).

and condition: Notwithstanding in danger, (were *God* extreame) *of endlesse torment: Therefore if* Salt *which* preserves *be good, the fire also necessary like th*[o]*se better to enter maim'd into* Heaven *then otherwise goe into fire* unquenchable *which goes not out, to our dayes without doubt* directed (*Marke the 9.*) *where so often repeated th*[o]*se words concluded,* have peace in your selves.

And therefore before that Parable *where mentioned the* gulfe *or fixed space, no other then a* prefixed space *of time. (Luke 15.) his* Elder *Brother* expostulating *reproves like* unnaturallnes *in others, without compassion of those undergoing the second death, in the lost* Son *instanc'd the second* brother, *as those words* saying: It was meet, &c. For this *thy* Brother was dead, and is alive again, was lost, and is found.

Approving of that Principle of every thing in the end, goes to its proper place from whence it came to returne. And so much for a doore in *heaven* opened; the mouth of Prophesie againe thundering out *Judgements,* (Revela. 4.) together *with these, the* Bottomlesse pit *opened* also, *hels* Epitomie & *their King over them,* where they not having the Seale of God in their foreheads (*some name given as it were*) These not killed seeking death fleeing from them where *so many months imprisonment shewd: as prisons never so fild as in those dayes:* Shall not need to add what yeare of God seald with, &c. where such innumerable Hors-men discribed to the life: *Currentium in bellum,* beside current *Coine* Half-Crown-peices, *super capita tanquam corone, & habebant capillos sicut capillos mulierum:* Revela. 9. *viz* &c.

And thus having cansel'd Purgatories numberlesse passes and pardons that take upon them to deliver others, and cannot out of such utter spirituall Darkn[e]*sse free themselves, deriv'd from hence:* thou *shalt* not come forth thence *untill paid the utmost mite. And hee without commisseration of his*

100

110

120

Line 109. **hels Epitomie:** the epitome or representation of hell.

Line 114. **Currentium in bellum:** running into war (Latin).

Lines 115–16. **super...mulierum:** on their heads as crowns, and they had their hair cut like the hair of women (Latin); Rev. 9:7–8.

Lines 119–20. **thou shalt...mite:** Luke 12:59; according to the doctrine of Purgatory, souls were condemned there until they had paid for their sins; also, prisoners were kept in prison until they had paid their fines.

fellow-servant served with the like *MEASURE:* delivered to the Tormentors, till paid all was due.

Al *ye* take to *your* comfort those armes *display'd, as said to the one, this day* Thou *shalt be with* ME, *&c.* So inferr another *like* day for the Other: And therefore, as the Lord lives that shall rayse us from the dust of death *so* the Lord lives (*let us say*) *that brings up out of the Jawes of* HELL *backe to Paradice,* and *increase our Faith.*

FINIS.

In *For the Blessed Feast* (Wing D1989), Lady Eleanor applies the message of the Book of Revelation to England. The present edition of this tract is based on the copy in the Beinecke Rare Book and Manuscript Library, Yale University (shelf number Mhc9 D743 F7).

FOR *THE BLESSED FEAST* OF EASTER.

Writs, By the La. ELEANOR.

Let the Heavens rejoyce, and let the Earth bee glad: Let the Field be joyfull, and all that is therein, before the Lord, for he commeth, for he commeth to judge the earth: he shall judge the world with righteousnesse, and the People with his truth.

Title. **Writs:** orders to institute legal proceedings; also something written.
Epigraph. **Let...truth:** Ps. 96:11–12.

TO THE ISLES OF Great *BRITTAIN* these;
From *PATMOS* ILE:

Because the time short, as here shewed, in the *NAME* OF GOD,
Amen: shall name the Child, Namely *the blessed LAMBE* extold so, *and*
magnified in the *Apocalyps:* Even the weeke of EASTER, (as much to
say) *when the generall RESURECTION time:* And this is the interpretation thereof; of which aforesaid Feast covered under NO few figures,
Metaphors and the like; Thus, <ye revelation>

    Given with such a speciall charge, *to keepe the things written therein;*
verse 3 (to wit) *contains Infalible fore-runners and signes, when the End of*
time at hand for the Churches Preparation *to stand on their* gaurd, *lest*
10 *surprised unawares.*

    And as here *Times* and *Seasons* mistery proclaim'd with *Times* treble
voices: *grace and peace from him which IS, and which WAS, and which IS*
to COME: And from the seven spirits before (or in sight of) *the THRONE,*
so shews withall His day of comming a GREATER then his proclaimed
BY great *BRITTAIN,* whose feast solemnized about the Resurrections
feast, *March* 27.: Those *first and last Princes, or Kings;* Of which last time
the Prophet *Daniel* Thus in his last; *And at that time shall* Michael *stand*
up the great Prince *&c.* who seales it *with* these, *Dan.*12. *And many that*
sleep in the dust, shall awak, &c. including those observed Feasts aforesh-
20 ewed, for an expresse token of the generall *Resurrection* in their Reigne,
and at that very time and season.

    Touching which turning again to the *Reve-*
    And with the Signe of the LAMB, *proceeding lation,* bearing the same
date, *vers.* 5. *And from Jesus CHRIST the faitfull* Witnesse, *the first begot-*
ten of the dead, PRINCE *of the* KINGS *of the Earth: That loved* US, *and*

Line 2. **the Child…LAMBE:** When John the Baptist saw Jesus coming, he said "Behold the
Lamb of God" (John 1:29, 36).

Line 11. **treble:** triple; also highest-pitched.

Line 16. **March 27:** the anniversary of the accession of King Charles I.

Line 22. **Touching…Reve-:** This line, which appears at the bottom of page 4 with the catch
word "lation", is perhaps an alternate beginning to the following whose first line on page 5 is
"And with the sign of the LAMB, proceeding".

washed US *from our sins in his own blood,* concluded With these, *and hath made us* Kings *and* Priests, *&c. To* HIM *be glory and dominion, for ever and ever,* Amen.

Behold HEE *commeth, &c.* Saying, *I am* ALPHA *and* OMEGA: Even so upon the LORDS day shewed unto that happie man: The Disciple whom the Lord above the rest entrusted, The likenesse of the dreadfull day of *JUDGMENT* standing in the middest of *Watch-lights,* saying; feare NOT, *I am the first and the last* King; *I have the* Keyes of HELL and DEATH: *Write the things which Thou hast seen, &c.* And he that hath an *Eare* let him heare the *Spirit of Prophecie, and repent.* Behold, I stand at the doore and knock, *to Supp with him who holds the seaven* Starres in his *Hand,* The evening of *TIMES* Ensigne.

And briefly beyond hope, that prevailed to open the seven Sealed Booke of Times Mystery; *after his much weeping, because no man was found worthy to read, or look thereon: No not the Prophet* Daniel, *who more then once was bidden go thy way,* (Dan.12.) *for the words are referred for the end of time.*

Thou shalt rest, &c.

Even so, Glory, Honor, *and* Peace, *be ascribed to the Lamb,* (Easter our Rest) *before whose face* (Rev. 6.) *Kings of the Earth, Mighty men, Great men, Rich men, and chiefe Captains, then taking their flight, as who able to stand in such a Storm of confusion, then commeth the great day of the wrath of the Lamb.*

Revel. Chap.7.

As here the yeare of Grace 1644. *followes, when. accomplished* (Or Seal'd) *those pernitious* Windes *till then not let loose.*

And the Seales *being sealed or oppened, thus proceeds.*

And after these things, I saw foure Angels standing at the foure corners of the *Earth,* holding the fower *Winds,* that the *wind* should not blow: Saying hurt not the *Earth,* nor the *Sea,* till *Wee* have sealed the Servants of God in the Foreheads. And I heard the number of them that

---

Line 37. **Ensigne:** standard or symbol. Line 43. **Thou shalt rest:** Dan. 12:13.

Line 50. **1644:** the year Lady Eleanor believed Judgment had occurred.

were Sealed, and there Was seald a hundred and forty &c. twelve times twelve, *serving both for the months and yeare, and the equall houres divided between day and night, when those unrestrained windes.*

60   *And as he heard the number of the one: Then after that (or the following yeare) which no man could number, so he saw of all Nations standing before the Throne, and before the* Lamb, *saying salvation to our God that sitteth upon the Throne, and unto the* Lamb, *the yeare of our salvation (to wit in the month of* March) *renown through the world beginning about* Easter. *And as by sitting on the throne expresses the* Rest *or* Sabboth *day when it began also, observ'd by Christians so long, likewise every one by those Palmes in their hands Ensignes of* Victory *and* Peace, *even proclaiming the Joyfull yeare 1645. this victorious time of such thanksgivings, wherein* Babylon *is blown up, and thus the last yeare, and the* New Model *signified hand in*
70   *hand who have washed their Robes in* the *bloud of the Lamb, and made them so fayre.*

Wherefore there needs no further question to be made of that *Albion Army,* who they are that serve him day and night, since not unknowne the condition of souldiers, companions of restles time, of whose service hard to judge between the state of prisoners, where desired, death flees away, and such liberty as they enjoy, which to be preferred or desired, (as the Prophets *Esay* 49) shewes or bindes them together here. That thou mayest say to the prisoners go forth, and them that sit in darkenesse, shew your selves. *They shall hunger no more, neither shall the heat*
80   *of the Sun smite them: The* Lamb *is their leader,* asmuch as to say *Easter* shall bid them welcom to the *L*ords table, and thus from their eyes teares wiped away by the *Lamb* in the midst of the throne, when peace and the day of judgement together going.

Lines 63–64. **yeare...beginning:** In the seventeenth century the English year began on 25 March.

Line 68. **1645:** the year of the parliamentary army's victory.

Line 69. **New Model:** Parliament's New Model Army had been established in 1645.

Lines 72–73. **Albion Army:** those in white robes (Rev. 7:14–15); also the British army.

Line 77. **Esay:** Isaiah.

Revel. Chap 14.

And following the *Lamb* whether he goeth, and his *Albion Troups* in their Virgin spring aray, his fathers name having in their foreheads, such a year of God, of the interpretation whereof as followes. *And loe a* Lamb *stood on mount* Sion, *and with him a hundred forty and foure &c.* where again the foresaid yeare of our redemption, witnes these words.

These are redeemed from among men, being the first fruits unto God and   90
the Lamb, And these whereas *singing a new song before the Throne, which song no man could learn but such a certain number a hundred forty foure which were redeemed from the earth, no other then some watch word given (as it were) shewing* When such a New time come to passe of Reformation, That then our Redemption drawes neere; As hereby shewed the houre come of his judgement, This for another signe *Babylons fall,* first her Numerous *Idols* cast downe its faln, its faln; The time exprest in that overflowing Wine presse of hers, a thousand six hundred bearing date.

Wherefore no marvell though *Syon* tunes up her Harps, so long out of tune, for such a blessed day where the Cup or Chalice of his indigna-   100
tion, not in a corner or in privat administred, but powred out in the Presence of the holy Angels, and in the Presence of the *Lamb:* Even NO more of their reall PRESENCE and the like, to wit, who have no Rest day nor Night, with sulphorous Smokes suffocated, in their own kind rewarded for the blessed Sabboth dayes violation, That solemne rest prophand.

Even so again on the other side *write, Blessed are the dead which dye in the Lord henceforth, that they may rest from their labours, and their workes follow them.* Shewing also for them with such Vallour and Courrage that have followed the Cause, these their everlasting Epitaph.   110

And so much for the NEW *Time,* and for *Babylons* judgement, the day of judgements forerunner, Her grapes being cryed full ripe, the

---

Lines 100–1. **Cup…administred:** God's wrath (Rev. 14:10); also the wine in the celebration of communion.

Line 103. **reall PRESENCE:** the belief that the body and the blood of Christ were really present in the bread and wine of communion, an interpretation of the sacrament associated with Archbishop Laud and others whom Lady Eleanor regarded as servants of the Beast.

Line 106. **prophand:** profaned.

houre unexpected Come, the Wine-presse trodden without the Citie up to the Horse-bridles, the horses too drinke their fill of blood without measure, the sixteen hundred yeares being fulfilled, serving for the measured compasse of this Island, 1600. myles also, Those furlongs. And this the contents of the *Apocalyps* 14. Chap. where Like the fruitlesse tree after the fourth yeare cut downe, sufferd to stand no longer.

And proceeding on, *Revela.* Chap. 19.

120 For the great dayes Preparation, as here: a greater priveledge then those *Writs* of Parliament to bee cal'd hether, to partake of The *Lambes marriage Supper;* A blessing to bee desired much more Then the *beauty of Lillyes,* to beare HER Company, granted she *should be arrayed in fine Lynnon, cleane and white:* As cleare by such *voices* and *Acclamation:* Of which marriage *Writs* to be published; briefly as followes: Requiring rather a quire of paper, Then circumscribed within the Narrow limmits of a sheet or two.

For such a meeting so long waited for: Represented (as it were) by the *ghests invited Now to the Lords table the* Easter-weeke: when as that
130 Deciple about to fall down and *worship, Charg'd; See thou do it NOT:* not the first caveat entred to flee *Idolatry.*

But going on with the *Season and Time,* a thing of such Consequence, as here the *Virgins day in Lent, after which, when Marriage licences so frequent,* accompanied with the *victorious Bridgrom, clothed in his Easter robes: a Vesture dipt in blood, proclaimed King of kings, and Lord of lords, that in righteousnesse makes war:* his Coronation feast then, as

---

Line 116. **furlong:** about an eighth of a mile; the distance the blood from the winepress spread (Rev. 14:20).

Lines 117–18. **fruitlesse tree…downe:** see Luke 13:7–9.

Lines 121–23. **Writs of Parliament:** the official summons to attend. **Lambes…Supper:** Those invited were blessed (Rev. 19:9). **beauty of Lillyes:** exceptional beauty (Matt. 6:28–9).

Line 126. **quire:** four sheets bound so as to form eight leaves. Line 129. **ghests:** guests.

Line 130. **Deciple:** disciple. Line 131. **caveat:** warning.

Lines 133–34. **Marriage…frequent:** The period after Lady Day was a popular time for marriage in England.

Line 135. **Vesture:** clothing.

crownd with so many Crowns, followed with his Saints, mounted or white Horses every one; a greater shew then *St Georges* his coming at hand, or any other. whose Name called the *Word of GOD,* that unknowne Name in another language (as it were) written, Not unlike those words: *Rex: Parliament: Peers &c. ver.* Where shewd lastly the fowls feasted on flesh, *the Storke and Crane &c.* Not ignorant of their time of comming, in the Spring time; *as the Horse* (Chap.14.) *swimming in blood up to the neck, which know their owner;* called unto the supper of the great God, to *assemble and muster* themselves *to eate the flesh of Kings, the flesh of Captains, the flesh of mightie men,* even Licenced by the *Lamb, all the fowls to bee filled:* All but so many *tokens, or Ensignes* displayed proclaiming when the houre of his *Judgement,* Come.

Revela. Chap. 21.

And as cald to witnesse here, a Reformation set forth before the *End;* a new Modell, a new *Heaven and a new Earth,* new *Jerusalem prepared as a Bride to meete her Husband, where no more paine, teares, and the like,* but like the Peacable Spring; when painfull Winter past, to such infirmities subject, as that heavenly voice making known; *Behold I make all things new, former things are past away, saying, it is done: I am* Alpha *and* Omega; seales it with that *unsearchable Name,* the quintessence of *Mistery* and *Mercy.*

And (in the second Moneth <The first vials> the Flood) of the dayes of *Noah,* returned in that *Angelicall name* inclusive Thus shewing *and, there came one of the seven Angels unto me, which had the seven vials full of the seven last plagues, saying, Come hether, I will shew the Bride the* Lambs *wife;* The seventeenth Century having its Vials, as from the Creation to the flood so many, being Baptismes figure, in the Fish preserved alive, those Creatures.

140

150

160

Line 138. **St George:** slayer of the dragon; patron saint of England.

Line 141. **Rex:** king (Latin).

Line 158. **second Moneth:** April was the second moneth according to the Julian calendar, which began the year in March. A handwritten annotation which reads "The first vials" follows the word "Moneth".

When the shining Bride at that time, preparing her person, *where-unto Solomon in all his* Lusture, Odors, *and* Ornament *not comparable;* as insues; no, Not the *Indies* and *Virginiæ* like the Churches glory before the End: accompanied then *with* the Spirit of Prophecie, to bee powred forth that odoriferous *Oyntment,* ever murmured at and envyed though.

170 And walking thus about *SION,* counting her Towers, also of that golden measure: Measured *a hundred forty and foure Cubits,* by the measure the Angel (*Winged time*) whose Viall or last glasse running: The meaning whereof having shewed afore, to be the accomplished yeare of grace 1644. So long before peace and truth to meet: shall passe by this point; where her Virgin reigne too of 44. years pointed at: together with those daies between *Ashwednesday* & *Easter,* as preparatives both, unmeet to be drowned in oblivion in this *divine* Calender.

Where the foure times three gates of that foure square City, even the foure seasons, each three Moneths allotted, and every gate, one pearle
180 (or Margarit) there one and thirty daies (to wit) So the moneths every one, with the Apostles names written in them, in this new Jerusalem, this no newes to shew it further, nor difficult to discerne by Sions impregnable Towers: the Tower of London its description: But then fin-ished in St. Johns daies: when Old Jerusalem at that time demolished, of which great store-house, with all its priviledges, let this suffice: These golden transparent streets being not unknown, letticed like glasse on both sides the mint: onely unlike in this, Those heavenly gates not shut at all: where no night there, no other then (as much to say) *This Booke to be unsealed of the Revelation; And faithfully interpreted, whether* or No
190 approved; Whether They heare or fe<a>re. <case>

Line 166. **Lusture:** luster; glow or sheen.

Line 168. **powred:** poured. Line 172. **glasse:** hourglass. Line 175. **her:** Elizabeth I's.

Lines 180–81. **Margarit:** margarite; pearl. **Moneths...names:** Lady Eleanor imagines a new calendar with months named for the apostles.

Line 186. **letticed:** latticed.

Lines 187–88. **gates...no night:** In Lady Eleanor's day, city gates were shut at night.

Line 190. A handwritten annotation obscures the printed text "They heare or feare"; written over "feare" is an "o", making it "fore", then "a[?] case". Lady Eleanor's meaning is unclear.

Revela Chap. 22.

And as afore: By such a lightsome Citty exprest, how clearly the *Truth to be revealed at Last:* SO againe, severall Demonstrations not wanting, and Similituds by a *Christall spring proceeding out of the* Throne *of God and the Lamb, that pure river of Life;* shewes the Resurrection *Time not unrevealed,* in that cleere Mirror shall see His face, as it were.

And so for this place, another Paradise, or Celestiall spring-garden set forth, let this suffice. A *Garden and a Cittie both,* where like the precious spring Times priviledge, no more *Curss,* there needs no Candle, there shall be No tedious *Night* vers 2. *As by the tree of life, on either side the* 200 *river: And in the midst of the street, &c.* Being this New Paradice its description. The present times face.

Where like Communion, and Fast-dayes; yeelding her fruite every moneth, also *Those golden* Leaves *for the healing of the Nations* in *such* endlesse *distresse and distraction* on every side, were it not for the Angels saying, *I come quickly:* Who takes his Leave as He began: *I am Alpha and Omega: Blessed is he that keeps the saying of this Booke,* even *the last Will and Testament of our Saviour given to his Disciple, who tooke and eate it up; that tree of life,* had the favour again to kisse his Masters hand that way, *with such a charg to read & hear the fame, commended by him to the* 210 *Churches;* only adding these, *because he comes so quickly,* now too <L>a<te> to repent or amend, *he that is unjust, and unholy, let him be so still; sleep on, and take their rest,* as it were, *the houre is come, when these Things come to passe: fulfilled* such a time.

And again, *John* so taken with these things, *seen and heard,* who could not forbeare or refrain; *but fell at the Angels feete,* again forbidden, *see Thou do it NOT,* worship God, concluding with that blessed time Thus. *And the Spirit and the Bride say come, and he that heareth These, let him say come:* Bearing date the blessed Virgins day, 1646. *And him that is athirst come; and whosoever will, let him take the water of life freely;* And 220 thus as invited to this Temple, forty-six yeares which was a building, the

---

Line 192. **lightsome:** radiant with light.

Line 197. **spring-garden:** pleasure garden. Line 199. **Curss:** curse.

Line 219. **the blessed Virgins day:** Lady Day, 25 March, the Feast of Annunciation.

Resurrections banquet to partake thereof. So these to be understood, together with the Sacraments divorce: (*the separation of the Cup from the Bread*) That he that shal take away also from the time prefixt of the Lords *blessed* comming, inclosed in this Booke, *shall not enter into, or be admitted his* Rest. Whose reward is with him, about *Easter,* to give them their wages every one.

The grace of our LORD, *&c. Amen.*

FINIS.

Lines 223–24. **separation…Bread:** an allusion to the Roman Catholic practice of giving the laity bread but not wine in the mass.

In 1646, as she had in 1645, Lady Eleanor made Whitsuntide the occasion of a tract. In *Day of Judgement* (Wing D1983) she interweaves the story of Noah (Gen. 7–8), the imagery of Whitsuntide in the ecclesiastical calendar, and Britain's experience as the first civil war draws to an end. She also draws heavily upon judicial practices then current in Britain. George Thomason dated his copy of the tract now in the British Library (shelf number E.337[23]) 25 May 1646. The present edition of *Day of Judgement* is based on a copy now in the Houghton Library, Harvard University (shelf number *EC65 D7455 B652t).

THE
DAY
OF
JUDGEMENTS
MODELL.

By the LADY ELEANOR DOUGLAS.

REVELATION, Chap. 7.
To day if yee shall heare his voice.

FROM THE La: *ELEANOR DOUGLAS.*
Upon the 7. Chapter of the REVELATION.

T*he* Time come to remove, the *Covering* having NO short space been shutt up in the *ARKE,* our *present* state *also* have *presented an Olive Leafe plucked from the* Tree *of* LIFE, *of the* Waters *abate dryed up,* as it were, *those* Teares *from the face of the Earth,* as appeares finish'd a tedious *Vale of Vanity:* for *soules* imprisoned without *release* and restlesse, till *Times* utmost minnit run out, or *Expired.*

    So of the *DOVES-LAST return findes rest for the* Sole *of her foote,* as
10 followes: Revealed even the most *holy and reserved of* Time *and* Seasons *conseald Mistery;* Except that of the unknown DAY and Houre imparted NOT to *Angels:* Namely, *NOT Yeares;* But forty *dayes,* The day of *Judgements* Last *Warning-peice;* AS the number of *forty* no stranger to the present either: which here bears date from *Easter-weeke* 1646. [*t*]or the *ASSENSION* thereabout, for appearance before the *Judge of quick and dead;* His great *Tribunall* extracted out of that *sealed* Number, *a Hundred forty foure &c.* Saying, *he heard the Number of Them* Revelati. 7. Chap. Wherefor the Keeper of the great Seal, and the Cryers voice, Thus (*verse* 2.)

20   Where farther contains These, belonging to Our *Clymate* or *Iland* described for a *Tryall before a Thron of Judicature,* NOT *heard till such an appointed* Time: witnessed by those restrained *Winds foure,* withall points at *Easter* Terme in *May,* the first Terme; Winesse the fresh Boughes in their hands, (*all in white Robes*) *Where the innocent Lambe,*

Line 7. **soules...release:** the condition of souls with no hope of general redemption.

Line 8. **minnit:** minute.

Line 9. **DOVES-LAST return:** see Gen. 8:11–12; Lady Eleanor's second husband, Archibald Douglas, occasionally signed himself "Arch Dove."

Lines 15. **ASSENSION:** the day of Christ's ascent to heaven, forty days after his resurrection.

Line 18. **Keeper...Seal:** the angel with the seal (Rev. 7:2); English legal officer who presided over the House of Lords and the Court of Chancery.

Line 23. **Easter...first Terme:** the first of the four terms into which the judicial year was divided.

Line 24. **white Robes:** see Rev. 7:5; the newly baptized wore white robes at Whitsunside; the boughs were covered with white blossoms in the spring.

as it were, *araignd before Them:* And by Them also evident, where the
Jury called by Name *Judah,* the *Fore-man* of those Twelve *godfathers* or
Elders sealed in the Foreheads, or *sworn-men;* And such innumerable
attendants as though the great day *Come: Such Legions of ANGELS
standing about the Throne, and about the Jury,* where *face to face the foure*
WITNESSES *all* Thronging *to heare their* Testimony, *Namely the foure* 30
Beasts, what they produce, These makes it plaine enough: About this
Prisoner, his holding up the hand at the *BARRE,* the very *MODEL* of a
Court, representing it: where shewes withall in the Peerlesse Lambs
Livory and posture; This his humble Servant, (*by the Lambe represented*)
presents his Person before the *Throne,* together with the woefull state of
so many Prisoners at this Time, being accompanied there-with:

But proceeding with this, the day of *Judgements Usher;* doubtlesse
where made by Them, such Lowe *Obeysance* to *HIM sitting on the
Throne, subscribing &* submitting to his Pleasure, saying, *Amen, &c.*
(verse) 40

And so the *Jury* also, those *Elders* No ordinary MEN: declares this
Prisoner one of their owne degree: NO *Common* ONE, pleading Not
guilty, neither deserving *death* or *imprisonment:* The *Lamb acquits HIM
here, though* Condemn'd. Nevertheless; *The white Robes* suffers, where
so many hands (as it were) held up; AS goes the *VERDICT:* SO the sentence *LORD have mercy on Them; And so theirs the* KINGDOM *of*
Heaven, as declared; *The* Lambe *hath Compassion on them;* HIM-SELFE
shall Lead Them to Living-Springs *and* Fountains: *Cœlestiall FOUN-
TAINS* and *SPRINGS, which never fayle, or shall be taken away,* intayld
so sure. 50

And in which portion of Scripture, as inclusive *Whitsontydes* mistery:

Line 25. **araignd:** arraigned; brought to trial.

Line 27. **sworn-men:** those who took oaths while participating in judicial proceedings; those who cried out, "Salvation" (Rev. 7:10).

Line 37. **Usher:** official or escort in the courts of law.

Lines 49–50. **intayled so sure:** To insure that land was preserved for descendants, lords entailed it or set up trusts so that no one holder could dispose of it.

Line 51. **Whitsontyde:** Pentecost; the celebration, seven weeks after Easter, of the descent of the Holy Ghost upon the Apostles.

Shadowed too under the *White Robe,* (as much to say) *The great and dreadfull day* in the Moneth of *MAY:* NO more *Whitsontides,* as by the Suns not *Lightning on them, &c.*

And so much for *Easter* and *Penticost,* a *feast* observ'd by *Jew* & *Christian,* cleerly exprest *by that sealed Number, and by the* others *without* Number *of so Many severall* Nations, *whereas* Noting withall; *Baptisme,* and the LORDS *Supper* adminstred (only) at those two Feast-times, as heretofore an Old custome: (*vers*) *So they shall* Thirst *no more,* NOR
60   *hunger* either *in that Kind,* an unlawfull restraint, without doubt points at the Present. Where *Virgins* excluded from *living Waters those.*

Herewith, one Thing more: Making known, touching That question By one of the Grand-jury-Elders, saying (*verse*) *What are These which are Arrayed in white, and whence come They?* Answered *HIM,* Sir, *Thou knowest,* (as much to say,) The present *Reigns character* or Colours: Serves both for the Yeare 1644. to bee accomplished before the Church her Triumphs or rejoycing shew: And his *Crownation* solemnized in *March* 1624. compleat about *EASTER:* HE, the foure and twentieth since the *Conquest,* of those *Elders In-Thrond:* As Not unknown, both
70   Father and Sonne about the aforesaid RESURRECTION *Feast* Crown'd. Who needs Then inquire what *STRANGERS* These? Much like as in the *Glasse,* one knew not *his owne FACE:* Or these in the SPRING, as it were, going a PRECESSION, *with those Palms in* Their *hands,* extended from the yeare, 1625. to the yeare, 1645. That deliverance *Time:* Hetherto forborn, (as it were, *the Winds restraind*) as since *Yeare,* 1605 so long since <for> that *Powder-Blowe* intended.

Line 63. **Grand-jury-Elders:** The Book of Revelation speaks of twenty-four elders (Rev. 5:8); a grand jury was composed of between twelve and twenty-three people.

Lines 67–68. **Crownation…March 1624:** Charles became king in March 1625, i.e., 1624. His formal coronation occurred the following February.

Line 72. **in the Glasse…FACE:** James 1:23.

Line 74. **1625…1645:** the time from Lady Eleanor's vision to the conclusion of the nineteen and one-half years that Daniel told her would remain until Judgment.

Line 76. **1605…Powder-Blowe:** the Gunpowder Plot; see note to line 130 on page 66.

Revelation, CHAP. XIIII.

And thus, abrupt for Expedition sake; Farthermore a touch *of This the finall blowe, for the sake of his Chosen: As* the *Time* shortn'd in consideration *of which,* the hastened *END,* So shewes how the WORLDS *mistical Weeke abated,* how much; *Before the houre COME* of HIS *Judgement:* By that great ARMEY *a hundred forty & foure Thousand, singing both one song,* with the former sealed Number, as *Chap.* the 7. informes: Extoling such a Yeare accomplished of our SALVATION, with these harping *The same* Note, *The yeare of our* Redemption, 1644. to bee accomplished, *Accompanying the Day of JUDGEMENTS houre, immediately which followes, Who before hand tune the* MARRIAGE-SONG, *so all following the* LAMB *whethersoever he goes.* Also <for> which Number includ[es]<ing> the 4000. *yeare* of the *world,* his Incarnation Then (*Chap.* 21)

[*And so much for*]<where> the Bride, prepared the *LAMBS Wife: Compared to such a uniform CITIE,* [*where*]<likewise> *a Hundred forty foure Cubits* the measured *wall;* (called *Salvation, Isaiah* 60.) Namely, the aforesaid Yeare of GOD, and serves for Dayes and Houres too, with the 4000 yeares (afore-shewed of the *World,* our Saviours being born of the *Virgin.*

A[*nd for*]<ll so for> the MISTICALL-WEEKE *of six* Thousand *Yeares* current, Thus exprest in the Number of the *Lambs followers:* The *Hundred forty and foure, &c. standing on the* Mount:

Even the *Houres* fulfilling of SIX DAYES, amounting to a *hundred forty foure Houres;* or Six times 24. (or 12 times 12.) As the equall Houres distributed to *DAY* and *NIGHT* about EASTER: *And six dayes, and six thousand yeares, all one with* HIM *Eternity,* so much suffices.

Where also <for y^e> *forty odd* DAYES, (*Chap.* 14.) between *Easter* and *Whitsontyd:* By his sitting on the *WHITE CLOUD* proclaimed, *One like the Son of MAN crown'd;* (to wit) *Whitsontyds figure or expression:*

Lines 80–81. **mistical Weeke:** the divinely calculated week, not the ordinary seven-day week.

Line 96. **Virgin:** An asterisk links this word to a handwritten annotation in the margin, which reads "wittness worship Him y^t made Heaven & Earthe &c :vers &c".

Line 100. **SIX DAYES:** the period immediately preceding Jesus' transfiguration (Matt. 17:1).

As this for another, *Cast in the same mould,* (Chap. 19. *&* 20.) *seal'd
with Him that satt on the White HORSE, with his* Albion-trayn. And
again, *Hee, who satt on the great white* Throne: from whose dreadfull
face, *EARTH* and *HEAVEN fled away;* And *hell and death delivering up
their* Prisoners, *as the* sand *of the* SEA: as the World *Then* to receive
Condigne reward, NO better which have improved their *precious Talent*
of *TIME,* sixteen compleat *Centuries* since *OUR blessed* Saviours
INCARNATION, proved by Scripture account.

Witnesse <since> that *Universall* imposed *Taxe,* in the Yeare ONE
and FORTY of *Cæsar August-reigne:* which OF the present heavie dayes
since (1641) *comes short:* Of whose difficult Number 666. so obscure.
The *truth of it,* even so many Moneths as stiled the Number of a MAN.
And the Moneths of *WOMAN* her *Reckning too;* So Fullfils HIS 55.
Yeares Reigne and a halfe. Wherein the *peace-maker, the Lamb of* GOD,
came into the World: confirm'd *by* the 42 *moneths* (or yeares 3. and a
halfe) of the cruell Beast, *bearing seven heads and tenne horns,* (*Chap.*
13.) That who needs then to be unresolv'd, *who the* Man *of sin; Or* what
date that writing <in Her fore Head> bears (*mistery Babylon*) Or whom
it Concerns (*Chap.* 17.) No lesse then the day of *Judgements* expresse
Character, by those *Sabbaticall heads, and sinfull horns ten:* when *as the
Man of sin,* the ROMAN *Beast* aged 17. *Centuries.* And <By> *the servants of the Lamb as sealed in the foreheads with his Fathers* Name: Likewise the *Beast with his marke* shews what *Communion* his Factors
(*papists*) have, with [ ]<the Name of> their *Father.* <yᵉ pope>

Line 108. **Albion-trayn:** see Rev. 19:14; also English armies. Line 112. **Condigne:** deserved.

Line 115. **Universall...Taxe:** tax imposed by Caesar at the time of Jesus' birth (Luke 2:1).

Lines 116–17. **heavie...since (1641):** years of civil conflict and heavy taxation in England.

Line 119. **55:** 666 months amounted to 55.5 years; Lady Eleanor was fifty-five in 1645. If one
calculates Caesar Augustus's reign from the death of Julius Caesar, he ruled fifty-five years. If
Charles I had lived until 1655, he would have been fifty-five.

Line 126. **Sabbaticall:** seven.

Line 127. **ROMAN Beast:** Lady Eleanor's description of the Roman Catholic church.

Line 129. **marke:** An asterisk links this word with a handwritten annotation in the margin,
which reads "yᵉ Agnus Dei". **Factors:** agents or representatives.

Line 130. [ ]: The deleted word is illegible.

And thus in the 15. Yeare of *Tiberius* Reigne, (as Saint *Luke* beares witnesse) Our *Saviour* about 30 Yeares of age *Then,* That was about the age of Yeares 15, When as *Augustus HE deceased,* since when the Moneth of *August* Continues in the Name of the *BEAST* ever since; So then the aforesaid Monethes his Numbred reigne. Who that Other, with *two Horns like a Lambe, That exerciseth all the Power there,* <of yᵉ first> *where NO Man buys or sels, &c.* No more but referred to themselves.

So prayse him the ancient of dayes, for ever-more Day and Night, his ancient servants, Hee that hath begining None or ending.   140

Lastly, for which premises concerning *Prisoners* araignd, *These keyes of darknes,* excluds Not these, of expressing the Churches power *of* binding & loosing: As here The Model or patterne Therof: What Discipline Agreeable with the APOSTLES, Rules Included: where The PEO-PLES approbation and Consent: As it were shadowed under That Multitudes Holding up their HANDS, with Those Sealed ELDERS Verdict or Judgement, joyning Their Voyces, saying; AMEN, &c. As directed to *Eastern and Western Churches* both, (Verse 2) By that *Angels ascending from the East.*

[*And thus*] concluding with the Number of *his* rageing Reigne, the   150
Antichristian Beast: Even since that *Sea-Monster* 88. With *that Admirable* Victory, *Just 666. monethes,* or 55. Yeares and a halfe; *So just and true are Thy wayes: Thou King of Saints. &c.*

FINIS.

Line 131. **Tiberius:** Roman Emperor (A.D. 14–37) following Caesar Augustus (Luke 3:1).

Line 133. **August:** named for Caesar Augustus.

Line 137. **sels:** An asterisk links the word "sels" with a handwritten annotation in the margin which reads "Except them of His Name or Haveing yᵉ crucifix adord:"

Line 151. **Sea-Monster 88:** the Spanish Armada that attempted to invade England in 1588.

For this tract (Wing D1972) Lady Eleanor uses a title very similar to one she used in 1641, but this is not merely a new edition of the earlier *Her Appeal to the High Court* (Wing D1971—page 75 in the present edition). Here she tells the story of her becoming a prophet and of her subsequent experiences, in order to show the preparations for Judgment and the Second Coming. The present edition of this tract is based on a copy in the Bodleian Library, Oxford (shelf number C.14.11.Linc.[14]).

THE LADY *ELEANOR*
HER
APPEAL.

Present this to Mr. *Mace* the
Prophet of the most High,
his Messenger.

2 PETER 3.3.

Knowing this first, that there shall come in the last days Scoffers, saying, Where is the promise of his coming?

JUDE 18.

Remember yee that they told you, there should be Mockers in the last time, having not the Spirit.

Subtitle. **Mr. Mace:** probably Thomas May, appointed secretary to the Parliament in 1646; a mace is a club or staff carried before an official, such as the Speaker of Parliament.

From the Lady *Eleanor* the Handmaid
of the Holy Spirit,

To Our beloved Brother Mr *Mace*,
the Anointed of our Lord.

Having in the burthen of his precious Word been my self a partaker,
made a publique Example, no mean one, concerning the way before the
Lords coming to be prepared, Have thought it not unnecessary by what
means it came to passe, to impart and publish the same unto your self,
in making known some passages, the truth of which unknown not unto
the whole world, almost ever since the Year 1625.

Shewing withall about a few dayes before the former Kings departure
this life, how first of all there came a Scotish Lad to this City, about the
age of Thirteen, one *George Carr* by Name, otherwise cald the dumb
Boy or Fortuneteller, so termd, that spake not for some space of time,
with whom it was my hap, upon a visit, to meet where some of them
would needs send for this Boy, although few more jealous of such
acquaintance or sparing, yet able to discern between such a one and
Impostures, making bold before my departure thence, to direct him the
way to my house, where care should be taken of him, not the lesse
because a Stranger, accordingly who there abode, where no simple people, but expert and learnd as any, try'd no few conclusions; some
instanced as here:

Sometimes who would take the Bible or a Chronicle, and open it,
and close it again, then cause the aforesaid Youth to shew by signs and
such like dumb demonstrations, what was contain therein; which
things he so to the life exprest and acted, as were it a Psalm or Verse then
feignd to sing, though saw not a letter of the Book; and sometime that
suddenly behinde him would blow a Horn, whereat never so much as
changed his look, seemd so hard of hearing. And again thus, to sound

---

Lines 11–12. **former…this life:** King James died on 27 March 1625.

Line 15. **hap:** happenstance or chance. Lines 19–20. **not…Stranger:** cf. Matt. 25:35.

Line 21. **try'd no few conclusions:** tests to determine whether George Carr was a fraud.

Line 27. **feignd:** pretended.

him farther, one must stop his ears fast, and then what [one] whisperd   30
at the other end of the Gallery, he must declare what they spake in the
ear, as often as they pleased several times.

Having by that time gotten a whistling voice, as plain as any can
speak, like a Bird; before that had used signs for the space of three
Moneths, then no longer dumb or deaf.

To conclude, whatsoever it were he able to manifest it, whether con-
taind in Letters enclosed in Cabinets, or by numbring how many pence
or pepper corns in a Bag or Box before it was opened, or any thing of
that kind fit for the vulgar capacity too; or when he was brought into
any place amongst Strangers, one should write in several papers every   40
ones Name, and he must give them accordingly to each his own Name,
at first making as though he were in some doubt which way to bestow
himself, where the chief Divines of the City present, some of them
bestowing a shilling on him, without farther consideration thought it
sufficient, &c. whilest others of that calling as liberal of their slanderous
tongues; that no longer might be harbored in our house, likened to
Friar *Rush,* Servants had so incensed their Masters, setting all on fire,
with Justices of Peace and Church-men, giving out he was a Vagrant, a
Counterfeit, or a Witch. Immediately upon which the Spirit of Prophesie falling likewise upon me, then were all vext worse then ever, ready to   50
turn the house upside down, laying this to his charge too: when laying
aside Houshold cares all, and no conversation with any but the Word of
God, first by conference with the Prophet *Daniel, cap.*8. *ver.* 13. I found
out this place, *Then I heard ONE Saint speaking unto another Saint, said
unto that certain Saint which SPAKE* (in the Ori[gi]nal (to wit) *The
Numberer of Secrets, or the wonderful Numberer* (Hebr. *Palmoni*) *How*

Line 39. **vulgar capacity:** the taste of the common people.

Line 43. **Divines:** clergy. Line 44. **shilling:** a coin worth twelve pennies.

Line 47. **Friar Rush:** *The Historie of Friar Rush* (1620) told the tale of a devil who deceived
people by representing himself as a friar.

Lines 48–49. **Vagrant…Witch:** all punishable by law. Line 50. **vext:** vexed; troubled.

Line 56. **Palmoni:** Palmowniy; a certain one (Hebrew); Dan. 8:13 refers to "that certain
saint."

*long the Vision concerning the daily, and the Transgression making desolate,
to give the Hoste, &c. And he said unto me, Unto Two thousand three hundred dayes, then shall the Sanctuary be cleansed.*

60   The sum of it this, as much to say, Inquired of such a one that spake
not at first, How long from the Vision before this Prophesie shall be
reveald, or whether I should be able, &c. as now about Two thousand
two hundred years complete since the Captivity, as here answered, *O
Son of Man, for at the time of the end it shall be: Behold, I will make thee
know in the last end of the indignation, for at the time appointed shall be
the end, Daniel, cap.* 8.

And thus not only providing for that aforesaid admired Guest, but
adored him almost; how it afterward came to pass, like that least of all
seeds, how it sprang up, as follows: Here following the Prophets their

70   order in these circumstances, Time, Persons, and Place, observed: Shewing,

In the aforesaid Year, 1625. the first of his Reign, the first of his
Name, in the Moneth of *July,* so called after the first Roman Emperor,
in *Berks,* the first of Shires, my self whose Father the prime Peer, or first
Baron, being at my House in *Englesfield,* then heard early in the Morning a Voice from Heaven, speaking as through a Trumpet these words;

*There is Nineteen years and an half to the Judgement day, and be you as the
meek Virgin.*

When occasioned through the plague, that heavy hand, like the Wise

80   mens coming from the East, the Term came down to *Reading* our next
Market town; and that first Parliament following it posting down to

---

Lines 68–69. **least...seeds:** see the parable of the sower (Matt. 13).

Line 72. **his Reign:** Charles I's.

Line 73. **first Roman Emperor:** Julius Caesar, who gave his name to the month of July. Historians usually call his successor, Caesar Augustus, the first Emperor.

Line 74. **Berks:** Berkshire, the county in which Lady Eleanor's home, Englefield, was located. **Father...Peer:** Lady Eleanor's father, Baron Audeley, claimed that he had been first among the barons when King James came to the crown.

Line 76. **Voice...Trumpet:** cf. Rev. 4:1.

Lines 79–80. **Wise...East:** cf. Matt. 2:1; because of the plague the law term was adjourned in the summer of 1625, and the lawyers and judges held their courts in Reading (west of London and not far from Englefield).

Oxford, not far off either: And somtime as in *Augustus* days, so in this of great Britains second Monarch, taxed likewise with no ordinary taxes levied; when this morning Star, this second Babe born, ruling the Nations with an iron Rod, no light Judgements foreshewing at hand: which words in a Manuscript annex'd to an Interpretation of the Prophet *Daniels* Visions, A few days finished afore, was then immediately for to be published, carried to *Oxfords* Parliament, that ancient'st of Universities, this golden Number heard, extending to the Year 1644. *January.*　　　　　　　　　　　　　　　　　　　　　　　90

Which Book perfected about the first of August, was with mine own hand delivered and presented to *Abbots* Archbishop, where the Babe signed in the presence of no few witnesses, with this token, That the great Plague should presently cease; that Curse so furiously pourd out on the desolate City, where grasse grew in her chief streets should be inhabited.

At which time the weekly Bill amounted to Five thousand; but because the next week it increased Six hundred, this Token of such deliverance was utterly cast out of remembrance: Howbeit before the end of August, scarce Five hundred of the Plague deceased, in such an　100 instant vanished, which somtime was grown up to that height as the Age of the World, Five thousand six hundred.

Concerning which aforesaid judgment or blow, foreshewed no other then the day of Judgements expresse forerunner, the worlds final blow at hand; upon farther consult with the Scriptures, the Book of the *Revelation,* understood how with the 7. Chapter it accorded, saying, *And I saw four Angels standing at the four corners of the Earth, holding the four Winds that they should not blow,* until expired such a time, such a year.

Line 82. **Augustus:** Caesar Augustus, Roman Emperor at the birth of Christ.

Lines 89–90. **golden Number:** used in calculating the date of Easter Sunday; a number with mystical significance. **1644. January:** nineteen and one-half years from July 1625.

Line 92. **Abbots Archbishop:** George Abbot, archbishop of Canterbury. **Babe:** Lady Eleanor's book of prophecy.

Lines 94–95. **Curse...desolate City:** cf. Rev. 18:19; London in the summer of 1625.

Line 97. **weekly Bill:** Bill of Mortality, a weekly report of deaths in London and the surrounding area.

Where that new prognostication beginning with the loud Moneth of
110 *March,* shews till 1644. those pernicious winds restrained under the
seald Number of One hundred forty and four, &c. the conseald time in
those Characters inclosed: So again Chapter 14. where those mustered
Troops on Mount *Zion,* seald in the forehead with the same Number,
One hundred forty and four thousand, encluding the fourth thousand
year of our Redemption, when he born of a Virgin not only, but the
year of Grace, 1644. when *Babylon* falls; *Shee's faln, shee's faln:* together
with the Kalender for that year, beginning with the blessed Virgins feast
(vers.) saying, *They are Virgins, &c. Redeemed from amongst men the first
fruits.*

120 And so much for the new Song, which none besides could learn, too
difficult for former Ages, too high a noat to reach.

To which the 21. Chapter answers, where she that virgin Cities walls
measured, *One hundred forty four Cubits,* the Churches preparation
then, or Reformation before the end.

And since prophesies Thundring Reign began, what judgments since
the year 1625 *July,* shal give you a list of some of them; beginning at
home first, where this Book of mine was sacrificed by my first Husbands
hand, thrown into the fire, whose Doom I gave him in letters of his own
Name (*John Daves,* Joves Hand) within three years to expect the mortal
130 blow; so put on my mourning garment from that time: when about
three days before his sudden decease, before all his Servants and Friends
at the Table, gave him passe to take his long sleep, by him thus put off, *I
pray weep not while I am alive, and I will give you leave to laugh when I
am dead.*

Accordingly which too soon came to pass, for contrary to a solemn

---

Line 111. **conseald time:** see Dan. 12:9.

Line 117. **blessed Virgins feast:** the Feast of the Annunciation, Lady Day, March 25, the
beginning of the new year under the old calendar.

Line 121. **noat:** note. Line 125. **prophesies Thundring Reign:** cf. Rev. 14:2.

Lines 127–29. **first Husbands…Joves Hand:** Lady Eleanor's anagram predicts Davies would
be touched by the hand of God, i.e., die.

Line 132. **gave him passe…sleep:** told him he could die. **put off:** dismissed.

Vow within three Moneths married to another Husband, who escaped
not scotfree: he likewise burning my Book, another Manuscript, a
remembrance to the King for beware great Britains blow at hand, shewd
him thus, *Dan.* 12. *And at that time shall Michael the great Prince stand
up, and there shall be a time of trouble, such as never was since a Nation,*   140
with the Resurrection in his time to be prophesied: & for a token of the
time, *At that time the people shall be delivered,* their oppressors put to
flight; where very Parliament-Stars shining for ever, as by such a solemn
Oath taken there sworn, &c. the contents of that last chap. verily concluding with the first year of the present Reign, 1625. signified in those
no obscure characters, *Blessed is he that waits:* And comes to Three hundred thirty five; which being added unto the former reckoning of Two
hundred and ninety, amounts to 1625. to wit, when this sealed Vision
before the end shall be revealed, witnesse the troublesome time.

And of *Daniel* signifying Judgement too: Thus about two years after   150
the Marriage, I waiting on the Queen as shee came from Masse or
Evening Service, All-Saints day, to know what service shee pleased to
command me; The first question was, *When she should be with Childe?* I
answered, *O portet habere tempus,* Interpreted by the Earl of *Carlisle:*
and the next, *What successe the Duke would have, who* (the queen said)
was intrenching, and much forwardnesse in? Answered again, As for his
honor, of that he would not bring home much, but his person should
return in safety with no little speed; which to neither side gave content,
satisfied not his Friends, much lesse such as look'd after his death.

Line 136. **another Husband:** Sir Archibald Douglas.

Line 137. **scotfree:** Douglas was a Scot.

Line 143. **Parliament-Stars:** cf. Dan. 12:3. Line 146. **Blessed…waits:** Dan. 12:12.

Line 151. **the Queen:** Henrietta Maria, wife to Charles I.

Line 154. **O portet habere tempus:** The time might come (Latin). **the Earl of Carlisle:**
James Hay (d. 1636), a courtier.

Line 155. **the Duke:** George Villiers, first duke of Buckingham, who commanded the English
fleet.

Line 158. **to…content:** satisfied neither supporters nor opponents; the duke had been the
focus of an impeachment effort in Parliament in 1626 and had both friends and enemies.

160   Besides, told the queen, for a time she should be happy, *But how long said she?* I told her, Sixteen years, that was long enough. But by the Kings coming in our discourse interrupted, saying, *He heard how I foretold my former Husband of his Death some three days before it:* Said I, I told him of a certain Servant of your Majestie: one extraordinary proper, &c. that forthwith was to come upon earnest businesse to me; and that he ask'd me the next day before his Death, when I expected My Gentleman: To which his Majesty replied, *That was the next way to break his heart,* who was pleased so much to commend my choyce without excepting any.

170   And so that time Twelve Months the queen conceived of a Son, and although had forgotten me, yet some about her I informed, that her Son should go to Christning and Burying in a day. <Coming before Her time.>

And the Duke accordingly too miscarrying, arrived safely the week after I had been there; of whose moneth of *August* to continue till then, not misinformed of it by persons of quality, told him from me; whereat Sir *Archibald* my Husband so much vext, ventured (at my motion) to lay the Breeches, before Mrs *Murrey* for one, and Mrs *Maxfield,* if I would be bound when it came not to passe, to abjure such my predic-
180 tions, wimzees, as he termd it, that sold the blessing was disappointed.

Whereupon seconded by his Uncle the Dean of *Winchester,* who wrote up to him to put me in minde *September* was at hand, *and that secret things belongs to God, &c.,* but shortly after craved me pardon, because it seemd I had added, *The Duke should never see a day in September;* (one bewaild on all sides, as though would throw the houses out at windowe, Worshipped so much before; But still pressing Great *Britains*

Line 160. **Besides:** An asterisk links this word to a handwritten annotation in the margin, which reads "shewing she should have a Sonn."

Line 175. **whose moneth of August:** Lady Eleanor predicted that the duke of Buckingham would not live beyond August 1628.

Lines 177–78. **to lay the Breeches:** to determine who is in power or who is right. **Mrs Murrey…Mrs Maxfield:** women at court.

Line 180. **wimzees:** whimsies.

Line 181. **his Uncle…Winchester:** Douglas's uncle, John Young.

blow, for which purpose to be near the Court, taking a house at Saint *James,* where the King not pleased with such Alarms, commanded one of his Bed-chamber, Mr. *Kirk,* to go from him, *and know what I had to do with his affairs; and if I desisted not; he would take another course:* To which my answer was, I would take my course against him, namely, Sir *Archibald Dowglas* that had burnt my papers to purchase his favor, and that he and all should know shortly.

In the conclusion Mr. *Kirk* said; *He was not carried with the vulgar, but prayed me to tell him whether the King should have a Son, or no:* unwilling to send him empty away, assured him a Son, and a strong Childe; which he not sparing to impart, accordingly solemnized was with Bonefires, &c. within a Moneth.

At which time, the first day of *June,* his Servant Sir *Archibald Dowglas* in *Martins* Church at the Communion, was strooken bereft of his sences, in stead of speech made a noice like a Brute creature, doubtlesse his heart changed into a Beasts too, for so would put his head into a dish of Broth, of Lettice or Herbs, and drink Oyl and Vinegar, and sometimes Beer all together, insatiable that way, knew no body but only my self, though it was not my hap to be at *London* then, nor when my former husband as suddenly dyed, but in *Berkshire,* through Gods providence the day before that saw them both.

Some three months before in the presence of the Lady *Berkshire* & the Lady *Carlisle,* who imputed it to want affection, that needs would have reconciled the businesse, declared sentence upon him, *Not so happy to be to dye, nay worse then death should befal him;* and so before all his Friends, who witnessed it with their Hands, the writing was drawn up, bearing Date in *March* 1630, &c. *That if in the Moneth of June next some such wonderful judgement from God came not upon him, then in a Sheet I would walk to Pauls barefoot;* whilest he boasting, *How with a Greyhound*

190
200
210

Lines 187–88. **Saint James:** area of Westminster near the court.

Line 200. **Martins Church:** St. Martin's in the Fields, the London parish church of Lady Eleanor and her husbands.

Line 208. **Lady Berkshire:** a near neighbor of Lady Eleanor in London.

Lines 214–15. **in…barefoot:** do penance at St. Paul's, the seat of the bishop of London.

he could run up a hill in the Snow, and the like. Where a witty Divine, one of the witnesses, saying, *Sir, give my Lady* Youly *for it:* And so though until the Moneth of *Youly* given, yet accomplished the first day of *June* on a Sunday at *London,* going up to give his Attendance at the

220　Princes Birth: his Uncle Dean *Young* when he saw him, saying, *I had turnd him now into his long Coats indeed;* And which aforesaid Divine was drownd, soon after the Boat cast away, that then lose his jest, would sooner lose his friend:

And as *Elisha* said to *Elijah, Hee would not leave him;* so passing on with what became of the house where those papers of mine at Saint *James* received Martyrdom, *Lex talionis,* immediately was burnt down, with no few of his Majesties choyce Books, re-edified since; And first of all as since in *Ireland* in a house of ours burnt eighty, all Scots; which unhappy house (left by me) Mr. *Patrick Yong* the Deans Brother would

230　needs take it, turnd to a Library, and he following his Brothers Text, *That reveald things belongs to us, Deut.* with his hand in Hebrew, Greek and Latine, written on a piece of the Book, having to the fire, like an old Sot for his pains, sacrificed the rest.

And not thus resting, shall give you a passage or two more; shewing the holy Spirit besides speaking with other Tongues, able to speak without a Tongue sometime, as by the Prophet *Ezekiel* to that rebellious Age, growing downward, by his portraying and the like: Shewing a few days before my deserting the aforesaid house, coming home, having been forth, and meeting with one seeming dumb, that came along with me,

---

Line 217. **give my Lady Youly:** extend the period during which her prophecy was to come true from June until July; accuse her to her face or give her "you lie" (a pun).

Line 221. **long Coats:** baby garments. **aforesaid Divine:** the "witty Divine" (Line 216, above), not Douglas's uncle, the dean, who lived until 1654.

Line 224. **Elisha...to Elijah:** see 2 Kings 2.

Lines 225–26. **papers...Martyrdom:** Lady Eleanor's prophecies were burned. **Lex talionis:** the law of retaliation (Latin).

Line 232. A handwritten annotation in the margin reads "ould scripsi scripsi", Latin for "I wrote, I wrote".

Line 233. **Sot:** habitual drunkard.

Lines 235–36. **speaking with other Tongues:** see Acts 2:4. **speak without a Tongue:** conveying a message through a vision. **Ezekiel...Age:** see Ezek. 2.

Soldier like, with a long garment or russet Coat, a red Crosse on the sleeve, by signs uttering his minde; where leaving him at door, without other notice, cold welcom, that had watched about the house all day, as they told me, calling to minde what trouble by such a one befel: presently after comes in Sir *Archibald Dowglas* my Husband from *Whitehall,* followed with a Chaplain and some six Servants, affrighted all, protested he had met with an Angel, whose custom always to give something to the poor, saying, He was come with him, a yong man very handsom, about his age, praying me to come forth; the Servants vowing he came out of Heaven, otherwise might (in the open fields) seen him afore suddenly who caught their Master by the arm.

Which man applying himself wholy to Sir *Archibald Dowglas* by such discoursing signs, of his late marriage, and former course of his life; would not a look vouchsafe me, till at last by locking, as it were, and unlocking a door, which I interpreting to presage prison, he assented unto this token bestowed on me; and Sir *Archibalds* back turned, then stept within the door as none should see him but my self, by pointing at him, and bending the fist, looking up as it were to Heaven, as though some heavy hand toward: About a Moneth after that lost both Reason and Speech, by like signs feign to learn his meaning, as he able to impart his minde, formerly shewd.

When this Messenger departing, as though had far to go, as swift as an arrow, having taken a shilling in good part, though promised as many pounds would he come again, by spreading the hands which he seemed to understand; where like conference to have, many of the Court sending after him, standing at St. *James's* gate to staid him; but no more of him heard, amongst the poor though inquired, whether knew any such. Moreover shewing us a Verdict should passe on our side for *Englefield,* pointing westward; about a fortnight after coming to passe in *Easter* Term: whereof all our neighbors at Berkshire house, and

240

250

260

Line 253. **vouchsafe:** give. Line 263. **pound:** English monetary unit of 20 shillings.

Lines 267–68. **Verdict...for Englefield:** Lady Eleanor and her husband were involved in lawsuits about claims to Englefield.

Line 269. **Berkshire house:** next to Lady Eleanor and her husband's house in London.

270 Master *Gwin* and the rest till it came in much expectation, the only
Tryal that gave us our right.

And since faln on this chronological Discourse, a passage or two
more that would fill almost a Library, were all written as that Disciple
wrote, the world would not contain the Books: Upon day visiting the
Countesse of *Berks,* where the Earl of *Holland* present and others, and
the Countess of *Carlisle,* who as I was informed by Lord *Andevere,* made
no secret of it; And some Relating of the Lord *Stewards* sending about
casting his Nativity to one at *Clarkenwel;* the wiseman had told he
should live to the Age of Fifty nine: But my judgement otherwise I told
280 them, for being born when the great Earthquake was, by the same token
his mother saying, *He would prove a Coward,* wisht him to harken to
me, for 49 was his <Jubile> time appointed, who suddenly a day and [ ]
<Yea>r deceased on his Birth day 49. *William* Earl of *Pembroke* by some
Citizens there weighing plate, on fames wing was mounted.

As this for another then blazed, being invited by the Lady of *Berk-*
shire to her Childes Christning, sent word I might not, nor would not
come; howbeit a fortnight after went, being Neighbors, finding there
the Lord *Goring* and the Lady *Carlisle,* the Lady *Berks* aspect somwhat
sad, relating my denial to her, saying, *She knew it boded something to her*
290 *child:* The Lady *Carlisle* saying, *He is well, is he not? Yes, I praise God said*
she, as any of the rest: Then quoth the Lord *Goring, I pray let us know*
what thundering thumping thing it is about my Lady Berkshires *Son:* To
which only thus before I went, enquired of her the Name of the other
born before this last, as I take it she said was *Philip,* then he must be
again the yongest I again replied, as after a few hours the same night the
Childe suddenly was gone and died, &c.

And though these things not done in corner or remote place,
restraind neither city nor court from such violent doings, vain laughter,
like the crack of thorns, as the wiseman, *cap. &c.* shews to be regarded

---

Line 275. **Earl of Holland:** Henry Rich, a courtier.
Line 277. **Lord Steward:** William Herbert, earl of Pembroke.
Line 278. **Clarkenwel:** Clerkenwell; parish in London.
Line 282. [ ]: The deleted word is illegible.
Line 285. **blazed:** proclaimed; made conspicuous. Line 299. **crack...thorns:** cf. Eccles. 7:6.

as much, of whose high presumption on record, such a blast from 300
Whitehall, bearing Date *October, 1633, &c.*

From the Court of *Whitehall, &c.*

His Majesty doth expresly Command the Lord Archbishops Grace and his Commissioners, for causes Ecclesiastical, That the Petitioner be forthwith called before them for presuming to imprint the said Books, and for preferring this detestable Petition.

Sidney Montague.

Which blasphemous accursed reference thus occasioned was upon their taking away of my Books printed at *Amsterdam:* But pressing to have them restored passages taken out of the Scripture concerning great 310 *Babylons* blow, *Dan. 5. And the Beast ascended out of the Bottomlesse pit, Revel.* 11. Applied to Great Britain, with the Hand-writing (*cap.* 5.) *Thou art found wanting, &c.* extended from that Marriage feast, ever since 1625. into the year 1645. or from the abomination, &c. *Dan.*12.

And of the aforesaid reference, thus; save Reverence his Grace the foreman of the Jury, 1633. *Octob.* 23. commanding first a Candle, he that would not be warnd; but said *No more of that;* burnt the Book, saying, *My Lords, I have made you a smoother of Dooms-day, to be in such a year about Candlemas, till then she takes time enough: What shall we do next?* when with one voice, *Let her be fined Three thousand pounds,* 320 *Excommunicated, no Bible alowed her, or Pen and Ink, or woman Servant; carry her away,* as by a Warrant under twelve Hands, confined to the Gatehouse for ever, where kept a close prisoner for two years, the Lords day unknown from another, the rest for brevity and modestly sake dismissed.

Line 301. **Whitehall:** the seat of the royal court.

Lines 302–7. **From the Court…Montague:** the text of the warrant summoning Lady Eleanor to a hearing before the Court of High Commission.

Lines 313–14. **extended…abomination:** Dan. 12:11.

Lines 315–16. **his Grace…Jury:** Laud, archbishop of Canterbury, acted as head of the Court of High Commission.

Line 319. **Candlemas:** Feast of the Purification of the Virgin Mary, 2 February.

Lines 320–22. **Let her…away:** the suggestions of the various commissioners about an appropriate punishment for Lady Eleanor.

Line 323. **Gatehouse:** prison at Westminster. **close prisoner:** a closely guarded prisoner.

To this day which sentence and remains of the smoked Book remain extant in the Office, Trophees of his Triumph, buried by this *Achan,* this golden wedge or tongue, he sirnamed the *Beast,* from *Oxford* deriving his Name, smothered as other things.

330   And *Irelands* Massacre, was it not *October* 23? and *Edgehil* fight the 23? Then *Octobers* Wine presse trodden; even shewing you a Mystery withal, *Rev.* 17. *The Beast that was, and is not, even he is the eighth, and is of the seven, and goeth into Perdition.* Even Kings and the Beast both put together; as from *H.*8. *H.* 7. &c. with his 7. years complete, and 8. current, the Archbishops lawless term before his going into prison, that Son of Perdition, translated to which place 1633. *September,* his ascending then, &c.

And twelve Bishops at once, were not so many sent to the Tower? hee likewise in the year 1644. *January* on a Friday put to death or killed,
340   according to the tenor of that Petition, stiled in such a probrious maner; composed as follows:

Most humbly shews to Your Majesty,
That the Word of God the first year of Your happy Reign spoken to the Peti-
tioner; upon Friday last did suffer early in the morning, the B. Beast
ascended out of the Bottomless Pit, seven Heads having signified seven years
his making War, hath overcome and killed them Books sealed with the
Prophets Testimony, &c.

ELEANOR. 1633, &c.

For unfolding the mystery of which referring unto *Rev.* 11.

Line 327. **Achan:** see Josh. 7:19–26.
Line 330. **Irelands Massacre:** October 1641. **Edgehil:** a battle, October 1642.
Line 331. **Octobers Wine presse trodden:** judgments in October; cf. Rev. 14:20.
Line 334. **H.8. H.7.:** Henry VIII, Henry VII.
Line 335. **his going into Prison:** Laud was imprisoned in 1641.
Line 336. **1633. September:** when Laud became archbishop of Canterbury.
Line 338. **twelve Bishops at once:** Twelve bishops were impeached in 1641.
Line 339. **1644. January:** 10 January, 1644, i.e., 1645, when Laud was executed.
Line 340. **probrious:** opprobrious; disgraceful, abusive.
Lines 342–48. **Most humbly…1633, &c.:** the text of Lady Eleanor's petition against Laud.

And so much testified in this Compenduary for this crucifi'd Book, containing the year of God 1644. for the treading down then his foes, suffering between Sir *Archibald Dowglas* on the one hand, and the Archbishop on the other; as both in one year, Sir *Archibald Dowglas* departing this life 1644. *July* 28. on Sunday the Lords Resurrection, interred in *Pancras* that Mother of Churches, Aged 44. the other on a Friday, the day our Lord descended, &c.

And with *Job* that good man with evil things, not unmindeful of the good, so of this mans double portion, living the flower of his days such a Monastical life, not admitting his own Brothers to see his face, sent from his parents out of *Scotland,* with such violence set upon the Kingdom of Heaven, wrestling like *Jacob,* his Candle till three in the morning not put out, he subscribing *Elisha,* calling the Clergy no other then *Baals* Chaplains from pregnant Scripture proofs; and at his death admitting none, saying, *His place without them was prepared,* with *Moses* injoying a view of *Canaan:* as in truth such despisers of Prophesie could not conclude them other then such, even forbidden to bid them *God speed,* it being stiled the testimony of Jesus, *Rev.* 19. and by shewing them of their saltlesse Collects out of season, praying as it were, Hear us for thy Servant St. *Andrews* sake, St. *Thomas,* St. *Bartholomew,* &c. without a word or mention how *Peter* served him, and St. *Thomas;* the ten like *Josephs* Brethen, so envying the other twain, all because they would be greatest as about the Keys, now at such strife: Turnd to the keys of the Gatehouse prison and Bedlem, those in their custody without question of such marvel may boast.

350

360

370

Line 350. **Compenduary:** compendiary or compendium; an abridgement.

Line 355. **Pancras:** St. Pancras; parish church in London.

Line 358. **this mans double portion:** Sir Archibald Douglas's woes.

Line 361. **wrestling like Jacob:** see Gen. 32:24–30.

Line 362. **Elisha:** Elijah; see 1 Kings 18. Line 364. **with Moses:** cf. Mark 9:4.

Line 365. **Canaan:** the promised land.

Line 368. **saltlesse Collects:** worthless prayers; see Matt. 5:13.

Line 371. **Josephs Brethren:** see Gen. 37:2.

Line 373. **Bedlem:** Bedlam; the London mental hospital named the Hospital of St. Mary of Bethlehem.

So lastly shewing of that writ served on the Kings house, *Dan.* 5. this also *Zech.* 5. serves for our meridian; *The flying rowl twenty Cubits in length, visiting the house of the false swearer, the thief;* appointed for plundring perjured witnesses and Jurors, their whole Estate of it, robbing no few: And with the Coat of the present, displayed too, directed to the
380   sign of the Flying Stork, not unlike the French vertugal like sails, the wind in their wings, mounted in the Air, that fugitive Mother (Sorcerers wickedness) and her Daughter, erecting Castles, old *Babels,* decaid Towers, (besides their *Sedans*) where the leaden weight bids beware the sheet of lead, *Zech.* as by her sitting in the midst of the Ephah carried, &c. So no farther of their cariage, his weighd in the Ballance, as hers measured by the Bushel.

And to like purpose, witnesse our Parliament LIKE-WISE daily visited, though shewd our God a Revealer of secrets, *Daniel 2. Sets up Kings, puts down, changes Times and Seasons,* by the great massy Image,
390   as that for ONE piece armed at all points (great Britains figure) points withal to Idolatries downfal for ever; And this although declared unto them aforehand, the *Whitsontide* before the Irish Rebellion brake forth, that the brittle iron feet of the fearful Image broken in pieces, served for the Kingdom of *Irelands* Sad Climat, the first blow to be given there; but so taken up, like the *Athenians,* every one hearing and telling News, passages coming forth every day cry'd, spending their time in nothing else but such Commentaries.

This the sentence of our aforesaid Wisemen, *What will this Babler say?*
400   That it might be fulfild, shewd & assurd also by our Savior, *There is nothing so secret and hid which shall be unreveald or not preacht on the house top,* from that below, even to that High Court or House, yet asleep

---

Line 380. **vertugal:** a verdugal or farthingale; a hoop for a woman's skirt.

Line 381. **fugitive Mother:** the Queen's mother, who had fled to England from France; cf. Zech. 5:5–9.

Line 383. **Sedans:** sedan chairs or litters.   Line 384. **Ephah:** a Hebrew measure.

Line 389. **great massy Image:** the image of the mass, the Catholic sacrament.

Lines 398–99. **What…say?:** Acts 17:18.   Line 401. **nothing so secret:** cf. Luke 12:2–3.

all, like the sleeper *Jonah,* or those bidden *sleep on:* So *that thee, O Father, that hast hidden from them* [ ] *these things* (of thy councel not made) *but to us reveald them.* Dan.2.19. *Then was the secret reveald to* Daniel, *Ver.* 21. & 28. & 47.

Anagr. $\left\{ \begin{array}{l} \textit{Reveale O Daniel.} \\ \textit{Eleanor Audeley.} \end{array} \right.$

FINIS.

Line 403. **the sleeper Jonah:** see Jon. 1:5. **sleep on:** Matt. 26:45.
Lines 407–9. **Eleanor Audeley:** Lady Eleanor.

In this tract (Wing D1996aA) Lady Eleanor explains her belief in General Restitution and presents her argument that the words "for ever" do not constrain God from redeeming the cursed. She developed this argument the following year in *The mystery of general redemption* (Wing D1996A). Her title *Je le tien*, a French phrase meaning "I hold it," which comes from her family's motto, illustrates the way she links her personal and prophetic identities to prove the authenticity of her claims to prophesy. The present edition of *Je le tien* is based on an apparently unique copy in the volume of Lady Eleanor's tracts in the Folger Shakespeare Library.

JE LE TIEN: THE GENERAL RESTITUTION.

Who then is a faithful and wise Servant,
whom his Lord hath made Ruler over
his houshold to give them their
meat in due season.

Title page. This page has extensive handwritten annotations. At the top of the page: "Gates of Heeven & Hell as if a palace [ ] a prison"; beneath the words "Je Le Tien": "such as we hear ye hell this age"; beneath the word "Restitution": "as ye numerous [ ] the sunn mone & stars Cor. 15 Father forgive them. Though they did god service in it"; beneath the words "their meat in due season": "so requisit" and then again the word "requisit"; beneath the words "Printed in the yeer": "sinister suspition they have murdered the [ ]". The bottom of the page is cut off.

Epigraph. **Who...due season:** Matt. 24:25.

Of the general Restitution.

As no few deceiving themselves, because of the day and hour no man knows, not Angels of the very day of judgement: conclude or conceive therefore the time unknown of the Lords coming, not possible to be reveal'd to any, in regard of a watchword given out, to keep such on their guard: otherwise, which would fail; or like the unwise Virgins, should let their lamps go out, &c. So this other mistake, upon parables or proverbs unnecessary now to be continued any longer, such sowre sawce out of season: The sayings of old time (namely) That *out of Hell is*
10   *no redemption:* Of which heavie sentence here revok'd, the deadly pottage heal'd as follows; this stone (the evening come of Time) from the well of Life its mouth rolled away, held not unuseful heretofore; but like the back parts, beheld in comparison of his reserv'd countenance, so full of grace and glory, first making known only, *I will be gracious to whom I will, &c.* And such passages <By> or straits, setting forth his prerogative, as with the potters power over the clay compares his: Though in another place thus, As wide as East is from the West, so far sets our sins from us; and not ours only, but the sins of the whole world; knows whereof wee bee made, remembers wee bee but Dust.
20   And where Mercy and Goodnes so immeasurable, and we but a grashopper, a shadow, &c. how stands it with so much equity, to make such bare near measure, even world without end, without compassion, out of remembrance to cast the world, the workmanship of his hands.

As by this attainder of *Adams* house suppos'd irrevocable, O far be it from him, after such deep protestations of old, and Heaven and Earth promis'd to bee renew'd; so to forget him, Man, for whom they were

---

Lines 2–3. **day…knows:** Matt. 24:36. Line 6. **unwise Virgins:** see Matt. 25:3.

Lines 9–10. **out…redemption:** a tenet held by those who believed in strict predestination.

Lines 11–12. **pottage:** food; Esau sold his birthright to Jacob for pottage (Gen. 25:29–34). **stone…rolled away:** see Matt. 28:2.

Lines 14–15. **I will…I will:** Exod. 33:19.

Line 16. **the potters…clay:** see Rom. 9:21. Lines 17–18. **As wide…from us:** Ps. 103:12.

Line 24. **attainder:** declaration of tainted blood as a consequence of a very serious crime.

made, to have dominion over them, for the first offence of our first parents deceiv'd, no better knowing good from evil in their minority.

Through a sleight of the evil angel, by his subtilty beguil'd, not of dust made, as man, whose doom to eat dust, yet beleev'd they forsaken, who without number, like as the sand of the Sea, so many millions of Legions, because over-reacht in state of Innocency, not only utterly cast out of sight, but left to exquisite torments, such as no pen able to express them, or tongue to utter, much lesse to number or measure, the bounds of that so far beyond all Ages and Times.   30

Even this proverb yet continu'd, *The childrens teeth set on edge for the fathers default,* so expresly prohibited; as suppos'd impossible for God to change or alter it, as it were the Decree of the Medes and Persians, whereas the Lyons mouths stopt, and the sevenfold heated furnace its furious flames of no force qualified.   40

And in that maner also forewarn'd, how incredible soever in the sight of men, as for a Camels going through a needles eye: that very point no more difficult with God in his appointed time, then for them to thrid a pack-needle, or to cast a wedge of Iron into the fire, taken forth again, and the like, all things with him as easie.

Whereas intolerable sinful *Sodom,* for so few their sakes had been spar'd prest, *Shall not the Judge of all the Earth do right?*

As by such a qualification admitted, which may be merciful as hee pleases, rather then unjust in the least.

And pardon'd *Ninivehs* great City, where like Hell out of the belly of   50
that great fish, he was heard and deliver'd: Also in tender consideration because of so many, the right hand not knowing from the left, for the

---

Line 29. **sleight:** trick.

Line 32. **Legions:** bodies of infantry (3,000 to 6,000 men) in the Roman army; thus, many.

Line 36. **childrens...edge:** Ezek. 18:2.

Line 39. **Lyons mouth stopt:** Dan. 6:22. **the sevenfold heated furnace:** Dan. 3.

Line 42. **a Camels...eye:** Matt. 19:24.

Lines 43–44. **thrid a pack-needle:** thread a large needle used for sewing heavy cloth.

Line 51. **great fish:** the whale (Jon. 2:10).

childrens cause the fathers preserv'd, lucky Babes, the state of Innocency, such respect had thereunto.

And here spreading his bleeding hands and arms, extended from paradice to hell, a greater then *Isaac* or *Abraham* either, saying, *Before Abraham was I am:* His onely begotten offering up himself, so did not *Isaac,* saying, *Here's the fire and wood, but where's the Lamb?*

60 And to be so well pleased in him, and so exceedingly displeased with them, The world, for whom he here prays; not for those given him out of the world, saying, *Father, forgive them, they know not what they do:* But all them in state of Ignorance, they who do they know not what. And therefore between them crucified, as it were, those two Thieves in paradise, which robd the garden of God, even forgave all the world at his death; that before knowing the power given him over all flesh, made that solemn prayer to his father, and thanksgiving for them which believ'd, &c. whose prayer *Steven* borrow'd, *Lord, lay not their sin to their charge, and fell asleep.*

70 Who them told afore, *If I be lifted up, I shall draw all men to me;* so to the one as saying, *This day thou be in paradise with me;* another day infers for the other: Howsoever, the contrary passes for currant, like that mistake touching that Disciple, that *He should not dye:* from some reserv'd meaning of our Saviors, misunderstood by the standers by.

As from this doubtfully given out, likewise of no inferior quality or consequence, concerning the fire not extinguished; where it follows not, their pains of like nature to be endlesse: the punishment, though granted inevitable, not avoided to be, yet the perpetuity thereof in suspence, uncertain how long to continue: as indeed the word *For ever* signifies but during pleasure, & so *Go ye cursed into everlasting fire,* in the
80 original, to wit, *length of dayes,* or *a long time.*

Lines 56–57. **Before…I am:** John 8:58. Line 58. **Isaac…Lamb:** Gen. 22:7.

Line 61. **Father, forgive them:** Luke 23:34. Line 66. **Steven:** see Acts 7:60.

Line 72. **that…Disciple:** see Matt. 26:35.

Line 75. **fire…extinguished:** eternal damnation.

Line 79. **during pleasure:** so long as the ruler wanted; many appointments, including those of the judges, were made on these terms.

Which mysterie of their restitution, The worlds general pardon, inferior not to their being made fellow-heirs the Gentiles, these Sacred Olive boughs (sayings of the Prophets and Apostles) make bold to go over them again, for the going forward with it, how impossible held soever, any such gleanings or multiply'd Fragments belongs to them, because long lay hidden, as taken here from the Tree of Life.

Proclaim'd, *Behold the Lamb of God that taketh away the sins of the world;* also the Angels first salute, *Behold, tidings of great joy to all people:* and of like healing nature, that *He the propitiation of our sins not only, but of the whole worlds:* and thus as at the first, *Behold the world made* 90 *whole; as, God saw every thing, and behold it was very good that he made:* so returns to their former or first estate; as *Dust thou art, and to dust thou shalt return:* confirm'd by the Apostle *Paul, If the first fruits and root holy, also the lump and branches.*

And again, *Who gave himself a ransom for all, to be testified in due time:* of which time *Peter* not unmindful gives command, *Therefore gird up the loins of your mindes, and hope to the end for the grace to bee brought unto you, at the revelation of Jesus Christ;* in whose Sermon, *Act. 3. Whom the Heavens must receive at the restitution of all things.* And concerning which grace of general Redemption, and the Lords second coming to be 100 reveal'd, as expresly shewed from good witnesse, to be waited for, and to prepare for it; moreover our Saviors charge, *Therefore be yee ready also, for in such a time as yee think not the son of man cometh,* (*Matthew 24. Mark 13.*) And as to the dayes of the unexpected flood, points to the same time, three periods and a half, a time and times and half, sworn in *Daniel* and the *Revelation,* as it were with him but evening, midnight, cock-crowing and morning, for his coming, then to expect it, saying, *Truly Eliah the Prophet first shall come and restore all things, before the*

Line 81. **general pardon:** a royal order or a statute providing pardon for all those who had committed certain offenses.

Line 82. **fellow-heirs the Gentiles:** non-Jews who became Christians and passed their beliefs to their descendants.

Line 87. **Behold the Lamb of God:** John 1:29, 36.

Line 91. **God saw every thing:** Gen. 1:31. Line 92. **Dust thou art:** Gen. 3:19.

Line 108. **Eliah...things:** Elias, i.e., Elijah; see Matt. 17:11.

great and dreadful day of the Lord, in whose sight a thousand years as yes-
110   *terday.*

According to *Malachi, Behold I will send you Eliah,* &c. And in
another place bears date thus, *Behold your house is left unto you desolate:
and ye shall not see me till ye say, Blessed is he that comes in the Name of the
Lord,* namely *Eliah* so cald, one after his spirit; for convincing them of
their hard sayings and opinions; *Who shall render them meat in due season, Mat.* 24. and by the same token how then it fares with them, even
the priesthood; *And in the day that I shall do this, saith the Lord of Hosts,
I shall leave them neither root nor branch* (to wit) the *Gentiles* Church
also cut off departed from the Faith, except a remnant that have not
120   bow'd the knee, or have declin'd their Antichristian Tenents, as this for
one, That the gift of Prophesie is extinguished; and that for another, the
root of Heresies, That there is no restoration from the second death,
which begat the popish purgatory, which begat the *Manichees* error
which begat *Arrianism, Pelagianism.*

Besides the abominable eating of blood authorised, against that so
solemnly inacted by the apostles, *Acts* 15 after such deliberation, & a
thing observ'd for a long time after, verily procreating that inhumane
opinion of Transubstantiation of the very Blood communicated in the
Sacrament; otherwise which never had bin broach'd such an Abomina-
130   tion, standing on the Lords Table adored: So *Rev.* 16. *Worthily ye drink
of the bloody Vials your fill, poured out now if ever.*

Now unto the aforesaid, what more may be said or added, then this,
If I be lifted up, I will draw all men to me; Though our Doctors prophecying out of their own Envious Spirit, would have it, as if the number of

---

Line 120. **Tenents:** tenets; beliefs.

Line 123. **popish purgatory:** Catholics believed in the concept of Purgatory, Protestants did
not. **Manichees:** Manicheans; third-century A.D. believers in a dualistic philosophy or
religion.

Line 124. **Arrianism, Pelagianism:** heresies in the early Church.

Line 128. **Transubstantiation:** the Catholic doctrine that during the mass, the wine and
bread are changed into the blood and body of Christ.

Line 130. **the Lords Table:** the Ten Commandments or Tables (Exod. 20:1–17); the
Protestant sacrament of communion.

Line 133. **If I be lifted up:** John 12:32. **our Doctors:** learned clergymen; doctors of divinity.

them to be heald, stung by the old Serpent, in comparison of the rest:
But as those in the last age which taste not Death, such a handful to the
dead since the world began, or as some Eight persons as it were saved by
Faith: Or like her houshold spard alive, destroyed not with the accursed
City; yet *Jericho built again, its foundation laid, and gates set up that lay*
waste.　　　　　　　　　　　　　　　　　　　　　　　　　　　　140

Though granted shadows forth, how few the number of the faithful
to others going the broad way, whose Antichristian plots prosper not,
shall not be able to stand in the Judgement that hold, Notwithstanding
the root our first Parents franckly forgiven, *Luke,* yet for their offence
their posterity cut off; the branches suffered never to grow again, against
Law and Justice, whereas recorded of that King concerning the mur-
therers of his Father, the children not put to death, 2 *Kings* 14. and *Deu-*
teronomy, &c.

He then which much more pardons, leaves not so much as a hoof in
Egypt, the very Beast the old Serpent sets him at liberty: Satan in process　150
of time unbound, reserved until the last day in chains of despair, though
supposed Sodoms captivity and her sisters never returns from endlesse
exile, much lesse those infernal spirits.

Because before the Tree of life tasted of, their future happinesse made
known, gives them a touch of the tree of knowledge, the Law.

Lets them know what he is able to do, as the Apostle *Paul* shews,
What if God willing to shew his wrath, and make his power known &c. So
after *Josephs* way, before making himself known, saying *I am Joseph* to
his unnatural Brethren: who notwithstanding foreshew'd how they
should all bow before him: yet possess'd with such spirit of misbelief,　160
whom they sold into *Egypt* knew him not.

Lest presumption, which knows no measure, take advantage of
unlimited mercy, a main point, for a long time permits them to wander

---

Line 136. **those…taste not Death:** see Matt. 16:28.

Line 138. **her houshold spard:** Josh. 2.

Line 142. **the broad way:** the route to destruction (Matt. 7:13).

Lines 149–50. **leaves…Egypt:** see Exod. 9:3–6. A handwritten annotation in the margin
reads "numerous as The [ ] in respects The others:" The edge of the page is cut off.

Line 158. **Joseph:** see Gen. 37–45.

in like ignorance, *Having sworn in his wrath,* first suffers fiery serpents
to vex them.

Much like the mist cast before their eyes, because their task increas'd
who mutin'd (*Exodus*) answerable but to that in the Gospel, by his Disciple being desired to send her away, answered, *I am not sent but to the
lost sheep of the house of Israel.* Where she cald dog, the *Canaan* woman,
which would not take it for an answer, but after him still cries out, partakes of the childrens bread, afterward the devil cast out of her daughter; The Gentiles forerunner and figure not onely, but those gone into
perdition.

And this his Kingdom, like *Davids,* reduced by degrees, made wait
for his promises; and that every one may come to the knowledge of the
Truth. Which Army a refuge for the distressed and discontented, as
Solomons kingdom a patern, after Judgment executed according to his
fathers command, of our expected rest. The peaceable new Heavens and
Earth, who though commanded a sword to be brought him, thought
not to take the Infants life; the standers by put in a doubt notwithstanding, and the mother of it much more.

But leaving him, that knew what he had to do with *Joab* and *Shimei,*
who excused not his own Brother *Adoniah* in such a nice point, for the
first fault, which was winked at by the Father.

For prosecuting of this nicety of the word *For Ever* and *Everlasting,*
such a stumbling block to them so blockish, that make us believe,
beyond these pillars or periods there is no passing or going farther, not
as much as a possibility of it will allow for this new Wine to drop down,
or to be drawn forth, reserved till the last, *Joel* the third and 18. v. such
a gift in misconstruing of Mysteries, have attain'd unto, with the Jews,

170

180

190

Lines 166–67. **their task...(Exodus):** see Exod. 16.

Line 169. A handwritten annotation in the margin reads "a reformd meaning His Hower not
yet come". **she cald...woman:** see Matt. 15:22–28.

Line 174. **his...Davids:** see 1Chron. 22:8.

Lines 177–80. **Solomons...life:** see 1 Kings 3:16–28.

Lines 182–83. **Joab...Shimei...Adoniah:** executed by Solomon for disrupting the kingdom.

Line 186. **blockish:** stubborn. Line 187. There is a large handwritten "S" in the margin.

so stumbled about their abolish'd Ceremonies and Ordinances, because said they, *Stand fast for ever* (*Psalms* &c) do not understand which way God is able to disavow or disanul them for the better: for example, because Circumcision cald an everlasting Covenant, *Gen.* together with the promis'd Land pass'd or given unto his seed for an everlasting possession: And yet so long kept out of possession, strangers there: no more strange then that for another, where such an express Deed canceld (saying) *I said indeed, Thou and thy Fathers house should walk before me for ever, but now far be it from me.*

So farther now for the aforesaid, in the Original signifying but for *Ages,* and likewise for *Ever and Ever,* for *Ages* and *FARTHER,* or *Et cetera,* as it were (to wit) with God during pleasure: The burthen of that gracious Psalm, *For his mercy endures* [*for ever*]<an Age>[ ] 200

And yet this burthen continued, supposed out of Hell there is no Redemption or Restauration, which also signifies *The Grave* (*Psalm* 16) one word expressing both.

Though elsewhere, as the Holy Ghost where he pleases able more abundantly to express it: In our Saviors being parareld with *Melchisedeck, Heb. 7.* mentions an endles life; in the Original (to wit) indisolvable; And again, *But this man because he continueth ever, hath an unchangeable Priesthood* (or) *which passes not away to another;* And to that end such passages. 210

So concerning the ability of our Savior, inferior not to *Adam,* with whom he is paraleld too; with *Adam* the first man, *Rom. 5. As sin entred into the world by him, and death by sin, which passed upon all men, for that all have sinned.*

Line 192. **Stand…for ever:** Ps. 111:8. There is a large figure "8" handwritten in the margin.

Line 194. **Circumcision…Covenant:** see Gen. 17:13.

Lines 200–201. **Original…Ages:** Lady Eleanor maintains that the biblical text has been wrongly translated.

Line 203. [ ]: The deleted handwritten words are illegible.

Line 209. **Melchisedeck:** see Heb. 6:20, 7:15–17. The word "&c" is handwritten at the bottom of the page.

Line 210. The word "&c" is handwritten in the margin. **this…continueth ever:** Heb. 7:24.

And by one mans obedience much more came upon all, *Justification to life,* so much prest by the Apostle.

And if ye will receive it, *Rev.* 14. resolves it, ordered by a voice from
220 Heaven to be written, where shews as there smoke ascends *For Ever and Ever,* that day and night that have no rest: so they that dye in the Lord from *Henceforth* rest from their labors or pains: The which besides useful for demolishing the aspiring walls of Purgatory, for any Saints ever coming there, to be partakers of such sulpherous smokes.

This Text of the Angels commanded to be preacht upon, farther informs, stiled *The Everlasting Gospel,* that the true meaning of it, even *For Ever and Ever,* it signifies but *From Henceforth,* a time determinable, and not infinite or unlimited, if credit may be given to the holy Spirit (*Revelations* the fourteenth, saying, *Yea* or *Content saith the Spirit;* so
230 what spirits soever resists it, or sayes *No,* touching those disobedient Spirits cast out of his presence, as if for those prisoners, ringleaders of rebellion, remains no hope or mercy; whereas Lucifer not excepted, confined though to extreme darknes, of whom *Jude* shews, *The Archangel Michael* DURST NOT *bring railing accusation against him,* being against the Law of prisoners to revile them, as indeed Hell no other then a prison, implying a Release thence, like as death cald sleep in respect of the Resurrection, to which end is shewed by *Peter* (3.) *He went and Preacht to the Spirits there imprisoned;* and therefore saying, *If I go down to Hell thou art there also,* Psalm, &c.

240 That each in his order; The first fruits redeemed from among men, for so *The everlasting Gospel* informs us: Then the latter Fruits or Harvest which follows, reserved for the hour of his Judgement, even 1600. bearing date, paced forth by time; howsoever exprest by the space of so many Furlongs for Centuries *(Revel.* 14.)

As hereof *(Luke* 16.) testifies where that distance between them termed a space fixt (or a Gulf) so much by our Adversaries insisted on; whereas the verity of it, a space of time prefixt, because otherwise (since

Line 234. The word "&c" is handwritten in the margin.

Lines 238–39. **If...Hell:** see Ps. 139.

Line 247. The word "&c." is handwritten in the margin.

time moves not) but an improper or unnecessary Speech; with that of *Abrahams* Bosom concurs, or like those Corn Ears interpreted so many years to come: Likewise his own Dream of *The Sheafs of Corn doing obeysance,* and the like.

Where touching his pedigree the *RICH* (man) *SON,* stiled by *Abraham,* some *PARSONS SON,* as is probable by that Reply, *They have Moses and the Prophets;* so without contradiction bids beware of lying, by his scorched tongue inflamed, testified *Psalm* 120. *Thou false tongue, &c.* So again a material point from *Abrahams* calling him *SON,* even points or refers us to her Story, after the Bottle spent, who had her eyes opened, saw a well of water, bidden *Fear not,* called unto from Heaven, *lift up the Lad* Ishmael, named so of the Angel, namely, *God shall hear,* when she again, *Thou God seest me.*

Where farther of what profession or Fraternity, he *lifting up his eyes saw afar off Lazarus in his Bosom:* whom he again calls, *Father,* whose last motion, that *Lazarus* then might be sent to his Fathers house to testifie and forewarn them (*Lest his Brethren, &c.* (to wit) Besides Arch.B. other Bishops, 25. in number, how they come there to have a care, as here in their formalities, that Brotherhood not alone, but those of the Law, their Coat displays herewith a chief Judge, who call Brothers too: This Stone or Bone cast amongst them, saying, *They have the Law and the Prophets, let them hear them.*

So then no ordinary Beggar taken up into Heaven, but one of the Prophetical order granted, who was to perswade them, coming in the Spirit of *Eliah* the *Tisbet,* DOUBTLES, whom they did not or would not know: And since he in Hell received no absolute denial, who knows but that it was obtained (to wit) a line of mercy from his finger top, as it were never so little of the water of life.

250

260

270

Line 249. **Abrahams bosom:** see Luke 16:22. **Corn Ears:** see Gen. 41.

Line 250. **The...Corn:** see Gen. 37. Line 252. **the RICH (man) SON:** see Luke 16:25.

Line 257. **her Story:** Hagar's story (Gen. 21:19).

Line 258. The word "&c" is handwritten in the margin. Lines 266–67. **those...Law:** lawyers.

Lines 268–269. **They...Prophets:** Luke 16:29. Line 270. "8" is hand written in the margin.

Lines 272–73. **Eliah...know:** Matt. 17:10–13. Line 274. **mercy...top:** see Luke 16:24.

And herewith the Prophetical Date shall proceed, which belongs to the preceding Parable to unfold, containing his discharge, shewed, he might be no longer Steward, accordingly whose Stewardship was resigned; where the measures of Oyl annointing him, for no common
280   Steward either, but how it shall come to pass in some wastful unjust reign, for his pass given him serves.

And so much for the testified present evil time, with the quaif-degree, and those of the Lawn sleeves, their fine Linnen, without doubt visited, holding it enough to have *Moses read and the Prophets,* though understand them not at all, so all watching thus with one consent, stopping their ears as their forefathers.

And thus it fares with this *Lazarus* whose ulcers Allegorical, those evil things received in his life time, *viz.* Imprisonments, Excommunications, and such like entertainment, by some forlorn suiters only licked
290   or visited, of whom well the blessed Virgin prophecying, shews how it shall fare with them in those rebellious days, *He hath shewed strength with his Arm, and he hath put down the mighty from their seat;* with whom the Apostle accords, *Corinthians* 15. *Puts all his foes under his feet before his coming:* And as this no news to him that hath ears, so this opinion as strange, for which serves the parable of that envious elder Brother that would not be perswaded either to see his lost Brother, or enter the house; of like evil nature bids others beware, lest like that Servant that obtain mercy himself, yet so unmerciful shew'd none at all to his fellow Servant, they be also rewarded with him (till the debt dis-
300   charged, every farthing accompted for.) And for the same purpose as *Peter* forbidden such remission by measure, *Not to pardon until seven*

Lines 277–78. **he…longer Steward:** see Luke 16:1–13; *Steward;* Stuart; surname of England's seventeenth-century monarchs.

Lines 282–83. **quaif-degree:** the sergeants-at-law; they wore the coif (a special hat). **those of the Lawn sleeves:** the bishops.

Line 287. The word "&c" is handwritten in the margin.

Line 291. **He…strength:** Luke 1:51.

Lines 295–96. **elder Brother:** A pair of asterisks links these words to a handwritten annotation in the margin, which reads "Like Jonah angrye to the death." See Luke 15:11–31.

Lines 297–99. **that Servant…fellow Servant:** Matt. 18:23–35.

Line 300. **farthing:** a coin, a quarter of a penny.   Line 301. **Peter…measure:** Matt. 18:22.

times, but until Seventy times seven; likewise in *Luke* 17. *Seven times a day to forgive;* where the Apostles replying, *Lord increase our Faith,* being by our Theologers termd a certainty for an uncertainty, what they please, yet not only points to very Easter, those weeks before it, when sent forth that first pardon, *The Messiah offered,* proclaimd Lord of Sabbaths; but as gives notice of this last pardon for the space of 1700. years hidden, so shews by the 70. times seven which amounts to the sum of Four hundred and ninety, the set time between the Prophet *Daniels* Visions and our Lord the Son of God his tasting death for every one, *The Lamb slain, &c.* without exception praying for all, a greater then *Daniel* praying then.

Which Four hundred and ninety years, seventy weeks, of years that fulfil, by seven years alotted to a week, after *Daniels* computation agreeing with *Jacobs,* said to accomplish her week too, (*Gen.*) in his seven years service for her.

And so the sum of the matter since by Scripture confuted this erroneous opinion, by breaking open Hel gates, or opening the meaning of such an intricate case, beyond any case in Law ever reported, consisting of such niceties, where since proved to be but prison, follows their remaining there no longer, but till the Debt satisfied, according to all Law and Justice imposed: As to him belongs only the mysterie of Times and Seasons, reserv'd in the power of the Father, reveal'd to whom he pleases, (*Acts* 1.) Therefore what hee appoints determinable, let none extend it to be without limitation, since *Rev.* 14. declares it; where the everlasting Gospel clears the mistake of the word *Everlasting, viz.* so long as day and night lasts.

And now moreover of the Book of the *Revelation* too, a word or two more, such an eye-soar to the Clergy; where too manifest what rottennes & Antichristian Abuses of late crept in, requisite to be purged out; as first, in our Bibles, where like *Jeroboams* policy, who made *Israel*

Line 306. **that first pardon:** Christ's resurrection.

Lines 310–11. **The Lamb slain, &c.:** see Rev. 5:6.

Lines 313–15. **seventy weeks...Jacobs:** see Dan. 9:24–27, Gen. 29.

Lines 330–31. **Abuses...Bibles:** Lady Eleanor's complaint about recent editions of the Bible. **Jeroboams policy:** see 1 Kings 14.

to sin, in this sinful Age have under colour of disburthening the congregation, testified and ordered by like Authority, That the New Testament shall bee read over every year once, with this proviso, Except certain Books which be least edifying, and may best be spared, and therefore left unread, as the *Revelation*.

And if he that shall think little of any jot or tittle of the Law, was to be least in the Kingdom of Heaven, what shall they be worthy of that have cast such a flood of Iniquity out of their mouth, as the dayes of
340 *Noah* not guilty of the like.

Having excluded that blessed book directed to the Churches, with *Blessed is he which reads, and they which hear the words of it, and as thus opened,* so closed with these, *For the time is at hand, Behold I come quickly.* Doubtles the days of the flood pointing unto, by the seven Vials poured out, filled with the seven last Plagues, in the seventeenth Century, so long after the creation, when as the world drown'd.

And so seven times cryed, *He that hath an ear, let him hear what the Spirit saith.* And last of all, *He that shall take away from the words of that Book, God shall take away his part out of the Book of Life.* Also, he that
350 shall adde (as much to say) shall say in his heart, The Lord delays his coming, not remembring the Flood time, God shall adde to him the plagues of *Egypt,* the waters turned into blood, &c. (*Revel.* 11.) And yet this Book by name cast out of the Church, under colour of being obscure, though assured nothing so covered or hidden which shal not be proclaimed or preached on house tops: And thus his promises waited for, the Holy Ghost knocking at the door, made to wait and stand without: which Antichristian Scoffers (in our dayes) without doubt *peter* testifies comes not short of them, 2 *Pet.* 3. in their proper colours of unbelief displayd, saying, *Where is the promise of his coming,* &c.

360 Even of the breed of the lawlesse seven-headed Beast with the Ten horns (to wit) in his head or Frontispiece, *Anno Dom.* 1700. who have annexed such open Blasphemy to the Bible. Nor this done in a corner, for a second of these unsufferable doings against the third Commandment, although all Heathenism Repetition forbidden, Notwithstanding

---

Lines 339–40. **Iniquity…Noah:** see Gen. 6. Lines 342–44. **Blessed is…quickly:** Rev. 22:7.
Lines 363–64. **the third Commandment:** see Exod. 20:4.

by a noise of Boys, that name rent in so many pieces in Churches where the Schools kept, indeed better much deserving to be whipt out then those defiling but the Temple, where that dreadful name taken in vain so, babbling at every word, *I pray God,* and *God grant,* and *Would to God we love,* &c. or have this or that, &c. upon any lascivious Lines of Heathen Poets their amorous Poems, when those children unlucky ones, 370 not held guiltles, so lesson'd for their mocking of him by unshorn Bears torn so many of them in pieces.

And moreover for a third course or piece of unsavory service; witnesse *Pauls* Churchyard, under the Noses of those reverend Masters, how close stools, those seats sir-reverence lined clean through with the Bible, from *Genesis* to the *Revelation,* those precious leaves for the healing of the Nations, polluted in that most base unmanerly maner, worse far then if burnt by the hangman: More sacred then *Sauls* Garment, when he coverd his Feet, (the modest Scripture phrase also worthy the observing) and was but cut off by *David,* that man after *Gods* own 380 heart, if his heart smote him for so doing: And *Moses* bidden to put off his shoes, because the very ground was sacred: And *Josuah* likewise: How comes it to pass no scruple made, by these Scorners, who fleeing Superstition, run upon gross contempt such prophanation: questionles then priviledge of Parliament being subverted, or infringed more material these which indure for ever, purchased with his Blood, any thing destructive thereto: a liberty far from that preacht by our Savior, in observing his severe stile, who stiles himself *The Preacher,* (*Eccles.*) that well blesses the day of death before the day of ones birth and mourning.

Lines 365–66. **Churches…kept:** Some of the most prestigious schools were associated with churches.

Line 367. **those…Temple:** see Matt. 21:12. Lines 369–71. **those…pieces:** 2 Kings 2:23–4.

Line 374. **Pauls Churchyard:** The churchyard of St. Paul's Cathedral, the seat of the bishop of London, was a center of news and commercial activity.

Lines 378–80. **burnt by the hangman:** the fate of books that were condemned. **Sauls Garment…David:** 1 Sam. 24:3–15.

Lines 381–82. **Moses…shoes:** Exod. 3:5. **Josuah likewise:** see Josh. 1:2–3.

Line 385. **priviledge of Parliament:** During the 1640s Parliament granted privilege or authorization for the printing of books.

Line 386. **purchased…Blood:** see Acts 20:28.

Line 388. **The Preacher:** The figure whose wisdom is contained in the Book of Ecclesiastes.

390   So where a rash word and a look awry extended to Murther & Adultery: referring us to the blessed Prophets before us *Antipodes* to the world in such contempt ever held, even blesses such and no other, who chuses the foolish things, and the weak, the Base, to confound and confute the Mighty.

But returning now to the former matter of his abundant love to all; by these men, how much so ever envied, beheld with such an evil eye this light extraordinary: So then for proving the *Affirmative,* (to wit) there is redemption for the *Damned;* confirmed though sufficiently by the Apostles Spirit, *Rom.* 2 *Cor.* 15. shewing as all dead in *Adam,* so all

400   made alive again, &c. yet this for an addition, *Rev.* 20. touching those that lived not again, being not unbound until such a space fulfilled of time, as known times bounds set also; where they that lived and raigned with Christ, whose part in the first Resurrection, as with them Antichristians no partakers; but of the second Death, implying a second Resurrection for those Children of Perdition; so shews like the lost Son, stiled so but in respect of being found.

Lastly notwithstanding the dreadful word for *Ever and Everlasting,* as mentioned by *Jacob* at his death, *Unto the utmost bound of the everlasting Hills, &c.* (*Gen.*) and *Jonas* in that danger, crying, *The Earth with her bars*

410   *was about me for ever;* So for the doubling of it for ever and ever, howsoever may serve sometimes to shew the thing established, as *Pharoahs* Dreams, or where he in stead of smiting five or six times, because came short, was shewd lost his pains by the coming shortly again of the Enemy.

Yet the truth of it, but like a Key that opens and shuts, serves also to give warning of some remarkable passage appertaining to the future for the most part, by him having *the keys of Death and Hell,* in due time made known: And hereof being ignorant unobserved, because of the unknown day and hour only mentioned, hold themselves not bound to wait for that time to be revealed.

420   Like as in the days of *Noah,* observe neither signs nor forerunners of it. As not without some mystery included (*Rev.* 20.) where several times

---

Line 391. **Antipodes:** opposites. Line 408. **Jacob at his death:** see Gen. 49:26.
Lines 409–10. **Jonas...for ever:** Jon. 2:6. Lines 411–12. **Pharoahs Dreams:** Gen. 41.

a Thousand years fufilled, repeated no lesse then six times; like that of the inextinguishable fire (*Mark 9.*) translated, Shall never be quenched, with the worm, &c. only (as much to say) Better there to indure any pain a long space, then to have had no being at all; where compared to some gangren'd member, *Better cut off then the body perish:* Instanced though in the case of the Kingdom of Heaven, & as explained that place here for the sin against the Holy Ghost, punished here and hereafter, where a possibility of escape, as the word Danger imports, *He shall be in danger, &c.* so concludes even *Judas,* though good had he been unborn, yet extends not to annihilate him.   430

Otherwise no such abounding blessing added to *Abraham,* without number to have a Seed or Generation as the Stars above, and the Sand of the Sea, if his mercy exceeded not much his Justice, *Merciful unto Thousands;* whereas but to a few, the third Degree, or fourth Generation, shewing hatred.

And as this relation thus concluded of the whole creation, accompanying the present Age, in the sufferings of late, groaning for so many Ages under the burthen of the word signifying but for *Ages,* or from *Henceforth;* so let this *Amoveas manus* serve: This Olive leaf for sinister   440
constructions, such illegal extent of unwarrantable words to make them accursed and void.

Forasmuch as should it repent God he had made man, &c. yet that ever he should reverse his own Judgment, God forbid, which no ordinary Judge can or will do, without a *Writ of Error* brought, since nothing but confusion brings; which *Writ* either upon any terms not feisible now as the state stands, a thing observable; so having pronounced every thing created and made was very good; then he which is the Word, not

---

Line 425.   A curling mark is handwritten in the margin.

Lines 429–30. **He…danger:** see Mark 3:29. **Judas:** apostle who betrayed Christ.

Line 432. **blessing…Abraham:** Gen. 17:7.

Line 440. **Amoveas manus:** remove the hand (Latin); a writ for legal relief. **Olive leaf:** a balm for healing. A spiral is handwritten in the margin.

Line 445. **Writ of Error:** warrant claiming that because of error, a case should be heard again by the court.

Line 447–48. **pronounced…very good:** cf. Gen. 1.

to make good his word, far be it from the Judge of all the Earth, the
450 God of all Gods, and let every one say to this confession, *Amen;* yea
saith the Spirit, by reason of the *Law and several Statutes,* since the
world hath faln in *DANGER* of such penalties and forfeitures: The King
of Kings, the grand Creditor, sends forth his Pardon, yea to the whole
Creation.

Je Elen: Ti:

I hold it.

FINIS.

Line 455. **Je Elen: Ti:** anagram of Je le Tien; also I Ele[a]n[or] Ti[chet], or Touchet, Lady
Eleanor's birth name.

In early 1647 Lady Eleanor was once again imprisoned in the Gatehouse at Westminster, where she had been held from 1633 to 1635. Printed in February 1646, i.e., 1647, *Gatehouse Salutation* (Wing D1991A) recalls Lady Eleanor's earlier experience there and, in the context of her expectations of the Day of Judgment, reflects upon the courts of law sitting at Westminster. Although the contents of this tract rhyme, only the last two lines are printed as verse. The present edition of this tract is based on the copy in the volume of Lady Eleanor's tracts now in the Folger Shakespeare Library.

THE
GATEHOUSE
SALUTATION

From the Lady *ELEANOR.*

Revelat. cap. 4.
Serving for Westminsters Cathedral, their old Service.
And Courts of Westminster, those Elders sitting, &c.

February, 1646.

Epigraph. **Westminsters...Service:** Westminster Abbey, where monarchs were crowned and buried, was the principal church at Westminster. By 1646 the order of service or liturgy was that from the *Directory for the Public Worship of God* rather than the *Book of Common Prayer* or the pre-Reformation missal. The bishop of London had used part of the Gatehouse at Westminster as a prison; another part had served as a public prison for Westminster.

Revel. cap. 4.

Post hæc vidi, & ecce ostium apertum in Cœlo, &c.

New PSALM or SONG;

The CONTENTS.

The Holy Ghost first knocks, so high extold, shews the end come, by New writ witnessed and Old; in whose Kalender the time set out, a week expired of Centuries thereabout: When as Twenty four from *Normand* Race sprung, cast their Crowns down, Times hourglasse (as 'twere) run.

10 So opend the aforesaid gate or door, what winged Beasts be those four; what restlesse eyes those day and night; The first ruff a Lyon like: The other smooth as a Calfs skin soft: The fourth an Eagle flying aloft: Midst them one visag'd as a MAN, which knot unloose he who can: what eyes these before and behinde, *Holy, Holy, &c.* all of one minde; *Which was, which is, which is to come,* say, *Glory to Father, Spirit, Son.* Inthroned, powther'd within whose Robe, in right hand whose the Starry Globe, the likenesse of the Judgment Day, as Resurrection robes display.

Benedicite omnia opera.

The four Beasts, *&c.*

20 *Bethlems* Manger sometime the Throne, as its describ'd, where she did grone; a Feather-bed cald otherwise, some Dormix curtains wrought with eyes; their work both sides alike doth shew, full of holes, besides all eaten so; A Rug and Blankets thereon laid, a woful prisoner, the aforesaid, whose companions tedious hours, no better Church then prisoners towers: As Elders white arrayed so shine, Four and twenty first crownd

---

Line 2. **Post...Cœlo:** After this I looked, and behold a wide opening in the sky (Latin); Rev. 4:1.

Lines 5–6. **The Holy...knocks:** Rev. 3:20. **by...witnessed:** shown in a new legal order.

Lines 7–8. **Twenty...sprung:** Charles I was the twenty-fourth king after William the Norman, who conquered England and became its king in 1066.

Line 16. **powther'd:** perhaps impowered or powdered; dusted and thus sparkling. **in right hand...Globe:** cf. Rev. 5:1.

Line 18. **Benedicite omnia opera:** Bless all works (Latin).

Line 21. **Dormix curtains:** warm woolen bedcurtains.

of time: Seasons four, also with Feast days, crowns resign; aloud him praise, all proclaiming Eternity, away with tyrant Time they cry.

All Blessing, Power, Honor, say, to him dedicate a third day; worship no Throne but his alone, besides whom King nor Priests is none: Like as with twain that covered their face, other twain with flying apace, their feet covered also with twain, Time past, present, and futures reign.

So Tabernacles three let us make, one for *Moses, Christs,* and *Elias* sake; as for those that adore the Beast, no Sabbath have, day nor nights rest.

Lo Moonday she cœlestial virgin Bride, as *Behold, I make all things new, Gates wide, new Earth, &c. Jerusalems* peaceable rest, Spouse of the Sun, our splendant new Moon's feast, Monethly, [*as*] the golden Tree of life like renders its fruit, no more pain, prison, strife: As spar'd a million of *Belial* Sons, better then touch one of those sacred ones: O kisse this precious Altar Coal, purges division, makes ye whole.

Away with former fashions old and past: New Lights appear, new Song record at last; he that is otherwise at his peril, as he that righteous is, be he so still.

So Gates and Prison Doors be no more shut,
The King of Glory comes, your souls lift up.

Farewell.

To the Tune of *Magnificat.*

FINIS.

Lines 30–31. **with twain...with twain:** the seraphim above the throne of God (Isa. 6:2).

Line 32. **Tabernacles...sake:** Luke 9:33.

Lines 34–35. **Moonday:** the day of the moon (Latin); Monday, as opposed to Sunday, the sabbath which Lady Eleanor believed was not properly observed. Diana or Artemis, the goddess of virginity, was also associated with the moon. **Behold...new:** Rev. 21:5.

Lines 36–37. **Monethly...fruit:** Rev. 22:2. Line 38. **Belial Sons:** sons of the devil.

Line 39. **Altar Coal:** from the sacrificial fire.

Line 46. **Magnificat:** Mary's song of thanks to God for choosing her to bear his son (Luke 1:46).

Lady Eleanor probably published two tracts about Ezekiel in 1647: *Ezekiel the Prophet* (Wing D1988A) and *Ezekiel, Cap. 2* (Wing D1988), neither of which has a title page in any of the known extant copies. They draw upon the same biblical text, but their contents and emphases differ. In *Ezekiel the Prophet*, the tract printed here, Lady Eleanor tells about her visionary experience in the Gatehouse in 1634. She apparently recalls that occasion and writes about it as a consequence of a similar experience on 2 April 1647, related in 1650 in *Appearance* (Wing D1972A—page 309 in the present edition), where she deals with the prophet's encounter with a rebellious nation. *Ezekiel, Cap. 2* is undated, and is three times the length of *Ezekiel the Prophet*. Two copies of *Ezekiel, Cap. 2* are bound just after *Ezekiel the Prophet* in the volume of Lady Eleanor's tracts in the Folger Shakespeare Library. The present edition of *Ezekiel the Prophet* is based on the copy in that volume; it is apparently a unique extant copy of this tract.

EZEKIEL THE PROPHET

Explained as follows.

So many having attempted the straits or passages of this Labyrinth, and lost their labor who went about it, could not but drop a word, have thought it not amisse or unseasonable, as wise as they are that missed their mark, a taste or touch to give them, of the tree of Life, otherwise cald the mystery of Times and Seasons, reserved for the last time, this Sacramental little Rowl, with such a solemn protestation bound touching times being no longer, which precious Manna, the Prophet *Ezekiel* and *John* the Evangelist both tasted of, not longed for a little (*Acts* I)

But hastning on *Cap.*1. now in the Thirtieth year, &c. *And I looked, and behold a Whirl-wind came out of the North, a great cloud, &c.* where 10 those winged living creatures four, &c. represented by the Tabernacle;

Title. **Explained as follows:** A handwritten annotation in the margin continues from this line, and reads "His writ served of Rebellion Lamentation Mourning and woe".

Line 6. **Sacramental little Rowl:** the bread given in the sacrament; also a roll or parchment containing important information. God gave a roll to Ezekiel to eat (Ezek. 3:1).

Lines 11–12. **represented…Curtains:** The details of Ezekiel's vision resemble those of the furnishings that God directed Moses to give to the Tabernacle (Exod. 26).

also the Lamp, &c. as it were those Curtains, every one of one measure joyned one to another with so many loops or eyes, and rings above so high, besides their running sideways, like those swift creatures who went on their sides when they ran, their displayed wings sending forth such a noise, of a spherical work, &c. And so much for these Curtains of his Pavilion, typifying the four Evangelists agreeing in one, said to kisse or touch, &c.

Whereof *Apocalyps* the Fourth thus, of the aforesaid four Beasts, and
20   the Lightning proceeding out of the Throne, shews first of the Lamp; *And there were Seven Lamps of fire, which are the Seven Spirits of God, &c.* Cap. 5. *The Seven Spirits and Seven Eyes sent forth into all the Earth,* as their Characters [ ] read through the world.

So to shew the truth of it, even the full Moon described its paleness in the Saphir-like Firmament, and no other likened to the Amber, and Fire its brightnesse, when this conception or gift of the holy Ghost, &c.

Giving withal to understand, received or rejecting it, notwithstanding how Prophesie ceased not, nor the Spirit (as the world would have it) totally is quenched; But the Writ or Label of this little sealed Rowl
30   being first served on them, cald a house of Rebellion, or a rebellious house so often; afterwards to be served again, reserved even for our days, as if any be pleased to observe, directed to our seventeenth Century, by the slain Lamb, Redemptions figure, *Cap.* 5. having seven Horns, and as many EYES; also witnesse the grand Jury, those Twenty four Crowned Elders, so many times mentioned, and as shewing since the Conquest Four and twenty Crowned, so Seven hundred years ago thereabout.

And thus going on when this sacred *Writ* to be served, how it came to passe; how distasteful to them, *hony in the mouth; bitter in the belly;*

Line 17. **the four Evangelists:** Matthew, Mark, Luke, and John.

Line 23. **their Characters [ ]:** At this point in the tract are printed symbols: a circle with a dot in the center, and a semi-circle; they may represent an eye and a horn or the sun and the moon.

Line 29. **Writ...Rowl:** The writ was the order attached to the document or roll.

Lines 34–36. **the grand Jury...Elders:** Rev. 5:8; a grand jury in England ordinarily had twenty-three people, not twenty-four. **since...Crowned:** Twenty-four monarchs had ruled England since the Norman Conquest of 1066.

Line 38. **hony...belly:** cf. Rev. 10:10.

compared to a womans travel, or as fares with Officers earning a Fee
venture their lives upon Arrests, even the sum of this Vision restlesse   40
Prisons description, clouded under the glory of the Tabernacle, sets
forth a Chamber-Bedsted and appurtenances, the Gatehouse prison, in
the year of Redemption, 1634. *September* 24. full Moon the everlasting
Lamp, prisoners fire and candle, who from the Angel sent thither the
Holy Ghost, that by the space of an hour, the Bed his throne rested
thereon, from his mouth for a farewel received a salute; and for another
farewel, that had on his right hand an Amber glove, left such an odoriferous scent when he was gone, all oyled with Ambergreece, the spirit
thereof proceeding from the Leather, so far beyond expression, as it
were invisible food, like when as said, *Cause thy belly to eat, and fill thy*   50
bowels, the hand being sent to him with the Rowl or Book spread, *&c.* a
Holy, holy, holy day, by whom observed ever since.

And for Lamentations, Mourning and Woe, such cryed up and
down: So much for this time cryed unto, *O Wheel, cap.* 10. besides proclaims winged Times reign includes years, containing the four Seasons,
Moneths, Weeks, Days and Hours, not returning restlesse time, with
the Clock wheel its motion, likewise Rings out the Abbey Bells, those
mounted wheels, *Verse* 18. *Verse* 19. like these living creatures likened to
burnished Brasse, with their ascending and descending; and for the
dreadful Rings so much, &c. *Cap.* 1. *ver.* 18. that were so high, their   60
sound or noise like great waters, the Voice of the Almighty coming from
Heaven, as it were: And so farther for that spacious round Window, the
glasse its curious work compared to the *Beril* of a Sea-green colour, as
the dreadful Christaline Heaven all with one voice proclaim the dreadful Judgement day reveald at hand, to a City most rebellious.

Given under the hands of those *Cherubs,* under their wings that had

---

Line 39. **travel:** travail; labor, child-birth.

Lines 40–43. **this Vision…September 24:** Lady Eleanor describes the vision she had in 1634
while a prisoner in the Gatehouse.

Line 48. **Ambergreece:** ambergris; secretion of the sperm whale used in perfume.

Lines 57–58. **those mounted wheels:** The bells were mounted on wheels.

Line 63. **Beril:** beryl; a transparent precious stone.

Line 66. **Given…of:** the formal ending of a royal writ or order.

hands, with that hand sent, &c. seals and signifies it, rings out Times farewel: And for the word of the Lord expresly so much. *Rev.* 1. *Write the things which thou hast seen, and the things which are, and the things which shall be hereafter.*

70 April 2.1647.   *Eleanor.*

FINIS.

Lady Eleanor addresses this tract (Wing D1987) to Oliver Cromwell. Although she has not yet met him, she looks to him to take up the cause of religion and thus bring the water of life, baptism, to the English people who have been deprived of it through the sins of their rulers, whom she compares to the beasts in Rev. 13. The present edition of the tract is based on the copy in the Bodleian Library (shelf number 12.0.1336 [1]), which has a single handwritten annotation (see page 231) and several phrases crossed out (see pages 231 and 233). As an example of Lady Eleanor's practice of inserting somewhat different annotations in the various copies of her tracts, annotations from the copy in the Houghton Library, Harvard University (shelf number *EC65 D7455 B652t) and the copy of the volume of Lady Eleanor's tracts now in the Folger Shakespeare Library have been printed in the footnotes to this edition. The most recent edition of Wing's *Short-Title Catalogue* lists two additional copies of *Excommunication out of Paradice* (both of which are also annotated), one in the British Library, the other in the Christ Church College Library, Oxford. The latter is quite different from the tract printed here, its thirty pages developing more fully the points made in the sixteen pages of the version now extant at the Bodleian, Folger, and Houghton Libraries.

THE
EXCOMMUNICATION
OUT OF
PARADICE.

By the Lady *Eleanor.*

GEN. 3.
So he drove out the MAN.

Title page. In the Folger copy a handwritten annotation at the bottom of the page reads "in the same Hower this given to ye Howse wth Her owne Hand. Not only a woemans Brains beaten out By the Abey doore &c But the Alderman Adams & the Lord Mayor". In the Harvard copy a handwritten annotation at the top of page reads "(Joh: 4) Except yee see signes & wonders yee will not Beleeve:". "Thes as seal'd or confermd since Septem^8 3:" is written beside the quote from Genesis. The date "3 September" may indicate that the note was written after the Battle of Dunbar (3 September 1650) or the Battle of Worcester (3 September 1651), both victories for the Commonwealth. Also in the Harvard copy, a handwritten annotation beneath the date reads "By John Feild". John Feild (or Field) was a London printer.

To the Honorable, *Oliver Cromwel,* Esq; Lieutenant-General, &c.

Noble Sir,

Your own high merit not onely, but that renowned Family of you[rs] (envied a little not) Lord Cromwel *Earl of* Essex, *such a Benefactor or Pillar of Church, begets this boldness in her to salute you, though farther to be acquainted have not the honor; but so much honoring them or their memory, through whose clemency or zeal, when the Faith lay at stake, we enjoy'd the Scriptures first in the vulgar or mother tongue, which began with the* 10 *Commandments and Lords Prayer, &c. She saying nothing but according to the Scriptures, whereof thus,*

August, 1647.   Being your humble Servant, &c.

The Excommunication out of Paradice, By the Lady Eleanor.

The Ark, Baptisms express figure (*Pet.* 3.) No such custom admits in Church, of those knowing not *good from evil,* to be Baptized a witness at mans estate all of them saved by water: where his three Sons, though married all, *yet had none born unto them till after the flood,* Noah *that* 20 *according to all the Lord commanded, so did he.*

Neither after our Lords example, of obedience giving to understand, *As my Father gave me commandment, so I do;* he at full age arrived: The Dove when as descended, or abode on him, who began then to be about

---

Lines 4–5. In the Folger copy a handwritten annotation in the margin reads "(Anagr̃. O: Cromwel Howl Rome".

Line 4. **Family of you[rs]:** In the Folger copy "Family of yours" has been emended by Lady Eleanor to read "Family of your name".

Line 5. **Lord Cromwel…Essex:** Thomas Cromwell (d.1540), minister to Henry VIII at the time of the English Reformation.

Line 9. **Scriptures…tongue:** the English Bible.

Line 13. **humble Servant:** In the Harvard copy "Excellencie" is handwritten above the line, with a caret between "your" and "humble".

Line 22. **As…commandment:** John 12:49–50.

Lines 22–23. **The Dove…descended:** see Matt. 3:16.

thirty of Age, thrice ten: Certainly had a great thing been commanded, as they replyed, *Naaman bidden, Go and wash in Jordan, &c.* How much rather this imposed, *But go ye and preach; He that believeth and is baptized, shall be saved* (vers.) according *who went forth and preach'd every where;* where thus (ver.) *Both men and women were Baptized:* As the Eunuch for another, *If thou believest with all thine heart, thou mayest be Baptized:* So he whose Father and Mother answering, *He is of age, ask him;* and again, *Therefore said his Parents, He is of age, &c.* (Joh. 9.) He bidden, *Go and wash,* as much to say, God-fathers and God-mothers needless.

The Church past non-age, hath need of milk no longer, such meat not belonging to Babes: Now (to search the Scriptures) the wedding Garment expected from none such under age; witness Marriage honored with his first Miracle; of *the good wine till last reserv'd,* himself the blessed Bridegroom watch'd so long for.

And *He that despised Moses Law* (Heb. 10.) *if dyed without mercy; what incur they that offer despite thus unto the Spirit of Grace?* alledging, because of Children brought unto him, *and setting one in the midst of them, saying, Who shall offend such one of these little ones, &c.* and *laying his hands on other;* and *except ye receive the kingdom of God as a little childe,* therefore the persons of men and women are excepted: wheras of another sort in truth signifie Babes and Sucklings, of whom said, *I thank thee, O Father, that hast revealed these things unto such and such,* hidden from the learned; whose weak Objections these, of *Little children to come unto me, for of such is the kingdom of heaven;* onely spoken after a comparative way, as afore shewed, little for their purpose: who produce Circumcision, appointed for Males, to uphold this Antichristian custom in times of Ignorance, through subtilty crept into the

30

40

50

Line 25. **Naaman…Jordan:** 2 Kings 5:10. Lines 26–27. **But go…saved:** Mark 16:15–16.

Lines 28–30. **Both men…Baptized:** Acts 8:12. **As the Eunuch…Baptized:** Acts 8:27–37.

Line 32. **God-fathers and God-mothers:** In seventeenth century England a child received godparents upon entering the Christian community at baptism.

Line 34. **non-age:** minority.

Lines 35–36. **wedding Garment:** appropriate clothing; see Matt. 22:11–12.

Line 37. **of the good…reserv'd:** see John 2:10. Line 50. **Circumcision:** Rom. 2:26–29.

Church, with the Serpent (as it were) yea, hath God said, *Ye shall not,* *&c.* the very forbidden fruit untimely tasted, as the Common prayer book partly confesses, in old time; but at *Easter* and *Whitsontide* administred, which custom, say they, out of use, cannot well for many considerations be restored, &c. without mentioning so much as one in behalf of their mock-Baptism, founded on Circumcision of Infants, a character not to be blotted out in the flesh, that impression even verifying the *Sows returning to the mire, and the Dog gone back, &c.* as accompanied
60 with a point of more concernment then *Joroboams* prefering to the priesthood the inferior sort, or his offering incense, those Mother Midwives *Joan Baptists* suffered to take that office upon them, because of *Ziporahs* circumcising her Son.

[*So turn ye to*] that warning piece (*Apocal.* 13.) of the Antichristian Beast *whose desperate wound was healed;* and the false Prophets description, [*and see*] upon what foundation both State and Church stands in the last days (vers.) *And I stood upon the Sea, and I saw a beast rise up out of the sea, having seven Heads and ten Horns, crowned, &c.* expresly bears date the present seventeenth Century, even the British beast also armed
70 at all points, from *Brute* its Name derived; where *Europia* (as it were) carried into the Sea: Besides *Cesars* adored Image, not to be drowned in

---

Line 53. **forbidden...tasted:** by Adam and Eve.

Lines 54–55. **at Easter...administred:** Formerly baptisms occurred only at Easter and fifty days later at the feast of the descent of the Holy Spirit.

Line 59. **Sows...back:** 2 Pet. 2:22. Lines 60–61. **Joroboams...sort:** see 1 Kings 13:33–34.

Lines 61–62. **Mother...Baptists:** cf. the story of John the Baptist (Luke 3).

Line 63. **Ziporahs:** see Exod. 4:24–26.

Line 64. [**So turn ye to**]: In the Harvard copy, "So turn ye" has been emended by Lady Eleanor to read "Not aware of" ("Not" is written over "So", "aware" is written above "turn ye", which has been crossed out, and "of" is written over "to"); a handwritten annotation in the margin reads "How pointing to K: Charles His faction surviving Him. &c:x:"

Line 66. [**and see**]: These words are deleted in the Harvard copy.

Line 67. **the Sea:** In the Harvard copy, "Sand of the" is written above the line, with a caret between "the" and "Sea".

Line 70. **Brute:** Brutus; legendary founder of Britain. **Europia:** Europa; in Greek myth, Zeus disguised himself as a bull and carried her off into the sea.

Line 71. **Cesar:** the Roman Emperor and thus secular authority; see Matt. 22:20–21.

forgetfulness, and tribute money from strangers, wounded sorest of all by *Brutus*, he of his own begetting foretold of the fatal *Ides* of *March;* by whom the year was set according to the Sun, Three hundred and sixty six days, corrected the Kalender, whose Names lives to this day both of them, *Julius Cesar,* the Moneth of *JULY* named after it. As for the Man of Sin, the other Beast his coming out of the earth, horned like the Lamb, but a Dragons voyce, the tythes (to wit) or fruits of those Rams, no few sirnamed, *Pope Innocent, he that runs may read it;* whose feigned Miracles, with Cross and Crucifix adored, like that of Gold, *whose*   80 *height sixty cubits, and breadth six* (Dan. 3.) and thus running over the Number of his Name 666 namely, *Julius Cesar* and *August,* whose numeral letters *Vic Lvvvi* about the fortieth year of which Reign (*Augustus*) who reigned 55 years and odde Moneths; *the Lamb of God came into the world,* aged 30: *in the fifteenth of Tiberius reign* (Luke, &c.) so that the aforesaid the 55 years and six Months, to Moneths 666 amounts the Grigean Account put into the reckoning; since which Empires rising (1600 compleat) as low declined; & whether or no our British Coat the Leopards spotted or pothered to be (vers.) be not as *Esaus* voyce from *Jacobs* to be discerned, or the Lambs from the Dragons language, even   90 paralleld with the ten persecutions, these days of ours the ten horns subscribes it; one Isle calling unto another, *Patmos*-Isle unto *Great Britains,* and *this great beast followed so, and admired of all the world;* said to *rise*

Lines 73–74. **Ides of March:** the date when Brutus and others assassinated Julius Caesar. **by whom…set:** Julius Caesar revised the calendar.

Line 78. **tythes:** Tithes were the tenth parts of income, traditionally agricultural produce, owed to the church for its support. In seventeenth-century England tithes were often monetary payments, and the rights to collect tithes had become property rights which, in some instances, were owned by individual laypeople.

Line 79. **no few…Innocent:** Several medieval popes had taken the name Innocent.

Line 83. **numeral…Vic Lvvvi:** the letters of a name which were also Roman numerals, in this case 666.

Line 85. **Tiberius:** Roman emperor who succeeded Augustus (Luke 3:1).

Line 87. **Grigean Account:** perhaps the Gregorian calendar, which was used in Europe but not England in Lady Eleanor's day.

Line 88. **Coat:** coat of arms. Line 89. **pothered:** powdered or dusty.

Lines 89–90. **Esaus voyce…discerned:** see Gen. 27:22–23.

up out of the sea; begins not too with that Founder of the Spanish Faction, *George* Duke of *Buckingham,* of the Order of Saint *George,* Master of the Horse, Admiral of the Seas, as by the Names of Ships, the one a *Leopard,* the *Lyon* another, the *Bear, &c.* he with a Butchers knife slain at *Portsmouth* in the Moneth of August 1628. having continued from 1625. March, beyond expectation; ten years that was a Minion to the former. And so much for *his three years and an half,* (ver.) together with the time exprest of his continuing how long, who went away from his Parliament (1641. *Jan.*) until *Nazebies* victory (1645. *June*) where the Dragons great Authority personates, S. *George* the patron of that Order; as count the number of his Name also, Viscount *Vuilers* (*Vic Lvvvi*) or *666.* wanting no open mouth, if standers by to be credited, his last words heard at *Portsmouth,* at whose dispose not onely high Offices, but the Crown Revenue, Six hundred thousand pounds and more *per annum,* the weight of *Solomons* Gold (*2 Chro. 9.*) 666 Talents aluding therto.

Where the treasureship the other Beast that *came up out of the earth,* spake as the dragon, not a true word as much to say, of late in the Clergies custody, as by the horns of the Lamb signified the two Archbishopricks bought and sold with the rest.

And as the story of 88 the Spanish Armado's defeat, witness in this catalogue, the Hangings of the House of Peers, bordered about with so

---

Lines 94–100. **Founder…former:** Buckingham received many tokens of favor from James I and Charles I, including the Order of the Garter. He was regarded by critics as a Spanish sympathizer and was assassinated in August 1628.

Line 100. **his three…half:** the time Buckingham lived during Charles's reign; cf. James 5:17 and 1 Kings 17–18.

Lines 101–2. **who went away…June:** Charles I left Westminster and Parliament in January 1641, i.e., 1642, thus about three and a half years prior to the parliamentary victory at the Battle of Naseby.

Line 103. **S. George:** St. George, England's patron saint, who was legendary for killing a dragon. **that Order:** the Order of the Garter.

Line 104. **Viscount Vuilers:** Viscount Villiers was one of Buckingham's titles.

Lines 110–13. **the treasureship…custody:** In 1636 William Juxon, bishop of London, became lord treasurer of London. **two Archbishopricks:** Canterbury and York.

Line 114. **88:** 1588.

Line 115. **Peers:** In the Folger copy an asterisk "Peers" calls attention to a handwritten note in the margin which reads "with His wounds in ye Head K: C: Heald others &c".

many Heads and Names, as it were (*v.*) *I stood upon the sand of the Sea, and I saw a Beast rise up, &c. with all those crowns,* &c. also in the House of Commons, those pieces of Tapistry, of Fruitage and Flowers, all in their pots coming out of the earth about 666 sometime in number; and so much touching that Allegory of their rising up, set between pillars, referred to the beholders, Hangings sometime belonging to the Abbey [*as it were the others up,*] and that spake, &c. (vers. xi.) the influence of the Ten Horns, [*pre*]tending to the French [*R*]. for another[,] with no inferior mouth 1610. mortally wounded, whose Faction revived by the Cardinal, lives and breathes to this day by his skill, such the mutable condition of all, *Behold, as he stood upon the sand,* though said, *Who is able to make war with the Beast?* As *Essex* behold too Viscount *Hereford* such another; from Heralds mystery deriving that appellation, as the Stag or red Deer bearing it for his Crest; and so count again, *Numerus ejus sexcenti sexaginta sex, Rev.* of whose rising from the generation of the *Walters: Walter Devorex* begetting *Walter:* and *Walter Dev. Walter* and *Walter, &c.* some six one [*after another*] of that Name.

Not without his sevenfold Blasphemous Titles, superscribed one as deeply interested in the Horns as any other, in the Forehead signed with the Horn; that married was in the year 1606, at the years of 16. 1636.

Line 121. **the Abbey:** Westminster Abbey.

Line 122. [**as…others up**]: This phrase is deleted in the Bodleian, Folger, and Harvard copies.

Line 123. [**pre**]**tending:** Lady Eleanor has changed "pretending" to "Extending" in the Bodleian, Folger, and Harvard copies. **the French [R]:** R[ex] (Latin) or R[oi] (French); Henry IV, assassinated by a Jesuit; in the Folger and the Harvard copies, Lady Eleanor has changed the "R" to a "K". **another:** In the Harvard copy, Lady Eleanor has inserted a caret over the comma that follows "another" and written "like monster" above the line; a handwritten annotation in the margin reads "As Dolphin Ludovicus 666 whose Brother SurNamd John Baptist". In the Folger copy a handwritten marginal annotation reads "That Sea Monster or Dolphin Lodovius 666. And monst. surname Joh. Bapt."

Lines 124–25. **the Cardinal:** Richelieu, who by 1624 had become chief minister in France.

Line 127. **Essex…Hereford:** The third earl of Essex, who also had the title Viscount Hereford, was general of the parliamentary forces at the outbreak of the civil war.

Lines 129–30. **Numerus…sex:** His number six hundred, sixty-six (Latin); Rev. 13:18.

Line 131. **Walter Devorex:** Devereux, first earl of Essex and second viscount Hereford (d. 1576).

Line 132. [**after another**]: These words are deleted in the Bodleian copy.

Line 134. **interested:** affected injuriously.

who father'd a son; and the year 1646. Sept. 16. aged 56. in the sixt year of the Parliament was stricken in the head by an an Apoplexy, that blow invisible too, whose Father, aged 36. that was beheaded, plotted by *Walter Rawley;* when as the Adored Image of the Beast, with those coat arms so adornd, as though he had been alive followed of all: In S. *John Baptist* Chappel interr'd for the *Walters* sake, the last of his name of *Essex.*

Lastly, in these troublesome Seas tossed Kings of the North and South, *French* and *Spanish,* such dutiful sons of *Rome,* the horns ten pointing that way not onely from *Cornu & Corona,* as *Carolus* derived, ten in number, four of the Race of *Charls the Great,* and six of the House of *Austria;* but from *Henry* the fourth of *Lancaster* House, unto *Henry* the Eight, and his progeny ten even Crowned; whereof the prophet *Daniel* thus, cap. 7. v. 23. of these devouring Tyrants, treading down Laws, &c. *And another shall rise after them, diverse from the first* (to wit) of another nation, *before whom three fell, by whom changed both the Name of the Kingdom, and their Liberties, &c.* no other then *Great Brit.* Scotish-horn, speaking with such a lawless mouth, *succeeding those three without issue,* Edw 6. Mar. and *Eliz. of whose time and times and half, or three years and half, the truth shewed afore of it, from the most supreme mystery that of times and seasons, signifying how long from his unhappy departure from his Parliament, until his being taken 1645. and outed, &c. of whom the last news, his Resurrection or rising out of the sea, brought to*

Line 136. **1646. Sept. 16:** death of the earl of Essex.

Line 138. **whose Father…beheaded:** Robert, second earl of Essex, was executed in 1601 as a result of a revolt.

Line 139. **Rawley:** Raleigh.

Line 145. **Cornu…Corona…Carolus:** horns, crown, Charles (Latin).

Line 146. **Charls the Great:** Charlemagne.

Lines 147–48. **from Henry…Crowned:** Ten monarchs ruled England between Henry IV and Elizabeth I.

Lines 152–53. **Great Brit. Scotish-horn:** When King James VI of Scotland succeeded Elizabeth on the English throne to become King James I of England, he took the title King of Great Britain.

Line 158. **his Resurrection…sea:** Charles I was taken from Holmby House to Hampton Court in August 1647; cf. Dan. 7:3.

judgement; so hitherto the end of the matter, as Daniel 7, *&c. onely these,*
Let him that is filthy, be so still, and he that is holy also, *&c.* and he that   160
is athirst, take the water of life freely, *which children and Infants [are] not*
[in]capable of, are free without it, cannot thirst or long for what they never
knew, the Spirit and the Bride saying, Come, and if any man thirst, *&c.*
out of his belly (*he that believeth*) shall flow rivers of living water, (Joh.)
proclaimed that great day, of it so much.

FINIS.

Lines 161–62. **Infants…[in]capable:** In the Folger copy, "are" has been crossed out; the first
two letters of "incapable" have been crossed out in both the Folger and the Bodleian copies.

Line 164. **rivers…water:** see John 4.

This tract (Wing D2005A), written in 1648 when Lady Eleanor was imprisoned in the King's Bench, adapts Ezekiel's message to Israel in order to prophesy imminent Judgment on England. The present edition of *Reader* is based on the copy in the volume of Lady Eleanor's tracts now in the Folger Shakespeare Library. Because no title page survives with that apparently unique extant copy, it is titled here with its first word.

READER,

The heavy *hour at hand,* that it should not *as a Thief surprize us in the night, Babylons* scattering whirlwind our final or utter blow; or lest should say, *There had not a Prophet been amongst them,* could not refrain giving thee warning, though like *rolling the restles stone, prove* but *labor in vain.*

Where *Line upon Line,* no vain repetition, stiles them *A house of Rebellion,* and *Most Rebellious,* Cap. ver. &c. Nay (as it were) had been sent to the house of *Austria* their Churches, replyed, *Had long ere this in sackcloth and ashes;* or to a People of *a deep lip,* of *another language,* &c.   10 The first-fruits of which Ambassage, shewing Israel being cut off, as by *Ezekiel* tasted of, *watchman over the rebellious house of Israel,* made to *eat the roll or writ, Lamentation, Mourning* and *Woe,* superscribed within and without; so by all signs and tokens without doubt served on our three sinful Kingdoms, home charged with open Rebellion, neither hearkning to the Prophet bidden, *stamp with the foot, smite with the fist, with the breaking of thy loyns sigh,* their musick but made and song, The

---

Lines 1–57. The base text of *Reader* is printed in italic type with roman emphases; the fonts have been reversed in the present edition for ease of reading.

Lines 2–3. **as a Thief…night:** see 2 Pet. 3:10. **Babylons…whirlwind:** cf. Zech. 7:14.

Lines 5–6. **rolling…labor in vain:** in Greek myth, the punishment of Sisyphus, who was condemned to roll a stone endlessly uphill.

Line 8. **Cap. ver:** chapter, verse.

Line 9. **house of Austria:** the Hapsburgs, the Holy Roman Emperors, who were supporters of Roman Catholicism.

Line 13. **superscribed:** written above; addressed or inscribed.

Lines 14–15. **our three sinful Kingdoms:** England, Scotland, and Ireland.

Lord of Hosts when uttering his thundring voyce, roaring as a Lyon, the
tokens of his coming, an end come on the four corners of the earth,
20   ready to fall asleep, *or sitting in the seat of scorners,* All their elbows
grown to the pillows, they and their fathers.

And so farther informing whether silent or otherwise, as it came to
pass in the fifth year of such a Kings captivity accomplished (*Ezekiel
Cap. 1.*) the hand of the Lord when upon him, his word coming
expresly to him, saw the great Vision of God, he amongst the captives;
Also from this place, the Kings Bench Prison amongst this Society, give
to understand, to accompany this warning piece of the *Turkish Armado's*
preparation, added a sign, as *Isaiah* sometime gave one of the *Suns going
back so many degrees retiring,* before their captivity at hand foreshewed
30   then; Another given of the *Moon,* from his giving the *Three half Moons,*
whose Army harbors at *Argier,* attending *Sions* being delivered up into
his possession: These *Islands* three to be under his lash of Jurisdiction,
drawn from which premises these, for his Crest or Coat-Arms who gives
the *Half Moon,* not far off his house called *Sion,* committed to whom
three prisoner Princes, one of no inferior estate, under *Babylons
Bashaws,* typyfying even our estate, those *Mahometans* our guardians,
the third Earldom of this Realm, assigned thereby to *Algernon* Earl of
Northumberland by Name, sometime Admiral of the Seas, paralleld
with that Northern scourge, *The Assyrian Army,* how given up into his
40   protection the houses of the Lord.

And so much (*Reader*) for this flight of ours, and this new sign of the
New Moon going before it, where cannot pass over *Ezekiels* portraying
our Cities siege, shewed by those battering rams or brazen Engines, so

---

Line 27. **Armado:** army. Lines 28–29. **the Suns...degrees:** Isa. 38:8.

Line 30. **Another:** the earl of Northumberland.

Line 31. **Argier:** probably Algiers, north African port of the Muslims.

Line 34. **his house called Sion:** After the Reformation the earl of Northumberland's family
acquired Syon, which had been a house of Bridgettine nuns; Zion was also the House of God.

Line 35. **three prisoner Princes:** The earl of Northumberland had custody of King Charles's
children.

Line 36. **Bashaws:** pashas or grandees.

Line 39. **Northern...Army:** see Isa. 10:5; the Assyrians lived to the north of the Israelites.

to the life their swift doing execution; and dreadful wheels motion and thundring voyce, in those living creatures (as shadowed under the *Seraphin work of the Tabernacles Curtains,* the Lord of Hosts Pavillion, each loop of which not without a Mystery, as observable *Fifty in one curtain, and fifty in the other, (Exod. 26.)* containing the mystery of winged time, the midst of the Century, even directed to, joyned like those Cherubin wings of theirs.

And of this your day drawing near, whose silver and gold the stumbling block, Author of unhappiness all, as he unto all the people of *Judah,* saying from such a year of the King of *Judah,* even unto this day; that is, the Three and twenty year (*Jer. cap. 25.*) Also the word of the Lord have I spoken unto you, rising early, but, &c.

1648. 23. of the present Reign.

F I N I S.

50

Line 56. **1648. 23…Reign:** By 1648 Charles I had been king for twenty-three years.

In this tract (Wing D2019) Lady Eleanor once again takes up the notion of restitution, which she had treated in 1644 in *The restitution of reprobates* (Wing D2008), in 1646 in *Je le tien* (Wing D1996aA—page 199 in the present edition), and in 1647 in *The mystery of general redemption* (Wing D1996A). This time she more explicitly links her own effort to obtain restitution of her property, the manor of Pirton in Hertfordshire, with the larger issue of restitution for those who have suffered under the rule of Antichrist. The present edition of *Writ of Restitution* is based on the copy now in the Houghton Library, Harvard University (shelf number *EC65 D7455 B652t).

THE
WRIT OF RESTITUTION:
By the Lady *ELEANOR.*

PSAL. &c.

Be wise now therefore, O ye Kings; Be learned ye that are Judges of the earth.

ACTS 3. 21.

Whom the Heaven must receive, till the times of Restitution of all things which God hath spoken by the mouth of all his Prophets since the world began.

THE Writ of Restitution:
BY The Lady *ELEANOR.*

And now in this his cause, *the Judge of all the earth, Prince of the Kings of the earth,* a case wherein all concerned; these are to pray three, who here sit in his place Judges: Give me leave to speak, and shew you a mystery, from this writ *Amoveas manus,* defended by the happy Mr. *Maynard,* notwithstanding opposed by Mr. Solicitor, with S. *John, not knowing what Spirit he's of.*

Before whom this day, the day of Judgements figure, shewing by rea-
10 son of a writ of Error, not executable, three stand charged with contempt of the Court, pleading *Ignorance,* notwithstanding the aforesaid
Amoveas manus writ being executed (as it were) the *forbidden fruit* tasted
untimely; these men yet each discharged and acquitted: as let it neither
be reputed impossible, how much opposed soever by others, for *All to be
saved at last, when the utmost mite or minute satisfied* or expired, the
worst of reprobates not excepted, in his time whose immense mercy
inscrutable: this is the argument, Against whom no writ of Error feisible
either or possible.

Who saw every thing very good at first made by him, reduced to be no
20 doubt to the same estate, as holds good from that *of dust return to dust,*
every thing to the place from whence it came; faln Angels and men
restored every one, not left a hoof, &c. or lost of that kinde bearing his
Image.

Of which general deliverance well understood to be an Article of the

---

Line 4. **these...pray:** the formulaic wording of a petition to institute legal proceedings.

Line 6. **writ Amoveas manus:** remove the hand (Latin); legal warrant. **Mr. Maynard:** John Maynard (1602–1690), attorney and judge who opposed the king's deposition.

Line 7. **Mr. Solicitor:** John Cook, solicitor and prosecutor in the king's trial. **S. John:** Oliver St. John (1598–1673), attorney and judge, chief justice in 1648, had been a leading parliamentarian, then sided with the army against Parliament, and subsequently refused to sit on the commission trying the king.

Line 10. **writ...executable:** warrant claiming that, because of error, a case should be heard again by the court; in this case, the writ could not be put into effect.

Line 19. **Who saw...him:** God at the creation (Gen. 1:31).

Christian Faith, famous *Origen,* from whose judgment other fathers erring, forced were to erect a Purgatory for Saints, that *Babel* edifice of
theirs; of whom the aforesaid ancient father, the worst they could say of
him was, *As he did worst of any when he wrote ill, so exceeded all men
when he did well.*

And so proceeding with this reported Case of this days Hearing,   30
where the fiery adversary upon their surmisings, pressing for a present
sentence, before the accused heard or answering, charg'd, that although
moved in open Court such a writ, the *Amoveas manus* to be respited:
and accordingly a *Supersedis* issued out, delivered to the Sheriff then in
being; the Tenants nevertheless outed of possession by the now under-
Sheriff of that county about three moneths ago: whereupon he cald and
appearing, demanded of whom, how those doors came to be opened,
denied not what he had done by vertue of such a sealed writ, by such a
Solicitor brought to him; as for other writs concerning them, pleads
Ignorance: One *Pomfred* by name, (*alias Pomum*) surprized in state of   40
inocency, like her *first in the transgression;* (for pursuing which Allegory
thus) shewing one *Massingal* cald, pleading ignorāce too as the man laying the fault on *Eve;* he (some three years since in that Office) onely had
a *Supersedis,* of what validity now he knows not; for other writ, none
came to his hand.

Also *Jo: Rand* Solicitor cald, he appears, no yong Fox, not to be foold
with pocket Errors, refers to the Judges, whether year after year that writ
like to be of much force, brought beforce such and such Officers;
namely the Treasurer, &c. when as in being none such, or like to be:
And so this the Epilogue or end of it, their stale Errors being quasht; the   50

Line 25. **Origen:** third-century church father.

Line 26. **Babel edifice:** see Gen. 11.   Line 33. **respited:** delayed or postponed.

Line 34. **Supersedis:** supersedeas; a writ ordering someone to cease or desist.

Line 40. **Pomfred:** John Pomfret, sheriff of Hertfordshire in 1648. **alias Pomum:** also known
as a fruit-tree (Latin).

Line 41. **her…transgression:** Eve.

Line 42. **Massingal:** Thomas Massingale, undersheriff of Hertfordshire in 1648.

Line 46. **Jo: Rand:** John Rand, Lady Eleanor's solicitor.

writ stands good for taking off or removing his Majesties unhealing hands, his Tenants cashier'd; moreover for strengthning which, another writ, a *Writ of Restitution* produced, brought in COURT, stops the Lyons mouthes, forced to put up their pipes, as let it happen to the ene-mie of *General Restitution*, sent to that parable of *the unnatural elder Brother towards his own flesh and blood*, Luke; and *murmuring laborers, because their fellows mads partakers with them;* endless unmercifulnes thereof to bid others beware.

And here to make an end with what penance imposed on those three for a presumption of that nature; these a touch of it: The under Sheriff *Pomfred*, somewhat of a low pitch, he never to aspire or take upon him the state or stile of a high Sheriff; the other sometime in the same imployment or Office, *Massingal* to return to his domestick function or calling deserting former dainties. The honest poor Solicitor *J: Rand* as for him unto other Solicitors an example his lot, besides to pinch him-self with hard and thin fare, never to attempt the Kings Solicitors place, or St. *John* to be cald like the wandring Jew.

And so farther, no jesting matter neither of mean consequence, where like Twins, this finished tedious Law Suit in Trinity term; and Gods word both sympathizing or joyned in wedlock, like the blessed Virgin and just *Joseph* Cousins, though abruptly in brevities behalf han-dled or penn'd, presaging without doubt, maugre the old Serpents plot-ting with his smooth outside, through the holy Ghosts power, the third person in Trinity, long silent though, or vaild under a cloud as it were, will immediately decide our Church-Differences, of such troublesom

60

70

Lines 53–54. **stops…mouthes:** cf. Dan. 6:22.

Lines 55–56. **unnatural…Brother:** see Luke 15:11–32. **murmuring laborers:** Matt. 20:1–16.

Line 63. **Massingal:** He became undersheriff when Pomfret became sheriff.

Line 67. **the wandring Jew:** person who, according to legend, was condemned to wander the earth with no rest until the Day of Judgment as a punishment for insulting Jesus on the way to the crucifixion.

Line 69. **Trinity term:** law term in summer.

Line 72. **maugre:** malgré; in spite of (French).

Times the cause, which Lord hasten, and teach them to discern the time better.

And so hastning on, shewing from hence how all shut up under ignorance, know not what they do; the man undone by the woman, aleaging for himself, suspected not, she unto him given, the Author to be of his ruine, having warning of it given him never; The woman on the other side again, The Serpents intents had she known, she had not been overreacht by such his falseness & flattery, to the overthrow of her and hers; so many: The Serpent his excuse, he came but to try her for his part; what would befal was above his reach, foresaw it not; no more then the old Prophet, that by means of him a Lyon by the way should tear his fellow Prophet: Or that such a mass of corrupted mankinde should succeed to perish, since the words to them twain being, *Touch it not lest ye dye,* importing but in danger of death.

And thus since all Original sin the root pardoned in that last prayer, *Father, forgive them, &c.* sealed with his own Blood on the Tree, Restitution of course follows, who can forbid it, or shew why the taking off, or removing of his heavy hand should not be an *Article of our Belief,* seeing this Son of *Adam* his administrator discharges all Debts from the beginning of the world to the end, which by that erroneous Opinion, Mother of Errors, they go about to annihilate that affirm, *Out of Hell is no Redemption;* who is able, having *Ages of Ages* (Rev. 1.) *even from the worlds beginning, the keys of Hell and Death,* to turn this *water into wine;* and where he hath given a being, to cause such judgements to be for the best, the onely Clay to regain the eye-sight, howsoever Excommunicated this Truth by envious times; of *Esau's* race, endeavoring to

80

90

100

Line 79. **aleaging:** alleging.

Lines 85–87. **the old Prophet...fellow Prophet:** 1 Kings 13:11–26. A handwritten annotation in the margin reads "for conferenc sake".

Lines 88–89. **twain:** two. **Touch...dye:** Gen. 3:3.

Line 91. **Father...them:** Luke 23:34.

Line 98. **turn...wine:** Jesus' miracle at Cana (John 2:1–11).

Line 100. **the onely...eye-sight:** see John 9:1–7.

Line 101. **Esau:** Esau sold his birthright to his brother (Gen. 25:29–34).

disinherit and strip the Son of God, *who gave himself a Ransom,* not for some, but *for All; All made alive in him: Forgive them, Father, &c.* as shewed afore, under ignorance concluded.

FINIS.

The date, January 1648, on the final page of this tract (Wing D1970A) suggests that Lady Eleanor wrote it at the time of the trial of King Charles I. The title page declares, "Printed in the yeer 1649," which may mean the tract was not printed until after 25 March, when England began the new year. She addresses this *Appeal* to Lord General, Sir Thomas Fairfax, the commander of the parliamentary armies. A few months earlier, probably in September, she had directed *Of the general great days approach* (Wing D1999A) to him and had also endorsed for him a copy of her new edition of *Given to the Elector* (Wing D1992—page 59 in the present edition). The present edition of *Appeal from Court to Camp* is based on the copy in the volume of Lady Eleanor's tracts now in the Folger Shakespeare Library; it is apparently a unique extant copy.

HER APPEAL FROM
THE COURT TO THE CAMP

Dan. 12.

Many shall be purified, and made white, and tryed: But the wicked shall do wickedly, and none of the wicked shall understand: But the wise shall understand.

The Word of the Most High:
To the Lord General, Lord FAIRFAX,
From the Lady *Eleanor.*

The generality or scope of this command touching *Prophesie,* though ceased a time, the Church bidden expresly, *Despise it not,* but *to try the Spirits,* needless to be insisted on. Let it seem not therefore strange or hard what is here desired, since nothing too hard for him whom ye serve, *The Lord of Hosts,* that you the Commander of the field, prayed *to send forth Harvest-laborers,* to be pleased to appoint some faithful by
10　name, the truth of these things for to examine, no true peace without it, concerning what she hath been a sufferer so many years for; no less then the burthen of his word to *Great Britain* (Anno Dom.) 1625. bearing date first of the present Reign, Three and twenty years since; shewing what year in as it were the general Judgment, speaking as through a Trumpet from Heaven: So that the Prophets testimony, the Scriptures which accords therewith, may no longer wait for their resurrection; that have by Antichristian authority been crucified and buried hitherto, like *that golden wedge or tongue,* hidden by him *Achan,* author of so much trouble: Even the Prophet *Daniel, that greatly beloved man;* and John,
20　*whom he loved, that bosom Disciple;* both testifying of great *Britains* visitation at such a time, as from his own mouth also (*Mat.* 24.) after such fearful denounced Judgements, the like never afore or again, bidden therefore, *watch,* &c. shews of that blessed *Manna* their *meat in due season,* when to be given them, doubtless something to be revealed, a forewarning plain enough.

　　As from *the Kingdom of Heaven being likened unto those virgins, five wise, and five foolish,* shall shew you a mystery, how points to the aforesaid acceptable year 1625. begins with the blessed Virgins feast (Five and twentieth of the moneth) witness when made at midnight *that cry*
30　*before the Bridegroom;* which as betokens the word of God in such a year

---

Lines 1–82. The base text of *Appeal from Court to Camp* is printed in italic type with roman emphases; the fonts have been reversed in the present edition for ease of reading.

Line 9. **send...Harvest-laborers:** Matt. 9:38. Line 18. **golden...Achan:** see Josh. 7:19–26.

Line 26. **Kingdom...virgins:** see Matt. 25:1–13.

Line 28. **year...feast:** Lady Day, Feast of the Annunciation of the Virgin Mary, 25 March.

so to such a Reign directed, that began then; and his marrying with such a one, with the late hour of wedding nights, &c. (*Mat.* 25.) *where the five Talents account given* up, a touch gives of the same year too; and for her wisdom anointed with *her lamp-oyl spent* so much: *Mary* likewise by name much like that, had a name, *She lives, but was dead* (Rev. 3.) *brought with her a curse in stead of a blessing, Pestilence,* never such, and Sword *Great Britains* portion; as blessings great set light by, unaccompanied with no smal corrections, where again upon his Prophetical Reply to our Saviour *Christ* (Luke 14.) *Blessed is he that shall eat bread in the kingdom of heaven* (as much to say*) lives to see him reign, his foes put under his feet for ever:* also *Sion, whoso toucheth her, toucheth the apple of his eye,* puts forth this Parable, *A certain man made a great supper, and bade many; and at supper time sent forth his servant,* that intrusted servant, saying, *All things are ready* (to wit) the Prophets wait, their visions are awake; when the unworthy wretches with one consent and voyce, all began to make excuse, one this, &c. another *that had married a wife, could not come without her leave;* as by *the five yoke of Oxen,* paints too unto his being Crowned and married such a year, in whose room *the maimed bidden, &c.* enough of whose company may be had (*Luke* 14.) in plain English, The careless *Stuart* by name, *justly turned out of Stewardship, what Trust to be repos'd in such a ONE? unto this day not weighing the many Caveats entered, and sacred Statutes, Matt. 24.* Noahs days, knowing not his own house, when hee sees it either: *as, had the goodman of the house known at what hour &c. would not suffred his house to be broken up,* his banqueting house especially, &c.

And again, like as in days of old what doings, when *the Son of man is revealed, thus and thus it shall be; marrying,* &c. bidden *Remember Lots wife* her looking back: *and where Lord being askt, shall be revealed that*

Lines 34–36. **Mary...blessing:** Charles I married Henrietta Maria in 1625.

Lines 41–42. **Sion...eye:** Zech. 2:7–8.

Lines 50–51. **careless Stuart...Stewardship:** see the parable of the unjust steward (Luke 16:1–13); the family name of Britain's seventeenth-century monarchs was Stuart.

Line 52. **Caveats:** warnings.

Line 55. **his banqueting house especially:** The Banqueting House at Whitehall, constructed for King James I, incurred damage in the civil wars.

Lines 57–58. **Lots Wife:** see Gen. 19:26.

secret, and these things be? wheresoever the body is, thither the Eagles resort.
60 The body of an army, those spacious quarters; *Therefore what I say unto you, I say unto all watch, have your lights burning, loyns girt, like men expecting, &c.* of which Oracles not so obstruse hitherto as obvious now. His farewel the prophet *Daniels* on the house top proclaims it, bidden *Go thy way &c.* (*Dan.* 12.) shewing, *And from the time the* Daily *shal be taken away; and the abomination that maketh desolate set up;* Altars adored; giving to understand, *As any have eyes may see;* Pauls no little one, thus computes the time, *There shall bee a thousand two hundred & ninety days: Blessed is he that waits, and comes to a thousand three hundred five and thirty:* whereby taking 1000. rests (the year of grace) 1625. call-
70 ing unto this Jubile year 1649. even *Behold I stand at the door and knock, if any man hear my voyce and open the door, I will come in and sup with him, and he with me shall sit, &c.* By your leave Sirs, which bars any more kneeling at the Table not onely, but from those words, *The daily taken away,* shews the Lords Supper how that taken away, unto the foorenoon translated: putting no difference between his and their own Suppers: well presaging the evening of time how discerned: what look-ing for and hastening, &c. would follow it, *Pet.* 3.

Resting, My Lord,
The humble Servant of your
80   Excellence,
January: 1648.   E L E A N O R.

FINIS.

Line 59. **wheresoever…resort:** Matt. 24:28.

Line 66. **Pauls:** St. Paul's Cathedral in London.   Lines 67–69. **thus…thirty:** Dan. 12:11–12.

Line 70. **Jubile year:** see note to line 85 on page 135.   **Behold…knock:** Rev. 3:20.

Line 73. **kneeling at the Table:** One religious dispute involved whether or not those taking communion should kneel.

Line 81. **1648:** i.e., 1649.

Lady Eleanor takes advantage of the occasion of the trial of King Charles I in 1649 to publish in this tract (Wing D1980, D1981) an account of the proceedings against her in 1633. She reprints a copy of the writ for her appearance which she had included in her 1645 broadsheet, *As Not Unknowne* (Wing D1973—page 139 in the present edition). To that writ she appends what appears to be a copy of a transcript from the records of the High Commission. Two editions of the tract appeared in 1649. Another version, which appeared in 1651, has been known as the *Dragons Blasphemous Charge* (Wing D1984), but is listed in the 1994 edition of volume one of Wing's *Short-Title Catalogue* as part of Wing D1993. The versions have different pagination and vary in the preliminary matter and annotation. Whereas the Worcester College and Harvard copies of *Blasphemous Charge* (Wing D1981) begin with a letter to King Charles as prisoner, page two of the Folger Library copy (Wing D1980) contains three points: the message Lady Eleanor heard on 28 July 1625; Laud's beheading in January 1644, i.e., 1645; the king's execution in January 1648, i.e., 1649. Page three of the Folger copy prints Lady Eleanor's 1633 petition to the king against Laud. The *Dragons Blasphemous Charge* has printed marginal glosses, which include but are not limited to those on the Folger version of *Blasphemous Charge*. The present edition of this tract is based on a copy of Wing D1981 in the library of Worcester College, Oxford (shelf number AA.1.12[3]).

THE
BLASPHEMOUS CHARGE
AGAINST HER.

Matth. 10.

And ye shal be brought before Governors and Kings for my sake,
against them and the Gentiles.

Title page. A handwritten annotation at the bottom of the page reads "[jer]emiah 51. the K: of B: Hath devoured mee. He Hath crushed: made mee an Emptie vessel. Hee Hath swallowed mee up like a Dragon. The violence don unto mee & my flesh, Bee upon [ ]." The bottom of the page is cut off.

For King *Charls* Prisoner, *these.*

SIR,

Upon a reference from you (1633.) *to these your Commissioners, I being Sentenced by them, as upon Record appears, because took upon me to be a Prophetess; first was Fined, and then to make publique Submission* at Pauls *so many times; that* Jericho *for ever cursed, and farther a close prisoner to continue at your pleasure.*

   So be it known, you are hereby required to make a publique acknowl-edgement of such your capital Trespass and high Offence; and first to Ask me foregiveness, *if so be you expect to finde Mercy in this world or the other.*

Jan. 1648.   Eleanor Douglas.

At the Court of Whitehal, Octob. 8. 1633.

His Majesty doth expresly command the Lord Archbishop of *Canter-buries* Grace, and His Highness Commissioners for Causes Ecclesiasti-cal, That the Petitioner be forthwith called before them, to answer for presuming to Imprint the said Books, and for preferring this detestable Petition.

Sidney Mountague.
Concordat cum &c. Tho: Maydwell.

Line 6. **Jericho...cursed:** see Josh. 6:26.

Line 9. **capital Trespass:** Lady Eleanor's connection of two conflicting legal terms: capital, punishable by death, and trespass, an action against person or property which did not amount to treason and was not ordinarily punishable by death; cf. Luke 17:3–4.

Lines 13–18. **At the Court...Petition:** the text of the warrant issued for Lady Eleanor's hearing.

Line 19. **Sidney Mountague:** royal official who issued the warrant.

Line 20. **Concordat...Maydwell:** Maydwell, the clerk who copied the warrant, testifies that it agrees with, i.e., is a true copy of, the original.

Registro Curiæ Dominorum Regiorum Commissionariorum ad Causas Ecclesiasticas. *Extract.*

Tertia Sessio Termini Michaelis, 1633.

Die Jovis vicesimo quarto viz. die mensis Octobris Anno Dom. millesimo sexcentesimo tricesimo tertio Coram Reverendissimo in Christo Patre & *Domino, Domino* Guilielmo *providenc' Diviná* Cantuar' *Archiepiscopo totius* Angliæ *Primate & Metropolitano,* Richardo *eâdem providenc'* Angliæ *Primate & Metropolitano Archiepiscopo Eboracensi, Honorandis & prænobilibus Comitibus* Portland, Dorset, *&* Carlisle, *Episcopis* Elien', *&* 30 Roffen' *&* Oxon', *Dominis* Johanne Lamb, *&* Nathanaele Brent *militibus legum Doctoribus,* Matthæo Wren *de Windsor,* Montford, *&* Worral *Sacræ Theologiæ professoribus Commissionariis Regiis ad Causas Ecclesiasticas apud* Lambeth, *Judiciarum seden' presente* Thomâ Mottershed *Regnerarii Regii Deputato.*

Con' Ellenoram Audeley.

Dr. *Worrall:* She appeared, and the Articles and Answers were publiquely read; She was Fined in Three thousand pounds, Imprisonment till she enter Bond with sufficient Security to write no more.

Mr. Dr. *Wren,* Dean of *Windsor,* he consenteth to that which is 40 already said.

Dr. *Montford, Similitèr* with Dr. *Worrall.*

Lines 21–36. **Registro...Audeley:** Register of the Lord King's Commissioners for Ecclesiastical Causes. Extract. Third Session, Michaelmas Term, 1633: On Thursday the twenty-fourth day of the month of October, in the year of the Lord 1633 before the court of the most reverend father in Christ and God, Lord William, Archbishop of Canterbury, Primate of all England and Metropolitan, Richard of the same province of England, Primate and Metropolitan Archbishop of York, the Honorable and very noble earls of Portland, Dorset, and Carlisle, the Bishops of Ely, Rochester, and Oxford, Lord John Lamb and Nathaniel Brent, Doctors of civil law, Matthew Wren of Windsor, Montford, and Worral, Professors of Sacred Theology and King's Commissioners of Ecclesiastical Causes at Lambeth, Judges being seated in the presence of Thomas Mottershed, deputy of the king. In the case of Eleanor Audeley. (Latin).

Line 42. **Similitèr:** similarly (French).

Sir *Nathanael Brent, Similitèr* with Dr. *Worrall;* and payment of Costs.

Sir *John Lamb*, and my Lord of *Oxford,* Agreeth with the highest, with the highest; and to acknowledge her Offence at *Pauls* Cross.

My Lord of *Rochester,* with the highest; and if the Court will bear it, he would send her to Bedlam.

My Lord of *Ely,* Three thousand pounds, Excommunication, con-
50   demned in Costs, and committed *ut prius,* till she give, &c.

My Lord *Portland,* and my Lord of *Carlisle,* desired to be spared from their Sentence.

My Lord of *Dorset* agreeth with the highest.

My Lords Grace of *York,* Imprisonment, and not to have pen, ink and paper, and so with the highest.

My Lord of *Canterbury,* Three thousand pounds, close Imprison-ment, and to continue till His Majesties pleasure be further known.

She was committed to the *Gatehouse.*

Officium Dominorum con Elleanorum Tichet, *alias*
60   Davyes, *alias* Douglas.

The Councel for the offence insisteth on her Answers, she to appear this day and place by Bond, to hear and receive the final Order and Judg-ment of the Court.

At which day and place the said Lady *Eleanor Douglas* being called for, appeared personally; In whose presence the Articles objected against her, and her Answers made thereunto were publiquely read, with certain printed Schedules & Exhibites thereunto annexed, which she acknowl-edged to be of her own penning and publishing in print; and the said Answers to be her true Answers, and to be Subscribed with her own
70   hand: By all which it evidently appeared to the Court, by her own Con-fession, That she had lately compiled and written, and caused to be

---

Line 50. **ut prius:** as [suggested] before (Latin). Line 58. **Gatehouse:** prison at Westminster.
Lines 59–60. **Officium...Douglas:** the office of the Lords [the Commissioners] vs. Eleanor Tichet, alias Davies, alias Douglas (Latin); a case initiated by the court rather than by an individual.

printed and published, the three several Schedules annexed to the said Articles, some containing Expositions of divers parts of the Chapters of the Prophet *Daniel,* some other scandalous matter, by way of Anagram or otherwise, against Ecclesiastical persons and Judges of eminent place, and some others, both derogatory to His Majesty and the State. And first as touching those matters of high nature, which concerned his Majesty, the Court did not any ways proceed against her, as holding them of too high a nature for this *Court* to meddle withal. But forasmuch as she took upon her (which much unbeseemed her Sex) not only to interpret the Scriptures, and withal the most intricate and hard places of the Prophet *Daniel,* but also to be a Prophetess, falsly pretending to have received certain Revelations from God, and had compiled certain Books of such her fictions and false Prophesies or Revelations, which she had in person carried with her beyond the Seas, and had there procured them to be printed without License, and after brought them over here into *England,* and here without License, vented and dispersed them, or some of them, contrary to the Decree of Star-Chamber, made in the xxviii. year of Queen *Eliz.* of famous Memory, for the restraining of unlawful printing & publishing of books, and to the manifest contempt & breach thereof, and to the great scandal of our Church and State, and the reproach of the true Christian Religion here professed, and established within this Realm. And forasmuch as by vertue of the Statute of *Primo Eliz.* and by vertue of Letters Patents under the Great Seal of *England,* this Court hath full power and authority to punish as well all transgressors and offendors against the said Decree of Star-Chamber, touching the printing and publishing of unlicensed Books, as such bold attempts as those of hers, in taking upon her to interpret and expound the holy Scriptures, yea, and the most intricate and hard places therein, such as the gravest and most learned Divines would not slightly or easily undertake, without much study and deliberation. For these her said bold attempts and impostures, tending to the dishonor of God, and

80

90

100

Line 87. **vented:** vended; sold. Line 94. **Primo Eliz:** the first year of Elizabeth's reign (Latin).

Line 97. **unlicensed Books:** books published without approval or permission.

Line 100. **Divines:** clergymen.

scandal of Religion, whereof she was found and adjudged guilty by the Court, she was thought well worthy to be severely punished; and was first Fined in the sum of 3000 l. to his Majesties use, ordered to make a publique Submission *in conceptis verbis,* at so many times, and in such places as this Court shall appoint, and as shall be delivered her under the Registers Hand of this Court; And she was further committed close Prisoner to the Gatehouse, and ordered there to remain during his Maj-esties pleasure, who had taken special notice of her and her Cause, and referred the Examination and Censuring thereof into this Court. And lastly she was condemned in Expences and Costs of Suit, which are to be paid before her enlargement: And the Keeper of the said prison was required and commanded not to suffer her to have any pen, ink or paper to write any thing, in respect that she hath so much abused her liberty in that kinde already.

Concordat premissa cum originalibus in veriâ predictâ facta collacione fideli per me

Jo: Donaldson, *Notarium Publicum.*

FINIS.

Line 105. **3000 l.:** three thousand pounds.

Line 106. **in conceptis verbis:** in particular words (Latin). The Commissioners specified the wording of the confession they ordered Lady Eleanor to make.

Line 107–8. **under the Registers Hand:** written by the clerk who kept the register or record for the Court of High Commission.

Line 113. **her enlargement:** release from prison.

Lines 117–19. **Concordat...Publicum:** This is a true collation of the original, made by me Jo. Donaldson, Notary Public (Latin).

Line 120. **FINIS.** A handwritten annotation at the bottom of the page reads "[ ] (And that it might Bee fulfilled under pretence of Longe prayer. theire fasting) devoure widows Ho[ ] mine of Englefield for ONE. Take Judgement the great [ ]". Several portions are illegible.

In 1644, soon after the execution of Archbishop Laud, Lady Eleanor examined the 1631 proceedings against her brother, Mervin, Lord Audeley and second earl of Castlehaven, in *The word of God* (Wing D2018). *Crying Charge* (Wing D1982A), which treats the same event, is in many respects a companion piece to the tract printed just above, *Blasphemous Charge* (Wing D1980, D1981), Lady Eleanor's exposé of the 1633 proceedings against her. The present edition of *Crying Charge* is based on a copy of the tract in the Houghton Library, Harvard (shelf number *EC65 D7455 B652t).

THE
CRYING CHARGE.

Ezekiel 22.

Now thou Son of man, wilt thou judge, Wilt thou judge the bloody City? yea, thou shalt shew her all her Abominations, &c.

To the High Court of Justice, appointed for the Tryal of *CHARLES STUART* King of ENGLAND.
By the Lady *Eleanor Douglas.*

SHEWS,

The Kings consent therewith, how *Mervin* E. of *Castlehaven,* Lord *Audeley,* unmercifully was sentenced to death *Easter* term *1631.* and in *May* cruelly executed a[nd]<ll> <X> Tower-Hill, accused falsly of two Crimes, what lewdnes could and malice produce; one, *Of his being accessary to a Rape committed on Ann his wife, done by a Page, one* Broad-
10   way; and, *Of Sodomy* (made death H:8.) *committed with an Irish Foot-man,* Fitzpatrick O Donel; which aforesaid Lord *Audeley* indicted of Felony, brought to his tryal at *westminster,* the K. Attorney where shew'd, *The King like God, would extend to the prisoner all mercy:* Like-wise the Lo: Keeper that day Lo: High Steward, *because the cry was great of Sodom,* would see whether those things were so; the Witnesses where-upon call'd to appear, she a common Whore her husbands accuser, without ever appearing in Court, or taking any Oath, had there con-trary to the Law, one of her consorts that said, *My Lady upon her Honor saith thus, &c. or, It was true.*

20   The other Witness, the *Irishman,* he a vagrant, had served under the Emperor, although a Papist, had contrary to Law, his Oath taken at the Bar, refusing the *Oath of Allegiance;* where askt by one of the Judges the maner, confest, *Not the act, but somewhat of a foul nature, &c.* what such malice & the like might invent, promised to be the Queens Footman. The Attorney, one not to seek of his Errand, saying, *Howsoever, it was an act of Uncleanness; prayed the Court to proceed upon it: My Lords,* said he, *you have heard this odious Crime, how dark and mysterious 'tis grown;*

Lines 1–88. The base text of *Crying Charge* is printed in italic type with roman emphases; the fonts have been reversed in the present edition for ease of reading.

Line 7. a[nd]...Tower-Hill: Lady Eleanor has written "ll X" over the "n" and "d" in "and".

Line 10. H:8: in the reign of King Henry VIII. Line 12. K.: king's.

Line 14. Lo: High Steward: officer who presided over the court.

Line 15. Sodom: sodomy; also a biblical city of sin (Gen. 19).

Line 22. Oath of Allegiance: statutory test of religious and political loyalty to the English monarch.

you must be curious therefore how you admit of any mitigation: who accordingly his counsel took, *&c.*

Upon which pronounced, *Lord have mercy upon thee the prisoner,* to 30 lose his life forthwith, of such promised mercy enjoyed the first-fruits.

All which undue sinister proceedings by way of humble Petition signified to the K. when perceived to what a low ebb the cry was faln and his Chaplains, Deans and others appointed to attend the prisoner, partly by their relation, he thrice in their presence had taken the Sacrament upon it, *He was not guilty of those criminals;* was pleased by them to let the prisoner know his gracious Answer, *He should dye like a Peer of the Realm, be Beheaded, and not Hanged like a common person: whose Servants, his Page the principal, who ought to have suffered, before the accessary; he and his fellow-servant the Footman were brought to their tryal* 40 *the next Term.*

In behalf of whom the aforesaid *Broadway,* came up divers Gentlemen of the County to inform the King, able to testifie of the Youths coming home to his Fathers house, more then six moneths afore the time put down by her of the Ravishment, this *Broadway* come away from his Lords service.

Who at last cast; when upon the Ladder so far protested both his Masters innocency that way and his own; taking God to witness, *A virgin he came into his service, and a virgin went forth of it.*

O Donel praying to St. *Dennis,* cryed out upon some of the Privy 50 Council that told him, *He must speak for the King,* and thought not to be served so.

And this mans house utterly ruined, chiefly, because had declined Popery, before his untimely death ever suspected; endeavoring to reform his Family, by which means cast himself upon the merciless times. *Mervin* Earl of *Castlehaven,* that faithful Martyr, suffering (as it were) between those twain, *one on the right hand, the other on the left,* the

---

Lines 35–36. **had taken…it:** had testified to his innocence by taking communion according to the rites of the Church of England. **them:** the king's chaplains.

Line 37. **his:** the king's. Line 40. **accessary:** one who aids or abets, in this case Castlehaven.

Line 50. **praying to St. Dennis:** an indication of his Catholicism.

Lines 56–57. **suffering…twain:** like Christ, who was crucified between two thieves.

honor having to be the first *entred into the joy of his Lord;* of whom notwithstanding the worst any in the [*world could*] world could say, was,
60   *He had the best things in him of any, and the worst:* Upon the Scaffold
making this his Confession;

In the Name of God Amen.

I *Mervin* Earl of *Castlehaven,* being in my full strength and memory,
thanks be given unto my Maker, having been branded and openly
accused for change, alteration and doubtfulness of my Faith and Religion; I thought fit, like a Christian man to give satisfaction upon what
ground I stand for my belief, and to express it under my hand, for the
satisfaction of all charitable people and Christians.

First, I do believe in the blessed and glorious Trinity, three persons;
70   one eternal and everlasting God, God the Father, God my Redeemer,
and God my Sanctifier.

I do relye upon the merit, death and passion of our blessed Savior
Christ Jesus, and upon his mediation for the remission of my sins.

I do believe and use with most humble reverence our Lords Prayer,
the Creed of the Apostles, and the ten Commandments, as they are set
down and allowed in the Church of *England.*

I do believe the Canonical Scriptures, and that they are written by
the inspiration of the holy Spirit.

And for the rest of my belief, I do refer it to the true Orthodox Faith
80   of our Church of *England.* And from the Articles received at this present
in the Church of *England,* and confirmed by authority of Parliament, I
do not differ in any point, renouncing all the Superstitions and Errors
taught or believed in the Church of *Rome* or any other Church; in
which Faith I will, God willing, continue to my lives end: In testimony
whereof, I have here unto subscribed my Hand this first of *May,* 1631.

CASTLEHAVEN.

Psal. 116. *Right dear in the sight of the Lord is the death of his Saints.*

FINIS.

In *New Jerusalem* (Wing D1997) Lady Eleanor links her personal story with those of England and Israel. Taking as her text the story of Saul, whom God made the Israelites' king when they demanded a monarch (1 Sam.), she makes her theme the loss of inheritance. Charles I's death deprived his children of their inheritance, and her second husband, Sir Archibald Douglas, whose prophetic spirit was never taken seriously, was unsuccessful in proving his claim that he was Charles's elder brother and thus should have been king. At the end of the tract, Lady Eleanor prints letters Douglas wrote questioning church practices. On the title page, beneath her name, she places her family's motto, *Je le tien* (French: "I hold it"), which she had used as the title of a tract (Wing D1996aA—page 199 in the present edition) three years earlier. The present edition of *New Jerusalem* is based on a copy in the Houghton Library, Harvard University (shelf number *EC65 D7455 B652t).

THE
NEW JERUSALEM
AT HAND:

By the Lady *Eleanor Douglas,*

Daughter of Lo: *Audeley,* Lo: *Touchet*
E. of *Castlehaven.*

JE LE TIEN.

MAT. 28.
Behold, I am with you all days, until the consummation of the age.

The Prophetess of the most High, to all
Nations and People, &c.

Shewing in stead of a *Charls* the second, gives ye the character of a second *Saul,* even *He and his for ever cut off,* unto that giving place, that everlasting, even proclaimed, *The first and the last* (to wit) Prophets the *beginning and the ending, Jure Divino,* afore Kings of the Earth: Certain inferences by, borrowed from dayes of old (*Sam. cap.* 10.) whose Reign confirmed by that ominous token, witness of *Rachels* Sepulchre (as much to say) such another he *mourning and weeping also for his children,* because they were not, or not him to succeed, read in letters of her Name, *Rachels,* otherwise rendred *Charls;* and thus running over the sum of it.

To whom on this wise shewed *cap.* he when little in his own eyes, above the rest how chosen to be a King so great, from *tending on Asses, Scotlands* former low Estate pointing thereto: & so farther of *Kings given in his wrath, in anger taken away:* briefly thus, but referred to the first of his Reign, *Anno* 1625. that heavy hand upon the City, an unparalleld Pestilence, concluded with our three Kingdoms Division; so that if ever all at their wits-end, now accompanying his departure, 23 of his bloody Reign; in making him King of *Great Britain,* evident the Lord repenting himself much more, well served for their Repining, whom *Nothing but a King would serve,* who blest were above all Kingdoms; so in a virgin *Queens* renowned Reign: And for them so much, *First and last of their Name,* both tasting of one sharp cup, their Heads cut off, and fastned their bodies in that maner to the wall, or nailed, &c. as to the Story referred (*Sam. &c.*) which had each three Sons: where this for another cast upon her, *Thou son of the perverse rebellious woman;* whether in right

---

Line 3. **Charls the second:** heir to Charles I, who would rule as Charles I had done.

Line 6. **Jure Divino:** by divine authority (Latin); the basis on which Charles I claimed to rule.

Line 9. **he mourning…also:** Rachel wept for her children (Jer. 31:15).

Line 11. **Rachels…Charls:** With this rough anagram Lady Eleanor suggests that Charles, like Rachel, will not be able to pass on an inheritance to his children.

Line 12. **cap.:** capitulum; chapter (Latin). Lady Eleanor is again referring to 1 Sam. 10.

Lines 14–15. **Scotlands…Estate:** Charles I's father, James I, had been king of Scotland before acceding to the English throne. **Kings…away:** Hos. 13:11.

Lines 21–23. **a virgin…Reign:** the reign of Elizabeth I. **First…Name:** James and Charles, as of 1649, were the only two Stuart monarchs; also Saul and his sons.

appertains not to our Scotish *Jonathan,* by his Mothers means stript of
his Royal means and Estate.

Passing over what between him passed and his ghostly Father or
Confessor, supposed to have been *Samuels* very Spirit, who fell all along   30
both of them upon the earth sore afraid, however feigned or carried out,
to make good the innocent blood spilt of such multitudes of his people,
who without question as participated of *Sauls* fits, *The evil Spirit from
the Lord* (to wit) the evil Counsel infused by the Clergy; so wanting neither in his Fathers Faith or Religion, spake truer then he wist, whose
wanton Minion bewitcht with, neither repented hereof; One *charged
with the life of his Father,* nor of his unmeasureable Swearing, which
amongst them sware *By their saul,* so long till verily conjured up his
Spirit, that not a little boasted of his Kingcraft, witness Familiar Spirits,
witches of late, transferr'd from *Scotland* hither: And as for that *Agag,*   40
the delicate *Buckingā* how his mother made childless, she author of his
unhappiness, she insnared by their *Spanish* junkets, cannot but adde
this to the Reckoning of *Phinehas* spirit, how it hath acted on these
twain, saying, *Righteous art thou, O Lord, that hast judged thus, Anno*
1628. as when *Buckingham* his deadly wound had given him, by such a
one transported, &c. so even *Charls* late King, 1648. at length paid
home that heavy Stroke or Blow of his, aged Eight and forty, like *The
flying Rowl, in length twenty cubins,* &c. twenty years, which had given
him to make his peace or repent him; and so much onely at this time
commended to the Reader, with this contained in the Prophet *Daniels*   50
confession (neither have we hearkned, &c. (*Chapter 9. v. 6.*) doubtless

---

Line 27. **our Scotish Jonathan:** Archibald Douglas. Line 35. **wist:** knew.

Lines 36–37. **Minion:** favorite. **One charged...Father:** Some people claimed that Charles I's
favorite, the duke of Buckingham, had poisoned King James.

Line 38. **By their saul:** by Saul (1 Sam. 10); also by their soul.

Lines 39–40. **Familiar...late:** 1 Sam. 28:7; there were claims that the duke of Buckingham
had dealings with familiar spirits. **Agag:** see 1 Sam. 15:33.

Line 42. **their Spanish junkets:** Charles and Buckingham went to Spain in 1623 in hopes of
completing the arrangements for a Spanish marriage for Charles.

Line 43. **Phinehas:** By his judgment the plague was stopped (Ps. 106:30).

Lines 44–45. **twain:** two. **Anno...him:** Buckingham was assassinated in August 1628.

Lines 46–48. **Charls...Stroke:** Charles was executed in January 1648, i.e., 1649. **The flying
Rowl:** see Zech. 5:1–3.

pointing to the people of this land alike with dumb & deaf spirits, &c. together with his lame confession on the Scaffold, like blinde Devotions Lesson, promised, *That he should say but very short Prayers,* who came not short of it none at all said that we hear of.

Nevertheless, unwilling to insult over the worm or grave; as his hard lot, *To morrow be thou with me,* said to *Saul,* so *This day be thou with me in paradice;* peradventure his pardon had folded up herein, which had not received in his life time altogether *those good times others had,* &c.
60 might at the last gasp or minute repent: And so much for *The Ax laid to the Root of the old Tree,* in a Reign of 23 years, which produced no better fruit. And for the title set forth of the Keys of *David* belonging to her, *Rev.* 1. 7 .

And as demonstrates a second *Saul,* so a second *Adam,* he first of the Kings of the Earth, his immediate woful fall shadowing it forth.

Witness she subject (*Heb.*) called *Chavah* or *Eve:* By whom had three Sons, where thus for her sake rewarded (*Gen. 3.) Even placed at the East a flaming Sword,* &c. turning every way, driven out as it seems Westward, from his Garden to the open Field, in their Leather liveries to
70 encounter travel, justly reaping the fruits of accursed mother Earth, war and strife, the Thistle and Thorn, its emblem in stead of the Olive and Grape: All our days as stubble but a blaze, vanished like a shadow: The sum or substance of which informing, formerly as he forbidden expresly the Tree of good and evil, notwithstanding took thereof; so again, when as offered the Tree of life, *its Leavs for healing the evil of the Nations,* or Kings Evil; a like Trespass or capital Crime guilty of, that rejects it, like

---

Line 54. **That…Prayers:** Charles I's remarks just prior to his execution.

Lines 57–58. **This…paradice:** Jesus' words to one of the thieves crucified with him (Luke 23:43).

Lines 60–61. **The Ax…Tree:** Matt. 3:10.

Lines 62–63. **Keys…Rev. 1.7:** an erroneous citation; probably should be Rev. 3:7 (the message to the angel of the Church of Philadelphia).

Line 64. **a second Adam:** Christ.

Line 66. **Chavah:** Eve (Hebrew).

Line 72. **stubble:** what is left in the field after the harvest.

Line 76. **Kings Evil:** scrofula, a disease which was believed to be curable by a monarch's touch; evils brought by kings.

Judgements draws upon their heads: *And therefore suppose not that those Galileans were sinners above the rest, because of late suffered,* &c. *Nay, but except ye repent, ye all likewise shall perish.*

And so from *Saul* and *Doeg,* deriving *Douglase,* here concluding as 80
began, how his bloody House cut off, also even *dyed for his transgression against the word of the Lord, &c.* and also for asking counsel of one that had a familiar Spirit, & enquired not of the Lord (to wit) his Bishops, &c. whose army how swarmed with Witches, never the like heard in any Raign visited in that kind, wherwith shewing lastly of the evil Spirit, when fell upon him, how the good Spirit (at the very same time) rested on another: The solitary Turtle-Dove as it were shut up, one of his own name (owned by King *James,* before the other of *Stuart*) and of his Age and Nation: Sir *Archibald Douglase,* the supposed Son of King *James,* the Elder Brother about a moneth, &c. also wrote *Anno Etatis,* 90
&c. as by a Legacy of a thousand pound *per annum,* out of his Crown-Lands appointed for him; whereof though disappointed or prevented by the said K. unexpected death, yet of the better part could not be disinherited, then any three Crowns a greater blessing: The holy Spirits anointing apparent by his Letters hereto annext, that not only in those days were accounted to be distraction; but to this very day, even with Learned Doctor *Sybald,* fulfilling what honor Prophets receive at home: By whose hand no few of these Manuscripts were burnt: This mans writing who wrote so long ago. From the *Hysope Nicity,* unto the Cedar Authority or Supremacy, conversing with no Books, but one the Book: 100
Sir *Archibald Douglas* right Heir of the Earldoms, howsoever of *Morton*

Lines 77–79. **And therefore…perish:** Luke 13:2–3.

Line 80. **Doeg:** the Edomite who oversaw Saul's servants. **Douglase:** Sir Archibald, Lady Eleanor's second husband.

Lines 85–87. **the evil…another:** Saul and David (1 Sam. 16:13–14); Lady Eleanor and Douglas. **The solitary Turtle-Dove:** see Ps. 74:19.

Line 90. **Anno Etatis:** in the year of age (Latin).

Line 91. **per annum:** per year (Latin).

Lines 94–95. **The holy Spirits anointing:** the designation of a prophet.

Line 97. **Learned Doctor Sybald:** a clergyman, Dr. James Sibbald, of St. James, Clerkenwell, London.

Line 99. **From…Cedar:** 1 Kings 4:33.

and *Douglas* the doughty; likewise of person a choyce yong man, and a
goodly, &c. That Nations Captain by his Birth-right himself a Soldier
by profession, in *Spain* and *Germany* no ordinary Commander, upon
whom the first fruits of the Spirit came.

Quæres or Questions To Dr. *James Sybald,* Minister of *Clerkenwel.*

And (whether) the very perillous time now, fulfilling what is written in
Pauls second Epistle to *Timothy, Men shall be lovers of their own selves,*
110 *more then of God,* &c. *from such turn away:* And what is written in
(*Mark.* 13.) *Of the troublesome last days:* (*ver.* 10, 11.) Of which I will
say no more, onely thus much: Had you demanded of me in how many
days, the change which I speak of should be, or known of what consequence it is, ye would not so suddenly have indangered me, as to have
spoken a word of me to that purpose, or where I was; when ye see what
will be, and what ye have heard of me; even very shortly you will be
ashamed, and heartily sorrow for your precipitate Opinion of me.

Now considering that you are preparing to morrow in the Forenoon,
on the uncertain Easter-day; Also to receive your part of the Passover,
120 even kneeling at the Communion-Table; consider these Texts, and prepare an answer to the same: *Deut.* 16. *There thou shalt sacrifice the passover at the evening, at the going down of the Sun, That thou mayest
remember it all the days of thy life:* 1 Cor. 11. *When ye come together therefore into one place; this is not to eat the Lords-Supper, for in eating every
one taketh afore his own Supper, &c.* John 13. *and Supper being ended,
&c.* Concerning which, tell me therefore in your Conscience; is not the
Lords-Supper in the Forenoon a most Belly-god invention: Also the
kneeling at the Communion Table doth not fulfil what is written in the
first Epistle of *Paul* to the *Corinthians, ver.* 20. 8, 21. *But I say, the things
130 which the Gentiles sacrifice, they sacrifice to devils, not to God; and I would
not that you should have communion with devils, &c.* Also is not the Title
of Doctors a most presumptuous thing (*Mat.*) *Which love the uppermost*

Line 102. **Douglas the doughty:** "Doughty Douglas" was the name of a character in the
popular ballad, "The Ballad of Chevy Chase." **doughty:** able or capable.

Line 120. **kneeling…Table:** a practice in dispute in seventeenth-century England.

Line 127. **Belly-god:** gluttonous.

rooms and chief seats, and to be called Rabbi, Rabbi, and Matth. 23 *Neither be ye called masters, &c.* As also the names of Saints, (*Psal.*) *When who knows how often he offends; much less knows the secret sins of another:* Also according to your Conscience let me know your opinion of the Ministerial Priests: Traditions hath not made the word of God of none effect, or to have no power, *Mark 7. ver.* 13. *and many such like things do ye.*

Also let me know what is their reward that do crouch and make cour- 140
tesies to boards; when as it is written, Keep thy foot, or have a care thereof when thou goest into the House of God; and be more ready to hear; then offer the sacrifice of fools (to wit) lest thou crouch and make a crooked courtesie to a board, which was but a stock, even a block: whatsoever it was, and whatsoever it is, and they worse then a block that make a cursed courtesie to it, a besotted beast and a devil (*Sam.* 28.) going even to the very Devil of Hell, with him *who stooped with his face to the ground, bowing himself;* likewise they try what reverence they can do unto him.

And lastly, what is the reward of addition and diminishing the word 150
of God, *Rev.* 22. shewing, *For I testifie, If any man shall add, God shall adde the plagues written herein; and if any shall take away, God shall take away his part out of the holy city.* So taking in haste leave, think of me what ye please,

Rest your faithful Friend,
ARCH: DOVE. *Elijah.*

Likewise know, I desire you not to speak a word of this till the appointed time, only have a care in the mean time of your own soul; *Acts 2. Save your selves from this untoward generation.*
From my Lodging at White-Fryers.   *Anno* 1638. your Easter-Eve.   160

Lines 134–35. **When...another:** Ps. 19:12–13.

Lines 140–41. **crouch...boards:** Lady Eleanor's view of bowing to the altar.

Lines 147–48. **him...himself:** see 1 Sam. 28:14.

Line 156. **ARCH: DOVE. Elijah:** Archibald Douglas, prophet; also archdove, in contrast to archbishop.

Line 160. **White-Fryers:** area in London, formerly the site of the house of the order of White Friars.

To my much esteemed worthy Friend, *James Sybald*,
Minister at *Clerkenwel*, this.

Loving Friend,

It seemeth your imployment is very much, for if it were not so, or if ye had remembred my desire, I should have seen you according to your Promise in two days, after that time ye was with me last: Certainly, if ye knew how near the Great Change is, which I spoke of, ye would have seen me before this: Which unexpected Change, whatsoever it be, it being so exceeding near, I request you, whatsoever ye have to do, let me see you this afternoon: But a few words. And likewise through *CHRIST* I charge you, not to speak a word of this, until you see what *GOD* will do shortly; whatsoever it be, unless a very Great Change be shortly, then think of me what ye will:

Exitus acta probat.

Ye may believe me, for I think ye know it had been better for the Lord Major of this City, *Anno Dom.* 1638. to have heard me from the *LORD,* then to have had the Plague of *GOD* amongst them, which came just then, how soon the seven Elected Eldermen did charge me, not to come near them, nor write any more unto them; which did so offend *GOD,* as his Plague hath continued amongst them until this day: Therefore do not vilifie my Request. So till I see you, Rest,

January 19.   *Your faithful Friend,*
Anno Do.   *Rev. 2. 28.
M.DC.XXXVIII.

THE MORNING STARRE.

I pray you bring no servant with you, near the place where I am; for I am exceeding loth for to be known, to be near the city until I be seen at *Court;* which now God willing will be shortly: I am sure there is none knoweth I am so near you, no not one, except my servants: Therefore I

Lines 163–220. The text in this section of the base text is in italic type with roman emphases; the fonts have been reversed in the present edition for ease of reading.

Line 174. **Exitus acta probat:** Death tests deeds (Latin).

Line 178. **Elected Eldermen:** the aldermen, officials in London.

request you let me not be discovered by you, nor by your words, con- 190
cerning the contents of my Letter.

Likewise do not think to lose much time with me, for one sentence
shall be sufficient.

> *To a Messenger of the LORDS, Dr.* James Sybald, *Minister*
> *at* Clerkenwel *at* London, *this.*

Loving Friend,

My self, though your Well wisher, hath constantly been committed willingly within the Chamber and Study where ye left me about two Year
since: It was not the Lords Will, know hitherto, that I should write unto
you, since the 20 of June, *Anno Ætatis,* 1638. Because the Great Change 200
which he moved me to tell you, was to be suddenly, know, it was not to
be accounted according to the computation of man, but according his
own (to wit) it was not plainly to begin, until some few days hence,
according to our computation; his mercies being above all his Works:
He gives his very enemies a space of time, for to consider their own
doings, that they might repent. Though now adays most of all the men
of this world, cannot possibly be moved lawfully for to be obedient
unto him, nor to be just: So saith *ELIAS* and verily *ELIJAH,* who
desireth you, if you love your self, or your own good, for to come unto
him about two a clock this afternoon: otherwise, assuredly the *LORD* 210
will not let me do you the good which I intend, who lets you understand, none of the unjust within this Kingdom before long will be able
to stay therein: So think of this, and do which I lawfully desire for the
best, till I see you. *Vale.* And so rest,

Decemb. 19.   Your faithful Friend,
Anno Do. 1639.   DOUGLASE.

From the JACOBIN or Carmelistain Fryers, to wit of old, From the

---

Line 208. **ELIAS and verily ELI JAH:** two forms of the prophet's name.

Line 214. **Vale:** farewell (Latin).

Lines 217–18. **JACOBIN...Frater:** Jacobins were Dominican friars, who wore black robes;
Jacobus is the Latin form of James. The Carmelite friars, or in French, "Carme Frere," were
mendicants who wore white robes, thus "white friars." Frater, meaning "brother," was the
Latin for "friar." The friars were dissolved in England at the time of the Reformation.

Carme, Freere, Frater; as Fray may be well applyed truly unto any one
of all the many many sorts of Fryers, whose Fray hath continued too
220 long; and now, it must, it must be returned to them.

And here happy Readers, with this Manna communicated (to wit)
the Divine Prophesies of this Man; know herewith ordain'd and enacted
as heretofore, a Rebel against the Father proclaimed, he that *Despised the*
Son; likewise (unable to gainsay it) they a Reprobate Church, *sitting in*
the seat of Scorners: which acknowledge not the fulfilling of these now,
(*John* 16. *All things which the Father hath are mine: Therefore I said, that*
he shall take of mine, and shall shew it unto you; and he shal shew you
things to come, as much to say, Even manifested the truth of those sacred
Mysteries, contained in the *Revelation of Jesus Christ which God gave*
230 *unto him,* &c. Cap. 1. Things for the future treasured up, by no other
Spirit to be unfolded, but by the same Spirit of truth, wherewith were
written at first, or penn'd; and for that purpose the same poured forth
again in the last days: And so these by that Spirit then persecuted, witness (*Rev.xi.*) *The Beast ascended out of the bottomless Pit,* or Abyss, one in
old *Samuels* likeness, Bishops, &c. Also which testifies, whosoever
despiseth the Spirit of Prophecy, guilty of all the Blood of the Prophets
shed: And therefore lest your sentence that, *Ye stiff necked, &c. ye do*
always resist the holy Ghost: as your fathers did, so do ye (Acts 7.) provoke
him not, who is *a consuming fire,* according to their works, Jew and
240 Gentile both high-minded, who rewards them, as referred to the
prophet *Malachi,* accompanied with what judgements (cap.4.) when
that blessed time, arising with *healing in his Wings,* (ver.2.) the meek
dove Messenger of peace, displaying her golden feathers, as the *lightning*
out of the East shineth even unto the West (Mat. 24.) the Spirit of Prophesie vouchsafing a visit, absent from the Church so long comfortless, saying, *I have the Keys of Death and Hell,* a Scepter of seven Stars in whose

---

Line 218. **Fray:** disturbance.

Line 221. **And here happy Readers:** At this point the text resumes, after a page break, in
predominantly roman type, with italic emphasis.

Line 224. **gainsay:** speak against. Line 225. **the seat of Scorners:** Ps. 1:1.

Lines 238–39. **provoke…fire:** Deut. 4:24.

right hand (*Re. cap.*1.) pointing to times Mystery, the present Century, and at this time so much for admonishing all: *He that hath an ear, let him hear, &c.* and fare him well that will not; a story by whom related of *Alexander the Great,* &c. on the Scaffold, as well might have told a tale   250
of his Horse.

These from Whitehall, *sometime*   Febr. 1648.
Wolseys *the Cardinal.*

FINIS.

Lines 249–51. **a story...Horse:** In his speech on the scaffold Charles I referred to a dialogue between a pirate and Alexander the Great, the emperor renowned for his conquests.

Line 252. **Febr. 1648:** i.e., 1649.

Line 253. **Wolsey:** cardinal and councillor to Henry VIII prior to the Reformation.

Lady Eleanor writes this tract (Wing D2012B) on the death of Henry Hastings, her eldest grandson. His death in 1649, on the eve of his marriage, shocked many contemporaries. A number of men, but no women, contributed elegies to *Lachrymae Musarum* (1650), a volume in his honor. Like some of these authors, Lady Eleanor uses the opportunity to reflect on England's history. She makes Zach. 12, from which she takes an opening quotation, the text for the first part of the tract and then uses a story from the Apocrypha (2 Esd.) that parallels that of her grandson and his mother. The present edition of *Sions Lamentation* is based on a copy in the Houghton Library, Harvard University (shelf number *EC65 D7455 B652t).

SIONS
LAMENTATION,
Lord *HENRY HASTINGS,*
HIS Funerals blessing,
by his Grandmother, the Lady *Eleanor.*

Chron. 34.
But Josiah *would not turn his face from him, &c. Harkened not unto the words of* Necho, *which were of the mouth of God.*

Title. **Sion:** Zion; the House of God; also England.

Epigraph. **Chron. 34...God:** 2 Chron. 34 tells how Josiah, who was eight when he became king of Israel, repaired the temple; but in the passage quoted (2 Chron. 35:22) Josiah died because he would not listen to Necho's words from God.

271

Zach. 12. *And they shall look upon him, whom they have pierced: And they shall mourn for him, as one mourneth for an onely, &c. and shall be in bitterness for him, as one is in bitterness for his first born.*

These as by way of comparison set forth: This prophesie appointed for a sign also requisite, since Faith in high things always slow.

  Jonas *as alotted then for the resurrections sign, of which took essay:* Such a three days rest and nights three; And the suns retiring so many degrees that high favor to *Hezekiah,* Likewise of the leavings in the cup, happy *Hastings* this first born, an onely Son, partakes one of no inferior Fam-
10 ily: Taking his leave of this life, whose first days rest taken, on the Lords day; *Saying my lovers and friends hast thou put away far from me (Psal.)* whose death and obsequies (bewaild of no few) assigned for a warning piece of those very perilous days stoln upon us: *When say peace and safety, then sudden destruction, Thes.x.* And they shall not escape even the general day of Judgements forerunner: whereof *Apocalips* thus, *Behold he cometh in the clouds, and every eye shall see him;* and they also that have pierced him; and all the Kindreds of the Earth shall wail, &c. And thus of one so hopeful committed to no simple Doctors, through too much suddenness or ignorance, as that way who can plead not guilty, by
20 letting blood was cast away; upon whom because of this cast suit of cloths bestowed on him of his Masters, *They shall look upon him whom they have pierced, &c.*

  Let none with an evil eye look thereon: And so passing on with several coats of houses born inclusive, adorning the Herse, as dedicated to our *Jerusalem* of the *Gentiles, And in that day there shall be a great mourning in* Jerusalem, *as the mourning in* Hadadrimmon, *in the valley of* Megiddon, the house of *Huntingdon* of which participates: Also in

---

Line 6. **Jonas…sign:** God caused the fish to vomit Jonah (Jon. 1:17). **took essay:** made a trial or test.

Lines 7–8. **three…three:** the time Jonah was in the belly of the fish (Jon. 1:17). **the suns…Hezekiah:** see 2 Kings 20:10.

Line 11. **Saying…me (Psal.):** Ps. 38:11.

Line 12. **obsequies:** funeral rites. Line 24. **coats of houses:** coats of arms.

Line 27. **the house of Huntingdon:** the dead boy's father was earl of Huntingdon.

London, every family apart mourning and their wives, &c. Of the royal Branches, like the *House of* David, all of them bewailing apart, &c. likewise from that ominous name, called *Megiddon* impart, *it is done, Behold he comes making the sable clouds his chariot:* solemnized Heaven and Earths Funerals, these great lights extinguished, The *Sun* become as sackcloth of hair, The *Moon* as blood, The *Stars* falling, &c. answerable to that loud voice, *Revel.* 16.

Done it is, gathered in that place called in *Heb. Armagedon,* when every yle fled away, &c. from whose Name importing diligence, *Hastings* who lost no time himself, declares much more what hastning required, and looking unto that day, at whose *appearing Heavens and Elements dissolves and melts, &c.* Wherefore, for instruction sake adds, when ye see these come to pass, *And I will pour upon the house of* David, *and upon the inhabitants of* Jerusalem, *the Spirit of Grace.* So be sure then time to look up, &c. And this for another, *and in that day I will make* Jerusalem *a heavy stone for all people, &c.* As extraordinary blessings rejected, no ordinary corrections incurring inseparable evermore, besides such distraction so giddy, that plague increasing daily too, or curse of tax leavied, as witness whether fullfilled: *and in that day* (saith the Lord) *I will smite every horse with astonishment, and the rider with madness: and in that day will I seek to destroy all nations, that come against* Jerusalem, &c. *and in that day* (saith the Lord) *I will cut off the names of the Idols out of the land.* And such like demonstrations shewing out of request, the name Saint drownd in oblivion, such an eye sore at this time unto many.

And passing forward also, whether that waiter on the latter days, *Esdras* testimony, termd *Apocrypha,* or miscalled, speaks not the present condition presaging, the sons of the Church, *Sion* her sons cut off that fraternity; whilst deeply musing upon their departure from the Law, grown to such a low ebbe or degree, the law though still in force, like the Spirit of prophesie supposed transmitted not beyond the primitive times, as gross as Romish miracles, without tryal *Esdras* informs, saw

---

60 such a mournful mother, chang'd his cogitations, she replying, *Sir let me
alone;* yet afterward thus after so long time, that had a son then nour-
ished by her with so much travel, grown up, came to take him a wife,
when fell down and died, the house turnd upside (as though) overthrew
the lights fleeing the city, &c. into which Park or Field fled, purposed to
take up her rest; whereupon her passion to divert, spreads that catalogue
of confusion the present case greatest of all *Sion,* the mother of all,
delivered into hands of hateful Jaylors a captive: Spoken to *Sion* her self,
at whose fearful voice cast out the earth shook, which besides her Sons
farewel, some future thing reveals, a prophetical voyce, &c. And new
70 *Jerusalem* in her place, &c. Whereupon *Uriel* the Angel signifying *Light,*
shews unto him. He in need of comfort himself the solution, thrice
over, who repeats these and thirty years, ver. *But after thirty years, &c.*
Lucy Lady of *Huntingdon,* the sackcloth and ashes Hers. *Ashbey's*
mourning for him, he born *anno* 1630. about nineteen years of age,
whose Epithalamiums to lamentations exchanged for Epitaphs: The saffron robe for sable mourning, whose mother coming to his bedside, a
little before his death, Thus *quomodo vales? quomodo non possum bene
valere cum proximus sim deliciis meis?* aluding partly to her Name of
Lucia, &c. And for the vissage mard or disfigured, wiped off so soon by
80 the resurrection hope, as matters not, though obvious to beholders at
such time; When beauty turnd into ashes, which Light about ten extinguished at night, injoyed no small happiness, in this the time of sickness, in scarce complained of pain, Heretofore inclining to the Royal
Party: *Hastings* prophesied of by *Esdras* the Prophet, as *Josias* his Birth,
so long before concerning that reformation, when those priests cut off,
foreshewed their judgement, &c.

Lines 66–67. **Sion...captive:** John 12:15.

Lines 73–74. **Lucy...Ashbey's mourning:** Lucy, the boy's mother, had lost her son; Ashby, a
country house belonging to the Hastings family, had lost one of its parts (the towers, which
were destroyed during the war).

Lines 75–76. **Epithalamiums:** marriage songs. **saffron robe:** marriage garment.

Lines 77–78. **quomodo...meis?:** how do I say farewell? how am I not able to say farewell
when I am so close to the chosen one? (Latin).

Line 79. **Lucia:** Lucy; light.   Line 84. **Josias his Birth:** 1 Kings 13:2.

And for *Esdras* that new song of his, so much suffice: And new *Jerusalem* at hand, no material city, whose face all *Light* and *Lustre:* And for these useful materials, *Giving all warning not unprovided to be of the wedding garment;* Threatning the downfal of the rough garment from   90
head to foot, soars and blains their candlestick reward: And so make haste Lord God, Amen.

FINIS.

July *the fourth, which Funeral train about noon passing through the City from the* Piazza *along those streets by the half Moon down the Strand, Temple-Bar, Fleet-street, up Ludgate and Old-baily to Smithfield and St.* Johns *street (worth observation) saw not the face of Coach, Cart or Car, which passed by, either that met us, or stood in our way, as witness can so many, Sun and Moon as when stood still,* Josh. *x.* Even so make no long tarrying, *Psal. lxx.*   100

Lines 89–90. **warning...garment:** see Matt. 22:1–14.   Line 91. **blains:** blisters.
Lines 94–98. **July...way:** Hasting's funeral procession through London.
Line 99. **Sun...still:** Josh. 10:12.

In 1649, when she was expecting the imminent arrival of the Day of Judgment, Lady Eleanor published *Sign* (Wing D2012AA). She says that she has reprinted, "with some words of addition," a tract that she had written and published in 1644. (Apparently no copies of that 1644 tract are extant now.) *Sign* tells the story of King James, whom Lady Eleanor views as the biblical King Hezekiah, whose life was lengthened because he heeded the warning of the prophet Isaiah (2 Kings 10; Isa. 39). King Charles, in turn, was Hezekiah's son, Manasseh, whose wickedness brought evil upon Jerusalem (2 Kings 21; 2 Chron. 33). The present edition of *Sign* is based on the copy in the volume of Lady Eleanor's tracts in the Folger Shakespeare Library. Also bound in that volume is another version (currently catalogued by the Folger as Wing D2012A.51), which I shall call *A Discovery*. Lacking the upper part of its title page, *A Discovery* follows *Sign* fairly closely through "*Manna* set at nought" on page 10 (although the break from page 9 to page 10 in *A Discovery* is one line after that in *A Sign*). The two copies diverge thereafter. The bottom half of the next leaf (pages 11 and 12) of *A Discovery* is missing. *A Discovery* then proceeds with pages 9–16, headed "Presented a Letter or Petition from their tedious Distraction for a speedy deliverance." That letter, dated November 1649, is another version of the letters appended to *Prayer* (1644) (Wing D2001—page 131 in the present edition).

A
SIGN
GIVEN THEM BEING ENTRED INTO
THE DAY OF JUDGMENT
TO SET THEIR HOUSE IN ORDER.

For the High Court of Parliament
assembled.
From the Lady *Eleanor*.

PSAL. 97.

The Lord is King (or reigneth) *let the earth rejoyce; let the great Isles be glad.*

A DISCOVERY
Unto what Nation the last Day aforehand to be in the last
days Revealed: Contained in the XX. of *Kings, Isaiah* 39.

As H[*ad*]<ee> no other assigned then *The word of God,* touching the
Resurrections then *being at hand,* but that of *Jonas* the prophet; so in
point of like incredulity at his return again turned *Sadduces,* appointed
no other, but this of King *Hezekiahs* days (*Kings, &c.*) that for a sign or
assurance had, the third day of his uprising, going up to the Lords
house to seal it; that of the *shadows going back,* for the thrid of his life
out lengthned, a lease made him of thrice five years, like a shadow when
past.

Without which token, not in a capacity of obtaining so high blessing
passed not without being by the prophet *Isaiah* advertised (the Lord of
Hosts Ambassador) his house afterward how swept; and sons under
what slavery issued from him, not for facility such onely, but difficulty
of belief dangerous not a little.

Of which days come about again, this great Revolution ushering the
day of Judgement, his coming in the Clouds; whereof as follows, of
Jacobs ladder reaching to heaven gate, thus, The express Epitomy of
King *James's* life of *Great Britain,* where beside no smal plague accompanying his first coming, afore never visited so with those tokens, of his
like recovery, here giving to understand beyond expectation; such a solemn Thanksgiving for which at *Pauls cross:* which long Sermon in was
related, how in his late sickness unto death, he likewise *justified his
upright walking with God:* and therewith how pluckt off his Cap, and
cast it on the ground, in such a passion professing in point of witting
Injustice, *he would not so much as ask God forgiveness;* by which way of
purging himself, as came not behinde *Hezekiah* neither in some gross
failings: like that good King his hearkning to those charming *Babylo-*

Line 5. **Jonas:** Jonah (Jon. 2:10).

Line 6. **Sadduces:** priests who did not believe in Christ's resurrection (Acts 23:8).

Line 9. **thrid:** thread. Line 19. **Jacobs Ladder:** see Gen. 28:12. **Epitomy:** representation.

Line 23. **Pauls cross:** outdoor pulpit in London, near St. Paul's cathedral.

nian Ambassadors or Spies with letters sent to congratulate from *Bal-*   30
adan son of Baladan.

Also who *shewed them all his store and armory,* coming from those
Austrian Philips, &c. overcome with like jugling flights, *a few figs and*
junkets, suffered that *Gundamore having surveyed the Tower, to carry*
away as many great Ordnance and Guns as he pleased, preserved for Truths
defence, and Kingdoms safety, in no less peril of home-bred friends such,
then forreign foes, requisite with Arms and Forces to be secured: And
then how sent his Son after, forced for whose *Ransom* to send over *All*
the precious things and goodly, laid up by his Predecessors, to be bestowed
amongst those insatiable Eunuchs and Officers distributed. And lastly the   40
good man himself, in whose days *flourished Truth and Peace,* thus over-
reached, for all his King-craft and Learning, that brake his heart shortly
after. *And the rest of his Acts, and all his might* (or greatness) *and how he*
brought water into the City, and made a Pool and a Conduit, <&> that
Idol[,] <the cross> *are they not written in the Chronicles, &c?*

And thus this *Hezekiah slept, and rested with his fathers, and Manasses*
his son reigned in his stead; that came not short of *Ahab:* and he awakened thus, for him so much suffices, become a sign himself, no inferior
one, had the Suns retiring for a sign, [*obeyed Joshuahs command (no*
feigned Phæton) [ ] *Moon moving neither they arrived that longed after*   50
Rest, so now before removed, carried thence away, shews them the way
accompanied [ ] *as it were, sets in the East: Moreover for whose additional*
years, fiveteen wedded to those ten degrees, these crowning the first of his
Reign, 1625. forbids any more Coronations of Kings: No] more rising or
setting here of theirs.

Line 33. **Austrian Philips:** the Hapsburgs, who ruled both Austria and Spain at the time.

Line 34. **junkets:** feasts. **Gundamore:** Gondomar; Spanish ambassador to England in the
reign of James I. He was thought to have had excessive influence over James.

Line 38. **sent his Son after:** James's son, Charles, went to Spain in hopes of marrying a
Spanish princess.

Line 50. [ ]: Several words in this long deletion are illegible, here and below.

Kings xxi. Chron. xxxiii.

And this *Manasseh twice twelve years old, when he began to reign over
Great Britain;* How he reared *Altars to Baal, and set up his Roman Altars,
built Altars in the house of the Lord, adored that Babylonian Image the*
60 *Crucifix, manifest are they not on record?* Beyond Heathenism abomination execrable: Moreover to the overthrow of them and theirs, how
many seduced, beside shedding so much Innocent Blood; insomuch
that the Catalogue of his sins, *Manasses* great wickedness, the hateful
Amorites Cup, wherewith paralleld and worse; which Tyrants but light
in comparison, weighed with this *MANS,* since 1625. the Remonstrance of the present.

To whom *the Lord spake, and to his people* likewise, but both by
regard alike improved in his Commandments; as the Suns course the
contrary way gone as many degrees astray, and so both alike whether
70 rewarded, recommended to the beholders, whose high looks brought
down, *here see whose Sons coat this? therefore thus saith the Lord, Behold, I
am bringing an evil upon them, that whoso heareth it, both his ears shall
tingle:* where thus again, whether *Jerusalems* line stretched over us,
CITY and Country both; *And I will wipe Jerusalem, as a man wipeth a
dish, which he wipeth and turneth it upside down;* as in a glass whether
presents not the face of the present, spares neither side; who not amiss
deriving from *Brute* their denomination, from the Ass as wel *who understands his owner,* no such stranger to the dumb. And so much for this
Manna set at nought, these judgements of the Lord foreshewed, light by
80 set; notwithstanding speaking the *Canaan* language unto this our Age,
to all whosover hath ears, in their Native tongue, shewed them their

---

Line 58. **Roman Altars:** English Protestants associated altars with Rome, Catholicism, and
superstition.

Lines 59–60. **that…Crucifix:** English Protestants identified Babylon, the enemy of ancient
Israel, with Rome in their own day.

Line 61. **execrable:** detestable.   Line 65. **this MAN:** Charles I.

Line 71. **Sons coat:** the coat of many colors (Gen. 37:32–33).

Line 77. **Brute:** Brutus; legendary founder of Britain.

Line 80. **speaking…our Age:** using a biblical parallel for the English experience.

unnatural motion gone backward how far, offended thereat or no, whereof as ensues.

This for another making up the number, he when made his supplication, how was heard, also returned to *Hampton-Court;* however mis-led by sinister Counsel, or betrayed, not unhumbled either, unknown not unto all who agreed to whatsoever, about two years after who slew him in his own house, attended with glowing ears not a few, such a spectacle.

And how *the people of the Land slew them again that had conspired, &c. Rainsborough* and our *Holland* Ambassador, taking essay of it, Drunkenness added to blood-thirstiness, were the first saluted with which unexpected cup.

And with expedition (a few words to the wise) on this wise passing on, what *Baptism* first past on his Sons, visible in the Seers book; withal how servile on the other side to his Priests Bishops, charmed by their subtile Gospels: whose Service book because allowed by his Father, what an Idol made of it, where that for another, recorded in their Prophetical Remonstrance, gave himself to them that had Familiar Spirits, bringing up whoso named by him, the gods and others; as Plays his night exercise.

And the rest of his folly, and other of his judgement, making his Prayerbook also equivolent with the Alsufficient *Scriptures,* evident as his grove made, daily at Ball where sacrificed his time, graced with one of his Fathers unhappy acts, that *Baals* or *James* Chappel, prodigious

90

100

Line 84. **he:** Charles I.

Line 90. **Rainsborough:** Thomas Rainsborough, an officer of the parliamentary army, was killed by some Cavaliers. **Holland Ambassador:** Isaac Dorislaus, English ambassador, was killed at the Hague in May 1649.

Line 94. **what Baptism...Sons:** Laud's baptizing of Charles's sons violated his marriage treaty, which specified that they were to be baptized as Catholics.

Line 96. **Service book...Father:** The *Book of Common Prayer* of 1604 was enforced more rigidly by Charles I.

Line 98. **them...Spirits:** Lady Eleanor's charge against Charles I's favorite, the duke of Buckingham.

Line 99. **Plays:** masques at the court of Charles I.

Line 104. **James Chappel:** In 1638 Charles I's mother-in-law, Marie de' Medici, took up residence at St. James and used the chapel for mass.

Twins, the other his *Babylonian* Theatre, from *James's* to which fatal
place made his last progress or march, erected in Commemoration of
the Ark as had been, also the seventeenth Century current; as from
Adam to the Flood so long, not unforewarned of it by him *that was the
son of Adam, that was the son of God;* that as were those days before
110 *Noah,* [*so shall be his coming*] again, [*concerning not onely Times golden
vial or glass, by which account its being at a stand: But how it stands or
fares with faith put to the question (Luke, &c.) whether* [ ] *found such a
thing as faith*], *how preparid then?*

[*As for the set time, or when. Lo, the present generation:* [ ] *Masters for
setting your house in order, who here discharges her calling or place by*] farther giving you in the next place notice, from *Manasses fifty five years
Reign,* of *his second coming at hand,* goeth hand in hand with that of
Cæsar Augustus his five and fifty years, in whose Reign *The Prince of Life,
The Beginning and Ending* of Monarchy, *came, about the fortieth year,*
120 *into the world, that began to be about Thirty years of age, in the fifteenth
year of Tiberius,* (Luke, &c.) even the sum of it bids turn to those sure
Chronicles, penn'd by the *holy Spirits command,* thus saith the Spirit,
from *the return of Manasses days to expect his coming again, aforehand,* as
shewed unto his servants the Prophets, expresly pointing to the year
1655. at hand, being the time when the flood came, 1655. from the
Creation, as computed by the Ancients and other *Noah* and his (*Baptisms* figure, at mans estate all) preserved in the *Whales womb, ten moneths* fulfilling, *before any window in the Ark opened:* and thus *one deep
calling to another,* as when the *waters prevail'd,* the snowy *Dove found no
130 footing,* the *Raven* afore sent forth, no other presaging then the *Spirit of
Prophesie,* at such a time again though ceased long at last salutes the
nations with the *Olive* leaf *in her mouth,* so seasonable now for their

---

Line 105. **his Babylonian Theatre:** the Banqueting House at Whitehall.

Line 118. **five and fifty years:** To arrive at this number, it is necessary to date Augustus's reign
from the Battle of Philippi in 42 B.C., rather than from the date customarily used by historians,
27 B.C.

Line 121. **Tiberius:** the Roman emperor who succeeded Augustus (Luke 3:1).

Lines 126–28. **Noah...moneths:** Gen: 8:5.

healing, without which Angelical leaves applied, an evil incurable, promised *The Tree of life, yielding its monethly fruit.*

And so be it known, That the aforesaid blessed period of years 55. containing Moneths 666. (*Rev.* 13.) called *The number of a MAN* (to wit) that *Roman* Emperors Reign, shewed afore the *Moneth* of *August* bearing his Name; by whose Predecessor for the Calender corrected: and 666 Hours fulfilling a *Moneth,* all bids Tyrant Time and his Generation or Offspring *Adieu,* subscribed with *Emanuel Jesus,* its Numerals   140
MVILV. Anno 55.

F I N I S.

Line 138. **the Calender corrected:** Julius Caesar reformed the calendar.

Line 140. **its Numerals:** the letters which are roman numerals.

Lady Eleanor published *Everlasting Gospel* (Wing D1986) in December 1649, almost a year after the execution of King Charles I, which she believed would bring redemption to England. In the tract she reflects on the history of his reign and on the history of her prophetic career which, like Charles's reign, had its start in 1625. The present edition of this tract is based on a copy in the Bodleian Library, Oxford (shelf number 12.0.1336[2]).

THE
EVERLASTING
GOSPEL.

Apocalyps 14.

And they sung a new Song before the Throne, and before the four Beasts and the Elders; ver. [*24.*] *And no MAN could learn that Song, but the* 144, &c.

Title page. A handwritten annotation above the title reads "Revelations".

285

The Holy Gospel, According to the Evangelist,
By the Lady ELEANOR.

Even the same, that which was from the Beginning, then believed in, magnified unto the end of the world, as until the consummation of the Age (saying) *Lo, I am with you, without end whose Kingdom.*

How it came to pass shewing, in the first year of his Reign, first of his Name, *Charles* of *Great Britain,* in *Berks* the first of Shires, she then at her House *Englefield* Manor, of *Englands* Realm, Daughter of the first Peer, *Anno* 25. the Moneth of *July* in, so call'd after the first *Roman*
10 Emperor, he slain, *&c.*

Where the word of the Lord of Hosts, when came to her, the Heavenly voyce descending, speaking as through a Trumpet of a most clear sound these words:

Nineteen years and a half to the Judgement, and you as the meek Virgin.

Awakened by which alarm early in the morning, whereof thus, signed with *Divisions* character, the years being divided, this magnified morning Star, story of *Jerusalem* of the *Gentiles, Great Britains* blow foreshewing, *Anno* 44. accomplished: The same though come to pass, who nevertheles in stead of their acknowledged error, like those *Priests*
20 *and Elders,* first who *setting a Watch,* then underhand by such large Doctrine endeavor to stop the peoples mouths, that do as they are taught, promised to *be saved harmless,* the old Serpents policy, *&c.* And with this Revolution thus going on, in the first of his Reign, the beginning in of the year, when a *Star* within the *Horns of the New Moon* enclosed, of

---

Line 1. **the Evangelist:** St. John the Evangelist, author of the Book of Revelation.

Line 5. **Lo...Kingdom:** Matt. 28:20.

Line 7. **Berks:** Berkshire. **Shires:** counties.

Lines 9–10. **July...Emperor:** July was named for Julius Caesar.

Line 16. **Divisions character:** see John 7:43.

Line 17. **morning Star:** Christ (see Rev. 2:28 and 22:16); Lady Eleanor's vision. **Jerusalem of the Gentiles:** Great Britain.

Line 18. **Anno... accomplished:** Archbishop Laud was executed in January 1644, i.e., 1645.

Lines 19–22. **those...harmless:** see Titus 1. **the old Serpent:** Satan.

some judgement at hand, the ominous Forerunner: First, of the Wise-men coming from the East, as follows; whose flight taken westward, through that heavy hand occasioned; the Cities unparalleld Plague, Bills to be Canceld never, or drowned in forgetfulness, encreased to no less then weekly *Five thousand five hundred and odde,* the Age of the world; decreased as suddenly about the midst of Summer: all one as their being 30 fed, that blessing thought upon, when the five thousand men with *those loaves five,* &c. no more then the fingers of their hand, any matter made of it, so thankful: Whereupon (the aforesaid Visitation) the Term kept at *Reding,* County of *Berks,* other Courts at *Maidenhead* Town, the Par-liament posting to *Oxford,* doing all homage to this *New born BABE, ruling with the iron Scepter,* them forewarning all in vain, *Be wise, O ye Kings, Be learned, ye Judges;* that in such security held themselves then, and so much first for that, and his powerful word displayed, the priority thereof, thou *Britain* not the least, *&c.* And of his wrath then kindled, shewed great Blessings and Corrections inseparable companions: 40 Where-with proceeding, namely, *without it done nothing that was done,* its mouth the Oracle, *Beginning* and *Ending* of *Monarchies,* inheritance whose from *East to West extends;* concerning the aforesaid golden num-ber, *Nineteen years and a half,* being in a Manuscript inserted, contain-ing *Germanies* woful Occurrences, and *Great Britains* both, with what

---

Lines 25–27. **Wise-men coming...Plague:** Lady Eleanor parallels the flight of Parliament and the law courts from plague-ridden London with the journey of the wise men to see the baby Jesus.

Line 29. **Five...odde:** deaths reported in the Bill of Mortality, a list published weekly in time of plague.

Lines 31–32. **those loaves five:** see Matt. 14:15–21.

Lines 33–34. **aforesaid Visitation:** the plague of 1625. **the Term...Reding:** The law courts adjourned from London to Reading in the summer of 1625. **Maidenhead:** town near Reading in Berkshire.

Line 35. **posting:** travelling by relays of horses. **this...BABE:** Lady Eleanor's prophecy.

Line 37. **Be wise...Judges:** Ps. 2:10. Line 39. **Britain...least:** cf. Matt. 25:40. **his:** God's.

Lines 42–44. **Beginning...extends:** see Matt. 24. **golden number:** the number used in calculating the date of Easter.

Line 45. **Germanies woful Occurrences:** in the Thirty Years' War (1618–1648).

sign confirmed; shewing further thus, who immediately after with her
own hand within two days delivered it to the Archbishop *Abots,* he then
at *Oxford,* of University the first, in presence of no few; with this for a
Token given, *the plague presently to cease;* of whom took her leave, the
50 Bishops *Amen* whereto went round.

The Bills obeying the same before the Moneth expired of *August,* witness when scarce deceased *One thousand* of all Diseases, whereas afore so
infectious, five children dying for one aged, next Term supplyed with
others fled returned; so that of its late desolation appearance, no more
then of Change or Amendment amongst them, none at all.

And so pursuing the Prophetical History in the next place, That it
might be fulfilled *out of the Low Countreys, &c.* as the Virgin when
undertook her voyage, she fleeing for the Babes preservation thither;
also constrained for printing the same, to go into *Holland,* those plain
60 swathing-bands for wrapping it in, pretending in her husbands behalf
the *Spaw* obtained a License, since none for printing to be had here,
inquisition and hold such, among them imprisoned about it formerly,
till afterward all as free, *Cum Privilegio* out of date become.

Where thus passing on the mean while ere her return thence, *George*
Archbishop deceased, *Anno 33.* unhappily whose hands imbrued in
innocent blood, Archbishop *Laud,* 19 of *Septemb.* translated, *&c.* reigning in his stead, successor of him, in stead of the Stag who shot the
Keeper, presaging what Murthers him coming after, when-as for
another her soul pierced in no mean degree, what honor to be *a Prophet*
70 *amongst their own nation and rank;* for example as specified on Record:

Lines 46–47. **her own hand:** Lady Eleanor delivered her prophecy. **Archbishop Abot:**
George Abbot, archbishop of Canterbury, 1611–1633.

Line 49. **Token:** sign or proof.

Line 61. **Spaw:** spa. **License…here:** Licenses were required for leaving the country as well as
for the printing of books.

Line 63. **Cum Privilegio:** with privilege (Latin); the phrase that appeared on licensed books.

Line 65. **imbrued:** stained; defiled.

Line 66. **translated:** moved from one ecclesiastical office to another.

Lines 67–68. **him…Keeper:** Archbishop Abbot shot a keeper while hunting in 1621.

Lines 69–70. **what…rank:** cf. Matt. 13:57.

no sooner arrived then apprehended, of her childe ravished, a greater then the Parliament, *the Word of God:* And how recompenced for their service, referred, *&c.* where after a Candle being sent for, about the third hour in the Afternoon, that with his own hand had burnt it, saying, *She hath taken good long time, till* 44 *. for Dooms-day then; My Lords, I hope I have made you a smother of it:* in truth his own fatal hour, those years of *Nineteen and a half,* reaching to his Execution Moneth and Year, *Anno* 44. *January,* when parted head and body, like that aforesaid divided year, shewed afore sacrificed by his ungracious hand, Author of this Division or Distraction, a cup filled to the brim afterward, as that 80 Judgement day, *June Anno* forty four compleat: The restrained four *Winds,* &c. *Apoc.* 7. signified by them, extending to forty eight, that Blow *January* also, all standing at the stroke of FOUR; the foursquare City *New Jerusalem* wherewith agrees: *Micah* the Prophet (*cap.* 5.) his alarm to awaken the Age, speaking no parable, [*by*] <So of> her goods seized on, wherewith given the Oath, such and such *ARTICLES* for answering to: In which case not much to seek, of *Scandalum Magnatum* in that kinde, against *those little ones,* the penalty of it, *touched by whomsoever, a milstone a fitter ornament,* &c. she not slow in appearing to receive their wilde Sentence; the Dragon of *Lambeth, Laud,* his venom 90

Line 71. **her childe:** Lady Eleanor's prophecy. **ravished:** seized; raped.

Lines 73–74. **a Candle…it:** Lady Eleanor is recounting the events of her hearing before the Court of High Commission in 1633, when Archbishop Laud burned her writings.

Line 76. **his own fatal hour:** Laud was executed in 1644, i.e., 1645, nineteen and a half years after Lady Eleanor's vision in July 1625.

Lines 82–83. **forty eight…January:** the execution of Charles I in January 1648, i.e., 1649.

Lines 83–84. **foursquare…Jerusalem:** Rev. 21:16.

Line 86. **the Oath:** the oath *ex officio,* whereby those brought before the Court of High Commission were to swear to respond to the articles against them.

Line 87. **Scandalum Magnatum:** legal offence of making a scandalous statement about someone who held a position of importance.

Line 88. **little ones:** An asterisk links this phrase to a handwritten annotation in the margin which reads "(order of ye prophets.)"

Line 89. **milstone:** millstone; stone used for grinding; a heavy stone that, if hung around someone's neck, could make the person drown (Matt. 18:6).

Line 90. **Lambeth:** the London palace of the archbishop of Canterbury.

discharging last of all, even *Anno Etatis* 33. measured out by our Lords age, when as brought to his Arraignment by wicked hands, how sacrificed this *Testimony* of his; a word also as ensues.

And [*thus*]<of> like measure *October* 23. she committed close Prisoner, Excommunicated, Fined to his Majesties use Three thousand pounds, and to make publique Recantation at *Pauls* Cross, as extant on Record, Twelve Hands Signed by; also *Edge* Hill fight, and the *Irish* Massacre 23 of *October,* and Twelve of them at once Voted to Prison, for that Order of theirs nothing to stand of force there done without them:
100 His Majesty lastly Fined his three Kingdoms to the use, *&c.* As for *Pauls,* a habitation for Owls, those Noats set up, to set forth the residue, where the time would fail how the first Blow at *Edge-Hill* in *Oxfordshire,* the second *Newbery,* fought within a stones cast of her house at *Englefield.* And thou *Bedlam*-House, too little the Thousandth part to contain of them distracted since thence her coming, *well knowing if the Master of the house called Devil, &c. what the Servant to expect;* where so much for this time, accompanied with the Universal Tax, no Inferior Rack set upon in these days *C. Stu.* his Reign, as sometimes in *Cæs. August.* second of that Monarchy, no small oppression, as the lineage of
110 *David* a witnes of it: closing it with these from her Name, *Rachels,* signifying a Sheep, rendring *Charles* <T>his foil for the Golden fleece bear-

---

Line 91. **Anno Etatis 33:** 1633, when Laud became archbishop.

Lines 91–92. **our Lords age:** Christ was 33 when he was crucified.

Line 94. **October 23:** the date in 1633 when Laud burned Lady Eleanor's prophecies.

Line 96. **Pauls Cross:** outdoor pulpit at St. Paul's Cathedral in London.

Lines 97–98. **Edge Hill fight:** the Battle of Edgehill, 23 October 1642. **the Irish Massacre...October:** in 1641.

Line 101. **Pauls:** St. Paul's Cathedral, the seat of the bishop of London. **Noats:** notes.

Line 103. **Newbery:** Newbury; site of battles in 1643 and 1644.

Line 104. **Bedlam-House:** St. Mary of Bethlehem, the mental hospital where Lady Eleanor was confined in 1636 and 1637.

Line 107. **Universal Tax:** at the time of Christ's birth (Luke 2:1); also in Lady Eleanor's time.

Line 108. **Rack:** instrument of torture; a manger. **C. Stu:** Charles Stuart, King Charles I.

Lines 108–10. **Cæs. August:** Caesar Augustus. **second of that Monarchy:** Caesar Augustus of the Roman empire and Charles I of the Stuart dynasty. **lineage of David:** kings of Israel.

Line 110. **Rachels:** sheep (Hebrew); an anagram of Charles.

Line 111. **the Golden fleece:** in Greek myth, the object of Jason's quest.

ing the Bell: so whom he hath joyned of her Lamentation, *& His Jacobs* saying, *Some evil Beast hath done it*, needs not ask *Whose Coat party-coloured?* also in pieces rent, since our *British* Union, *&c.* not without cause *weeping, because they are not;* and so all doing they know not what, *even forgive,* [*&c. And again thus*], since *Thus it was written, and thus it behoved to suffer, and to rise again.*

The New-Years-Gift *to all Nations and People,* Jubile.

Decemb. 1649.

FINIS.

Line 113. **Some…it:** see Gen. 37:20.

Line 118. **New-Years-Gift:** gift traditionally given at the beginning of January, though the British still officially began the year in March. **Jubile:** see note to line 85 on page 135.

In this tract (Wing D1979) Lady Eleanor claims for herself both the episcopal power of excommunication and Parliament's legislative authority in order to abolish Sunday, the much abused sabbath. In its place she proposes a new sabbath, Monday or Moonday. Her prophetic messages to English institutions of her own day compose the second part of the tract. For these she adapts the text of the messages to the angels of the seven churches (Rev. 2–3). The present edition of *Bill of Excommunication* is based on the copy in the volume of Lady Eleanor's tracts in the Folger Shakespeare Library. The annotations on its title page make some of the same points she made in *Sign* (Wing D2012AA—page 277 in the present edition).

THE BILL OF EXCOMMUNICATION,

For abolishing henceforth
the SABBATH
Call'd *Sunday* or *First day.*
By the Lady *ELEANOR.*

Apocalips, cap.1.

Title Page. The title page is heavily annotated with handwritten additions as follows: at the top of the page: "Daniel Rest &c. What if Hee tarry till I come" (John 21:22–3); down the right-hand margin: "The floods A[rk] 1655 & times reign Caesar Augustus moneths of 56 years 666 Howers of ye monethe"; across the bottom of the page: "Have no rest daye nor Night [ ]captivitye." The edge and bottom of the page are cut off.

293

The Bill of EXCOMMUNICATION

For abolishing henceforth, The Sabbath called Sunday or
First day, from the Lady *Eleanor,* (*Apoc. cap. 1.*)

As shewed by whom (when passed by) in his admonition: *Whom ye
ignorantly worship, him shew I unto you,* (*Acts*) so understood of you
even alike Prophesies Mistery, especially this Book of *Apocalips: The last,
&c.* times and seasons preordained bounds, whereof the sum, in season
now; of which obtruse Oracle by Her as ensues; a blessing far from
every one of you neither; the most Supreme and reserved.

Containing three Articles or Arguments first Prophesie, like the *Eagle*
renewing its strength. Secondly, of a new Sabbath instituted, namely
Moonday, *One for Thee,* as it were, *one for Moses, and one for Elias.*
Lastly, *Of the Lords second coming in the last days,* revealed to be, also of
time, persons and place, no unnecessary circumstances.

The Book superscribed thus, *Reader and Hearer, both with a blessing
crown'd, keep the words hereof, for the time is at hand.* ver. a sufficient
Motive.

Which passages profound till come of full Age, under custody of
Metaphors and Figures, by him Secretary to the Holy Ghost, on this
wise, under his Hand *Joann.* The grace of God signifying, *Anno Dom.*
These Visions when awakened, that alone Peace-maker.

Ver. *John to the seven Churches, grace and peace from him which was,
and which is, and which is to come, and from the seven Spirits in presence of
his Throne:* Times voices past, present and future, bids farewel him, a
Father become of many Generations, bearing date the last seven hundred years, those in the rear next to eternity: *That sits not on Thrones by
hands erected.*

As in the next place *Easters* Anniversary day, the Resurrections
comemoration (*ver.*) *And from Jesus Christ and first begotten of the dead,*

Lines 4–5. **Whom...you:** Acts 17:23.

Line 8. **obtruse:** abstruse; difficult to understand.

Lines 10–11. **Eagle...strength:** see Ps. 103:5.

Line 12. **Moonday:** Monday, day of the moon, rather than Sunday, day of the sun.
One...Elias: Matt. 17:4.

Line 20. **Joann:** St. John the Evangelist, author of the Book of Revelation.

that washed us in his Blood, &c. implying (Jesus CHR:) even Lord of   30
Sabbaths three, from his rest; a greater then *Cæsar* slain then, or CH:R:
either of *Britains* three Isles, stiled Defenders or Saviors, &c. whose
Coronations father and son both about *Easter, J.* and *C.* those first and
last.

And so he cometh he cometh, (*Psal.*) *Let the great Isles be glad therof,*
To him be glory and dominion for ages of ages, even so Amen. (ver.) *A.* and
O. All and Some, beginning and ending of the *Roman* and *Norman*
Tiranny both, also pointing to the Hebrew Language and Greek, Old
and New Testament, where the one begins, the other *Finis* subscribes.

And so a brief Remonstrance of whose Sabbath or First day, not only   40
how of late prophaned, but accompanied with a mass of abomination as
far as these narrow limits permit.

To steal the hearts of the people, *Absoloms* policy like, consecrated to
Maygames and Wakes, when crowding and piping to fall to their Heathen exercises, needs not be awakened, to give ear to these lessons, like
him that made *Israel* to sin; such a care had of the people, least weary
themselves that way, answerable to those presumptious prefaces annext
to Bibles, lest it troublesome either, that except the Revelations Book,
and other like least edifying, and such as may be best spared, allowing
the rest once a Week to be read; Doubtless in process of time, not with-   50
out an intent to poyson the rest likewise of those living Fountains, by
like aspersions.

Pretending it only concerns *Rome,* as by their Marginals all upon that
Dragon laid and his Red Livery. And thus proceeding with that Ivory
Box, dissolv'd those Spirits oderiferous Oyntment alike acceptable, to

---

Line 30. **CHR:** Christ. Line 31. **CH:R:** Charles Rex; King Charles.

Lines 32–33. **Britains three Isles:** probably England, Scotland, and Ireland, three kingdoms, as Lady Eleanor notes elsewhere, even though only two islands. **whose…Easter:** James and Charles both acceded to the throne around Easter.

Lines 35–38. **Let…Amen:** Ps. 97:1; Rev. 1:6. **A. and O.:** Alpha and Omega; first and last (Rev. 1:8). **Roman…Tiranny:** the rule of Rome (the papacy) and of the Normans.

Line 43. **To…policy:** 2 Sam. 15:6.

Line 44. **Maygames and Wakes:** parish festivals that included sports, which the Puritans considered irreligious.

Lines 53–55. **Marginals:** marginal notes. **that…Livery:** Rev. 12:3. **Ivory Box:** see Rev. 18:12.

the world as when she of everlasting memory, afore his Burial then brake the other, no less then before times departure prefiguring the Spirit of Prophesie distilling that dew on *Mount Sion,* &c. a threefold testament importing.

60   But leaving that, *like to the three measures of meal taken by her, wherein hidden, &c. till the whole leaven'd again return* where left him; after had his ample Salutations signified; Relates by what Authority sets out the insuing Proclamation or summons to appear all before the Throne of his rest.

Where shews first of all when and where (*ver.*) *I John even your Brother, on the Lords day transported,* &c. *in the Isle called Patmos,* &c. as a subverter of the World thither exil'd, that Disciple voyced, He should not dye because of that ambiguous Speech: *If I will he tarry till I come, &c.* Suddenly behinde him like a Trumpet, a great voice; *I am A. and O.*
70   *the first and the last,* Affirmative and Negative both, as much to say, before Parliaments: *What thou seest, write,* &c. turned about, who saw such a dreadful apparition, the day of Judgements very likeness, saying, *I am he that was dead,* &c. the Resurrections voyce, that posture in, standing in midst of seven golden Candlesticks, the seven Planets in his right hand, bidden dread neither Tyrants Scepter or Jaylors Keys, both are his, Keys of Death and Hell.

As moreover a Books description in Paper, Ivory white, gilt about, bound and brazen clasps in relation thereto, a PEN razen like; The Liquid Sword with two edges coming out of the Standish mouth, even *Rev-*
80   *elations* sacred Representations, with its lightning Aspect: a voyce, as many waters, emblem of troublesome times: as the Flood about the midst of such a Century the seventeenth, not unknown, Shepherds advertis'd all, vigilant to be then even from the Lord of Sabbaths presence, (evident) whose eyes like the Moon at full, a flame of fire likened unto, as the Sun in its full strength, his countenance with the seven

---

Lines 60–61. **three...return:** see Matt. 13:33. Line 68. **If...come:** John 21:22.

Lines 78–79. **razen:** sharp. **The Liquid...edges:** the sharp pen (Rev. 1:16). **Standish mouth:** a mouth serving as a standish (a stand containing ink, pen, and other writing materials).

Lines 82–83. **Shepherds...all:** see Luke 2:8–12.

Stars or Planets in his right hand: *Saturn, Sol* and *Lunæ,* who fell dead at his feet, he of that new Name *John;* no stranger to our Nation, or uncertain Author: The Name given by the Angel to him, last of the old Prophets, first of the new.

And as for the first day of the Week become the last, shadowed out without question by those displeas'd Laborers, told them the last should be first, and first last, (that Reciprocal reply) complained had born the heat of the day, demanded whether unlawful for him to dispose of his proper Goods, when that Evenings account finished, a peny to each, amounting to seven pence, *&c.* Displaying thy splendant Locks; O our Sundays Sabbath, our Sunday, our Sunday Sabbath, under a total Eclipse; O Sabbath, our Sunday our Sunday; as when he hid his face, set up that *Epanalepsis* noat of his, told except come forth, not a man would tarry that Night, *&c.* 90

Thou *Absolons* Pillar, weep *Pauls* for thy cashiered day *Apolo's* Temple, this Dragons Tail, where worshipped no more, in whose Churchyard, save-reverence, worse then burnt by the Hangman, whereas the lap of his Garment cut off *Sauls,* smote *Davids* heart, witness set out those unclean seats, there lined with the Scriptures clean through, not only, but the House of Prayer turnd to School Houses, Ringing with a noise of boys such a charm, *I pray God and God grant we love;* upon any lascivious Poem or Fable, rent in pieces that Name 100

Line 86. **Sol and Lunæ:** sun and moon (Latin). Lines 91–92. **the last…first:** Matt. 19:30.

Lines 93–94. **demanded…Goods:** Matt. 19:21–23.

Line 95. **splendant Locks:** splendent or shining hair.

Line 97. **as…face:** see Exodus 3:6.

Lines 98–99. **Epanalepsis:** rhetorical figure in which the same word or clause is repeated after intervening matter. **noat:** note. **except…Night:** see 2 Sam. 19:7.

Lines 100–1. **Absolons Pillar:** see 2 Sam. 18:18. **thy cashiered day:** when St. Paul's Cathedral, seat of the bishop of London, no longer enjoys such power as it once claimed. **Apolo's Temple:** The Greek god Apollo was associated with the temple at Delphi, whose oracle reputedly became silent at the birth of Christ.

Line 101. **Dragon's Tail:** Satan was often represented as a dragon (e.g., Rev. 20:2).

Line 102. **burnt…Hangman:** the fate of condemned books in seventeenth-century England.

Line 103. **the lap…heart:** 1 Sam. 24:5.

Line 105. **School Houses:** There were schools associated with many of the English cathedrals.

lessoned by others not, but miscalling a Prophet, what befel, doubtless then sellers of Doves (*Simonis Caveat*) deserves the Whip much better.

110 But in comparison of the rest, like palms of her Hands, and soles of the Feet *Jezebels*, for brevity forborn: So in sweat of thy face, both return to eat Bread and Fish, cry Oynions and Garlick, those Hymns, the Day and thou droven out together.

Apocal. Cap. 2.

As the generality or scope of which informs, how much qualified above others, the more adds to their failing in what Point soever, so shews herewith to such an Age abounding with fulness: Of the gift of Prophesie added beyond all the rest for a multiplication.

Thus, where every word hath its weight: *Unto the Angel of the Church*
120 *of Ephesus,* &c. *I know thy works* (ver.) *Besides these thou shalt do no maner of work,* &c. viz. exempted labor implies this Islands denomination, derived from the Angels Name, otherwise called *England,* containing Bishopricks about twenty seven; Seald with the seven Lamps or Golden Candlesticks.

Who although had suffered Martyrdom, disproved them, to wit, Bishops of *Rome* false Prophets, with feigned Miracles had discovered such: Nevertheless, guilty of no less than their first love forsaken, because for a time the gift of Prophesying ceased given, gone totally, whereby gives to understand, not enough to hate where God hates,
130 except love too, whom he loves, who may say they had a Candlestick, *except repent and amend.* As for the seven Stars born, times Antiquity displaying, requires no farther pursuing.

The Prophetical *Oyes* following it to all persons in general shewing,

---

Lines 108–9. **what befel...Doves:** see John 2:13–16. **Simonis Caveat:** beware of the simonist (Latin); a simonist is one who buys and sells church offices.

Lines 110–11. **palms...Jezebels:** see 2 Kings 9:35.

Line 112. **cry...Garlick:** complain and displease God; see Num. 11:1–5.

Lines 121–22. **this...England:** Lady Eleanor argues that "England" was derived from "Angelland." Although the early Anglo-Saxon historian, Bede, tells a story that also identifies England with Angel-land, it was not a common association.

Line 126. **Bishops of Rome:** the popes.

Line 133. **Oyes:** hear ye; a call to silence by a public crier or court officer.

Thus saith the Spirit of Prophesie, *To him that overcometh, endureth to the end,* &c. Stands out the storm, gives them the Sacramental Tree of Life, in the midst of Paradise: The true Vine, the Word its mystery signified, revealed to be about the midst of the present Century, as from his walking in the midst of those golden Lamps not onely, but by this Trees standing in the midst likewise, *&c.*

Where follows to *Smyrna's* Angel, down weight, *I know thy works, saith the first and the last, He that was dead,* &c. Again sounding the Resurrections alarm, notwithstanding their poverty, saying, *Thou art rich,* by that seeming paradox, shewing the estate of Prophets: The Supreme Authority, difficulties rather kindling, then daunting generous Spirits, such as between the Arch-Angel and the Tempter, in Infancy of that Church: such a like bout or dispute, as (sometime) about *Moses* Body, so here with the father of falshood, like blasphemies the Devils Deputy, breathing out; as informs for casting out the Holy Ghost, *(ver.)* Behold, *The Devil shall cast some of you into Prison, that ye may be tryed,* like *Daniel in the Lyons Den:* which Ambuscado's and Inquisitions inhibits to fear them. The Crown that none can dispose of, suffices the limited ten days, (to wit) the *Jubiles* release or return.

And going herewith on the Churches Map, or several Parishes by name, in what estate it stands when reproclaimed, *Make plain the way,* &c. Even explained by his Messenger, the very Age or time at hand of his coming.

Thirdly, *To the Angel at Pergamos,* time for them to be let Blood, sends this Challenge from *him with the two edged Sword,* unworthy of their ears, cowards and dastards, as it were, that hide themselves: knows their service and where they abide both, *ver.* where Satans Throne, his Courts were kept, preying daily on widow and fatherless not onely, but their Spiritual Dens also, setting Fornication of both kindes at sale, adding Doctor *Balaam* Excommunicating to make up weight, *curse*

140

150

160

Lines 134–36. **To him...Life:** Rev. 2:7. Line 136. **The true Vine:** John 15:1.

Line 146. **dispute...Body:** see Jude 9. Line 150. **Ambuscado's:** ambushes.

Line 152. **Jubile:** The Jubilee year, every fiftieth year, was to be a year of restoration and liberation (Lev. 25:10).

Line 154. **Make...way:** Prov. 15:19.

where should bless, in such a milde way reproved, *ver.* hath *a few things against them,* none of the sharpest Wits or Spirits, yet as of no inferior consequence; as again, others appointed to visit prisoners, or rather sift, *&c.* persons condemned, in making report contrary to their conscience, guilty not onely of innocent blood, but have drawn the never departing Sword, instruments of it: *Except repent,* may say, *They had a dwelling:* will shortly try with them, the two edg'd Sword none spares: The paper Field, its Excision to beware: *He that hath an ear,* &c.

170

Moreover, *To him that overcomes,* stands it out, *ver. Will I give to eat of the hidden Manna.* That Sacramental Cordial for all Maladies, a present cure, beyond Chymistress extolled works, under their Ænigmatick terms concealed, equivolent not with this *Unium Necessarium,* this Donative, not of man, but from him, assuring nothing so secret that shall not be discovered, not a little of it failing.

Inlarged thus, (*ver.*) *I will give him a white stone, therein a new Name written, which no MAN knows but he that receives:* beside the gift extraordinary, of discontinued Prophesie restored, alludes to him, *a Prophet and greater, &c.* His written *NAME,* where so real a demonstration of the aforesaid Immunity and Name, needless further to be insisted on, or for displaying, further quotes of such Antiquity, with their several distinguishing Motto's, figuring *Daniels* reserved visions. And these of the *Apocalips,* a *Phœnix,* one of great *Babylon;* the other an *Eagle,* taking its flight from *Patmos,* both of a feather, the inspired Pen: withal shewing these speaking the *English* Tongue, with *Hebrew* and *Greek,* either equivolent, preferred to be the Holy Ghosts Interpreter, discovering future things, even ours the Angelical Golden Language: And so much for that Super-Philosophical *Elixir* or multiplying Stone, of such a profound penitrating Nature; this secret gift, hearts obdurate,

180

190

Line 173. **Cordial:** a medicine invigorating the heart. Line 174. **Chymistress:** chemistry's.

Line 175. **Unium Necessarium:** One necessary thing (Latin). Line 176. **Donative:** gift.

Line 184. **Daniels reserved visions:** see Dan. 12:9.

Line 185. **Phœnix:** a bird which, according to legend, burned itself after living five hundred years and then arose from the ashes to a new life of similar length. **great Babylon:** the city of sin which fell and would be no more (Rev. 18:21).

Line 189. **ours…Language:** Lady Eleanor's claim that "English" derives from "Angel-ish."

Line 190. **Elixir:** substance that could turn base metals into gold.

as hardest Mettal or Adamant, expels the Old Serpents poyson, them reduces to a glorified estate, others to whom but dross in comparison.

The fourth writ served on *Thyatirus Angel,* so stiled from inspiring their Auditors, *ver. These things saith the Son of God, that hath his eyes like a flame of fire, his feet as fine brass,* viz. The refining Word, or Spirit of Prophesie, knows their works or laborious service, neither on the decreasing hand.

And thus all to make up their account, against whom notwithstanding *a few things,* whose Angel currant neither, where shews implyed a true Prophet or Prophetess, from a false one mentioned, *Jezebels* Sorceries tollerated and Idolatries: And Father *Balaams* Magick documents confided in, whilest true miracles faithful signs as nothing reputed, though not inferior to *Elias* Spirit, when vanquished *Baals* Priests, with those companies or fifties blown up, and their Commanders, on which Church imposed no other Assessment or Burthen, but exchange of the Sabbath: No more burthens by Porters upon Moondays, no longer a working day, not without a touch of their Mother Priests, namely, those laying in Childebed suffered to Baptize.

From him whose eyes likened to the Moons fiery visage: But to hold fast that *Magna Charta* from the beginning, then *Westminsters* tryal, or *Guild-hall,* of more importance, concerning what attention due, when the holy Ghost commands audience, things to come shews; as here every Church like the days of the week called by name, *&c.* This for another addition, not the least, together with the Morning Star, whose Patron not as *Lucifer* faln, or mans invention, like a common sign, but evident manifestation of the Spirit, from him the Father of Lights, accompanyed with the Iron Rod: Kingdoms turned upside down, others like a tottering Wall, unlike Ensigns of Magistracy, the Mace, *&c.* expresly signifying withal, for the publishing of this News-book, or

200

210

220

Line 193. **dross:** impurity. Line 204. **Elias…Priests:** 1 Kings 18:21–37.

Lines 207–9. **No more…Baptize:** Lady Eleanor's examples of profanation of the sabbath and senseless church practices.

Line 211. **Magna Charta:** great charter (Latin); document guaranteeing English liberties, signed by King John in 1215. **Westminster:** seat of Parliament and the courts of law.

Line 212. **Guild-Hall:** London's city hall.

Line 219. **Mace:** ornamental staff, symbol of authority.

Revelations. Together with the Press, the Art of Printing so requisit, (of late by a Soldier, one free of the Military profession, found out) this exquisit work, as compared to a Potters Vessel broken in shivers or pieces; Their breaking every Letter (so not a little ominous) The Iron scouring Rod, Pieces or Guns belonging unto, invented by a Monk those Ordnances, the Iron Age foreshewing therein, *How the powers of heaven shaken between them:* foreknows thus all Sciences and Crafts, Liberal and Mechannicks, from the Goldsmith to the Blacksmith, also Heralds and Alumists, those mysteries.

230   And thus of their Angels faln asleep for company: *The Church of Sardis* Angel not found perfect, prophane rather, after the former calm way admonished: *These things saith he with the seven Spirits of God, the seven Stars in his right hand,* viz. *Die Lunæ,* The Spiritual day saluted with the Resurrections voice, *(ver.) Be awake,* &c. where Possession being eleven Points of the Law, *bidden to hold fast.* Not enough, they had the white Garment, or had faith, *Repent,* &c. *I know thy faith,* as much to say, *by thy works: He that hath an ear,* &c. be watchful, plain as the Bellman speaking what hour or time of the Night, (signifying times glass run out) or suffices either to confide in the Name, naming the childe after

240   *Peter,* or the like; as much to the purpose, as their Gossips cup and white sheet. Beggerly Traditions prefering, whereas in times of old among the Kings and Genealogies those, not two of one Name hardly read of.

    Sixthly, *Philadelphia's* Writ, their good Angel saluted, *from him that is*

Line 223. **shivers:** fragments or splinters.

Line 226. **Ordnances:** artillery; perhaps also a pun for ordinances, i.e., orders. **Iron Age:** the era preceding Judgment.

Line 229. **Alumists:** people who work with alum, a mineral salt; perhaps also a pun on "alchemists."

Line 233. **Die Lunæ:** Monday (Latin); literally, "Moonday."

Lines 234–35. **Possession...Law:** Lady Eleanor's variant of the legal maxim that possession is nine points of the law.

Lines 236–37. **Repent...ear:** Rev. 3:3–6. Line 238. **glass:** hourglass.

Lines 240–41. **Gossips...sheet:** The gossips were the women present at childbirth; the cup, the warm drink they gave the new mother; a white sheet was traditionally worn by someone doing penance for incest or adultery.

Line 243. **Writ:** a written letter or command.

aluding to *Holy and True:* Their name shews, *Had loved them:* though slow, had some strength or faith, whose upbrading foes to do Homage at their feet who they are. No more difficult then of this universal Tryal (from which they delivered or escaped) to discern of what nature, stiled the hour of Temptation, strengthned so by the preceding Proofs: *Behold, I come shortly, hold fast that no MAN,* &c. implying, because said, *Of that day and hour none knows:* Therefore such an offence, his comming to be revealed aforehand, as though because the moment of Execution uncertain, therefore the Sessions or Sizes.

Where lastly, Of the NAME how called or subscribes, as follows. Shewed them more or less, *They had denyed his Name, and had a few Names,* &c. inferring not onely their denying Baptism, (imposed on Infants) but the Prophets Name figured from his, *A King and a Prophet, Davids,* ver. *These things saith he that hath the keys of David, shuts and no MAN opens,* &c. further, *as Seals it with the Cross:* That *Eloi, Eloi,* &c. supposed *he called Elias,* by a *Paranomasia;* as these to corroberate the mystical expressions of the Prophets Name, witness, *ver. And I will make him a Pillar in the Temple of my God, and will write upon him the Name of God, and of the City of my God, coming down from my God.*

So take all, Crown and Keys both, a better Title whoso shews, with New *Jerusalem,* whose Name of old called *Elia,* that *Homonymia* for another. *Eli-Amor vincet,* That all things indures. For the everlasting Diadem, worth the holding fast, *Je Le Tien.*

Lastly, with *Amen* who begins, *These things saith he,* &c. *Unto the Angel of the Church of the Laodiceans:* To whom a short Sermon also, as

250

260

Line 252. **Sessions or Sizes:** The quarter-sessions were courts held four times a year in the counties; the sizes (assizes) were circuit courts held semi-annually and presided over by judges of the central courts.

Line 258. **Eloi, Eloi:** the cry of Jesus on the cross (Mark 15:34–35).

Line 259. **Paranomasia:** paronomasia; a pun or word play.

Line 264. **Elia:** God. **Homonymia:** homonym.

Line 265. **Eli-Amor vincet:** God-love conquers (Latin); or, loosely, "Eleanor conquers."

Line 266. **Diadem:** regal power. **Je Le Tien:** I hold it (French); Lady Eleanor's family motto.

Lines 268–9. **as much…Candlestick:** not paying attention; Puritans claimed that the use of candles and candlesticks in church services was a Catholic practice.

much Ears as their Candlestick, *Neither cold nor hot:* Even *Pauls* with its
270   Aspiring fired Steeple, and their *Amens* hallowed out, naked and filthy
both: Though carry his Name that Apostle, none of his Spirit upon
them, after the cold fit off, as violently hot: Confesses was afore exceeding mad.

These Hour-glass Doctors how fervent aludes to Alcumists, glass
Stills or Limbecks, knows their Lukewarm temper, *I counsel thee to buy
of me gold tryed in the fire, and white rayment,* &c. *and eye salve:* pointing
both to Buying and Selling those places: Also better seen in *Plato* and
Hypocrates, then in the Prophets or Apostles, whose arrogancy begeting
incurable blindeness: likened to them taken with a vomiting com-
280   monly, as in Agues, shortly come to be spewed or discharged, loathsom-
est of all other: By their Sophism laboring to anoint with the Spirit of
ignorance: Fruit of their stale Orations, what Tyrant Custom Priviledges, or for their own pleasure or benefit, best serves. Unto that given
in the same hour, above violence or robberies reach that treasure. Strangers and Forreigners ought to have bought rather the other permanent.
Then arrayed in that rag of Heathenism: Hypocrasies Livery, by whom
so different from the expedition wherewith the Spirit writes, (witness)
have with mixture, like Water put into Wine agrees as well: Intermin-
gled senceless *Heterogenium* Parenthesis, but answerable to faultless
290   Marginals as poor.

And these no times to sleep in, or secure, with no flattering Pensil, or
falsifying Pen, inhibited neither Sex to unsheath that two edged Sword,
where portrayed from head to foot both: *The World, the great MAN, and
the Word, whose horrible Throne, the Creations Fabrick,* for the snowy

---

Lines 270–71. **Amens…both:** prayers offered (or shouted out) in an impious way.

Line 274. **These Hour-glass Doctors:** clergy who timed their sermons rather than preaching
for as long as the spirit led them. **aludes:** alludes. **Alcumists:** alchemists.

Line 275. **Limbeck:** alembic; device used in distilling.

Line 277. **places:** ecclesiastical offices.

Line 278. **Hypocrates:** Hippocrates, ancient Greek physician.

Line 280. **Agues:** acute fevers. Line 281. **Sophism:** appearance of wisdom.

Line 288. **Water…Wine:** the miracle at Cana (John 2:2–11).

Line 289. **Heterogenium:** nonmatching (Latin).

Fleece, likened for its purity and softness: So many Lights about it. The Elements, those Coats of Antiquity displaying: *Like a flame of fire his eyes: Out of his mouth like the piercing ayr, a voice as waters, such a noise: The footstool earth as dumb, likened to brass,* those veins Mines: rings out precious times adieu or lamentation, like those extinguisht Lights, so many Candlesticks signified by: *Signed with the seven Stars in his right Hand, even like the old garments drest anew, Heavens and Earth ready to vanish:* Whereof so much for manifestation, though much more affords touching the Title and Reign of a Prophet over this Kingdom, to put al rule under his own feet, even when altogether by the Ears; as much to say, *He that hath an ear, Then,* &c. Shut up so long under no ordinary Locks on this wise set on, by unlucky Door keepers, of whose providing: Behold, like to have a warm Supper: Their leavings at Noon, understood like the rest, &c. their own Suppers like laid aside: Informing, he as commanded to say, *I am hath sent me,* &c. So here again, *which was, which is, and which is to come,* commanded these things to be written unto you, from *A.* and *O. He that hath an ear:* After the vulgar strain: *To our loving Friend, at the Angel or Sign of the Crown,* &c. *with speed these, subscribed yours,* &c. *Da: & Do: These are to let you understand: so trusting shortly,* &c. *bears date, Anno* &c. The Sabbath or Resurrections witness, sealed with the seven Tapers: First, to *Westminsters* Church, expressing without vigilancy, the rest but all void. As secondly, with the Keys, testifying these, saith, *He that was dead,* &c. For the Holy Ghosts cause them put into the Gate-House, forbidden to fear those infernal furies. So thirdly, Those Advocates maintaining any Title or Cause: To Judicature Courts at *Westminster-Hall.* The Sword of

300

310

320

Line 296. **Elements:** earth, water, fire, and air. Lines 301–2. **even…vanish:** Isa. 51:6.

Lines 311–12. **After…strain:** in everyday terms. **To…Crown:** standard formula of letters.

Line 313. **Da: & Do:** Davies and Douglas, Lady Eleanor's names by marriage.

Lines 315–16. **Tapers:** candles. **Westminsters Church:** Westminster Abbey, where English monarchs were traditionally crowned.

Line 318. **Gate-House:** prison at Westminster Abbey where Lady Eleanor was imprisoned, 1633–1635.

Line 319. **Advocates:** attorneys.

Line 320. **Westminster-Hall:** portion of Westminster palace which held the central courts.

Justice, with intrusted: By *Balaams* example, Bryberies snare, to flee or to beware: Signed with the Swords point two edged, pointing to the Throne of Tyrants, lest pride receive a fall.

To redeem the time, spurring on to repentance, whose all-searching eyes, *likened to flames of fire, and feet like brass,* Sign of the Gun: The Cities Church, *Peters.* Fourthly, its warning piece, for cleansing or scouring their Lodgings, those Common Sewers or Stews. Also, to *White-Hall* Chappel, to make clean theirs, winking at the like, willed to be awake, *&c.* have regard to a good Name, under colour of late meet-
330   ings, lest pollute themselves.

And thus according to the signs born under, here to that ensign worn out at Elbows: Every one in his order addes to the seven Stars Impression: *The seven Spirits, those before the Throne:* The wedding Garment, that Robe not to defer it.

To the House of Parliament, Sixthly, *Thus saith he that is Holy, an open door that hath set before them, &c.* Prophesie discontinued Parliaments, both under a notion: *Have kept the WORD,* wherefore escape that stumbling block of the Sabbaths change: Also knows the work of their Hangings, shews, *I will make a Pillar, &c.* because a little strength
340   in them. Lastly, with their lowd *Amen,* the Sabbath witness: To *Pauls,* with its Church-yard Drapers, what lack ye: *Buy of him white rayment,* that the filthiness of their nakedness appear not, all to be rayed in plain English, fitter for to sell sackcloth, more in season: remove those offices out of the *House of Prayer:* And thus knows all their Parishes, how many

---

Line 321. **Balaam:** see Num. 22:5–41. **Bryberies:** briberies.

Lines 325–26. **The Cities Church, Peters:** St. Peter's Cornhill, where the Lord Mayor and aldermen attended Whitsun services.

Line 328. **White-Hall Chappel:** the royal chapel where Hugh Peter preached to the court trying Charles I.

Line 331. **ensign:** emblem.

Line 339. **their Hangings:** the tapestries in the Houses of Parliament.

Lines 340–41. **Pauls...Drapers:** Cloth merchants transacted business near St. Paul's Cathedral.

Line 342. **rayed:** arrayed; dressed.

Line 343. **sackcloth:** garments made of rough cloth used for mourning or penance.

within the Walls, *&c.* as though had lost either their keys or ears, *that let him to stand without or knock,* who (however flatter themselves) serves them thereafter.

And knocking here louder and louder, *like the Trumpet on Mount Sinai,* concludes with this Royal Patent, as formerly declares, received of his Father, *The morning Star, &c.* with a touch given of their Morning   350
Suppers: *So again to him that overcometh, will I grant to sit on my Throne at my right hand, or rest, even as I overcame, and sate with my Father, &c.* as much to say, That maintains the cause witnessed with the Prophets awakened Visions, like her Son, who opened his eyes, seven times sneezed, came out of his long sleep: So even prescribed the present Century, whenas out of that *Chaos* or *Hyle,* its quintessence comes to be extracted: Through the Holy Spirits Co-operation, wherewith at first written, ordains for it a day of acknowledgement or remembrance.

Where lastly, for these Allegory Doors, both of entrance and utterance, his messengers knocking thereat early and late, *He that hath an*   360
ear, &c. Behold, comes shortly, at the door, &c. so much for that: That cannot be accounted but long: That *day and hour,* to be so much longed for, and for this no small favor to shew the Door, only this Postscript by the way, *cap.* 4.

> *Post hæc vidi ecce ostium apertum in Cœlo, &c.*

Witness, the Trumpets voice, a door or passage no longer shut, *ver. Come up hither, and I will shew thee things to come to pass,* &c, As immediately saw about the Throne, he holding those precious Tables, like a Book open, the Grand Jury set: All seting forth a rest day, even the fourth Commandment, *the four faced four beasts,* eye witnesses, testifie no less: 370
Where like as when the Law given, like Lightnings, Thundrings, and Voyces, proceeding out of the Throne, accompanying the Trumpet with their

---

Line 345. **within the Walls:** within the City of London.

Lines 348–49. **Trumpet…Sinai:** Exod. 19:16. **Royal Patent:** royal letter sent open rather than sealed closed.

Lines 354–55. **her Son…sleep:** 2 Kings 4:35. Line 356. **Hyle:** matter (as opposed to spirit).

Line 358. **a day…remembrance:** the sabbath (Exod. 20:8).

Line 365. **Post…Cœlo:** After this I looked, behold a door opening in the sky (Latin); Rev. 4:1.

displaying Colours, or Ensigns, pouthered *full of eyes before and behinde, rest not day nor night, which was, and which is, and which is to come: Holy, holy, holy, another rest day, &c.* agreeing with that of *Isaiah, When the posts of that door shaken, the Seraphims displaying those wings of theirs, with twain covered his feet, with twain did flee, with other twain covered their face,* crying Moonday, figured in those three solemn Feast-days, *The Passover, Pentecost, and that of Tabernacles, fall down before him that sate on the Throne,* give up the verdict, *ver.* saying, *Thou hast created all things, and for thy pleasure these were and are created:* Witness, *The Rainbow Fringe over his head, before him the emrald Earth, his Cushion; and fire and ayr, those burning Lamps and Spirits, &c.* The Chrystial *Ocean Sand* his Hour-glass, with hours 24, and four seasons: The Conquest four and twenty, in their old Cathedral way prostrate, making such low obeysance in white, &c. say all glory be to the Holy Ghost also.

The Prophetess his Messenger   From *White-Hall,* fatal 30 *of January, Jubile.*

FINIS.

Line 373. **pouthered:** perhaps powdered, or sparkling.

Lines 375–78. **Isaiah...face:** Isa. 6:2–6.

Line 379. **Passover...Tabernacles:** three biblical feasts whose dates were determined in part by the phases of the moon.

Lines 384–85. **The Conquest...twenty:** Lady Eleanor compares the twenty-four elders (Rev. 4:4) to the twenty-four monarchs who had ruled England since the Norman Conquest of 1066.

Lines 387–88. **fatal...Jubile:** the first anniversary of King Charles's execution.

Line 389. **FINIS:** There is handwritten annotation at the bottom of the page which reads "wch daye about [ ]". The bottom of the page is cut off.

In *Appearance* (Wing D1972A) Lady Eleanor again recites the evidence which convinces her that the Second Coming is at hand. She mentions not only her experience at Englefield in July 1625, but also one on 2 April 1647, the day she wrote *Ezekiel the Prophet* (Wing D1988A—page 221 in the present edition). The copy on which the present edition of this tract is based includes only the first sixteen pages of *Appearance;* it is apparently the only extant copy of this tract. Heavily annotated, it is bound in the volume of Lady Eleanor's tracts now in the Folger Shakespeare Library.

THE
APPEARANCE OR *PRESENCE*
OF THE
SON OF MAN.

PSAL. 48.

Thy right hand is full of righteousness, Let Mount Sion rejoyce, and the daughters of Juda be glad, because of thy Judgements.

Title page. There is a long handwritten annotation in the right margin, the edge of which is cut off, and which reads "As the fat[her] justifying the Sonn: the Sonn like[wise] justifis He[ ] Hee the Im[age] of God: Sh[ ] The sonn o[f] mans & both one w[ho] dispises them dispises Him & so Him & His father both [ ]".

309

Even as I received of my Father, &c. He that hath an ear let him hear.

And proceeding herewith in another place what he saith, *who had not concealed it were it otherwise; That in his Fathers House were many mansions:* reserv'd Mysteries, all revealed not at once, as much to say, [*Men therefore left without excuse: of the iron rod the Ax bid beware, reiterated so*] even *He that hath an ear* (to wit) on pain or peril of his head, *&c.*

Proclaiming no other then the Supreme Order or Authority, their unlimitted Commission: The Spirit after absent so long, how (as it were) *stands knocking at the door:* whereof these the sum or substance of

10 no inferior consequence: A greater then the Conquerer, Parliaments Prerogative not exempted: saying, *To him that overcomes, and keeps my works unto the end, I will give power over the Nations, shall rule them with a rod of iron:* His insulting Enemies necks made his footstool.

Who speaks the word of the Lord, and done it is: Those Heathen Potentates, but like to Potters brittle Vessels broken in pieces, scattered, suddenly a Printers Press like. As the aforesaid herewith consenting shews expresly (*Psalm*) *The Lord said, Sit thou on my right hand, until I make thine Enemy, &c. shall send the rod of thy power out of Sion, Be thou ruler, &c.* And so much for this the prophetical everlasting Order.

20 Whose Prison-commons put into the reckoning, *In the days of thy trouble* (saying) *shall the people offer thee free-will-offerings, &c.* Bread (to say) for the Lords sake, and runing-water: *Therefore shall he lift up thy head: The Lord thy keeper, hell gates shall not prevail against her:* and clear truths as Noon-day, not unknown come to pass: Notwithstanding by you, *As for this Moses we wot not what is become of him:* with one consent afraid all to come nigh him, terrified with them, because of that lusture,

---

Line 1. **Even…hear:** Rev. 2:27–29 (Geneva Bible).

Lines 2–4. **who…mansions:** John 14:2.

Lines 8–9. **Commission:** An asterisk links this word with a handwritten annotation in the margin, which reads "That wch wa[s] from the Beginning; Things before Hand shews". **The Spirit…door:** Rev. 3:20.

Line 10. **the Conquerer:** William I, who conquered England in 1066.

Lines 11–13. **To him…iron:** Rev. 2:26–27. Lines 14–15. **Those…Vessels:** Rev. 2:27.

Lines 17–18. **The Lord…ruler:** Ps. 110:2. Lines 20–21. **In…free-will-offerings:** Lev. 23:38

Lines 22–23. **Therefore…head:** Ps. 110:7. **hell…her:** cf. Matt. 16:18.

Line 25. **As…Moses:** Acts 7:40. Line 26. **lusture:** lustre; sheen or gloss.

on his vissage, *&c.* The two renewed Tables coming down with in his hand: Shadowed out directly in those revived Witnesses two (*Revel.* 11.) when supposed to have heard no more news of them: Those lights deem'd had utterly been extinguished, like to the day of Judgement,   30 when those rebels at the same time swept away in that cities earthquake: And sacrificing all to your own inventions, how requisite some real Demonstration then extraordinary, such unruly winds, where broken loose Trees whose fruit withers: Not for ought good without applyed means supernatural, not to be tamed or ordered: Even appointed this anointing faithful and true saying: These from her overshadowed with the same hand, as he *Aarons* god that was ordained, like Beams of Divinity participating, and Oyls odirefferous, an Elixer not of man or flesh and blood: *She whose Throne heaven, earth her footstool from the uncreated,* saying, *I am A. and O. first and last, both beginning and end-*   40 *ing, by whom all things were done: Not without her any thing done or made; Trinity in Unity, of Manhood the head: Who of Death have the Keys and Hell:* Then the Queen of the South a greater, born a greater not of *Women: Melea,* by Interpretation, *Queen of Peace,* or She-councellor. And so much for this without contradiction, she his Executor, *Made like unto the Son of God,* the ancient of days likeness: owner of that Title of Tythes, to whom the Patriarch offered a Tenth, from the slaughter being returned of those Kings; preceding that Cities day of Judgement prefiguring the final; for which interceding none might avail: *Even the Lord upon her right hand, wounding even Kings in the day of his wrath;*   50 *judging among the Heathen: Heads of divers Countreys smiting assunder:* [*such headships of the Church,*] of such no more.

Line 27. **The two...Tables:** God gave Moses two tables of laws (the Ten Commandments) and renewed them after they were broken (Exod. 34:1).

Line 37. **Aarons god:** a golden calf; see Exod. 32.

Line 38. **odirefferous:** odoriferous; sweet-smelling. **Elixer:** substance that turns stone to gold.

Line 39. **She...footstool:** cf. Acts 7:49. Line 40. **A. and O.:** Alpha and Omega (Rev. 1:8).

Line 42. **Trinity in Unity:** a phrase from the Athanasian Creed, c. A.D. 400.

Line 43. **Queen...South:** "shall rise up in the judgment" (Matt. 12:42).

Line 44. **Melea:** one of Jesus' ancestors (Luke 3:31). A handwritten annotation in the margin reads "a compound of His Name Melchisidec". Melchisedec was a priest of Salem (Heb. 7:1).

Lines 45–46. **Made...God:** Heb. 7:3. Line 47. **to...Tenth:** Heb. 7:4.

And weak sights [*moreover*] lest offended overcome with light, for quallifying the said Deity, or to moderate the same. *Imprimis,* first and formost saying I am *A.* and *O. alias, Da:* and *Do:* by her first and last marriage so subscribes, that beginning and ending *Dowger,* &c. in the next thus. *Item,* Daughter of *Audleigh,* or *Oldfield,* in the *Saxon* Tongue, [*also*] no created Peership: a *Saxon* Baron afore the Conquest, As unto this day, preferring the act of time Antiquity, before Titles subject to be
60   revers'd; and so far for that beginning and ending, of Kings and House of Lords.

Also Baron *Touchet* of *France,* *Castlehaven* in *Ireland,* *Douglas* of *Scotland:* Honors three, consisting in a fourth, *Audeley:* Of those Nations no obscure Denominations, which late ruined old house of this Kingdoms fall a forerunner, *Je Le Tien* its Motto, *Hold fast till I come* (*Rev. &c.*) a derivative therefrom: like unto the Tabernacles work to a loop, and holy Garments or Coats adorned with several precious Stones, following that patern in their true fiery colours display'd, [*consuming dross so a Refiners fire, like*] of whose discent, Genealogy of his noble Prophets no novelty
70   to be kept, suffices so much in refference to the Morning-Star, usher of the day: That honor received from him, giving the seven Stars or Plannets: The Creations coat, arms born: By vertue hereof, (*ver.*) *He that keeps my works unto the end, as I received of my Father,* &c. [*whom*] invincible Prophets, his followers with whom no shrinking or back-drawing, till they have made it good: so much for their Charge.

Where lastly, by consequence, Heaven how comes to be her Joynture, place, being no unnecessary circumstance thus going on: Thou *Bethlehem* or *Berkshire,* not the least, first of Counties: Even shewing the

---

Line 54. **Imprimis:** printed (Latin).

Line 56. **Dowger:** dowager; a widow who enjoyed property or title from her deceased husband.

Line 57. **Daughter…Tongue:** Lady Eleanor's etymology of her father's title, Audley.

Lines 62–63. **Baron…France:** Lady Eleanor claims that her birth name connects her with a French baronage. **Castlehaven in Ireland:** the earldom bestowed upon Lady Eleanor's father in 1616. **Douglas of Scotland:** Lady Eleanor's second husband claimed connections with this Scottish clan.

Line 66. **like…loop:** Exod. 26.

Lines 72–73. **He…Father:** Rev. 2:26.

Line 76. **Joynture:** jointure; property set aside to support a woman after her husband's death.

word[s] of the most high God, at *Englefield* Mannor-House: That
Morning-Salutation for ever blest, where that voyce came unto her, 80
speaking down as through a Trumpet, these words.

Saying, *There is Nineteen years and half to the Judgement day, And you
as the meek Virgin.*

Where farther, by way of Priority thus walking about *Sion,* counting
her Towers, those Right-hand years, in the first of his Reign, *A*° 1625.
first of his name of these Dominions, moneth *July,* 28. so after the first
Roman Emperor called: He slain, *&c.* shewing not to vulgar apprehen-
sions difficult, in this Cosmographical Table of New Heaven and Earth:
How under the Gallery of the aforesaid *Englefield*-House, where awakened with that unexpected Alarm in English: The Western Road lies a 90
Thorowfare under a high Arch for Travellers: Also a place called Hell of
old, a Mile or two distant therefrom, full of pits within the royalties:
The Harbor of such decrepid with age, and their Associates blinde and
halt, craving relief nigh the Highway-side, no Critick observation in the
county of *HARTFORD:* whose Joynture the Manor of *Pyreton* (fire in
Greek) consisting of a Tythe or Impropriation, shews *A*° 48. the same
year of that Kings slaughter or execution: she restored *Trinity* Term put
into Possession of the said Tythe: By the Sheriff a Writ *Moveas Manus,*
by vertue of it, to that Patriarch, sometime appertaining Abbot of St.
Albons: sold away *A*° 33. in the days of her durance, not difficult a little 100

Line 79. **Englefield Mannor-House:** Lady Eleanor's estate in Berkshire (where she had her
vision in 1625).

Lines 82–83. A handwritten annotation in the margin reads "even Mene Mene &c." "Mene
Mene" are the words written on the wall during Belshazzar's feast (Dan. 5:25).

Line 84. **Sion:** Zion; the House of God. Lines 86–87. **first...Emperor:** Julius Caesar.

Lines 90–92. **Western...royalties:** places in the vicinity of Englefield. A long handwritten
annotation in the margin reads "[w]ch maner [s]old awaye [b]y the E: of Huntingdon bought
by [th]e Marques [of] Wincester [a]nd since made [an] Example [so] it hath [f]ired wth
[th]eirs Ashbey House: & Bazeing to Towers".

Line 95. **HARTFORD:** Hertford; the English county where Lady Eleanor's manor of Pyreton
(Pirton) was located.

Lines 96–98. **A° 48...execution:** By the calendar then used in England Charles I was
executed in January 1648. A handwritten annotation in the margin reads "(Her Wedd[ing]
portion". **Trinity Term:** The legal year was divided into three terms; Trinity term began in the
early summer. **Writ...Manus:** the legal instrument used in the tithe proceedings.

Line 99. **appertaining:** belonging to. Line 100. **durance:** confinement, imprisonment.

to regain it; the oftner Argued, the more Ambiguous, until by the Barons of Exchequer, in writing the same appointed to be put down; so Intricate, *&c.* Of which holy Appurtenances Consecrated, things too exactly which cannot be observed, *A°* 1625. Since when, not any thing acted or come to pass: From *Germanies* Desolations, *Rochels* Siege, until *Irelands* Blow, and what since followed; like one waves pursuing another, forerunners of the moments great change and general Judgement, [*when persons or Sex; without such respects*]: even which Passages not unforeshewed by her hand, together with the aforesaid Golden

110 Number of *Nineteen years and a half to A°* 1644. extending [*the ABB*]<to Laud> his *January* Account not onely, but the late *Charls* when became a prisoner, *Nazeby, &c.* That day of Judgement, *A°* 45. current; afterward tasting of the said fatal Moneths cold Cup: as *Buckinghams* August Moneth, him foreshewed, whereupon (boading to that Nation a lash) she wan that wager to his smart: The typifying Breeches of the *Sotch* man her Husband, against such wimzes of hers who laid them, as he then termed it, passing not scotfree, *&c.*

Lines 101–2. **Barons of Exchequer:** judges in the court where Lady Eleanor's case was heard.

Line 103. **holy Appurtenances:** rights or privileges belonging to the church.

Line 105. **Germanies Desolations:** Germany was laid waste in the Thirty Years' War (1618–1648). **Rochels Siege:** Rochelle, the Huguenot (Protestant) city, was besieged by French forces in the 1620s.

Line 106. **Irelands Blow:** In October 1641 civil war erupted in Ireland, and the English received reports of atrocities committed against Protestants..

Lines 109–10. **Golden Number:** the number used to calculate the date of Easter.

Line 111. **his…Account:** Archbishop Laud's execution as a traitor in January 1644, i.e., 1645.

Lines 112–15. **Nazeby:** site of Parliamentary victory over royalist forces, June 1645. A handwritten annotation in the margin reads "[ ]an: the stone cut out wthout Hands. not all frustrat Malachi all the prophet refreshing and watch all etc. Peter appearing of our Lord &c."

Lines 113–14. **Buckinghams…Moneth:** George Villiers, first duke of Buckingham, was assassinated in August 1628.

Line 115. **she…smart:** Lady Eleanor's husband Douglas suffered because she won a wager with him that Buckingham would not live beyond August 1628. She had promised to give up prophesying if she lost. A group of handwritten annotations at the bottom of the page reads "Acts And a prophet like mee", "fa[ ] and relent the base shall not see him 'till Blessed. etc. And Elijah restoring all things Husbandmen."

Lines 116–25. A long handwritten annotation in the margin reads "Imprimis Dr. Giffords wife so ma[ ] for many y[ ] presently [ ] perfectely [ ] Item captain m[ ] the next. Item Mr Jandey so long in [ ] &c. Item cast. out of a [ ]". The text is illegible in several places, as indicated by [ ]; the edge of the page is cut off.

And these with other like, a world not able to contain them: also this for another, 1647. by the same token that Night a bold Star facing the Moon (April. 2.) passed through her Body, at which time served that Writ, bearing date the second of April: *I send thee to a rebellious house, &c. Ezek.* 2. and *cap.* 12. she prefixing Penticost ensuing, as when such a mighty rushing wind, to beware them like as when they all assembled, *&c.* witness *Southwark:* That Mornings ghests unexpected accompanied with such a Thunder-clap from above, and darkness: To the upper House a warning piece their discharge.

And lastly, a second like unto it, witness, 1650 *July Jubile,* that judgement by fire in *Holborn,* and other parts of the City: Instantly in the same week she cast out of her lawful possession of *Englefield,* by that Counties Sheriff, being by due course of Law put into the same: But in the Whitson-week, the like unheard without being impleaded: for the same Sheriff with pistols and Weapons to break up doors, done as he said by a mighty power: All he had to say for himsef, authorized by Committees Order, for swallowing a Widows Estate up after that maner: And fasting, under pretences,

120

130

Lines 119–20. **1647…(April. 2.):** another of Lady Eleanor's visionary experiences.

Line 121. **Writ:** order concerning her tithe litigation.

Line 122. **Penticost:** Pentecost, also known as Whitsunday; the celebration, seven weeks after Easter, of the descent of the Holy Ghost upon the Apostles.

Line 124. **Southwark:** borough on the south bank of the Thames, across the river from London. **ghests:** ghosts; blasts. A handwritten annotation at the bottom of the page reads "And att supper time Hee sent out a servant to a crye att midnight Hee y^t Hath an Eare."

Lines 125–35. **upper House:** the House of Lords. A handwritten annotation down the margin of the page reads "[an]d after Her [hus]band Sr [Ar]ch. Dowglas [wa]st strikne maddness the physician [ ]ld of an [in]cureable [n]ature [ ]t the spirit [of] prophisie in Him obscure [ ] merlins riddles." The edge of the page is cut off.

Line 128. **Holborn:** northwestern area of the City of London.

Line 131. **impleaded:** arraigned or accused in a court of justice.

Line 135. A handwritten annotation at the bottom of the page reads "[A]nd Lastly theire skirmish By Sea eshewd from Tobias fishing with his Rod. &c."

In *Before the Lords Second Coming* (Wing D1974), Lady Eleanor recites once again evidence from her own time that corresponds with biblical prophecies to indicate that the Second Coming is at hand. She offers additional evidence in her annotations. The present edition is based upon a copy in the volume of Lady Eleanor's tracts now in the Folger Shakespeare Library.

BEFORE THE *LORDS* SECOND COMING,
OF
THE LAST DAYS
TO BE VISITED,

Signed with the Tyrant *Pharaohs* Overthrow.

ACTS 3. 22, 23.

A Prophet shall the Lord your God raise up unto you of your Brethren, like unto me, &c. And it shall come to pass, Every soul which will not hear that prophet, shalbe destroyed among the people.

Title page. A long handwritten annotation in the margin reads "revela: cap: [ ] which Ro[me?] Him &c.; Imp[ ] Huc[ ] & as [ ] &c. allso t[o] present Jul[y] moneths [ ] Septemb: 3 Decemb. Blowe the Woe pas[sed]. Thes as gi[ven] understand Latin & other to et in illa terre mortu[ ] et septe[ ]. et septem[ ] et Thes bea [ ]". The first part of the annotation, through "allso to present" is crossed out. Square brackets indicate material cut off the page when its edge was cut away. The "et in illa…bea" is Latin and perhaps means "and in that land having been killed and divided and Seven."

The most Mighty his Messenger,
ELEANOR DOUGLAS, *Dowger; Daughter of Lo:*
Audeley, *Lo:* Touchet, *E: of* Castlehaven:

To them of *England, France, Scotland, Ireland* and *Wales;*

Brethen of these distracted Dominions, hereof in a word \<prophicye>
without which, that tryed Gold in the fire coveted, and whitened Rayment, eyesalve, of that sort or anointing, do but bathe an Ethiopian,
spur *Balaams* ass, since other Balm or way none beside, when have tryed
all, but by the word to try the Spirits, whether counterfeit or current,
Scriptures to search, those Mines, a business worthy of as serious dispute as whatsoever: namely, whether for blaspheming against the holy
Ghost hath not brought upon us this judgement unexpected, wherein
delay no less perillous then heretofore pernicious, untimely tasting that
paradice fruit, whose precious gates when as come to pass set open, The
chrystal flowing living fountain to all passengers free, supposed to have
been dryed up: The reserved Tree of Life likewise given gone, monthly
rendring its golden Largess, attain'd not to its maturity till now: whose
wholsom leaves [*dispersed daily*] for asswaging the Nations festered
wounds assign'd, so requisite those Supernaturals against unnatural
waged wars: These not the first time pressed, But *Gallio* cared for none
of these matters, (*Acts* 18.) although deny the holy Ghost; by consequence The Lord that bought them. Moreover accompanied with frequent Blasphemies, by the Trade called *Religion* set abroach, Scriptures
not more in thraldom to *Romanists,* their state of Ignorance, then the
holy Ghost endeavored to be enslaved (Arrogancy the worst) by them
stiled *Our Reformers and Deliverancers,* distraction of no common consequence, destructive to concord among Brethren-Nations, in their
Brothers eye narrowly observ'd, discern a mote: Execrable Opinions

10

20

Line 2. **Dowger:** dowager; a widow who enjoyed property or title from her deceased husband.
Lines 6–7. **that tryed…anointing:** Rev. 3:18. **bathe an Ethiopian:** see Acts 8:27–39.
Line 8. **spur Balaams ass:** see Num. 22:20–33. Lines 13–14. **tasting…fruit:** see Gen 3.
Lines 15–17. **chrystal…now:** Rev. 22:1–2. Line 24. **Romanists:** Roman Catholics.
Line 28. **mote:** a speck or particle of dust; see Matt. 7:3.

theirs, nevertheless a Beam such a mountain in their own, esteems it not considerable: Foes of our grand Freedoms and Liberties, [*whatsoever they pray, Thy Kingdom come say in their hearts, Torment us not before our time*]; not onely intrenchd *Sion* about, have scaled new *Jerusalems* wals, undermined her Bulwarks: But outstripping Savages of late have slain most barbarously our two Sacred Ambassadors, Those Witnesses as impeached (*Revel.* 11.) The last days, whose Ringleader the foul Beast ascended out of the Abyss, by undeniable evidence chargd with the gift of Prophecies Lamp extinguisht, troden under foot that holy City, &c. exchangd for their gifts sent one to another, or Symony, triumphing over their corps, because tormented them with their published Commission, testified that solemn Oath taken, (*Rev.* 10.) of Tyrant times being cut off, and unhappy generation, such to be no more.

And so much for these precious passages, all plainly speaking of Prophecies return or resurrection, like the Eagles renewing her strength, immunities not inferior to former times, withal informing what Mutiniers in Court and City, against these 2 books in special of the Prophets, *Daniel* and *John,* both which men revived but by a touch, &c. the one continuing until King *Cyrus,* the other until the Cities destruction, Types and Figures before the Churches Deliverance time: How long in captivity under Tyrants, Lawless wretches, not unlike those ruines of the Temple, darksom uninhabited Vauts in the possession of Owls and their Mates, whose Houses and Riches become their Heaven and god.

And so come to Times Mystery, his golden Hour-glass, whereof thus, (*Revel.* 11.) he where bidden to arise, &c. his casting it up to be forty two Moneths, in short as much to say, By three yeers and a half, pointing to the number of Seven, extends not onely to the Seventeenth Century, but expresly to the present *Jubile,* from that moiety or dividing of Time, so over and over prest by those sealed Writs of theirs: The

---

Line 32. **Sion:** Zion; the house of God.

Line 38. **Symony:** simony; the buying and selling of ecclesiastical offices.

Line 43. **like...strength:** see Ps. 103:5.

Line 47. **Cyrus:** king of the Persians during Daniel's time (Dan. 10:1).

Line 56. **present Jubile:** 1650, the date of this tract, was the century's jubilee, or fiftieth year; see Lev. 25:10. **moiety:** half.

Prophet *Daniel* his multiplyed weeks, as informs, saying Seven weeks, and Seventy weeks are determined, &c. And in the midst of the week,
60 &c. but several voyces all in one, expressing the aforesaid *Jubile* or fiftieth yeer, appointed that of pardon, whereof our Lord on this wise, *It is impossible but that offences will come,* (Luke 17.) *But wo unto him,* &c. no less then *Great Britains* neck-Verse, that shall offend one of these, stiled *his Little ones,* a Mill-stone then other Ornament more proper for such a one, as in reference hereto, bears date even his last return (*an.* 49.) seven times seven. *And if he trespass against thee seven times in a day, and seven times in a day turn again, thou shalt forgive (or receive) him:* bear witnes the Disciples, *Lord increase our Faith,* to wit, Defenders of the Faith stiled, never at so low an ebb, as that sure Oracle replyed, *had*
70 *they Faith as a grain of mustard, &c.* Need not fear the day of Judgement tydings, or *Worst of Tyrants* concluding it, how faring with them when the Son of Man revealed, *vers.* 24. one taken the other left, demanded where Lord such Massacre, and woful wars <as> refers them to the Roman Ensign, the Eagle, where the corps, &c.

And so much for this, be it known to all, *Touch not mine anointed, do my Prophets no harm,* with a touch of Times week its Mystery, the most Supreme, set at nought for Onions and Garlick, those anointings in sted of *Canaans* Grapes and Olives, by *Oxford-Naamans,* are not the Rivers of *Damascus* better.

Line 63. **neck-Verse:** biblical verse (usually Ps. 51:1) that one needed to read in Latin to prove entitlement to the legal benefits of being a member of the clergy. These benefits included exemption from the death penalty in most instances; thus people could save their necks by reading the verse.

Line 65. **his:** Charles I, who was executed in 1649.

Lines 68–69. **Defenders of the Faith:** a title given to King Henry VIII by the pope and retained by the English sovereigns.

Line 74. **corps, &c:** An asterisk after these words links them to a handwritten annotation in the margin which reads "Aquila also pointing to the North."

Lines 75–76. **Touch...harm:** 1 Chron. 16:22. Line 77. **Onions...Garlick:** see Num. 11:5.

Line 78. **Canaans...Olives:** the fruits of the Israelites' promised land. **Oxford-Naamans:** servants to King Charles whose headquarters were at Oxford; Naaman was a servant to the king of Syria.

So proceeding with *Sodoms* Map of those two Prophets crucified, 80
exposed like some Malefactors not suffered to be interr'd, where three
days and half (and years) beside sounding the general Resurrections
Alarm, Months forty two, theirs contributing thereto, for a time, times,
and dividing of Time, with one consent crown the Seventeenth Century, 500 years fulfilling a period, shadow'd under Hyerglypick figures,
how honor'd the Spirit of prophecy then powred out, as by those two in
Sackcloth Liveries, their agreeing in one, and them whoso hurts or dis-
honors with untimely death repaid, fire proceeding out of their mouths.

At whose word (that wine) Waters turned into Blood, Wars foreshewed, restrain the Heavens, smite the Earth with Plagues as often as 90
they please, stiled *The two Olive Trees,* and *Two Candlesticks,* expelling
darkness; the healing nature of Oyl not unknown, requires no farther
amplification, shewed to be the Books of the greatly beloved Man, and
that Disciple whom the Lord loved: So, *Come, saith the Spirit,* and
Come, saith the Bride, and those will take *gratis:* and *If any man take
away,* &c. for I testifie unto every MAN: Lest the last Error worse then
the first, when the bad Spirit tempting, and the woman.

Thus passing on, when the Spirit powred out a passage when opened
in Heaven, the Holy Prophets giving thanks, the time come of their
awakening, opened also the gates of Hell; such an uprore about Father 100
Times being cut off, those tydings the City setting on fire, the Nations
stung, their time come for[*th*] to be judged, (*Rev.*) the Devil wilde for
company, loses no time by Sea and Land, because his but short greatly
wrath.

On all sides thus, how the Mystery abounds of Iniquity, witnes our
wandring Stars, visible in this horrible Age, so many though charg'd
with abusing their Tolleration or Liberty of conscience: no wonder,

---

Line 80. **Sodom:** evil city; see Gen. 19.

Line 85. **Hyerglypick:** hieroglyphic; ancient Egyptian writing; difficult to decipher.

Line 87. **Sackcloth Liveries:** Sackcloth was coarse cloth used for mourning or penance; liveries were uniforms or insignia of employment.

Lines 94–95. **Come...Bride:** Rev. 22:17. **gratis:** without obligation (Latin).

Line 106. **wandring Stars:** Jude 13.

when higher Powers express no better use made of theirs, then by leas-
ing and scoffing to abuse the Holy Ghosts long-suffering, of whose
110 Apostacy and Erroneous actings, extending to delay of the day of Judgment, not sensible of our entrance thereinto: And detaining the Kingdom of Heaven from the true owners, By reason of certain Reserves or
doubtful Speeches, matter of Reality failing, our fluent *Tertullus's*
inform: Because said, *Of the day and hour knows no man,* and to Thieves
approach likened by night; hold forth, need not be beholding, or farther consolation expected for *Sion,* that fear causless, lest set at nought
their Trade, no farther watch requisite, teach the good man of the house
may take his ease, (*Mat.* 24.) as upon that mistake went abroad of that
Disciples not dying, taken for a second *Elias, Joh.* &c. Because of the
120 conceal'd day and hour, which matters not: Go on in deferring amendment, sufficient tokens come forth of the last Day, though pricking the
hearts of very Jews.

   Of which store not all expended, *Aarons* distillings, or her renowmed
anointing to the end of the world, <Herewith> tendred not by way of
ostentation or self ends, seasonable as looking towards *Sodom:* Shewing
<How> extant on Record in several Courts since *an.* 1663. and afore to
a year, a Month, and the very day, under her hand, foreshewed matters
then of highest nature of late executed as by so many years durance
undergone, since then when deem'd impossibilities or distraction.
130   As farther, by credible persons to be testified, no few about the City,
how accompanied with Miracles no inferior ones: Beside Devils, also
dumb Spirits cast out, most outrageous of all other, with as ample commission and convincing testimony, as ever *Moses* and *Elias,* if not a

---

Line 113. **Tertullus:** Tertullian, Roman theologian (c. A.D. 160–230).

Line 114. **Of…man:** Mark 13:32. Line 119. **taken…Elias:** see John 1:21.

Line 123. **distillings:** extractions or drippings. Aaron used his rod to turn the river Nile to
blood and to bring other plagues upon Egypt ; see Exod. 7.

Line 125. **looking towards Sodom:** When Lot's wife looked back towards Sodom, in
violation of God's command, God turned her into a pillar of salt (Gen. 19:26).

Line 126. **on…afore:** Lady Eleanor maintains that her prophecy about when Judgment
would occur could be found among legal records dating from 1633 and before.

Lines 133–34. **Moses…greater:** see Luke 9:30–35.

greater, except the Age become more deaf or unmoveable then that pillar of Salt, *Lots* metamorphosed wife, her Execution sign, or then our *Wyldshires* stonage wonder, as proper for *Pharaohs* of these days.

And as closes (displaying his pedigree off-spring of the Prophet *David,* saying, *I come shortly*) with that Benediction, *Blessed are they that do his Commandment,* that they may have right to the Tree of Life, whose Leaf withers not or changes: And may enter in through those everlasting gates, twelve of the new City, so Monethly Humiliations and other like Superstitions observ'd, no other then (*Dan.* 3.) when ye hear the sound, &c. *Whoso falleth not down,* &c. and *If any man buy or sell, save he that hath the mark of the Beast,* &c. alike acceptable, leaving the other undone, (to be excommunicated with Dogs, &c.) Be it ordain'd (even) upon pain of Death.

140

Deo sit gloria, &c.

From the Queens Bench.
2 September, &c.

FINIS.

Line 136. **Wyldshires stonage wonder:** Stonehenge is in Wiltshire.

Line 138. **I come shortly:** Rev. 22:7 (Geneva Bible).

Line 141. **Monethly Humiliations:** Lady Eleanor's description of the monthly fasts decreed by Parliament.

Line 147. **Deo sit gloria, &c:** Glory be to God, etc. (Latin).

Line 148. **Queens Bench:** Lady Eleanor's name for the prison which, in 1650, was called the Upper Bench. Its name was changed from King's Bench after the execution of Charles I in 1649; not since the reign of Elizabeth I (d. 1603) had it been the Queen's Bench.

Elijah the Tishbite, whose story appears in 1 Kings 17 to 2 Kings 2, enjoyed a special place among the prophets of the Old Testament: he was carried up to heaven in a chariot of fire, and his return was expected. When John the Baptist saw Jesus, he immediately thought Jesus was Elias, as Elijah is called in the New Testament. In this tract (Wing D1985), Lady Eleanor invokes her birth name, Elinor [Eleanor] Tichet [Touchet], to associate herself with Elijah the Tishbite. She also sees herself as the widow Zarephath or Sareptas, whose son was restored to life after she helped Elijah. The present edition of this tract is based on the copy in the volume of Lady Eleanor's tracts now in the Folger Shakespeare Library.

ELIJAH THE *TISHBITE'S* SUPPLICATION

When
Presented the likeness of Hand, &c.

(*Kings* 18.)

MARK 13.

But when ye shall see the Abomination of Desolation (or maketh desolate) *spoken of by Daniel the Prophet, standing where it ought not; Let him that readeth understand,* &c.

Title page. The title page is heavily annotated as follows: the word "was" has been written after the word "When" in the title; "a" has been inserted between "of" and "Hand"; after "Hand, &c." are written the words "for a prese[nt]"; below "Kings 18" are the words "As Likewise this Hand or monster Foot.", and in the right margin the words "(Dan9[ ] Abomina[ble] Armey (or [ ] in yᵉ origina[l]". The edge of the page is cut off.

Elias Intercession preferr'd.

O Lord of Hosts our God, *How long thou Lord of Sabbaths,* thus shall silence be in Heaven? How long whilest they suppose *like their sitting Gods* thou likewise *faln asleep,* slumbrest, or hearest not at all; as theirs *pursuing the Enemy, or on a march;* thy thundring Voyce refrain no longer: O this day be it known That <Thou> art God, I beseech thee, I thy Servant also, hear me for thy Words sake, above all hasten to Answer, hear me, bidden in thy Name but ask *Fire, fire, from the Wheels of thy Seraphin Throne,* vouchsafe the light of thy presence, a spark
10 thence to lick up at once or Reconcile (a Deluge such of Divisions) threatning no less then quenching Celestial flames; Thy Incense smoke to extinguish thus arm'd to re-edifie *Babel*-Rout these Gyants then as fared with those false Prophets both of one Spirit, Lo crying from morning to night too, *Let none escape either,* despising not the Birthright onely (sure Promises) But where thou blessest, filling up with inveterate hatred the measure of such Long-suffering, the World, made believe thy Spirit confined in the Hemisphere of their Studies; That the *Jews* how much blest, uncalled in such revolted times, where beside Confusions Mark set on the Age present, confounded alike as that first Generation
20 after the flood, their aspiring Towers Erecting when scattered, whether then turned *Turks* and *Saracens,* that Mother of Abomination, bear witness, *Mahomets* Blasphemous *ALCORAN* also, at *Pauls, Cum Privilegio* the Great Whore stilled well *Babylon,* never more Bruitish after once inlightened, the Night past, that *whoso runs may read,* not a tittle failing, whose presence likened to Lightning out of the East, even shining unto

---

Lines 8–11. **Fire...Throne:** cf. Ezek. 10:6 and 1 Kings 18:38. **spark...flames:** see 1 Kings 18:38. A handwritten annotation in the margin reads "wittnes B[ ] so many B[ ] August 23: 1651 That Thunder &c". Square brackets indicate material that is missing because the edge of the page is cut off.

Lines 12–13. **re-edifie Babel:** rebuild the tower of Babel (Gen. 11); or rebuild Babylon, the city of the Antichrist. A handwritten annotation in the margin reads "1651 As Mr. Love &c.:"   Perhaps the reference is to Christopher Love, a minister who was tried and executed in 1651 for plotting against the Commonwealth.

Line 20. **Towers Erecting:** the Tower of Babel. Line 21. **Saracens:** an Arabic people.

Line 22. **ALCORAN:** the Koran. **Pauls:** St. Paul's Cathedral in London. **Cum Privilegio:** with privilege (Latin); the phrase that appeared on books that had been licensed.

Line 25. **whose presence:** the Muslims.

the West, coming not short of the *Jews* Visitation, notwithstanding in as much want (if not more) to be reingrafted standing themselves, to *Babylon* lo returned.

As moreover witness to this day in the first place, without Baptism; supperless both; Nuld by them such a Deed of Gift bestowed on those Masters of Art our Rabbies, whereas in the Ark its first figure all at full Age, till after the Flood none born unto them; imposed nevertheless by these *Gog* and *Magog* Administrators on such, knowing *not the right hand from the left,* retaining other Character, none but hearsay; together with the other left off, or taken as some morning potion, and other like Tradition: armd with thy Brimston Bow, appeal to thee, O righteous Judge, thus where turned into Wormwood, the *Waters of Life* no few perishing that way the Springs of Justice answerable, if weighs not *Naboths* Case down *Ahabs* sword, instead of *Solomons* season'd in the strife of that now despised Sex, of *Turkish* slavery more then a taste partaking, Widows Estates put into the Ballance, in the Worlds state of Infancy, that if repentest at the heart, thou madest him not a Beast. Rather, leave it to the world [*also*] of such an Expression the extent how much since concerned in it, that in Expectation of *New Jerusalems* Nuptials were it not, better a Thousand times the Gentiles Church since the Apostles Age, to have perished in that foreshewed Siege and Destruction, not a *stone left on a stone,* also they as obdurate.

Which Petition wherein without farther Process, not like Attorneys BILLS, supposing to be Heard for their much Repetition.

Where lastly to be short with the time like that *little dark Cloud a Hand like,* to the waiting Prophet no small welcom token, as gathered therefrom these of Palmistries Science, extending to the present *Jubile* or Number of Fifty; so points to a Blow when as much attention lends

---

Lines 29–30. **without…both:** Baptism and Communion or the Supper were the two sacraments retained in the Protestant church. **Nuld:** annulled.

Line 31. **Rabbies:** rabbis. Line 33. **Gog and Magog:** see Rev. 20:8.

Line 36. **Brimston:** brimstone; sulphur; highly flammable substance; see Rev. 19:20.

Lines 38–39. **if weighs…Solomons:** Lady Eleanor contrasts Ahab's injustice to Naboth (1 Kings 21) with Solomon's just decision (1 Kings 3:16–28).

Line 47. **not a…stone:** Matt. 24:2. Lines 48–49. **Attorneys BILLS:** pleadings in a law case.

Line 52. **Palmistries Science:** prognostication or prediction.

to their Note, as they of such took notice sent from him, those *Baals* Sons the Image of God both alike, as the Baboon or such like theirs carried with the current of the Cormorant Times. And so far for them drinking at the Brooks side their farewel, Four hundred and fifty, for Fish and Fowl such an unexpected evening Banquent. And for the peoples hearts turned back, trusting in heartless Leaders, attended with that blessed *shower* expected as little so long after the Heavens restrained; and in *Israel no few Widows too, but unto none of them, save to Sareptas Widow of Sidon,* &c. As thereby that line behold measured the present Abominable Age its coming to it self again, cleansed the unparalleld Leprous Time.

60

October   By *Eleanor Tichet.*

FINIS.

Line 56. **Cormorant:** greedy.

Lines 57–59. A handwritten annotation in the margin reads "1651 [ ]anishd & this sold att Chelsye &c". The edge of the page is cut off.

In this tract (Wing D1996bA), Lady Eleanor expresses her hope that the fiftieth year of the century will be a biblical Jubilee (Lev. 25:10) and bring restitution. She parallels her own unfulfilled claims to inheritance to those of the godly, and the misdeeds of the Stawell family to those of Britain's rulers, the Stuarts. The present edition of *Her Jubilee* is based on the copy in the volume of Lady Eleanor's tracts now in the Folger Shakespeare Library. Apparently the only extant copy of the tract, it has no title page.

The Lady Eleanor Douglas, *Dowger,* *Her Jubiles Plea or Appeal,* A°&c.

Even [*she*] a Prisoner so many years that hath been for the Kingdom of Heaven; shews this Prisoner called to the Bar, Sir *John Stowel* Knight, He the Herald appointed for displaying her Title, as in this Looking-glass presented or appears; in the West Parts one of no mean Quality or Means: Four and twenty Knights since the Conquest, he the last of them: His Mother the onely Daughter in being of that Queen, bears that Virgin Name, *Eliz.* The said Prisoner aged *November* last, Fifty years; moreover well known, whose Grandfather Sir *John Stowel*, unhappily that had his hands in blood, *&c.* Had two wives living at once, begetting no Common Suits at Law, between the Divorced's Suing for Dower after his Decease, and others of the Name to carry the Inheritance, *&c.*   10

Title. **Dowger:** dowager; a widow who enjoyed property or title from her deceased husband. **A°&c:** In the year etc (Latin); perhaps a shortening of a more complete title.

Line 2. **called to the Bar:** brought into court for judgment. **Sir John Stowel:** Stowell or Stawell (1599–1662); a Somerset gentleman whose mother was Lady Eleanor's sister. He was tried for treason in July 1650.

Line 3. **the Herald:** The College of Heralds oversaw claims to gentility and to titles of nobility. **her Title:** her claim to rank and property; also the recognition of her claim.

Line 4. **in the West Parts:** Somerset, Stowell's home, was in the west of England.

Line 5. **Four...Conquest:** Stowell's family, like the monarchs of England, included twenty-four holders of the title since 1066.

Lines 8–9. **whose Grandfather...wives:** He divorced his first wife (see G.D. Stawell, *A Quantock Family* [Taunton, 1910], pp. 71ff.).

Line 11. **Dower:** the part of a deceased husband's estate which by law goes to the widow.

Thus paraliz'd here with the *Stuarts* Line, the late *Charls* aged *Novembr.* 48. *Anno redempti*, 1648. He since the Conquest the four and twentieth Crowned of these Western Isles, whose father (that made it death in like case) King *Ja:* had himself his *Leah* and *Rachel* also, two Wives, lived with both; the first, she Daughter of one Sir *Peter Yong:* His Son *Charls* about a Moneth yonger then Sir *Archibald Douglas deceased*, *&c.* to one of his own name, who married her as K. *Ja:* ever disclaiming

20   that of *Stuart, &c.* alway Stiling the said Sir *Peter* his Father with due reverence every way; whose eldest Son the Dean of *Winchester,* K. *James* his Executor made, *&c.* about a month before his death, appointing out of his Revenues about 10000 *per annum* for the said Sir *A: Douglas;* with no pleasing Aspect by the *Buckinghams* look'd upon.

And how it hath succeeded, witness such slips what root have taken: His eldest Son *Henry* at full age cut off: His eldest Daughter a Fugitive: Her eldest drowned, *&c.* as better for him too, then his person prostituted so to the Iron rods lash: That token bequeath'd his Son a Milstone in the place, even he and his extirpated, with *William* Conquerer, Bas-

30   tard as began, concluded with *Charls, &c.* By whose unseasonable Ele-

---

Line 13. **paraliz'd:** paralleled.

Line 14. **Anno redempti, 1648:** in the year of redemption (Latin); Charles's execution in January fell in 1648, i.e., 1649.

Line 15. **Western Isles:** the British Isles.

Line 16. **King Ja:...Rachel:** Leah and Rachel were the two wives of Jacob (Gen. 29); Jacobus is the Latin for James. Lady Eleanor charges that King James had two wives, but there seems to be no substantiation for this claim.

Line 17. **Sir Peter Yong:** Sir Peter Young (1544–1628); a Scotsman who tutored King James I and was the grandfather of Sir Archibald Douglas.

Line 18. **His Son Charls...Douglas:** If this claim is true, Archibald Douglas, Lady Eleanor's second husband, should have succeeded King James to the throne rather than Charles.

Line 21. **Dean of Winchester:** John Young (1585–1654).

Line 24. **the Buckinghams:** George Villiers, first duke of Buckingham and favorite of King James and then King Charles, procured titles and grants for many members of his family.

Line 26. **His eldest Son Henry:** James I's son, Henry, Prince of Wales, died in 1612, while his father was still king. **His eldest...a Fugitive:** Elizabeth, queen of Bohemia, was exiled from the Rhine Palatinate and Bohemia in 1620, during the Thirty Years' War (1618–1648).

Line 27. **Her eldest drowned:** Frederick Henry died in 1629 at the age of 15.

Lines 29–30. **William Conquerer, Bastard:** Before he conquered England in 1066, William I was known as William the Bastard.

vated thoughts, others bidden be wise: The *Germain* Empires Ebb, for his forewarning who had, and superfluous many words. Lastly, But put it their proper Case; likewise in those Courts of theirs, whether require not of Tenants, an Oath of Fealty, without questioning Possessions, Title of those owners (as whereunto referred) suffices point of Law; so for deciding other-like doubts: Bars striving with that of Justice, one or the other, the Sword with two Edges.

December, &c.

FINIS.

Line 31. **The Germain Empires Ebb:** The Peace of Westphalia, 1648, which ended the Thirty Years' War, reduced the power of the emperor and increased the power of the constituent states of the empire.

Line 34. **Fealty:** loyalty.

In this tract (Wing D1995), Lady Eleanor tells the story of her arrest and imprisonment in London's Wood Street Compter in 1646, when Thomas Paine, the London printer who had printed her *Prophetia de die* (Wing D2005) in 1644 and may have printed others of her tracts, sued her for debt. Citing the error in her name on one of the legal documents in the case to illustrate the corruption of the English judicial system, she discusses biblical texts, such as Matt. 8, Mark 5, and Luke 4, where naming (or distinguishing between good and evil) leads to Judgment—condemnation of the evil and healing of the good. The present edition of *Hells Destruction* is based on the copy in the volume of Lady Eleanor's tracts now in the Folger Shakespeare Library. Its pages eleven to sixteen differ slightly from those in the copy in the Houghton Library, Harvard University (shelf number *E65 D7455 B652t).

HELLS DESTRUCTION.
BY The Lady *Eleanor Douglas.*

Apocal.

Behold, the Devil shall cast some of you into Prison, that you may be tryed; and you shall have tribulation ten days, &c.

Epigraph. **Behold...ten days:** Rev. 2:10.

333

Hells Destruction.

Behold, the Devil shall cast some of you into Prison, that ye may be tryed;
and ye shall have Tribulation Ten days, &c. Apoc.

Most Learned and Honored Judges, with whom so precious restles
Time, of which as who can be over frugal, shunning therefore Multi-
plicity; long process but wearisom to the wise: Seeing then our Laws
how ballanced with Gods Law its profound Precepts, said to be founded
thereon, and Reason in its purity consonant thereto, otherwise hath
with it no affinity.

10   Emboldens to present this Paradice Posey, durable presidents which
too circumspect wherein ye cannot be, hereof as ensues.

Adam that first Lord Chief Justice or Judge, before whom *the Lord*
God brought every Creature formed of the Earth, to see what he would call
them; and whatsoever he called every living Creature, that was the name
thereof: of a certain admits of no wrong or contrary Names whatsoever
in any Courts of Record to be legal or answered unto. As these inform,
accords with the former, the Judge of quick and dead; where demanded
first, *What his Name was?* before obtain'd a pass for that Baptized Herd
the Gentiles Prototype doubtless, the Devil his Godfather; who made

20   answer, saying, *Legion, for they were many;* he resident (as it were) in
Hell, among the Graves distracted, *&c.*

Thus as we see and know irrational Creatures, these of several kindes

---

Line 4. **Most…Judges:** a prisoner's appeal.

Line 8. **consonant thereto:** in harmony and agreement with.

Line 9. **affinity:** relationship.

Line 10. **Paradice Posey:** a bunch of flowers or poetry from paradise.

Lines 12–13. **Adam…every Creature:** see Gen. 2:19–20.

Lines 15–16. **admits…Record:** Errors in names were one basis for legal challenge in the
English courts.

Lines 17–20. **the Judge…dead:** see Acts. 10:42. A sidenote printed in the margin reads
"Consisting of about 6000 Foot and 700 Horse, the length of Times Foot, the distracted Time
Aged near 6000 years, he Legion also, &c. The Dutch stiled Gravs and Boors their late loss put
into the Reckoning, Mat. 8. Mark 5. Luk. &c." Gravs and Boors were nobles and peasants,
respectively.

retain their proper Names; and very Devils not debarred theirs. Nevertheless that Dominion have over them, Man the *Little World,* to Angels not much inferior, deemed no little Wonder, as though confined to a lower Region then they, suffer our selves, worse then Bruits undergo Names enjoyned utterly false, instanced as here the dead childe like in stead of the living laid in her Bosom, disputed in *Solomons* presence; whereby no less then bereft both of her good Name and Liberty, witness this their erroneous Warrant of Arrest, *Ecce vera copia.*   30

Eleanor Lady *Davers* alias *Douglas,* committed to *Woodstreet-Compter* by *Steedman* Officer to the Lord Major (*July* 17.) 1646. As true that might have stiled her *Lord Major,* &c. for any relation between *Davers* and *Douglas:* But by a Non-sence *Alias* a seeming connexion far from Holy Writs Example, Slime in stead of Morter, and Brick-bats for firm Stone, with it dispenses not; Confusion of that consequence.

Whence follows next *Simon Magus* alias *Peter,* &c. Saints and Devils become fellows; also Fool and *Racha:* what not? as out of the path of his Commandments: of warrants that latitude allowed them, one Name because lighted on, matters not how many false beside, so at all with   40 Logicks definition or Reason, agrees not, authorized by the proviso (*Alias*) the meaning of it; sometime or otherwise *&c.* though she never afore at any time called by the aforesaid Name belonging to another Tribe or Family; *He that calls the Stars by their Names* (as it were) Male and Female, those lights: where joyns names, no such Bills of Divorce tolerates neither what Antiquity or Custom either occasions, as referred to those judicious, the Sequel of what concernment.

Lines 24–25. **Man...much inferior:** see Ps. 8:5.

Lines 27–28. **the dead childe...presence:** see 1 Kings 3:16–27.

Line 29. **good Name:** cf. Prov. 22:1. Line 30. **Ecce vera copia:** Behold a true copy (Latin).

Line 31. **Eleanor...Douglas:** the name on the warrant for Lady Eleanor's arrest.

Line 35. **Holy Writs Example:** the biblical example in contrast to the writ for her arrest.

Lines 35–36. **Slime...firm Stone:** cf. Gen. 11:3.

Line 37. **Simon Magus alias Peter:** an absurd pairing; see Acts 8:9–20 and Matt. 16:18–19.

Line 38. **Fool and Racha:** absurd pair; see Matt. 5:22. Line 44. **He...Names:** see Ps. 147:4.

Lastly wherwith even whose additionals *Abraham* & *Sarahs,* consists but of a letter both alike old and new consenting in one. Also *Paul* for
50 *Saul,* one so cautious that way, witness in mentioning the said Patriarks Blessing as well observes, saying, *Not Seeds, as of many,* &c. *but Seed,* &c.

And so much for that, *They would have said,* &c. in stead of *Alius:* All they can alledge or say for themselves so contradictory to Sense and Verity, better to be justified by some blinde slow Belly *Cretians* such Vipers, then by those interested in the Name of Christians, who would be unwilling to Subscribe to any other.

And hereupon of her false Imprisonment undergone; so many years, *If when the cause of the Law ceases, then ceases the Law it self:* wherefore
60 when the Adversary detains the work, for which the Bond was entred into, occasioned it, why should he keep it, and her person in hold both: or by what Justice and Equity stands such an Execution any longer afoot or in force, she having been since put to the charge for Imprinting the same all over, for which was acknowledged the said Obligation of Sixty pounds, no benefit whereby accrewing to her, by a certain Printer, one *Pain,* upon whose importunity and protestation 'twas obtained.

Another *Quære* thus, since Scandalous Names bear Action to be termed Bankrupt, *&c.* why unjust Cut-Throat Actions so many as the Adversary pleases, no Redress in that case; as amounting to Hundreds
70 no few by this Broken Printer and his Consorts, the Burthen of them, no short furrows plowed, *&c.* By City unmerciful *Adonizebeks,* unmindeful of his Confession, *as he had done, God had requited him, Threescore and ten had dismembred them,* &c. And *Abimelech* how rewarded, *doing execution on his Seventy Brethren,* a woman his Executioner (*Judges* 9.)

Lines 48–50. **Abraham...Saul:** Although their names have some of the same letters, the individuals are very different.

Lines 51–52. **the said...Seed, &c.:** see Gen. 22:17.

Line 53. **They...Alius:** an argument about the wording of the writ for Lady Eleanor's arrest.

Line 55. **some...Cretians:** see Titus 1:12. Line 59. **If when...it self:** see Gal. 2:16–19.

Line 66. **importunity:** annoying persistence.

Line 67. **Quære:** question (Latin). **Action:** legal action.

Line 71. **Adonizebeks:** Adonibezek; see Judg. 1:5–7.

laying on himself (as it were) violent hands, *caused one to slay him,* not impertinent here.

The Milstones lighting on his Head, unominous either to the Press, with *those several Tables under which so many fed by him, sealed with his Thumbs and Great-Toes,* to unmerciful Executions of all kindes which extends. 80

And what Figs and Grapes such Thistles and Thorns produces, proceeding therewith the plot of this Cut-Throat Fellow; which aforesaid Arrest in his own House, who to draw her thither fain'd had lost the Copy, *&c.* The ready way for compassing their desperate Ends, supposed in having her life at mercy, being sent to the Compter, lock'd into her Chamber by the Keeper: Not long after (she all unready, *&c.*) between two of them carried down thence, instantly shut and bolted was into the Dungeon-Hole, Hells Epitomy, in the dark out of call or cry, searching first her Coats pockets, at least expecting she should have made some proffer, *&c.* Frustrate that way, with the Key took away the 90 Candle, there left on the wet floor to take up her lodging, beyond any draught, by so many poysonous Vermin harbored: Like disquieted Spirits setting up fearful several Notes, coursing about, *&c.*

About an hour after, when as no need of Sun, Moon or other (*Anno* 1646. *July* 17.) whereof notice Extraordinary taken about the City, they brought her again to a Chamber, That Night till day break, the Heavens without intermission flashing out Lightnings, as Noonday; The Element like a Casemate standing open, without Thunder at all, or any Rain, those continued fireworks notwithstanding.

Which time Twelve-Moneth that *Adonizebek* the Lord Major was 100 committed to the Tower, and his Brethren (*Anno* 47.) when the Armies unexpected arrival at the *Whitsontide, &c.*

As for the perfideous Printer how hapned with him, soon spued out

---

Line 76. **impertinent:** irrelevant.

Line 82. **Cut-Throat Fellow:** Paine, the printer.

Line 90. **proffer:** present or offer; bribe.

Line 98. **Casemate:** vaulted chamber, built in the ramparts of a fortress for defense.

Line 103. **perfideous:** perfidious; treacherous.

of House and Home, his Wife within few days dead, in whose Brothers unhappy Name the Bond taken, he dead also.

And so when the smoaky Bottomless Pit to be opened, oppressed Captives, when seasonable for Elevating their Heads, not to despair longer, *Signs in Heaven and Earth, Sea and Waters* as recommended, contribute their testimony, no obscure Tokens, like *the floods voice utter-*
110 *ing theirs,* unbound as it were, *clapping their hands for company;* perplexed people at their Wits-end (*Luke* 21.) on all sides in that unparalleld Thraldom, That *better unborn,* then the Uncircumcised their Commissions date expired.

Of which shortned Days for the Elects cause thus, not unparalleld with the ten *Persecutions, Ten days shall have Tribulation;* The Mysterious Beasts Reign, Crown'd or Mitre'd with *his Ten Horns,* no less then charged with *open Blasphemy, against the Tabernacle,* the presence of God (to wit) &c. *opening no narrow Throat,* repaid *Lex talionis,* that *leads into Captivity,* &c. *Rev.* 13.

120 And so much for the year of Redemption, *lifting up your heads,* &c. Tokens of it likened to the Springs infallible Messengers of Summers approach, *the Fig-tree and the rest,* proclaimed to be by Heavenly Heralds, higher Powers that bids beware the Tree, shaken like those Boughs, *&c.* so to expect fruit forbids it, of the Nations unspeakable travel, until those wonders, *&c.*

Where not to be drowned in Forgetfulness, our New Star in *Cassiopei,* the French taking essay of its influence, that *Herodian* Massacre not long after it, seen 74 years before the year 1644. our day of Reckonings forerunner; of which Great-Seal day *John heard the number*

Line 112. **Thraldom:** slavery. Line 114. **the Elect:** those predestined for salvation.

Line 116. **Mitre'd:** wearing the cap of a bishop.

Line 118. **Lex talionis:** the law of retaliation (Latin).

Line 122. **the Fig-tree…rest:** see Luke 21:29–31. Line 124. **travel:** travail; labor, suffering.

Line 127–28. **Cassiopei:** Cassiopeia, northern constellation in which a new star had appeared in 1572. **the French…after it:** On St. Bartholomew's Day, 1572, Catholic conspirators massacred French Protestants. Lady Eleanor compares this event to Herod's massacre of all children in Bethlehem and its environs who were two years old and younger (Matt. 2:16).

Line 129. **Great-Seal day:** Judgment Day; see Rev. 7:3.

(*Rev.* 7.) even sealed the year of God *Anno Dom.* 44. observing the 130 motion of the former, that in the East 74 years afore *Jerusalems* Judgment, *sworn in his wrath* as it were *By Heaven,* &c. the numbred Time of our Captivity or coming out of *Heathen Babylon,* of whose *Habeas Corpus* Writ out of the smoky *Abyss,* (Rev. 9.) commanded *not to harm any, but those not sealed* (viz.) *marked as for Murther and Theft,* ver. 20. And for mysteries those *Oracles* however grown out of request among our *Rabbies,* prefixt or set times said to be but a certain time for an uncertain, & the like, questionless of highest concernment those undervalued most, because flatters not or torments them, termed *wilde notions and brainsick,* &c. as much attentive and grateful *for precious* 140 *things cast before such:* suffices these, and like that Dispute about *her having five* (Joh.) Bidden *Go call her Husband:* whence follows, if *Davers* one, then (*Alias*) otherwise called *Douglas,* he none of hers either. As farthermore for their farewel, tedious Apprentiships canceld forthwith; together with that granted, *What is not true is false; Ergo,* Libel bastard slips, and sinister actions imposed on his people, unlawful to be fathered on Gods Word, his Law thereon either erring not in a tittle. *Easter* 1651.

FINIS.

Lines 131–132. **74 years… Judgment:** see Jer. 25:12.

Lines 133–37. **Habeas Corpus:** writ used to require authorities to explain why they are holding a prisoner. A sidenote printed in the margin reads "Shewing they have a King over them, &c. (of the Roman Faction) where those cald Cavaleers or Royalists, and coyn Dollors and Half Crown Pieces adored (Dæmoniæ) (he heard the Number of them) with Pieces of Ordnance, the Fleet or Navies preparation by those hideous Hieroglyphicks signified, &c." Dæmoniæ are idols or demons; see Rev. 9:20. Ordnance is artillery.

Line 135. **ver. 20:** Lady Eleanor's citation should be Rev. 9:21.

Line 137. **Rabbies:** Lady Eleanor identifies England with Israel, and thus clergy with rabbis.

Line 141. **her:** the woman Jesus met at the well (John 4:17–18).

Citing the letters "A" and "O" which link her with Almighty and Omnipotent God, in this tract (Wing D1975) Lady Eleanor bestows her blessing or benediction on Oliver Cromwell, whose initials she also believed had prophetic significance. The other editions of this tract (Wing D1975A and D1976) differ only in their title pages. The present edition of *Benediction* is based on a copy in the British Library (shelf number 1389.g.49).

THE BENEDICTION.
FROM THE A:lmighty O:mnipotent.

I have an Errand to thee O: Captain.

2 Kings 9. 5.

Title. **A:lmighty and O:mnipotent:** also Alpha and Omega (Rev. 1:8).

For the Armies GENERAL, His EXCELLENCY.

MY LORD,

Your Interest in the Nations unparaleld Troublesom Times: The Flaming Sword for *expelling the Man* in your hand, which Crowns with no Inferior Honor that Name of Yours: Hereof by her Hand a touch presented. Derived from his own, namely, *A. & O.* Letters of no mean Latitude: Armed beside with his Sword: Sun and Moon when as stood in Admiration, witness [ ] their Golden Characters, stiled Eyes and Horns of the Lamb, *&c. Their voice gone out into all Lands*, Psal. (Rev. *5.*) Like
10 theirs here, every one when the fifty days at an end, heard in his proper Language, *&c.* (*Acts 2.*) The Prophet *Joel* as foresaw and others: By whom Decypher'd that Generals Thundring Donative his the Crown and Bended Bowe (*Rev. 6.*) That Seal or Box of Nard opened; as much to say, *O: Cromwel,* Renowned be Victorious so long as Sun Moon continues or livever.

Anagram, *Howl Rome:* And thus with one voice, *come and see, O: C: Conquering and to Conquer went forth.*

My Lord,
OCtob. 28.   Your Humble Servant,
20 A°*1651.*   ELEANOR.

Lines 1–20. The base text of *The Benediction* is printed in italics with roman font for emphasis; the fonts are reversed here for ease of reading.

Lines 3–4. **The Flaming Sword:** cf. Gen. 3:24. Line 7. **Armed…Moon:** cf. Rev. 12:1.

Lines 8–9. **witness [ ]:** At this point in the tract are printed symbols: a circle with a dot in the center, and a semi-circle; they may represent an eye and a horn or the sun and the moon. They also resemble the letters O and C, Oliver Cromwell's initials. **Eyes…Lamb:** "O C" also could represent the eyes and horns of the lamb; the Lamb standing in the midst of the elders had seven horns and seven eyes (Rev. 5:6).

Line 10. **the fifty days:** the time between Easter and Pentecost.

Line 13. **Nard:** aromatic plant.

Line 16. **Howl Rome:** a rough anagram for Cromwell; the prophets frequently exhorted the sinners to howl (e.g., Isa. 13:6).

Lady Eleanor wrote this tract (Wing D2007), which had fifty-two pages in its original edition, when she was a prisoner in the Fleet. In it she addresses both her own situation and Britain's. She uses the parable of the talents (Matt. 25: 14–30) to treat the theme of restitution more fully than she had in *The restitution of reprobates* (1644; Wing D2008), in *Writ of Restitution* (1648; Wing D2019—page 239 in the present edition), and in tracts such as *Before the Lords Second Coming* (1650; Wing D1974—page 317 in the present edition) and *Her Jubilee* (1650; Wing D1996bA—page 329 in the present edition). She had emphasized restitution in 1650 because it was the Jubilee year, which, according to the Old Testament (Lev. 25:10), was supposed to be a year of restitution. The preface of *Restitution of Prophecy* bears the date 25 December; its conclusion shows Candlemas (2 February). Both dates, the celebration of the birth of Christ and the Feast of the Purification of the Virgin Mary, marked a woman's (Mary's) role in restitution (by giving birth to Jesus). The present edition of this tract is based on the copy in the Bodleian Library, Oxford (shelf number 12.0.1336[4]). The Rota Press published an edition in 1978.

THE RESTITUTION OF PROPHECY; THAT BURIED TALENT TO BE REVIVED.

By the Lady *Eleanor*.

John 16.
He shall glorifie me; for he shall receive of mine, and shall shew unto you.

To the Reader:

This *Babe*, object to their scorn, for speaking the *truth*, informing of things future, notwithstanding thus difficult to be *fathered* or *licensed*. That *incission* to the *quick*, hath under gone; without their *Benediction*, in these plain *Swathe-bands*, though commended unto thy hands.

No spurious *off-spring* of *Davids*, but the *Son* of *peace*. This *Oblivions Act, Messenger* thereof. *Be of good cheer, O my people*, (Isai. 40.) *O ye Prophets*, saith your *God*, Tell her, That her *Travel* is at an end; Her *Offence* is pardoned, our *Jubiles deliverance:* Sirs, to be plain, as in the
10 first place, *His Commission*. He first of the *new Prophet;* so his and hers both: She the last of the *old.* Confesseth likewise, or beareth record of his *presence, Born in the flesh;* of whose *Kingdom* no end.

Although not in a *Stable* brought forth, yet a *place* like *restless;* a hard choice between *extreams* or *streits* of that kinde to distinguish. No *Inferior Prison,* or of obscure *Denomination;* whereof that street carrieth the *name:* not the least, honored with no less then the *Temple* for one.

Where belonging to passages of *Inns;* The one frequented all Hours, and Drinking, not more free then the others darksom *grates close;* famished there no few. But requisit *Bridges,* and the like, the true *Narrow way*
20 (by suffering) *that leads to life:* From him a proper *passage* or mention. Straits of the *Virgins-Womb* had passed; besides Seafaring-persons his followers in that way not unexperienced, afore arrive the *welcome Haven.*

And so far *Reader,* for these excluded their *Approbation,* where paral-

---

Line 2. **This Babe:** Lady Eleanor's prophecy of Judgment for England.

Line 3. **licensed:** having received official permission for publication.

Line 4. **That incission...quick:** the birthing or publishing process. **Benediction:** blessing.

Line 5. **Swathe-bands:** swaddling bands; a baby's wrapping.

Lines 6–7. **spurious:** illegitimate. **Oblivions Act:** An act of oblivion was a formal means, especially in political cases, of declaring offenses forgotten.

Line 8. **Travel:** travail; labor, suffering.

Line 10. **His Commission...Prophet:** her babe or book's message.   Line 14. **streits:** straits.

Lines 14–16. **No Inferior Prison...name:** the Fleet in London. **the Temple:** in Jerusalem, built by Solomon; also the Inner and Middle Temples, the societies which trained lawyers, located along Fleet Street.

Lines 17–18. **The one...close:** Fleet Street and the Fleet Prison.

Lines 19–20. **the true Narrow way:** see Matt. 7:13–14.

lel'd the *Broad-way, Ebrieties* leading to destruction: Those *Gates* put into the reckoning, and such holds *chained* up, *&c.* and for this *nonplus* also; unwilling to transgress the bounds of a *Preface,* Shewing as by those *Vigilent Shepherds* (published) a *Saviour* to Them *peace* then required likewise a *pass* for these from ours as appears, witnessed thus, *I give thee charge in the sight of God. which quickneth all things,* &c. *That thou keep the Commandment until the appearing of our Lord Jesus Christ;*   30 which appearing in his time, he shall shew, *That he is King of Kings, and Lord of Lords,* (1 Tim. 6.) So in another place, *For the testimony of Jesus,* in the Spirit of Prophecy, *King of Kings, and Lord of Lords,* the Holy Spirits presence namely: But arrogancy begetting incureable *blindness,* these savored but as *non scence,* not material. *Galio* cared for none of these *matters, &c.*

December 25. The Fleet.

Postscript.

But blessed is he not offended, &c.

Line 24. **Broad-way:** servant of Lady Eleanor's brother, Mervin, Lord Audeley, second earl of Castlehaven. Castlehaven was accused of being an accessory to Broadway's rape of Lady Audeley, Castlehaven's wife. **Ebrieties:** intoxications.

Line 25. **nonplus:** puzzle. Line 28. **those Vigilent Shepherds:** see Luke 2: 8–11.

Lines 28–30. **I give…Christ:** 1 Tim. 6:13–14. Line 36. **Galio:** see Acts 18:14–17.

Line 39. **blessed is he not offended:** see Matt. 11:6.

MATT. 25.

The Book of the Restitution of Prophesie:
the great Account, *&c.*

The secrets of the Gospel under Allegories covered and Parables, precious Leaven, generality or scope whereof reflects, although on the day of Judgements severe account, unknown day and hours reserve: Nevertheless, days preceding their proper Lesson, a warning piece for them.

Which *Unum Necessarium* inestimable Pearl, the Kingdom of Heavens purchase, that Manna, the unknown Bdellium likened to: who sold 50   all to compass it, requires Artificials none either, presumes cannot be frustrate, or by all troden under foot: of which an essay as ensues tendred, as to watch all or wait: so to beware if wise, how they quench the Spirit, where not unlike his dream of good consisted and bad, both because the thing Established repeatable not; then their Decree, much less to be changed, *&c. Dan.*

That consists not in meat and drink those Externals, unto a wedding likened so many Handmaids, his Kingdoms Epitomy at hand, or forthwith to appear Virgins, their's the priority: five perfection of Numbers: Her quickning time, till when concealed, *&c.* (*Luke*) a prime period, 60   alluding to the Sences.

Five were wise, other five were foolish; no lame similitude, ten in number, its full time (as it were) or reckoning had gone out: To whom how befel those that were out of the way; saying, *Our Lamps are out or quenched,* dreamt not an answer that way insufficient a point of what consequence to say, They had not thought or supposed, *&c.* cast in the teeth with Spiritual Chandleries an Item thereof.

Lines 44–90. The base text for this section is in italic font with roman emphasis; fonts have been reversed here for ease of reading. Fonts follow the base text again beginning at line 91.

Line 45. **Leaven:** that which makes bread rise; see Matt. 13:33.

Line 48. **Unum Necessarium:** one necessary thing (Latin).

Line 49. **Bdellium:** gum resin similar to myrrh; see Gen. 2:12.

Lines 53–55. **his dream...changed:** see Dan 4. Line 58. **Virgins...Numbers:** see Matt. 25:1–12.

Line 59. **Her:** the Virgin Mary's; see Luke 2.

Line 61. **similitude:** comparison, symbol, allegory. Line 63. **Our...out:** see Matt. 25: 3–8.

Line 66. **Chandleries:** makers and sellers of candles, also of provisions more generally.

In what obscurity all without the Spirit manifesting without contradiction as appears: *The Bridegroom while tarried all slumbred and slept, bidden be watchful: Therefore watch, for ye know neither the day nor hour,* &c. as that for another, *Could ye not one hour refrain:* our caveat bids, *sleep on,* who allow the Spirit not transmitted beyond the Primative bounds, what real demonstration soever, as if any thing impossible with him: and thus the blinde conducting the blinde, emblems what postare Synods and Church-men found in: How provided of the wedding garment: when that summons, *Come now for all things are ready:* The Spirit and Bride, saying, *Come, gates of Paradice wide open, no more curse,* &c. *the Tree of Life,* attain'd its Maturity, living waters *gratis Aurum Potabile* as free, no longer to be fasting then.

And so much for their farewel restless good night, *Lord, Lord,* &c. knows their voices as much as they discern (read by them) the Prophets theirs, *&c.* unworthy of the oderiffrous Mariage-gloves, or a taste of those transcendant Confections, even departed from the faith: *Depart ye follish Galatians, who hath bewitched you:* wherewith verily, The Kingdom of Heaven expresly unto what Nation or Kingdom to be revealed obvious as those Solemnities: under the notion of a Wedding, Revels not returnable often: When as some supernatural anointings or Conception, as by that Mid nights Alarm shaddowed forth, in due time administred: After the way of old illustrated, when the Word of the Lord came unto them, Recorded in such a Year of their Reign, and in what Moneth; pointed to a Jubile's moiety, *Five times five.* The years prime *Anniversary Feast,* blessed throughout all Generations: her Wedding-day; faithful Handmaid the Virgin *Mary,* her Five and twentieth of the Moneth, as bears date 1625. Year of Grace: His very Proclaimed

---

Line 68. **The Bridegroom…slept:** Matt. 25:5.

Line 70. **caveat:** warning. Line 73. **the blinde…blinde:** see Matt. 15:14.

Lines 74–76. **provided…garment:** see Matt. 22:11–12. **The Spirit…Come:** Rev. 22:17.

Line 77. **gratis Aurum Potabile:** free gold that can be drunk (Latin).

Line 81. **oderiffrous:** odoriferous; sweet-smelling. Lines 82–83. **Depart… you:** Gal. 3:1.

Line 90. **a Jubiles…five:** a jubilee is fifty; its half, twenty-five.

Lines 91–93. **Anniversary…Moneth:** Lady Day, the Feast of the Annuciation of the Virgin Mary, was 25 March, the beginning of the English year in the seventeenth century. **His:** Charles I's.

Reign, Coronation accompanied with unhappy *Nuptials:* He aged 25. she Fifteen, *&c.* graceless voice, Twenty four from the Conquests Bastared Generation (compleat *Anno* 24.) marched with a Yoak-fellow; and could not come in five Yoke of Oxen of his *Oxford* Commons an item, must attend on her Ladiship, roaring Sabbaths Mid-nights works: No Stranger subject to be unmaskt, and Farmer Bishopricks weekly
100 Alarms.

While she as free with her impostures to communicate our *Heavenly Saviors* homage to Idol blocks doted on painted Popets, for whose name, wo to the House suffices the Dogs in the same place licking his Blood: Moreover as in his Maps Circumference contained, of unhappy memory, Her five years Fiery Bloody days, of the name such knows none charming Letanies (*good Lord, good Lord*) they know not what, *ave gratia,* &c. *Pater Noster* and Creed alike intelligible, to her sorrow Matched in her after days.

By her *Virgin Sister* succeeded, in the Five and fortieth of whose
110 unmatchable Reign was Interred at the *Virgins Annunciation;* &c. those plentious times farewel: The *Bridegroom Sun* and his *Virgin Spouse,* parting the hours ushering the *Obsequies.*

So proceeding with the subsequent parable, whose Divine Nature as descended to a habit of Flesh: So by this way of Domestique Affairs,

---

Lines 95–96. **she:** Henrietta Maria, the French (Catholic) princess, whom Charles married. **Twenty four...Bastared:** Charles I was the twenty-fourth monarch after William I, who was known as "the Bastard" prior to conquering England in 1066.

Line 97. **could not...Oxen:** see Luke 14:19. **his Oxford Commons:** the royalist Parliament.

Lines 98–99. **her Ladiship...unmaskt:** the queen's court entertainments (masques) described as witchcraft.

Lines 101–2. **she as free...blocks:** an allegation that the queen worshipped idols.

Lines 103–4. **the Dogs...Blood:** see 1 Kings 21:19.

Line 105. **Her five years...days:** Mary Tudor's reign (1553–58), when many Protestants were burned as heretics.

Line 106. **Letanies:** litanies; prayers.

Line 107. **ave...Pater Noster:** Latin prayers beginning "hail gracious one" and "Our Father."

Lines 109–10. **By her...Annunciation:** Elizabeth reigned for forty-four years and died in March at the time of the Feast of the Annunciation; she succeeded Mary Tudor.

Line 112. **Obsequies:** funeral rites.

unto the vulgar capacity condescend: the Kingdom of Heavens Title to coroberate, presidents produce: of the present the five Talents (to wit) in what Reign.

Where those three of no obscure quality: Their Lord as though returned from a far Country, had acquired some great Prize or Victory, otherwise some Merchants return. 120

Called in the first place a prime Peer of the Land, so highly preferred *Audeley* E: of *Castlehaven,* even to hold up his Hand at the Bar, with two of his Servants Arraigned and Excuted all three on this wise.

He charged with the Rape, a Page protested at the last cast, a Virgin came into his Lords Service, and went away a Virgin thence. The other an Irish Papist, a Vagrant: The Footman said, had he thought Lords of the Councel bade him speak for the King; have served him so, would otherwise been advised for his Pardon called on St. *Dennis,* whose Oath taken contrary to Law and Justice, refusing an Oath of Allegiance: As Hers not at all, upon whose Accusation before the Privy Counsel; taken 130 away her Husbands life, that in Court appeared neither that day.

Anne Strange Heretrix, of that extirpated House, Isle of *Man:* In which preferred Bill, this long Proces wherein shuned, Anatomized that mankinde Grandams mery, and hers like Daughter, *&c.*

As shews in the day of his wrath, wounding even Kings, *&c. Sit thou on my right,* &c. thy Sentence (as much to say) until upon them be accomplished (*Revel.* 13.) *Even the brutish Beast wounded in the head,* his mortal wound: *And Hers* (*Rev.*17.) *where one of the seven Angels which had the seven vials* (namely the last of them) saying, *Come, I will shew*

Line 118. **those three:** the servants in the parable of the talents (Matt. 25:14–30).

Lines 121–22. **a prime...Castlehaven:** Lady Eleanor's brother, tried and executed for sodomy and accessory to rape in 1631.

Line 124. **a Page:** one of Castlehaven's servants.

Line 126. **an Irish...Vagrant:** the other of Castlehaven's servants.

Line 128. **called on St. Dennis:** demonstrated his Catholicism by praying to a saint.

Line 132. **Hers:** Anne Strange, Lady Eleanor's sister-in-law and Castlehaven's wife, whose testimony was important in his conviction.

Lines 133–34. **shuned:** perhaps shunned. **that mankinde...Daughter:** Anne Strange's mother was also grandmother to Lady Eleanor's son-in-law. Lady Eleanor vented her rage against the family in *Woe to the House* (1633—see page 57 in the present edition).

140 *thee the Judgement of the great Whore or great bellied Harlot sitting on many waters:* The Cities Bridge on Arches, this Map as displayed person, and place, Circumstances none more necessary: And some Haven Town from whence derives her Title of Honor. So from the Title great infers a Grand-mother. Then that imperious Hell-hound, more Mother *Jezebels* then one.

And with the Holy Spirit moving on the waters: Thus proceeding dispelling Mists and Darkness, saying, *Wherefore dost thou wonder, or marvel'st thou* (as it were) at this *Sea Monster,* not more strange then true, *The Mother, &c.* I will shew thee the *Mystery* of the *Woman.* And 150 the *Beast* that *beareth* or *carrieth her , &c.* Expresly *Herals* their *Mystery* which *demonstrates:* And present *Century* the seventeenth. *As behold whose Arms? And they shall eat her Flesh and burn her with Fire,* besides hers some four-footed rather. *Skull, palms and feet,* no Dog would touch, in reference to *Feasts.* What *Bruit* or *Flesh* of Beast in most request, *Eaten, &c.* Points to so many *Stags Heads* born in a *Bend,* or their *Skulls, &c.* Touching whose *Arms* suffices so much refer'd to *Sign Posts:* the *Red Deer* that Scarlet *Beast* also; and *Babe* in its *scrimson bearing Clothe,* a Relique to these days; in her custody: Who cried out as much as she. (*Gen.*) him solicited daily: By whom his garment laid up, 160 *&c.*

And so what dost thou hero *Elijahs enlightning days, founded* in

---

Line 141. **The Cities...Arches:** London Bridge.

Lines 142–43. **Haven Town:** Castlehaven.

Lines 144–45. **Mother Jezebels:** see 1 Kings 21:23–25.

Line 150. **Herals:** heralds; officials who oversaw the coats of arms and pedigrees of the English gentry and nobility.

Line 155. **so many...Bend:** The arms of the house of Derby, the family to which Lady Eleanor's sister-in-law belonged, included a stag.

Line 157. **the Red Deer...Beast:** Lady Eleanor compares the red deer in the arms of the house of Derby to the whore of Babylon (Rev. 17:3). **scrimson:** crimson; see Jer. 4:30.

Lines 158–59. **Relique:** a piece of the remains of a saint. **Who cried...as she:** see Gen. 39:14–18.

Line 161. **Elijahs enlightning days:** Elijah convinced the people to believe in God and to slay the prophets of Baal (1 Kings 18).

whose, Our Capital City *LONDON*, of old called *TROY*, A compound of *Babylon* the Great: As written Son in her Forehead or Frontispiece. Where from *His Greatness* or *Lord Mayorship*, not onely derived Title of *Great Cuckold;* but Great *Britain* its addition; since exchanged *Anglia* for *Brute*, no less then undone, most proper from him (one *change* pursuing another) embrewed in that way of his *Hounds* and restless *Hunting* to prefer the Beasts name, accords but with his *Minions* that of *Buckingham.*

So running with him *Ahimaz*, The way of the *Plain* or present *Wavering Gothes, Sarazens,* and *Knights* of *Rhodes* out of date, and *Romes* scituation remote: As they to their Father. See whether this thy *sons coat, &c.* whose City on a River no slender one, with its Appurtenances (from which *Allegory* of carrying) *Ships* called *Bears* and *Tygers, Sea-Horses,* fraught with *Tyrian* in *Grain, Pearls, Precious Stones, Gold,* and *Wines* in that abundance, *&c.* With Her Cup of poyson arayed *Cleopatra* like, sitting on Seven Headed *Nilus:* The Beast with so many Heads and Horns.

The *Woman* and *Beast* with so many *Heads and Horns, &c. Church, Court,* and *Cities* description, with *Kings,* their obeisance to her; beside in what *Century:* Also his Seventeen years Reign, until (*Anno* 41) Load

170

180

Lines 162–63. **LONDON...TROY:** Brute, the legendary founder of Britain, was a Trojan. **A compound...Great:** Lady Eleanor conflates Babylon and London in her manuscript tract "Bathe Daughter of Babylondon" (1636—page 71 in the present edition). **Frontispiece:** the front, or the first page of a book; cf. Rev. 17:5.

Lines 164–66. **Lord Mayorship...Cuckold:** If London was Babylon, the whore, London's ruler, the Lord Mayor, was a cuckold. **Great Britain...Brute:** When James, king of Scotland, became king of England (Anglia, the land of the angels) in 1603, he took the title King of Great Britain (the land of the Beast or Brute).

Line 167. **embrewed...hunting:** King James was a great huntsman.

Lines 168–69. **the Beasts...Buckingham:** "Buckingham" contains the letters of buck, a beast that one might hunt; one of James's favorite, George Villier was the duke of Buckingham.

Line 170. **Ahimaz...Plain:** cf. 2 Sam. 18:23.

Line 171. **Gothes...Rhodes:** warlike peoples of the Middle Ages.

Line 172. **See...coat:** the question posed to Jacob (Gen. 37:31–34).

Line 173. **City...River:** Rome; London; Babylon (Rev. 17:18). **Appurtenances:** belongings.

Line 181. **his:** Charles I's.

away not unknown, by what means: our *Domitians* days: in whose, this City made an open example: As behold whose Bridge fired, shunning the *fire* to cast themselves into the water, forced; Eaten by *fish,* their *flesh.* Since when others suffering, no few. The *Towers* Blow for an other, with *Lightnings* and *Thunder-claps,* like *Dooms-day, &c.* the *Bridge* at the same time Burnt: when she no ordinary *Whore,* charged with a *Husband, Blood:* worthy of no other *Cup, Naked* and *Burnt.* Credible *Witness* of the *Churches Apostacy, Figures* in her later *Days* what a faithful

190   *Spouse;* sealed with *Sabbatical Heads* of the Scarlet coloured *Beast* (*Cruelties Character*) with *Oxford* and *Cambridge,* no mean *Strumpets,* whose Denomination interrested in the *Ten Horns:* Their *Tithe* an *Assembly* sitting at *Westminster;* also carried by Water in their *Gowns,* belongs thereto.

   Furthermore, as this Cities Feastivals and Funerals all set upon this reckoning, such flocking then to behold her Pomp, stiled, *The great Whore with her Cup of Drugs:* Carried in what State, By *Cerberus* Headed Hounds, her black Steeds. She siting on the *Waters, Her Habitation* or *Title:* By Kings at Arms and others, To give attention to

200   *Preaching Parasites:* whereas compared to the *Block-headed Beast* going

---

Line 182. **Domitians days:** a time of turmoil and violence in Rome which ended with the Emperor Domitian's murder in A.D. 96.

Lines 183–85. **whose Bridge…Blow:** Lady Eleanor interpreted fires and storms that struck London as being divine warnings.

Lines 187–88. **she…Blood:** Lady Eleanor's sister-in-law, Anne, Lady Castlehaven.

Line 189. **the Churches Apostacy:** its abandonment of its principles.

Lines 192–93. **Their Tithe…Westminster:** The learned men contributed their tenth (tithe) by participating in the assembly at Westminster, which discussed reform of the church. **carried…Gowns:** The clergy (and university men), whose gowns were a mark of their position, often travelled to Westminster by water.

Line 196. **Pomp:** ostentatious display, associated for Lady Eleanor with Catholicism.

Line 197. **Cerberus:** in Greek myth, the three-headed watchdog of the underworld.

Line 198. **her black Steeds:** in contrast to the white horse of the Lamb (Rev. 19:11).

Line 199. **Kings…Arms:** heralds responsible for coats of arms and pedigrees.

Line 200. **Preaching Parasites:** clergy more concerned with collecting tithes than with pastoral duties.

to the slaughter. *Man in Honor,* as easie *for a Camel to go through an Needles eye, as for such to enter, &c.* When made notwithstanding the Beasts Image: Laid before them: Adored Obsequies for costly *Blacks* bought at such a price. Welcome *Image* of the *Beast, Saint,* or *Devil, Whore, &c.* Honored a like, Sackcloth when more seasonable then *Muld Sack* of late. Of which Sexes more remarkables then one deceased.

So withal (part of the Bag and Baggage) of *Saints-days* abused as much by the rotten *Whore: Eaten, &c.* That *Mistress* of mischief, and her Servant the roaring *Beast* wel-matcht: *Vermillian* Livery in Grain, then *Simon* and *Judes* Commemoration: The *Floods* doings rather and *Sodoms;* crowed on both sides, as though never seen afore or heard their *Horn-pipes* attended; whose going by water retained to these very days *Trojean* Games: a world of Coaches, Belconies filling and Windows, *Spectators* and to be seen; because *Jacobs* Flock spotted, like *marks* by the foul *spirit* set on them: the *tokens* imitated, *Churches* by *Pastors* thus prepared; a like for *Theators* and *his Temple. Varnished* with poysonous *spells,* or *paint* (she trodden underfoot) her accursed *Pictures;* or some carted like dasht, *&c.* fit *Guests, &c.* On the other side *restless-swearing Cooks* about *Firs,* and other like *Catch-poles;* appurtenances of the *Scarlet Beast,* for this narrow *Table* too *voluminous:* Also *Christmas-boles,* All nights *Game-boles; Dancing* and *Dicing,* scored on the *Horns,* with *Goldsmiths-hall* and *Skinners,* from the *Cup* of beaten *Gold;* a *health* to them too.

Through whose *streets* formerly carried in *state* by *Scarlet Liveries,*

Lines 201–2. **Man…enter:** cf. Matt. 19:24. Line 203. **costly Blacks:** mourning clothes.

Line 205. **Sackcloth…Sack:** mourning clothes (sackcloth) more appropriate than drinking wine (mulled sack).

Line 209. **Vermillian Livery:** bright scarlet clothing.

Line 210. **Simon…Commemoration:** the Feast of Saints Simon and Jude, 28 October, one of the feast days retained by the Church of England after the Reformation.

Line 213. **Trojean:** associated with ancient Troy; boisterous, dissolute.

Line 214. **Jacobs Flock spotted:** see Gen. 31. Line 219. **Catch-poles:** sheriff's officers.

Lines 220–22. **Christmas-boles…Dicing:** activities which Lady Eleanor deemed contrary to true religion. **Goldsmiths-hall…Skinners:** halls of two of the London Companies or guilds.

from all parts flowing to have sight of her *person* or *presence:* Totally
stript of *Purple array, Margaret Pendants, Bracelets* and *Chains:* some
Kings Daughter as though, or *one of the Blood:* became as *deformed, dispi-
cable* and *desolate:* Hated as formerly, followed with their *Leopard skins*,
the naked *House of Lords,* concerned not lest; beside plundered Pay:
230   *Houses, Kings* and *Lords,* those.

As moreover, *she* none of the lest, that *mother* of *Witchcrafts,* branded
for a Baud, whose *Babel-Pyramid* fired. Fictions of fresh *edition, University Excrements* daily, whereby *oppressing Shops* and *Presses* with them:
overflowing too shameful, whilest *Close-Stools* set to sale, lined through
with *Scriptures old* and *new:* When *Turks,* lest *Gods name* therein, refrain
to set their foot on a leaf of Paper, whose *Alcoran Mahomets* the false
Prophets, Cum Privilegio, &c. Accursed *Jerocho's* reedified *Gates,* in the
mean while *Jerusalems Walls,* waste, *&c.*

So sends greeting *Pathmos* Isle, to this Islands City. He when unexpe-
240   rienced in those *Hieroglyphick* Demonstrations *Saints* dayes, signifying
beyond *Paganism* Rites celebrated. St. *John* stricken or transported with
such *admiration* and *marvel (O strange)* and ugly: What *Strumpet, Baud,
&c.* As *points* to that *fiction:* of ravished *Europia,* carried on the *Bull* into
the *Sea:* true as the others *Rape, &c.* in *Maps* and *Tapistries* ordinary; so
to another not long since no *fiction* on this *River.* Those Brace of *Span-
iels, Her Graces* swimming match. And *Knight* Errand, no small *Bull:*

Line 226. **Margaret:** margarite; pearl.

Lines 231–33. **branded for a Baud:** taken as a bawd or whore. **Fictions…daily:** an attack on
some current publications.

Line 234. **Close-Stools:** chamber pots.

Lines 236–37. **Alcoran…Privilegio:** a complaint that the Koran had been authorized for
publication. **Accursed…Gates:** see Josh. 6:26.

Line 241. **St. John…transported:** According to Tertullian, St. John was thrown into a
cauldron of boiling oil at Rome and then exiled to Patmos.

Line 243. **Europia:** Europa; in Greek myth, Zeus disguised himself as a bull and carried her
off into the sea.

Lines 245–46. **Those Brace…match:** a pair of submissive servants who, according to Lady
Eleanor, complied with Lady Castlehaven's proceedings against her husband. **Knight
Errand…Bull:** like Zeus in the tale of Europa.

supported by his Hand; laid upon her, *&c.* Requisit as any in our Cities Map to be displayed. That *Esprit* Order, conjured up again, entered in them as into that *Cities Swine:* because the good *Spirit* moved on the *waters* also *Apishlike* by the evil *spirit,* and *Witches,* those, *&c.* With his   250
Venetian, she free of the aforesaid three *Stags Heads;* the *Horns* his too, *&c.* with her *Cup* of *Viper Wine,* that never awakned, whether Drunken or no, *&c.* The *Floods* days not equivolent.

All which copied out by that *Piece,* when his *butcherly birth-day* kept, bound himself, *&c.* Instructed by her *Mother Baud,* dancing her lacivious *Jigs* and *Tricks:* beheaded the *Baptist;* late by her, and her Ladies not onely Hermophrodite acting *mankinde;* but sworn by his *precious, &c.* And *wounds* by their base *Players. Let us eat and drink, to morrow is our last:* More true then aware of, notwithstanding a *Mote* in anothers Eye perceive, so returning to his last account, made *even,* or *confession* on   260
Tower-hill, arrived the *Haven* above, *This day be thou with me,* &c. *Enter thou into thy Lord and Masters joy. Easter* Term, *An. Dom.* 31.

Between those twain Sacrificed, he charged but as an accessary: Had the honor nevertheless, of first entrance. Next Term theirs *Bradway* the innocent *Page,* and the other, *&c.* Who in those times thought full little of *(Jud.) Bradshaw.* When thirsted after his *Vineyard, Mervin* Earl of

---

Line 248. **Esprit:** spirit (French).   Line 249. **as into...Swine:** see Matt. 8:30.

Lines 250–51. **With his Venetian...too:** Lady Eleanor suggests that the tale of Kenelm Digby (1603–1665) and his wife Venetia Stanley parallels that of her brother and sister-in-law. The arms of the house of Derby, with which both women were connected, contained three stag's heads; both women were alleged to have cuckolded their husbands.

Line 252. **Cup of Viper Wine:** Rumors circulated that Digby caused his wife's death by having her take such a drink.

Lines 254–55. **butcherly...Baud:** Digby eventually became Queen Henrietta Maria's servant.

Line 257. **Hermophrodite acting mankinde:** Digby's religious convictions seemed to vary according to convenience; those of Lady Eleanor's brother were at issue in his trial.

Line 259. **a Mote in anothers Eye:** see Matt. 7:3.

Lines 260–61. **confession...Tower-hill:** that of the earl of Castlehaven; Lady Eleanor printed it in *Word of God* (1644) and in *Crying Charge* (1649—page 255 in the present edition).

Line 264. **Next Term theirs:** Castlehaven's servants were tried and executed in the legal term following his execution.

Line 266. **Bradshaw:** the judge who presided over the trial of Charles I.

Castlehavens. So many *Manor Houses*, to few or none inferior: This
Kingdoms forerunner; or what should him befal: His *Enemies* likewise
those of his own *house* (to his last) *swearing* at every word *cursing, &c.*

270   This man never once charged with *Oath,* other *then truly and verily:*
Taxt with *injustice* neither, or owing unto any: Paid and rewarded all.

By means of alteration in his *Religion,* as much disclaimed; and mis-
matching himself: scandalized by others *misdemeanor.* They who worst
reproached him, was, *That he had the best things in him, of any man,* as
well as the worst.

Stumbled at the *Church* upon *point* of *Antiquity:* By reason whereof
stood in *Poperies* defence, or *Romes.*

That *Fathers* aspersion undergone, *Origens, That when he wrote well,
none could do better; when he wrote ill, no man so bad.*

280   Envied among them, *Court* Motions that ever distasted, stiled to be
Pharoahs Son, or accounted *the Creature of Fortune;* to whose potent
adversaries, no *slender* or *mean advantage.* Cast by a *Jury* of Peers: His
unnatural *Jury of Brethren,* as sold him, *figure* of the *Lamb,* called the
Dreamer: scorned and *stript* of his *Garment.* Also between those two,
through her lust. Blood of the *Grape,* as sealed. The ones *pardon* the life
therein. So the other the heavy *Famins* forerunner hanged up: by Birds
betokened on the *Wing,* his flight, *&c.*

In the end tasted *Egyptian slavery,* themselves *Straw-gathers: Types* of
the scattered *Jews* not onely; but of a *spiritual Famin,* proceeding from
290   forgetfulness, *&c.* Parables, consisting of a twofold-like *Construction;*

Line 270. **never once...Oath:** Lady Eleanor alleges that Castlehaven's wife's allegations
against him were not made under oath.

Line 276. **Stumbled...Antiquity:** Castlehaven had difficulty accepting the Church of
England as the true church.

Line 278. **Origen:** early third-century Greek Christian scholar.

Lines 280–81. **stiled...Son:** see Exod. 2:10.

Line 283. **unnatural Jury...him:** a comparison of the peers who condemned Castlehaven
with the brothers of Joseph (Gen. 37). **figure of the Lamb:** a representation of the Lamb
(Christ).

Line 288. **Types:** representations; biblical typology, popular in the seventeenth century,
identified people and events in the Old Testament as types of those in the New Testament.

are those aforesaid *Fellow-servants,* in one day said to have their *Heads* lifted up both, who advanced so. *All knees to bowe, &c.* Afterward biding them not be sad; for their preservation sent thither: So much for the word *throughout all ages,* and the *world* through. Also touching his leave taken at *Tower-hill,* so highly rewarded. *Well done good and faithful servant.*

Follows the second a Lieutenants turn next of *Ireland, Strafford* no *shallow Brain-piece,* over-powered by the *old Serpents* policy. *Papist* by reason in highest *Offices,* had his *quietus est, Easter* Term *(Anno* 41.) Sealed with no ordinary *Arms,* the *Ax:* Neither wanting after his *ability* of what *Faith* or *Belief, Kingdoms* slippery places, as unto her a second *Eve;* for her forwardness, ye know not what ye ask: Whilest on the other side as backward. This piece interlined, as shews, when presented the *Lord General* herewith, a *Manuscript prayed to be priviledged,* by him; referred to the *Bar:* Lodging in *Ax-Alley,* where about three *weeks* spare waited on. Other *use* of which (as though) had not made, returned them, not vouchsafest the value of a word. No *Babe* in long *Coats,* though bewrayes, *barbarous* alike, not to *bless* where they ought, and to *contemn* or *curse:* No less then *cowardize* also in a high degree, what should be improved to *Hide, &c.*

In the mean time unburied *Lord Deputy Iretons,* sad welcome rung out, landed, whose *Corps.*

Farther giving to understand, had advertiz'd him what befel immediately afore, signed with *Whitehals Powder mischance.* Bidden to shake of

300

310

Lines 294–96. **his leave...Tower-hill:** Castlehaven's execution. **Well...servant:** Matt. 25:23.

Lines 297–99. **a Lieutenants...Term:** Sir Thomas Wentworth, earl of Strafford and lord lieutenant of Ireland, was executed as a traitor in May 1641.

Line 302. **ye know...ask:** Matt. 20:22.

Lines 303–4. **when...Manuscript:** In 1648 Lady Eleanor reprinted *Given to the Elector* (first printed in 1633—page 59 in the present edition) and gave a copy of the tract to Lord General Fairfax.

Line 305. **Ax-Alley:** probably Lady Eleanor's invention.

Lines 307–8. **No Babe...bewrayes:** nothing unexpected revealed.

Lines 311–12. **unburied...out:** Henry Ireton, Cromwell's son-in-law, died in November 1651 in Ireland, after the capture of Limerick.

their dust, that have but *ears* for a shew: How in the same moneth *October, &c.* about the same hour at *Night, &c.* wherein delivered to *His Excellency* by her a *Book,* Entituled, *Babylons Hand-writing,* bearing date *Anno* 1633. Printed beyond Sea; by the same token with *Specticles* put on, read by him. That *watch word* superscribed, *Is a Candle to be put under a Bed, &c.* (useless and unsafe) He that hath Ear hear this *Piece. Contents* of the said Book (*Dan.* 5.) contained in a sheet of *Paper,* sometime served on the late K.C. after his return from *Scotland, Anno* 33. Crowned, *&c.* concluded with *Charls* Be, from his name, attended with his Riotous *Lords, Belshazer* the last (to wit) *Beheaded, &c.* to beware his *Banquetting Houses salutation; Great Babylons* exchanged *Feast,* into such confusion, instead of *kissing hands,* stampt a *hand writing,* subscribed, Great *Britains Lamentation Mourning* and *Wo.*

Whereupon like his *killing* and *slaying Decree, Dan.* 2 *&c.* She to *appear* and *answer* forthwith, as by that *Babylonian* reference annext, Signed *Sydney, Mountagne,* for *presuming* to *prefer* and *imprint, That detestable,* &c. *An. Dom.* 1633. *October, Whitehals* no petty Trespass.

Of which *Babylonish* Garment hidden as it were in his *Tent* to this day.

So much by the way for that, and of his *Kingdoms* no delay admitting, as by the foresaid *Advertisement* to the speechless Dr. *Ba. Balams*

Lines 315–17. **October...Book:** Lady Eleanor's encounter with Fairfax in 1648.

Line 321. **Contents...Book:** The book interpreted *Dan.* 5, which treats Belshazzar's feast.

Line 322. **K. C.:** King Charles I. Lines 324–25. **Charls Be...Belshazer:** a rough anagram.

Lines 324–25. **his Banquetting...salutation:** Charles I was executed at the Banqueting House at Whitehall.

Line 327. **Great...Wo:** words on the title page of *The Dragons Blasphemous Charge* (1651).

Lines 328–31. **She to appear...1633:** the warrant for Lady Eleanor's hearing before the High Commission in 1633. **Whitehals...Trespass:** Lady Eleanor blames Whitehall, that is, the royal government, for the proceedings against her.

Line 332. **which Babylonish Garment:** the anti-Christian evidence; see Gen. 39:18.

Lines 335–37. **the foresaid Advertisement...Ass:** In a printed marginal note to *The Dragons Blasphemous Charge* (1651—see the headnote to *Blasphemous Charge,* page 249 in the present edition), Lady Eleanor claims that Dr. Reeve, the king's advocate at her High Commission hearing, was speechless at her answers; cf. the story of Balaam and his ass, Num. 22-24.

madness reproved, when served or sufficed from those Ears. *Did I ever serve thee so before:* put to silence by the *dumb Ass:* all as swift that way; but *Midas* Ears, their long Hair hides not, or Perwigs either.

And thus in reference to the *premises,* from a *Wedding,* its late hour. That cry also after a long time his return, of a cried *Court-day.* Officers they called to appear, called *Thou slothful servant Dr.* Laud, as appears, He the last Arch. B. of *Canterbury.* The one Talent even buried by his hand, *Achans* graceless Scholar.

In the Earth: he buried in the *Valley* of *Achor:* a heap of Stones *Dunghil*-like; his Monument and theirs consenting thereto: Had not alone troubled *Joshua,* expostulating in *rent clothes:* Wherefore, *&c.*

Root of all Evil, filthy lucre confesses did covet: *Thus and thus, &c.* In the *Valley* of *Trouble,* took up his Lodging. Sign of the *Spade,* fitter for it.

And thus after a *verbatim* way, for our *hiding days* in season: Servants such of *Mammon* or *Money. Weeping* and *howling* their Portion: Of the *Spiritual Calling,* or *Clergy voice,* as follows: Called *Thou sloathful, &c.* One in ten theirs, reaped where *sowed* not; gathered where had not strawed. A severe or hard *man,* counted every *Sheaf,* &c. *Tythe* gatherers (to wit) far and near; with usury ten in the hundred; not wanting their *Trade;* known in others Name.

In relation to whose *Name* these, even the *Beast* out of the *Loathsome pit* ascended (*Rev.* 17.) *And they shall wonder whose names not in the Book of life, &c.* (or *Church-book*) namely, That of *Canterbury* derived from some *Grace-makers* occupation, below the *Dung-hils* office. As at first every *Creature* after its properly.

340

350

360

Line 338. **Midas Ears:** King Midas angered Apollo, who caused him to grow a pair of ass's ears in punishment. **their long Hair...either:** The Royalists were known for wearing their hair long or wearing wigs.

Line 340. **a cried Court-day:** Criers announced the holding of court.

Lines 341–43. **Thou slothful...hand:** cf. Matt. 25:26. **Achans graceless Scholar:** an allegation that Laud, like Achan, aroused God's anger against the kingdom; see Josh. 7.

Line 347. **lucre:** profit. Line 348. **Sign of the Spade:** symbol of burial.

Line 352. **One in ten theirs:** the tithe claimed by the clergy.

Lines 358–59. **Canterbury...occupation:** Archbishops were referred to as "Your Grace"; they were also supposed to be concerned with salvation or grace. **Dung-hils office:** see Dan. 2:5.

As hence appears how had occupied, *&c.* That *digged and interred,* shrowded it in the ominous *Napkin* to their *Napery* pointing, or *ghostly* array withal.

And one thus unfolding another, as that *farewel* of his Bidden, the *dead* to *bury the dead.* Either because *rich* and concealed it, or might *allude* to his *name:* In like case as *Canterbury* or *Salisbury.*

The Title of *Grace Buried,* neither in *silence* or *forgetfulness.* That *Paradox* for another, as implies.

His own bare measure meted or returned him; he without excuse, 370 knew his *Lords* severness nevertheless: Lo there, *That is thine,* &c. As from *him that hath not,* saying, *Even that he hath shall be taken away.* Of Parentage obscure, as much to say, *His Graceship digraded shall be (Jan.* 10.) a day and hour not aware of, to Preach his own *Funeral Sermon,* not mentioned in his *Diary.* That *Fridays Christmas Cup, gnashing of Tieth:* Who hated the light, depended upon the former days *provission, Star-Chamber* Decrees and Articles; was cast into the prison of utter darkness; besides *Extortion* added to *Usury; Covetousness* very *Idolatry,* also with *Gluttony* charged: Emblem'd the *Napkin,* their excess and concealed *Bags;* so of which one *Talent* assigned; in short thus, saying, *Lord* 380 *he hath ten:* Disputed as though some other better deserved it; answered, *He that hath, more shall be given him,* or *shall have abundance,*

Lines 361–62. **digged...Napkin:** Luke's version of the parable of the talents (Luke 19:20).

Lines 362–63. **Napery...array:** household linen; the white robes of the archbishop.

Lines 364–65. **the dead...dead:** Luke 9:60.

Line 366. **Canterbury...Salisbury:** These titles of bishops include the letters of the verb bury.

Line 369. **His own...him:** Luke 6:38.

Lines 371–72. **Of Parentage obscure...be:** Laud, executed 10 January 1644, i.e., 1645.

Line 374. **Fridays Christmas Cup:** Lady Eleanor believed that Laud's execution, which occurred on a Friday, was fulfillment of Daniel's prophecy to her in 1625; the Whore of Babylon had a cup full of abominations (Rev. 17:4). **gnashing of Tieth:** a sign of the last days (Matt. 25:30).

Lines 375–76. **Star-Chamber...Articles:** Prior to its abolition in 1641, the court of the Star Chamber's decrees regulated printing; the court's articles were its charges, e.g., of sedition or libel, against offenders.

Lines 377–78. **Extortion...Napkin:** Laud's wrongdoings; cf. Ezek. 22.

&c. Even *Anno Dom.* 1631. *Easter,* (to wit) had the *superabundant* honor to be *the heavenly Lamb;* ancient of days *Figure,* foreshewing by a *Harlot Spowse,* Remonstrates not onely *Romish Massacres,* that *Smoaking Clarret;* but by *Protestants,* how to the *brim* filled, *&c.*
Wherewith a word of the said *Prisoners* present release, by the figure Ironia, commended, *&c.* delivered by *His Majesties Chaplains,* His gracious *Message* and *royal Favor* toward him.

He whereas was to have suffered as a common person should die, now like a *Peer* of the Land, *beheaded, &c.* appointed to sist him, no 390 others admitted, having been under *Inquisition* so long; upon their *information,* had thrice taken the *Sacrament* upon it, was innocent of those *crimes* for which adjudged to lose his life: whereupon thanks not omitted, replied, *Would esteem it a coller of precious Stones should draw him up to him, embraced the Tree, to his Feet.*

And by these *Jews,* our *High Priests,* in what *Execrable* manor *Crucified* on their *Altars,* prepared for that purpose; roaring with one consent, *Sacrifice* and *Eat,* both one, or indifferent; also *Altar* and *Table.*

Like as in *Golgotha,* That fatal *Fridays* dismal day, (end of the week) *bowed then the knee. Chams* accursed *seed,* by whom a *Giant crucifix* 400 *Goliah* like, not the value of a *Napkin* to cover, &c. Horrible to behold,

---

Lines 382–83. **Anno...Lamb:** the trial of Lady Eleanor's brother, the earl of Castlehaven.

Lines 384–85. **Harlot Spowse:** Lady Eleanor's sister-in-law. **Smoaking Clarret:** the burning of the whore of Babylon (Rev. 18:9).

Line 386. **word...release:** Lady Eleanor was writing from prison.

Line 387. **Ironia:** the rhetorical figure of irony; perhaps also a reference to the rod of iron (Rev. 19:15).

Lines 389–90. **die...Land:** King Charles sent word that the earl of Castlehaven might enjoy a death according to his rank.

Line 392. **had thrice...Sacrament:** the earl of Castlehaven's proof of his religious faith and his innocence.

Line 395. **embraced...Feet:** cf. Acts 5:30.

Lines 396–98. **And...Table:** The significance of the sacrament of communion and the issue of whether it should be performed on an altar or a table were topics of considerable dispute.

Line 399. **Golgotha...day:** the place and time when Jesus was crucified (Matt. 27:33).

Line 401. **Goliah:** Goliath, the Philistine giant slain by David (1 Sam. 17).

eclipsed light, covered the *Ten Commandments,* under colour of an *Altar Hanging,* wanting no *nailing* either: Of course *Woollen, Purple, &c.* fastned down, lest those precious *Tables* an eye sore. Whilest mounted over the *Lords Table,* to kneel before it, with the *Centurion:* No *Dwarf* mounted on his *Courser* or *Beast,* to be worshipped to, superscribed a true *Copy,* brought over by *Father, &c.* in his *Holiness* Chappel done thereby; *Lietchfield* Minster for one, were forced afterward for fear of the *Parliament Forces,* those *Clerk-Vicars,* to bury it in the *Dunghil,* not

410   one would harbor it. As this added, the very hidden *Talent,* his *Lords buried Goods,* accords with the *Tables* of the *Law,* from no causeless jealousie, as Extant in our *Bibles* ordered, except the Book of *Apocalyps,* and other like, least edifying, may be best spared; allow others read every *Sabbath, &c.*

Besides how many silenced imprisoned, other some *Crucified* on *Pillaries,* whilest he and his *Panders,* eating and drinking with the *drunken.* *Item, Oxfords* Roast, three hundred *Dowes* or *Deer* at a *Chancellorships* dinner, with *Spiritual Courts* abominable *Bribery* taking on both *Hands* from those stripped of their *livelihood, Widows,* but *Tenants* for life; no

420   Commiseration for such, especially, present pay, or else turned out.

Unto which annext his *vow* of *Chastity,* stiled, *Pater in Christi, &c.*

Lines 402–3. **eclipsed light:** cf. Matt. 27:45. **covered...Hanging:** changes in the cathedral at Lichfield which Lady Eleanor protested in 1636.

Line 404. **those precious Tables:** the Ten Commandments, also referred to as the ten tables of the law; Laud and other bishops objected to using a table rather than an altar for communion.

Line 405. **kneel:** Kneeling to take communion was another issue of controversy. **Centurion:** Roman soldier present at Jesus' crucifixion (Matt. 27:54).

Line 407. **true Copy...Chappel:** The papal envoy who came to England in the 1630s allegedly brought an altar-hanging which Laud used in his chapel.

Line 409. **bury...Dunghil:** The altar-hanging to which Lady Eleanor had objected was buried during the civil war.

Lines 412–14. **except...Sabbath:** a protest that current ecclesiastical policy treated the Book of Revelation as less important than other parts of the Bible.

Lines 415–16. **how...drinking:** the "godly" clergy prosecuted by Laud and his associates.

Lines 417–19. **Oxfords Roast...dinner:** the feasts associated with Laud's service as head of the university. **Spiritual...life:** Lady Eleanor's personal grievance, as well as a more general contemporary complaint against the church courts.

Line 421. **vow...Christi:** an allegation that clerical celibacy was a relic of Catholic priesthood.

Verily, false *Christs* shall deceive many, *whose names not written from the foundation, &c. (Rev.)* Exchange *commodities;* those *Virgins* Canonized in his *Tables* admire, *Laud* his name, *&c.* the apprehended old *Serpent, alias Satan,* whose false *Keys,* as though his *saecession* Iron Gates opened of their own accord, were in their custody (*Apoc.* 20.) *The Key whereas of the sealed Abbyss, whose proper Seal.*

And thus proceeding a compleat *Jury,* their *Verdict* with one consent, *Prophet* and *Apostles;* Touching our *Nations story. English, Irish, Scotish* and *French,* every one as heretofore heard in their proper *Languages,* fulfilling nothing so *secret* and *covered,* that shall not be revealed and made manifest. 430

Including withal *Times* reign or reckoning, *Five thousand five hundred years compleat since the Creation.* Secondly, *Two thousand years before the Laws, and Two thousand under the Law.* Lastly, Compleat *One thousand under the Gospel,* from those in trusted Servants account, which would have amounted (had not he faln short) to *One thousand* years more, or had it not happened into slothful hands. The *Three Ages* otherwise equally *Two thousand* years unto each allotted.

Whereof thus (*Apoc.* 17.) concerning *place, time* and *persons concomitants: Five are faln, one is, the other is not yet come: And when he cometh, shall continue a short space:* Namely, *the fifteenth century past and gone; the sixteenth bears the name, the other not compleat to be, but shortned.* Here is the minde that hath *Wisdom (viz.)* to number the time, *Psal.* reflects on King *James* the Sixth. Others as weak as he wise. From a *Parliament* called by himself, to absent *his person,* here signified, *Of one minde,* called by *write;* others by most *voices, Chosen ones.* And as 440

Line 424. **Laud…name:** a pun on Archbishop Laud's name and the verb laud (praise).

Line 428. **a compleat Jury:** the twenty-four elders (Rev. 19:4).

Lines 429–30. **our Nations…French:** Until 1714, the English claimed to rule France. **every one…Languages:** see Acts 2:6.

Line 431. **nothing…revealed:** Luke 8:17.

Lines 433–39. **Times reign…allotted:** calculations of time based upon biblical evidence.

Line 444. **the minde…time:** Ps. 90:12.

Lines 445–46. **King James the Sixth:** James VI of Scotland was James I of England. **From…person:** Charles I left Westminster and Parliament in 1642.

rewarded for the most part afterward, who hate the *Whore* and make her desolate: A *Widow,* as much to say, *Utterly stript of all, by the Ten Horns,* fulfilling such a time, amounting to ten years space. As moreover, *For God shall put into their hearts, to fulfil his will,* &c. repented as it were; alluding to which words, *Have mercy upon us, and incline our hearts,* &c. or *Write thy Laws in our hearts we beseech thee;* where *acts* against *Idolatry* and *Adultery,* made death that *act,* put into the *list* of the aforesaid *ten Horns,* so many years fulfilling.

And so proceeding with his *relation* hereof, who wrote to her stiled so highly, *The Elder, To the Lady Ele:* &c. in our *British* Language, as to the full exprest, *Apoc.* where accompanied with insatiable *Tyrant Times Mystery (Eating all things)* his displayed *Arms:* also the *Stuarts Arms* or *Coat;* The *Bulls-head* blazoned, that sign in *Taurus,* giving to understand farther of *Europes* Apostate Churches, returned to *wallow in the mire,* all from her sitting on the waters of *Babylon,* with inlarged *skirts,* those of *hers* as afore shewed; computed by the *floods* execrable *Age, Hearts* as *Buff:* Signed and sealed with *Babylons* Great Seal, The Beasts heart: That fulfilled seven times, not to be Cancelled either. How long afore his *reason* to him returned a *Jubiles* seven times seven, where included.

Lastly, What affinity between them, fixt place as signified from her sitting posture, &c. So *restless time* by the weary *Beast.* Names written on both their foreheads, That *City Mistress* as upon Hers, *Mystery Babylon* or *London:* Also *Mars, Mercury, Venus,* &c. Names of *Blasphemy* on *his,* all *her most humble Servants.* The *Scarlet Beast, Anno Etatis,* &c. when her downfal withal.

By persons represented of no obscure *decent:* Namely, House of

---

Line 456. **his:** St. John the Evangelist's (2 John 1).

Line 457. **Lady Ele:** Lady Eleanor.

Lines 458–59. **Tyrant Times Mystery:** the answer to Daniel's question as to how long it would be till the end (Dan. 12:6–13).

Line 460. **The Bulls-head...Taurus:** Taurus is the astrological sign of the bull.

Line 461. **Europes Apostate...mire:** cf. 2 Pet. 2:22.

Line 463–64. **Hearts as Buff:** in military attire, armed.

Line 471. **Anno Etatis:** in the year of age (Latin).

450

460

470

Derby, matcht with the House of *Oxford,* armed on both sides with the *Horns: no secret,* either he bearing the *Stags heads* metamorphized into a *Bear:* Father of him who suffered: On all *four* acting in their *likeness;* and other of that kinde on *Stages* in *Pastorals,* tumbling to the admiration, *&c.* A *blessing* by the *mothers* side: So *wherefore wonderest thou at signs, &c. Rev.* 17.

And sotish *Bathe,* another like *odium* of the *Beast,* forerunners of Great *Britains* unlucky derivation, not onely from *Brute,* but of *Cities* names their sympathizing, called after theirs, or participating. 480

And so far for these literally prefigured, The present *Age* sent to *School* to the *Ox, Ass,* and *Camel;* In their *Litter* knows its owner, better observes the time, and for *times Mystery* and *Seasons.* The weaker *Sex* preferred more proper for them, requisit for former days neither: To whose Disciples not a little earnest (answered) *A thing not in his dispose, he was but the Word;* but *his Fathers* where he pleased, a *Conception;* as much to say, By *special Grace:* Witnessed to be by them though.

And shunning *Circumlocution,* where like theirs under terms *Enigmatical,* concealed by way of *Numbers* and *Figures* numberless. Whosoever understands any one; serves for the *master Key* to that *hidden Treasure* or *Quintesence.* 490

Of the *third* or *last similitude,* as follows, The last days dreadful *alarm* likened unto that *Sessions* day, attended with a guard of *Angel,* by a *King* sitting on his *throne:* On the *right hand* faithful to *him* that stood in defence of the *cause;* on the *left* that took up *Arms* against him: which *remarkable* days of ours compared to a *Shepherd, Jacobs* separating the *sheep from goats.* Our *Nations* prime Commodity, *Wool, Sheep,* no mean fence against *Hunger* and *Cold;* also pointing to such a *year* and *season:* 500

Lines 474–76. **House…Horns:** in the coat of arms of the family of Lady Eleanor's sister-in-law. **he bearing…Bear:** cf. Rev. 13:1–2.

Line 480. **sotish Bathe:** In her "Bathe Daughter of BabyLondon" (1636—page 71 in the present edition), Lady Eleanor associated Bath with the whore of Babylon.

Line 484. **Ox, Ass, and Camel:** proverbially stubborn animals.

Line 495. **Sessions day:** when the quarterly courts met in the counties; Judgment Day.

Lines 498–99. **Jacobs…goats:** see Gen. 30:33.

viz. The distance between the *Suns* entrance into *Aries,* the crowned *Ram;* probable when as the *Worlds Creation.* And that of the Tropick *Capricorn,* the *Hoary bearded Goat:* Character of *Spring* and *Winters* approach; whereby slaughtered sheep as betokens an execution day, at hand; from the *fold* to the *scaffold, &c.* So foreshewed to be the very *year,* aforehand *revealed.*

His *sinister reign* shadowing forth from 1625. *March,* until his *arraignment* after *Christmas,* the late *Charls* his doleful *note,* imprisoned, harborless, not worth a House: A Stranger (to wit) of another *Nation,* where by way of retaliation as he had close imprisoned others, unresisted *The blessed Lambs voice,* and *Decembers,* &c. Made it his own case, in as much, *Had not visited the least of those his Lambs, Hunger, Starved* and *Cold:* For any *mercy* on their part, *Rebels* proclaimed to his *Kingdom,* alluding to the *flaming sword;* That *Doomsday* when they expelled thence, whose *Valediction* depart, *&c.* The never departing *sword* and *smoake* their portion. The *Righteous* on the other side, or *Roundheads* pointing to *Paradice* their return to *peace:* As those *Thunderclaps* then, and *Lightnings, August* 23. *A°* 51.

So much for mitigating this *Mittimus* to *Hell,* exprest by way of *Terror,* his *Judgement day,* the *Scape Goat,* no *Purgatory* pardon: whose Funeral attended with those three, *Hamilton* and *Holland, &c.* made by them; No private Account, Extends to oppressed Prisoners *Christmas* Cry, Verily *Sterved* and *Rotting,* so over charged those *Penfolds;* under any *colour* or *pretence* buried quick, by accursed *Cut-throats* daily, and imprisoned *Anno* 45. Whose Twenty three years Reign, from *Anno* 25.

510

520

Line 501. **Aries:** the ram; astrological sign of spring.

Line 503. **Goat:** Capricorn, astrological sign of winter. Line 505. **fold:** where sheep are kept.

Line 512. **Had not visited...Lambs:** see John 21:15. Line 515. **Valediction:** farewell.

Line 516. **Roundheads:** the king's opponents in the civil war.

Lines 517–18. **Thunderclaps then, and Lightnings:** see Rev. 11:19.

Line 519. **Mittimus:** a writ sending someone to prison.

Lines 520–21. **no Purgatory pardon:** the Catholic belief in Purgatory was deemed superstitious by Protestants. **whose Funeral...Holland:** Three peers, Hamilton, Holland, and Capel, were executed two months after the king was beheaded.

Line 523. **Penfolds:** pinfolds; places for confining sheep or cattle.

until *Anno* 48. The *Scepter* when resigned the Hand: *Table of bounty* turned to a *blow;* as by the Fruitless fatal *Tree Mythologised,* of three years standing afore came under the heavy *lash;* besides a *Lease* of three years more ex-pired; Also a warning to *Churches,* his *House,* for usurped *Keys resignation.* Enemy to the *Nations cure,* the *Tree* of *Life: Scepter* and *Keys* both. The *Epilogue* or *End* of which *subject* or *excommunication,* concluded with his *voice,* The inthroned *Lamb* in *Bethlehems* Manger, concerning othersome in this *burthensome age;* as unto those groaning restless *Companions,* overcharged by their unmerciful owners. *Come unto me also ye heavy laden, and* (your intolerable Tax)*I will ease you,* and insupportable Bonds, those *Yokes,* saying, *Behold I come quickly. Whose righteousness like the strong Mountains, &c. Judgements like the great deep,* to be manifested, *&c.*

Thus much for their *Analogy* or likeness, unexpectedly also come upon us unto the last great days account likened. And for this *Antichristian Beasts* sevenfold names of *blasphemy,* namely *Saturn* and *Jupiter, &c.* Days of the week *christned* in theirs, and Moneths in their *commemoration Ethnicks;* after *Julius C* and *August,* containing VICLVVVI. Those *Members* no inferior ones of the *Roman* breed, Hours of the Moneth 666, whose number also pointing to the days of *Noah* 1656. By so many Moneths amounting unto 55 years and a half. Then *Treasure* lyable to *Plunder,* of more consequence to count those at hand, including his reign of 55 years and odde Moneths succeeded him, wounded not least by his begotten *Brutus.*

So then how passes for current, or accords together, that such taking upon them to be qualified with *humility* and fear of *God,* do *prohibite*

530

540

550

Line 527. **Fruitless fatal Tree:** the fig tree (Luke 13:7).

Lines 528–29. **a Lease...ex-pired:** Charles I lived three years beyond 1645, the year Lady Eleanor had believed Judgment would occur.

Line 532. **The inthroned...Manger:** see Rev. 22:1; also a reference to Lady Eleanor's confinement in London's mental hospital.

Lines 534–35. **Come...laden:** Matt. 11:28. Line 536. **Behold I come quickly:** Rev. 22:7.

Lines 541–42. **blasphemy...Moneths:** these had pagan (non-Christian) names.

Lines 545–56. **the days...half:** Noah's age in months (Gen. 9:29).

Line 548. **his reign...Moneths:** Julius Caesar's. Line 549. **Brutus:** Caesar's assassin.

swearing in others and *blaspheme* themselves. Make *Laws* for strict keeping the *Sabbath,* notwithstanding so stupid and carnal, stop the *ear*
against his *Word* and *Law, Thou shalt have no other gods.*

Whilest the *simple* deluded by *assumed Titles* of *Saviours,* and the like;
called *Defenders of the Christian Faith,* An *Antichristian* Authority otherwise called, *The Blood thirsty devouring Beast,* rising out of the *Water* in
the *Lambs* Rose coloured *Robe;* wounded (as it were) with the Crown of
Thorns: whose *Baptism* and *Sabbaths* exercise, edifying as their *Bells,*
560   *Feasts* and *Fasts,* part of the Forty and two *Moneths* reckoning and
breathing the *Holy Ghost,* witness the three abominable *Frogs* for
another; with the *gift of healing, Miracles* by *succession,* the *Image* of the
Beast worn, *&c.* So of *Elias* Alarm, *Fire* causing to come down, *&c.*
(*Apoc.* 13.) in the sight of men by *lightning* as *burnt* so many *Barns,* last
Harvest fulfilling; also the *Harvest* great, but *Laborers* few: Put to their
Heels for the Press then, not to be forgotten. Subscribed I am *A & O*
&c. And have the *keys, &c.* As our *Liberty* proclaims and the *Holy Ghosts*
reign for evermore, sent in his name the *Spirit* of truth, otherwise called
The Lamb, likewise by their *Synagouges* how confined within *Iron gates:*
570   Whose *Angelical* presence signifies as declares, *He was in prison; Depart*
you cursed: so blessed are they, called unto Lambs marriage supper .

> *Qui se humiliaverat, ipse exaltabit*

Ele: Da. *&* Do.
Fleet.
Candlemas.
Her *Purification.*
1651

Principium & Finis.

Line 566. **A & O:** Alpha and Omega (Rev. 1:8).

Line 572. **Qui se…exaltabit:** Who humbles himself shall be exalted (Latin); Ezek. 21:26.

Line 578. **Principium & Finis:** beginning and end (Latin).

Bethlehem (Wing D1978) is probably the last of Lady Eleanor's published tracts. She died early in July 1652, a month after the date at the conclusion of the tract. In this tract Lady Eleanor uses the parable of the talents (Matt. 25:14–30) to discuss sin as disease and to show how prophecy, which had been devalued in Britain, provides information necessary for healing the evils that have plagued the nation. In this context, she addresses directly for the first time her confinement almost twenty years earlier in London's hospital for the insane, the Hospital of St. Mary of Bethlehem, popularly known as Bedlam. The present edition of *Bethlehem* is based on a copy in the Bodleian Library, Oxford (shelf number 12.0.1336[6]).

BETHLEHEM
SIGNIFYING THE HOUSE OF
BREAD: OR WAR.

Whereof informs, Whoso takes a small Roul to taste cures forthwith Distraction in the supreamest Nature; with such vertue indu'd.

By those TORMENTERS Firy SERPENTS as they when stung, were heal'd a view by taken of the Brazen ONE.

Ezekiel 16.
Cause Jerusalem to know her Abomination, &c.

Title. **Bethlehem...War:** Bethlehem was the site of Jesus' birth. He told his disciples that he was the bread of life (John 6:35); his second coming would mean Judgment and war (Rev. 19:11). St. Mary of Bethlehem was London's hospital for the insane. **Whoso...Distraction:** cf. Ezek. 3:1. **indu'd:** indued; vested or endowed. **By...ONE:** see Rev. 9.

Touching the healing of the present Evil.

Shews (as not unknown their *influence*) the better that we may judge of
things to come; from Examples in vain not recorded of things past:
Achan as his story for one *Epitomizes:* By whom the *golden Wedge* or
Tongue hid, wch trespass until discovered of his, *thus and thus, &c.* no
peace or presence of the *Lord* any more. So whence as follows, *Cause the
city to know, &c.* for recovery of *health,* to have knowledge of the *disease*
since the first step thereto.

   Acters or consenters, know ye or be informed, of one and the same
10 nature: that of the one *Talent buried also by him or not improved, &c.*
where so much for the better ordering the *Medicine* or *prescribed Rule:*
shewing how in days of those late *high Priests* it came to pass *Anno Dom.*
about 36. By them after what *execrable maner Crucified the Oracles of
God,* their late *Altars* for that purpose prepared; to be short over which a
Gyant Crucifix being erected: *The value not of a Napkin to cover,* &c.
exposed to the view of all to *kneel before it:* like as in *Golgatha that Fridays dismal Day bowed the knee:* Then his humble Servants also.

   Which Goliah *portray'd with the Crown of Thorns,* wanting neither *its
Superscription,* done by that in his *Holyness Chappel,* a true *Copy* brought
20 over by *Father,* &c. Whilest that *Original* as shamefully covered the *Ten
Commandment* at the East end plac'd: to their low *obeysance* at every
turn, least an *Eye-sore.*

   Had contrived under colour of an *Altar Hanging,* fastned down to
the wall of course *purple Woollen,* even to *Ecclipse that Light of Lights:*
whereby to cover the *Ten Commandments* no *obscure business* as befel:

Line 4. **Achan:** see Josh. 7:19–26.

Lines 13–14. **Crucified…Altars:** After William Laud became archbishop of Canterbury, he
intensified the campaign to convert communion tables to altars and introduce other changes in
church furnishings and services; Lady Eleanor alleges that his actions destroyed true religion.

Line 15. **The value…cover:** cf. Luke's version of the parable of the talents (Luke 19:20).

Lines 16–17. **in Golgotha…Day:** at the crucifixion of Christ (Matt. 27:33).

Lines 19–21. **in…Father:** At Archbishop Laud's trial, allegations arose that he had a Roman
missal and had altered the furnishings and service in his chapel to conform to it. "His holiness"
was the title of the Pope, not the archbishop of Canterbury, who, by English usage, was
referred to as "his grace." **Ten…end:** In the *Constitutions and Canons* (1603) the Convocation
of the Clergy had prescribed that "the Ten Commandments be set upon the East ende of every
Church and Chappell." **to…obeysance:** The Laudians insisted on bowing to the altar.

Brocht in *Litchfield Minster:* where this *Monster Table* appointed with the *Centurion,* armed at all points, mounted on this *Courser:* the *Beast* worshipt too.

Unsufferable to behold, the one not more *ignominiously exposed,* then the other *obscured:* to give free passage to whatsoever abomination.

Whereupon, *O accursed,* as obliged for bringing to light the same *Court* and *City* to awaken: Their *Lord Major* that *year* a *Litchfield man:* resolved to set some *mark* upon their *purple Covering,* whereon she cast a *Confection* made but of *Tar,* mixt with *wheat Starch,* with fair *Water* heated, *&c.* Them possessing with such outrage flocking about it, some *Gunpowder Treason* as though: upon whose *fright,* post a *Sergeant at Arms* was sent down at *Candlemas* to carry her up: Carriers unable to pass after that *Summers drought,* when as much wet again: At whose *Arrival,* though *Higher Powers* certified by the *Sergeant at Arms,* of such causless *Panick Terror:* yet said, in regard *who knows what she may do in other Mother Churches:* Held it fit to commit her to the *Cities Custody;* one as it were buried quick in *Bedlems* loathsom *Prison,* infected with those *foul Spirits* day and night *Blaspheming:* where was shut up by the space of two years sufficiently published or bruted by that time.

When began, the *War* kindled in *Scotland:* And so much for that

---

Lines 26–27. **Brocht...Minster:** embroidered in the cathedral at Lichfield. **this Monster...Courser:** The altar table was decorated with a centurion, a commander in the Roman army, mounted on a horse. A centurion was present at the crucifixion (Matt. 27:54).

Lines 29–30. **the one...obscured:** The crucifix and altar were displayed, the Ten Commandments hidden.

Lines 33–35. **resolved...heated:** Lady Eleanor is describing her vandalism of the new altar-hanging with hot tar and wheat paste.

Lines 35–36. **some...though:** as if comparable to the Gunpowder Plot of 1605, whereby the Catholics allegedly planned to blow up king and Parliament and take over the kingdom.

Lines 37–38. **Candlemas:** Feast of the Purification of the Virgin Mary, celebrated on 2 February. **Carriers...again:** Flooding, due to rains as excessive as the summer drought, kept the messenger carrying the order for Lady Eleanor's confinement from reaching Lichfield.

Lines 40–41. **in...Churches:** Laud, in his report upon the state of the church for 1636, commented about his belief that Lady Eleanor must be confined lest she commit elsewhere acts similar to those she had done at Lichfield.

Lines 42–44. **infected...Blaspheming:** Bedlam's patients were noted for their loud cries. **shut...years:** Elsewhere Lady Eleanor says she was in Bedlam for a little over a year. **bruted:** talked about; also treated like a brute or a beast.

Line 45. **the War...Scotland:** the First Bishops' War, 1639.

designed place *Bethlehems Hospital*, alias *Bedlem: Bethlehem* the *House of Bread signifying, or War, &c.* undergon in behalf of that *crying cause,* causless *Jealousie* of hers.

Never that was called to appear or *answer* whether *Guilty*, but *sur-*
50 *prized* in that sort, or the *Adversary* against her appearing: *Conscious* of their abominable *Cause*, of whose proceedings by *Luke* thus recorded: in which aforesaid City dwelt a *Judge*, saying within himself not difficult to judge when *Though I fear not God nor reverence Man:* yet least this never ceasing *Widow* by her *Writing, &c.* inlarged thus no ordinary *Assessment* were mentioned: who by casting into their *Treasury those two mites*, from that seeming *Paradox* outstript them all, as *Englefield Manor* for one devoured, *&c.* accompanied with the unparalleld last *troublesom times Description:* when that *Famine of Faith* a fore-runner of his coming.

Return shall to the former of those *precious Tables*, able to dissolve
60 *Millstones: Like as when rent the Templevail, Stones and Graves unable to contain*, &c. men whilest more *obdurat* as in the Bladder of uncircumcised *Hearts*, which nothing *penitrates*.

Oyes, himself *Westminsters Cryer*, in the mean while much *People* gathered, several *Soils* those, proclaims *Earth, Earth*, in relation to her *Ears* not few: how difficult to bring forth fruit in kinde, three for one miscarrying: *He that hath ears*, &c.

Which *Ten Commandments* lastly how were Restored; although yielded not to *pluck down* the aforesaid *Cloth* that *Altar Ornament*, appointed nevertheless in an *Azure Table* the *Law engraven* to be in *gold*
70 *Letters:* Hanged up in all *Churches*, bearing date, *Anno 37*.

Line 49. **Never…appear:** Imprisoned by a summary procedure, Lady Eleanor had no hearing.

Line 51. **by Luke…recorded:** cf. the parable of the importunate widow (Luke 18:2–8).

Line 55. **casting…mites:** see Luke 21:2–3.

Lines 56–57. **Englefield…devoured:** Lady Eleanor claimed that she had lost possession of Englefield, where she heard Daniel speak to her in 1625.

Lines 59–60. **those…Millstones:** see Rev. 18:21. **when…Templevail:** see Matt. 27:51.

Lines 61–62. **whilest…penitrates:** see Acts 7:51.

Lines 63–64. **Oyes:** hear ye; a call to silence by a public crier. **much…those:** cf. Mark 4:33.

Lines 69–70. **appointed…37:** In 1637 there was an order for the Ten Commandments to be hung in all churches.

To be buried in silence neither, where by accident in the *Prisoners Chamber:* when brought into it, beheld on the wall *the two written Tables in Moses hand coming down out of the Mount,* the onely *Ornament* or *Picture* there, hang'd up on a *Nail:* not long after rent down by the *Keeper;* because unto some shewed or as a token then what done by them in *Churches:* not calling to minde; *As visits unto the third and fourth Generation, That hates them, so mercy shews to Thousands that love his Commandments.*

And so return to their *sufferings:* As testifies (*Apocalips cap.* 11.) The *Tables* of the *Law* those *Lights* inclusive with the two invincible *Witnesses, Where the Lord Crucified, &c. Waters* converting into *Blood:* whose insulting *Enemies* rewarded thereafter with *Core* and his Companions in that *Earthquake,* &c. as when *Prebends* and *clerk Vicars* forced, were afterward for fear of the *Parliament Forces* to bury it in a *Donghil,* not one would harbor it, so low obeysances had made thereto afore: And this in *Stafford*-shire their *Lord Major* aforesaid of that County, fulfilling what *honor* his *anointed ones* to expect: *If the Master of the House call'd Devil or Beelzebub: Bedlem* no dishonor for them, especially whilest *Grandees* in that measure their *House* infected.

As moreover for that aforesaid Shire or intire County of *Stafford,* not long since belonging to whose *Ancestors* the house of *Audley* of no

80

90

Lines 72–73. **beheld...Tables:** Lady Eleanor found the Ten Commandments hanging on the wall where she was confined.

Lines 75–76. **as...Churches:** an allegation that the keeper's tearing down the Commandments in Lady Eleanor's cell was a violation like those that had occurred in churches.

Lines 76–78. **As...Commandments:** see Exod. 20:5–6.

Line 81. **Waters...Blood:** see Exod. 7:21.

Line 82. **Core...Companions:** Korah and his company; see Num. 26:9–10.

Lines 83–84. **Prebends...Donghil:** During the civil war the cathedral clergy of Lichfield buried the altar-hanging to protect it from the parliamentary armies. Lady Eleanor is perhaps alluding to the parable in which Jesus said that salt which had lost its savour was not even fit for the dunghill (Luke 14:34–35).

Line 86. **Stafford-shire:** the county where Lichfield was located.

Lines 87–88. **If...Beelzebub:** see Matt. 10:25.

Lines 90–91. **Stafford...Audley:** The baronage of Audley, which Lady Eleanor's father had inherited, held lands in Staffordshire.

obscure *Denominations. Audley* of *England* from whence derives her *Antiquity. Touchet* of *France,* the *Paternal Name. Castlehaven* in *Ireland,* thence her *Precedence* alike concerned in each. From the *Province* of *Wales* that of *Davis:* and *Douglas* of *Scotland* the *Doughty:* such a one of the several *Nations* as intimates no less: *A Prophet shall the Lord like unto me raise up unto you of your Brethren, him shall you hear, &c. And every soul which will not hear, shall be destroyed from among the People:* (Acts 3.) so a *Deliverance time,* whose word a *Law:* stoops to no *Bulls* or other 100   like actings: *Prophets* howsoever buried in the *Land* of *Oblivion:* which *Nations,* as much to say, avenge her shall of her Adversary thus supported: *My hand shall hold him fast and my arm shall strengthen him, nor gates of Hell shall not prevail against her: O Hell or Fleet-Prison* (to wit) *where is thy Victory* now.

   And for a leading touch, these suffices for this *spreading soar,* its swellings to asswage threatning, no less then *Ears* and *Throat:* By our *Achans* for the accursed thing put among their own *stuff,* as upon his *Humiliation shewed them:* And for this Analogy between the *Times* of spiritual *Egypts* Map. And for that prophet parallel'd with *Moses,* by whom the 110   Golden Calf conjured down by his *Serpent Rod: Those first and last of Prophets.* Containing a Brief of a like Dispute as between them about *Moses* Body. *Jude.*

June.   *Elea: Aud: Touch: Castleha.*

                                                        Da: & Do:

Lines 92–93. **Audley...Antiquity:** The title "Audley" was an ancient one; "old" is part of the literal meaning of Audley.

Line 93. **Touchet of France:** the name of Lady Eleanor's family. **Castlehaven in Ireland:** the Irish earldom held by Lady Eleanor's father.

Lines 94–95. **Precedence:** rank. **From...Davis:** Lady Eleanor's first husband, Sir John Davies, was of Welsh ancestry. **Douglas...Doughty:** Lady Eleanor's second husband, Sir Archibald Douglas, was a Scot.

Line 99. **Bulls:** papal orders.

Lines 102–4. **My hand...her:** cf. Matt. 16:18. **O Hell...now:** cf. 1 Cor. 15:55; Lady Eleanor had been imprisoned in the Fleet.

Line 110. **Golden Calf...Rod:** see Exod. 32.

Lines 111–12. **Dispute...Body:** see Jude 9.

Lines 113–14. **Elea...Do:** Eleanor Audeley Touchet Castlehaven Davis and Douglas.